Women's Organizations and Democracy in South Africa

WOMEN IN AFRICA
AND THE DIASPORA

Series Editors

STANLIE JAMES
AILI MARI TRIPP

Women's Organizations and Democracy in South Africa

Contesting Authority

Shireen Hassim

The University of Wisconsin Press

The University of Wisconsin Press
1930 Monroe Street
Madison, Wisconsin 53711

www.wisc.edu/wisconsinpress/

3 Henrietta Street
London WC2E 8LU, England

1   3   5   4   2

Printed in the United States of America

Library of Congress Cataloging-in-Publication Data
Hassim, Shireen.
Women's organizations and democracy in South Africa :
contesting authority / Shireen Hassim.
p.   cm.—(Women in Africa and the diaspora)
Includes bibliographical references and index.
ISBN 0-299-21380-3 (cloth: alk. paper)
ISBN 0-299-21384-6 (pbk.: alk. paper)
1. Women in politics—South Africa.
2. Women and democracy—South Africa.
3. Feminism—South Africa.
4. Women—South Africa—Societies and clubs.
5. South Africa—Politics and government—20th century.
I. Title.   II. Series.
HQ1236.5.S6H37   2005
306.2´082´0968—dc22   2005011887

For

SAMIR and AISHA,

with love

Contents

Preface

This book is based on archival research, secondary sources, interviews, and participant-observation. It contributes to existing scholarship on both social movements and gender in South Africa by developing a narrative about the trajectory of women's politics within the national liberation movement in the last two decades of the twentieth century. To do this I have brought together scattered and somewhat parochial reports, articles, and testimonies from the pages of alternative media such as *Speak, Work in Progress,* and *Agenda.* I am indebted to the reporting done by the *Speak* collective, especially Shamim Meer and Karen Hurt, who were committed to letting women speak their own words. Their work over many years has created an invaluable archive that has preserved women's voices, both individual and organizational, for future scholars to use. Without this magazine's short reports on organizations and their activities, and its interviews with politically active women at the local level, researchers would have great difficulty reconstructing the tenor of gender politics in the 1980s.

Few scholarly studies of women's organizations cover the gender politics of the 1980s and 1990s in South Africa. Pingla Udit's dissertation is a
notable exception, although she did not benefit from access to archives and
she was studying a different period. Articles by Gay Seidman[1] and Sheila
Meintjes[2] provide useful but brief overviews of the period. In addition,
I benefited from perceptive articles by four astute participant-observers:
Leila Patel on the Federation of South African Women,[3] Gertrude Fester on
the United Women's Organisation in the Western Cape (UWO),[4] Nozizwe
Routledge-Madlala on the Natal Organisation of Women (NOW),[5] and
Sheila Meintjes[6] on UWO and NOW. In my effort to gain deeper insight
into the women's organizations discussed in chapter 2, I was fortunate to
be able to consult a range of archives, several of which were not available to
researchers before South Africa adopted democracy in 1994. However, the
records were not all in good order or condition, and this limited the extent
to which I could offer documentary evidence of particular events and decisions. The standard of record keeping reflected the repressive conditions of
the 1980s. The archives of the UWO are meticulous for the first five years.
Thereafter the states of emergency and the general disruption of the organization resulted in irregular record keeping, and then a fire in the office in
1986 destroyed some records. Compared to UWO's, the archives of NOW
and the Federation of Transvaal Women (FEDTRAW) are thin. NOW did
not keep proper records because its leaders considered this a security risk,
particularly as police continually raided the office and confiscated minutes
and financial records. The last NOW executive had lost track of the few remaining documents, but these were eventually tracked down to the Killie
Campbell Library in Durban. Record keeping in women's organizations
was also dependent on the extent of middle-class participation. In UWO in
particular, the efforts of the historian Anne Mager, who served as secretary,
had a tremendous effect on the archives, as all the records were relatively
well ordered and she preserved even small scraps of original notes. In addition, my own notes and record of participation in NOW, the United Democratic Front (UDF), and the Women's Charter Alliance of Southern Natal
were invaluable in reconstructing events and analyzing particular incidents.

The South African Historical Archives (SAHA) are located at the Cullen
Library at the University of the Witwatersrand. There I had access to the
extensive UDF Papers, the FEDTRAW Papers, and the collected papers of
Helen Joseph. At the University of Cape Town I was able to consult the
newly archived papers of Ray Alexander (Simons), which contained many
reports sent by underground activists in the women's movement and Simons's own notes and assessments of developments based on secret meetings. She also kept her own copies, with commentaries, of documents and

notes from the Women's Section of the African National Congress (ANC). Her papers, as well as the private notes and papers of Jacklyn Cock, a member of the ANC's Emancipation Commission, and Sheila Meintjes, a member of the Strategising Group of the ANC Women's League, helped me to fill in the gaps in the official archives of the ANC, which are stored at the Mayibuye Centre at the University of the Western Cape and the Cullen Library. The Women's National Coalition (WNC) Archives, located at the organization's offices in Braamfontein, are substantial but not yet properly organized and appear to be incomplete. Again I was fortunate to be able to supplement the official archives by perusing the private papers of Sheila Meintjes and Catherine Albertyn, key participants in the WNC. I am grateful to Jackie, Sheila, and Cathi for their generosity.

I supplemented my archival research with interviews with key informants between 1998 and 2000. These were qualitative, open-ended interviews, some lasting well more than two hours, and almost all interviewees were willing to respond to queries and in some cases read draft chapters after the interviews. I did not attempt to interview a representative sample of participants in women's organizations but endeavored to obtain a diversity of viewpoints. I hope that this broader study will facilitate research on the internal cultures of the organizations; this would necessitate a wider and more representative range of interviews. The timing of this research, a few years after the first democratic elections and within the broader environment of the Truth and Reconciliation Commission (TRC), was crucial in that interviewees were willing to speak openly about their participation and their views on developments within the different organizations. I thank all interviewees for their trust and openness in speaking to me.

Research on the institutionalization of gender in the new democratic state was facilitated by my work at the Human Sciences Research Council during 1997 and 1998 when I led a project on this topic. With research support from Marit Claasen, Ordelia Nkoenyane and Santha Naiker I was able to interview women in the national machinery in all nine provinces during 1998. I was also able to access internal reports and preliminary assessments of the progress of institutional development.

I was fortunate to have the enthusiastic support of good friends. I would like to thank the following people who generously read several draft chapters of this book and offered perceptive and encouraging comments: Cathi Albertyn, Jo Beall, Jacklyn Cock, Stephen Gelb, Beth Goldblatt, Amanda Gouws, Natasha Erlank, Cynthia Kros, Tom Lodge, Sheila Meintjes, David Pottie, Gay Seidman, Raymond Suttner, Pingla Udit, Linda Waldman, and Cherryl Walker. John Saul supervised the original thesis on which this book is based, and he brought to the project care, dedication, and a refreshingly irreverent eye. Without their faith and generosity of time, spirit, and intellectual advice, I would not have completed this book. Of course, all errors are mine.

I would like to thank the Faculty of Humanities at the University of the Witwatersrand for two generous grants that allowed me time off from teaching to concentrate on writing.

Finally, I would like to thank Bill Freund for believing in me long before I ever imagined an academic career. My most grateful thanks for their many acts of support also go to Adila Hassim, Anice Hassim, Anisa Hoosen, Sheila Meintjes, Sandi Savadier, and Di Stuart and to my parents, Aziz and Zohra Hassim. Above all, I thank Stephen Gelb for his deep and enduring love, for his willing sharing of the joys and burdens of parenting, and for giving me room to be the best I can be.

Abbreviations

ANC	African National Congress
ANCWL	ANC Women's League
AZAPO	Azanian People's Organisation
BWF	Black Women's Federation
CASE	Community Agency for Social Enquiry
CEDAW	Convention on the Elimination of All Forms of Discrimination Against Women
CGE	Commission on Gender Equality
CODESA	Convention for a Democratic South Africa
COSAS	Congress of South African Students
COSATU	Congress of South African Trade Unions
FEDTRAW	Federation of Transvaal Women
GAC	Gender Advisory Committee
GEAR	Growth, Employment and Redistribution strategy
IFP	Inkatha Freedom Party

MK	Umkhonto we Sizwe
MPNP	Multi-Party Negotiating Process
NEC	National Executive Committee
NIC	Natal Indian Congress
NNP	New National Party
NOW	Natal Organisation of Women
NWEC	National Women's Executive Committee
OSW	Office on the Status of Women
PAC	Pan Africanist Congress
PLAAS	Programme for Land and Agricultural Studies
RDP	Reconstruction and Development Programme
SACP	South African Communist Party
SALGA	South Africa Local Government Association
UDF	United Democratic Front
UWCO	United Women's Congress
UWO	United Women's Organisation in the Western Cape (formed in 1986 following merger with the Women's Front Organisation)
WNC	Women's National Coalition

Women's Organizations and Democracy in South Africa

Introduction

Autonomy and Engagement in the South African Women's Movement

Feminist politics should be understood not as a separate form of politics designed to pursue the interests of women *as* women, but rather the pursuit of feminist goals and aims within the context of a wider articulation of demands. . . . Feminism . . . is the struggle for the equality of women. But this should not be understood as a struggle for realizing the equality of a definable empirical group with a common essence of identity, women, but rather as a struggle against the multiple forms in which the category "woman" is constructed in subordination.

Chantal Mouffe, "Feminism, Citizenship and
Radical Democratic Politics"

This book analyzes women's political participation during a dramatic period in South Africa's history, when movements for social, economic, and political justice overthrew one of the most vile regimes in history. It traces the ways in which women articulated their political interests within the broader struggle against apartheid and, in some instances, against capitalism and in the process sought to articulate a set of interests based on the particular experiences of gender oppression. The book follows the emergence of the women's movement as an important social movement in South Africa; it seeks to identify the participants in women's organizations, the organizational structures that were developed, the political and ideological resources that such organizations were able to command, the changing nature of political consciousness, and the capacity of the women's movement to exploit the various external opportunities and transcend the constraints imposed by the political environment within which it operated.

3

The book offers one lens on the extraordinary history of women's political struggles in contemporary South Africa. It does not seek or claim to be comprehensive. Although I have attempted to be exhaustive in archival research and have sought to interview as widely as possible, the sheer size of this undertaking has limited my ability to include all the voices and issues that I would have liked. It is thus one perspective, seeking not to be definitive but to illustrate the tensions, challenges, and achievements of one of the most complex and fascinating women's movements of the twentieth century.

This book takes the approach that the South African women's movement must be understood as made up of heterogeneous organizations, rather than being viewed through the lens of a single organization, an approach that I will outline more fully later in this introduction. I also use a particular definition of *strong social movement.* A strong social movement has the capacity to articulate the particular interests of its constituencies and to mobilize those constituencies in defense of those interests; it is able to develop independent strategies to achieve its aims while holding open the possibility of alliance with other progressive movements. This definition suggests that a strong social movement requires a degree of political autonomy in order to retain its relative power within any alliance. In addition to these organizational capabilities, the ideological influences of feminism are vital in building robust women's movements. My approach to studying the South African women's movements draws extensively on Maxine Molyneux's articulation of the notion of autonomy.

Defining Women's Organizations and Women's Movements

Attempts to define *women's movement* raise a peculiar set of considerations, as this is not a movement in which subjects, interests, and ideological forms are self-evident. First and perhaps most obviously, women do not mobilize as women simply because they are women. They may frame their actions in terms of a range of identities, whether as worker, student, African, white, and so on. In other words, women do not mobilize for a single reason. Indeed, as several theorists have pointed out, attempts to disaggregate gender identity are nearly futile, as the cultural meanings of *woman* shift in relation to the numerous other markers of identity and in different contexts. Second, no one agrees on how to define the notion of *women's interests,* given the interactions of race, class, and other objective and subjective interests. Gender is simultaneously everywhere—gender differences are inscribed in practically all human relationships as well as in the ordering of the social, political, and economic structures of all societies—and

nowhere—it is difficult to apprehend as an independent variable. And finally, the women's movement takes different forms in different contexts,
operating at some moments as a formalized structure and at others as a
loose network. This variety of organizational forms is accompanied by a
variety in the range of tactics used, from assimilative to confrontational
and even violent.

Although some women's movements, and some forms of feminism,
have identified as their common interest the elimination of patriarchy
(understood as the system of male domination), in many postcolonial
countries the notion of patriarchy has been unhelpful as it fails to account
for the particular intersections of class, race, and colonial forms of domination with the oppression of women. Postcolonial feminists have criticized the emphasis on patriarchy and on the sameness of women's interests
for reflecting an ethnocentric and middle-class bias that privileged the
Western model of women's political struggles as the standard by which to
judge all other women's political strategies. As Mohanty and other postcolonial scholars have argued, feminism and the ideological content of feminist consciousness should not be specified a priori according to the abstract
definitions of universalist theory but should be defined in the context of
particular social formations and should have resonance in the historical experience and political culture of specific societies.[1]

In tackling the difficult of issue of how to define women's interests in
the face of these differences, Molyneux has offered a conceptual distinction
between "strategic gender interests" and "practical gender needs" that has
been influential for the analysis of postcolonial women's movements. Molyneux defined *practical gender needs* as those that arise from the everyday responsibilities of women, based on a gendered division of labor, while *strategic gender interests* are those interests that women share in overthrowing
power inequalities based on gender. While Molyneux has acknowledged
that these distinctions might be difficult to pin down in practice, the value
of her contribution lies in offering a conceptualization of women's movements that recognizes and allows for the diversity of women's interests.
Given this definition of women's interests, it is possible to conceive of a
women's movement as containing within it conservative elements that organize women from a particular social base but do not seek to question
power relations within that base, let alone within society more generally. By
contrast, feminism has a direct political dimension, as it is not only aware of
women's oppression but also seeks to confront male power in all its dimensions. In this broad formulation of women's interests, the task of feminism
is to examine the particular ways in which power operates within and
between the political, social, and economic spheres of specific societies—in
effect, this is a political project of transformation.

A more limited approach to defining women's interests focuses only on women's relationship to formal political institutions. In this view the most stable interest that cuts across the range of differences between women is women's exclusion (or at least marginalization) from the political arena, as it is conventionally understood.[2] Regardless of race, class, ethnicity, and other factors, women are consistently defined as political outsiders or as second-class citizens whose entry into the public sphere is either anachronistic and short term or conditional upon their maternal social roles. Here the emphasis is on women's interest in accessing arenas of public power and less on debating the policy outcomes of such engagements. The task of feminism, in this more constrained approach, is to challenge exclusion. The political projects that are associated with this approach are, for example, women's enfranchisement, struggles around women's representation in national parliaments, and the emphasis on electoral systems, quotas, and other mechanisms for overcoming political-systemic obstacles. Inclusionary feminism—or equality feminism—may be seen to create some of the necessary conditions for the removal of gender inequalities, but it is reluctant to tamper with the structural basis of inequalities. This reluctance stems in part from a strategic imperative to maintain minimal conditions for unity among women and in part from the ideological underpinnings of liberalism, which regards family and market as lying outside the realm of state action.

Like the distinction between women's practical needs and strategic gender interests, the transformatory and inclusionary approaches to defining women's interests are not mutually exclusive. Rather, they need to be seen as part of a continuum of women's struggles for full citizenship, which may take a linear historical form (that is, a shift from inclusionary demands to transformative demands over time) or may be present within a single movement at a given moment, with some sectors pursuing alliances with political elites for inclusion and other pushing toward a more radical set of demands. As this book shows, in South Africa both these approaches have been used in order to advance gender equality claims, at times with striking synergy. However, although these approaches may coexist within women's movements, they are in tension with one another in many ways. It is important to note that each approach has long-term implications for what *kinds* of political alliances are built, which may in turn affect internal relations of the women's movement. In the case of the inclusionary approach, women's movements need access to political power to pursue the interests of representation effectively. Although they can gain this access through effective mobilization, they also need linkages with power brokers within political parties in order to ensure ongoing attention to the political system.

Consequently, inclusionary politics tends to become increasingly elite based. Transformatory feminism, on the other hand, is more likely to be conducted in alliance with other social movements, such as social movements of the poor, that seek structural transformation. This kind of politics may bring certain sections of the women's movement into contestation with elite and party-oriented members, as it is a form of politics that is likely to take a more confrontational approach to party platforms and state policies. The outcome of such alliances may be a marginalization of these actors from the state and political parties.

Given these differences, analysts of women's movements have attempted to classify them into different types.[3] The most dominant of these, based on Latin American experiences, distinguishes between women's movements that are *feminine* and those that are *feminist,* terms that evoke Molyneux's distinction between practical needs and strategic interests. Both feminine and feminist movements mobilize women on the basis of the roles conventionally ascribed to women, such as their reproductive and domestic responsibilities. However, feminist movements seek to challenge those roles and articulate a democratic vision of a society in which gender is not the basis for a hierarchy of power. This distinction is a heuristic device; in practice many women's movements embrace both forms of activism. Molyneux's distinction recognizes that acting as women does not necessarily imply that the gender identities that are invoked are progressive, in the sense of seeking to eliminate hierarchies of power.[4] The advantage of making the distinction, however, is that it enables a movement to develop in an inclusive manner—accommodating women who are less convinced of confrontational politics while at the same time holding out a vision for transformatory politics. Feminine consciousness develops from the connections between cultural experiences of gender and the everyday struggles of poor families and communities to survive, impelling women to political action. While nevertheless "emphasising roles they accept as wives and mothers [they] also demand the freedom to act as they think their obligations entail," Kaplan has noted.[5] The ideological interventions of feminist activists enable the shift from feminine to feminist consciousness, where the aims of the movement shift to eliminating power relations based on gender.

The extent of inclusiveness is particularly important in countries where women are organized around a wide range of issues that fall outside conventional definitions of the political as well as Western-centric notions of feminism. For example, in South Africa many forms of associational life, such as women's religious groups, stokvels (savings clubs), and burial societies, have provided solidarity networks for women. These forms of organization need to be recognized if a more fluid and inclusive understanding of politics is to be developed. It is important to note here that social movements do not merely "activate" preexisting identities and consciousness; they also create consciousness. Solidary associations such as these often provide the arenas in which women develop a collective consciousness that can be mobilized when the survival of a community is at stake, and in many cases collective consciousness developed within these arenas forms the bedrock of indigenous feminist mobilization. As Temma Kaplan has pointed out, although the activities within these forms of organization are unspectacular and may seem politically insignificant, they can be important sources for the emergence of social movements (not only women's movements).[6] Thus definitions of women's movements should not be so prescriptive or inelastic that they exclude the kinds of organized activities that involve the majority of poor women. Nevertheless, a critical factor in shaping whether women's movements aim to transform society is the existence of feminism as a distinct ideology within the movement, emphasizing the mobilization of women in order to transform the power relations of gender. Feminist ideology is pivotal in women's movements, as its relative strength determines the extent to which collective action is directed to democratic ends.

These difficulties have shaped the divergent forms that women's movements have taken in different contexts. Women's movements are not homogeneous entities characterized by singular and coherent sets of demands. Rather, by their nature they tend to be diverse, embracing multiple organizational forms, ideologies, and even at times contradictory demands. Indeed, some activists prefer to speak about the existence of many women's movements in South Africa, reflecting these different tendencies.[7] Despite these diversities, however, it is possible to name and loosely bind together as a women's movement organizations that mobilize women collectively on the basis of their gender identity. Like other social movements, women's movements wax and wane in the context of particular political, economic, and social crises. What needs to be understood is why and when women's organizations act in a coordinated way—that is, defining at what moment disparate groups within the movement coalesce in such a way that they *act* as a *movement*, distinct from other political forces. Some analysts have referred to this moment as tipping.[8] Tipping—the point at which disparate acts of protest cascade into a mass movement—occurs "when people come to believe that their participation becomes necessary or even required.[9] This point can sometimes be identified by a particular event, such as the 1956 Women's March on the Union Buildings, which then becomes an iconic moment for further acts of movement mobilization, or by a distinct period, such as South Africa's transition to democracy, which opens possibilities for institutional reform that have long-term consequences.

Women's Movements and Autonomy

The extent to which women's movement activists in South Africa were able to harness and develop feminist consciousness was determined by the extent to which nationalist movements and other social movements were willing to allow feminist approaches to thrive. This condition may be described as one of organizational and discursive autonomy. While autonomy was highly valued in Western women's movements—and in many was seen to be a condition of existence—autonomy is less highly valued in postcolonial countries. Because women's political activism in postcolonial contexts has been enabled by larger struggles against colonial and class oppression, the result is a more highly developed politics of alliance rather than autonomy. Yet even in the context of alliance, the precise nature of the relationship between women's organizations and their allies is defined through ongoing negotiation. As Molyneux has argued, "From the earliest moments of women's political mobilization, women activists in political parties, trade unions, and social movements have argued that they needed a place within which to elaborate their own programmes of action, debate their own goals, tactics and strategy, free from outside influence."[10]

Aili Mari Tripp, in her study of the Ugandan women's movement, has identified a number of reasons why autonomy is an important issue for women's organizations.

- Women's organizations are able to determine their own goals, even when these are in conflict with dominant political organizations.
- Women's organizations can select their own leadership, free from interference of political parties or government that might wish to choose women leaders who are loyal.
- Organizations can engage in direct collective action to improve their situation.
- Women can challenge discriminatory distribution of resources and power.[11]

She lays out here an important set of reasons why the idea of autonomy should not be dismissed as inappropriate for postcolonial women's movements. However, the concept still needs further theoretical specification. Clearly, the term means more than *separate* women's organizations, since separate women's organizations have frequently coexisted with nonfeminist goals. There is no simple definition of what defines autonomy, nor is autonomy a static characteristic of organization. Autonomy may differ in strength, may be achieved and lost, or incrementally gained over time. Nor is its strategic virtue self-evident: women's organizations may make enormous gains through the patronage of other political organizations. A high degree of autonomy may indeed confine women to a political ghetto in which they are so marginalized from national political processes that they are unable to shape political outcomes to favor women. Autonomy cannot therefore be simply asserted as an a priori value of feminist organization.

These dilemmas demand that the issue of autonomy be addressed with greater theoretical rigor if it is to be legitimately treated as a crucial variable in the success of women's organizations. What kind of autonomy is desirable, and under what conditions can it be achieved? Maxine Molyneux has offered the most sophisticated feminist understanding of autonomy, a useful schema of types of autonomy. She distinguishes three ideal types of direction in the transmission of authority: independent, associational, and directed. Independent organizations are those in which "women organize on the basis of self-activity, set their own goals and decide their own forms of organisation and forms of struggles. Here the women's movement is defined as a self-governing community which recognizes no superior authority, and nor is it subject to the governance of other political agencies."[12] Molyneux warns that while this definition is most often used by feminists, it should not be unproblematically assumed that independence will result in the best expression of "women's real gender interests."[13] Women's organizations may be autonomous from other organizations but may pursue a wide range of goals with conflicting interests. She also points out—pertinently, in the context of this study—that in some cases women have been organized independently "to help realize the broader goals of nationalist or revolutionary forces: Such forms of activism may have a special meaning and clear implications for women (which accounts for why they gain their support), but the goals of such movements are typically formulated in universalistic terms, and are seen as indissolubly linked to national independence and development. Such movements are not therefore pursuing gender-specific interests, but they have involved independent collectivities of women in the field of national politics."[14]

Even where women's organizations may be formally independent of other political forces, and therefore not subject to the procedural rules or political direction of male-dominated organizations, the effectiveness of the women's organizations may be limited by informal power structures (e.g., cultural biases in favor of men) or by political discourses that are seen as authoritative (e.g., national liberation). In short, while women may be organized independently, it is not self-evident that this form of organization will necessarily produce a movement that will advance women's gender interests, that is, their interests in eradicating imbalances in access to power and resources between women and men.[15]

A second conception of autonomy defined by Molyneux is associational autonomy, which refers to a situation in which independent women's organizations "choose to form alliances with other political organisations with which they are in agreement on a range of issues."[16] Here women retain control of their organization and its agenda while linking women's issues with universalistic goals. "Power and authority in this model are negotiated, and co-operation is conditional on some or all of women's demands being incorporated into the political organization with which the alliance is made. . . . This process of negotiation from an autonomous base is the key to democratic politics; it acknowledges that interests are diverse and sometimes conflictive, and that they cannot be defined in unitary terms and imposed from above."[17]

While the idea of associational autonomy avoids the Manichean dilemma of "integration versus autonomy," there are two conditions for its success. First, as Molyneux suggests, success requires that women's organizations constantly maintain a strong bargaining position if they are not to be co-opted. If the terms of the alliance have to be constantly negotiated, women's organizations have to maintain their capacity for independent agenda setting while being alert to opportunities to insert their aims into universalistic struggles. Second, the external political environment has to be conducive to the achievement of feminist goals. In other words, this strategy needs potential allies that share not only immediate political goals but also broad democratic values that can accommodate feminism.

Finally, Molyneux draws attention to the political mobilization of women in which there is virtually no autonomy: directed collective action. Here, authority and initiative clearly come from outside and stand above the collectivity itself. The women's organization or movement is therefore subject to a higher (institutional) authority and is typically under the control of political organizations and/or governments. There is little, if any, room for genuine negotiation regarding goals.[18] Typically, a directed women's organization is primarily concerned with nongender-specific goals such as overthrowing the government or supporting particular political parties. Directed action may have the possibility that women can make incremental gains. For example, many modernizing nationalisms may support some form of gender equality as part of their broader goals, but the women's organizations are nevertheless subject to the authority of either the party or the state. On the other hand, fundamentalist religious movements or fascist movements may explicitly mobilize women in defense of women's subordination.

I have described Molyneux's schema at length because it offers a useful framework within which to locate different strands of and moments in the South African women's movement. For the South African women's organizations, the dilemma of autonomy versus integration was particularly invidious. On the one hand, political resistance against apartheid was the crucible in which women's activism was born. On the other hand, women's organizations had to define both *what* political purposes they were organizing women for as well as the *form* that organization should take. Although separate women's organizations emerged in the three key provinces of the country in the 1980s, their emphasis on and degree of autonomy from other regional as well as national political movements needs to be explored. What was the nature of their autonomy within Molyneux's schema, and how effectively did they negotiate the benefits and constraints of their chosen mode of interaction with their political allies or superiors?

Molyneux's analysis suggests that in the South African context three key areas need to be addressed: the nature and extent of autonomy of women's organizations; their internal capacity to direct goals and strategies; and the nature of the external political environment within which women's organizations were located. First, then, we need to specify what types of autonomy were proposed by different sectors of the women's movement and the degree to which they were able to make political gains. This issue is directly tied to the extent to which women's organizations developed their internal capacity for decision making and agenda setting. In order to explore the question of autonomy and the internal characteristics, strengths, and capacities of women's organizations, I examine in chapter 2 three key women's organizations (the United Women's Organisation, the Natal Organisation of Women, and the Federation of Transvaal Women) in some detail. I explore the context in which these organizations emerged, the nature of their aims, the types of organizational forms adopted, and their relationship to the civic movement and, especially, to the United Democratic Front. Within Molyneux's schema I argue that these organizations pursued forms of associational autonomy. Although they maintained independent structures and decision making—in other words, they remained identifiably separate organizations—they tied their concerns and their fate to those of the broader internal resistance movement. This alliance offered the opportunity to universalize the aims of the women's organizations and to assert the need for a more thorough-going transformation of the social order as the precondition for women's liberation. Struggles to ensure that their demands became part of national liberation goals laid the basis for more long-term constitutional and institutional gains in the transitional period.

However, as Molyneux has argued, such alliances also extract costs from the women's organizations. The strategies of the male-dominated organizations were often inimical to the building of democratic grassroots women's organizations, and women's leadership was siphoned out of women's organizations into the broader movement. Women's organizations were increasingly unable to negotiate between the demands of building a women's movement and those of the antiapartheid movement. Within two years of joining the alliance with the United Democratic Front, women's

organizations shifted from being able to define goals and strategies in relation to their primary constituency of women to being auxiliaries of the
United Democratic Front with the responsibility of mobilizing a "sector" of
the masses into the larger organization. Women's organizations struggled
to maintain an increasingly fragile associational autonomy, articulating
women's interests as relatively distinct from those of national liberation but
in practice heavily bound by the strategies and mobilizational language of
the United Democratic Front. As I discuss in chapter 4, autonomy was completely abrogated in 1990 in favor of joining the ANC, although the question of independence was held sufficiently open so that within two years a
new cross-party coalition of women's organizations was formed under the
leadership of women from the ANC.

In chapter 3, I examine the role of women within the ANC in exile itself,
characterizing the ANC Women's Section as an example of directed collective action. As Molyneux has pointed out, in this situation women's associations are directly under the control of a higher political authority, in this
case, the ANC, and have very little room for negotiation about goals. However, even within this framework it was apparent to women activists in exile
that some form of independent decision making was important if women
were to negotiate more favorable terms within the national liberation
movement, and beginning in the 1970s there was an increasing, but unsuccessful, demand for autonomy of the Women's Section. By 1990, when the
ANC was unbanned and a new period of transition to democracy opened,
these struggles for autonomy remained unresolved, but in response the
ANC expanded its conception of liberation to include gender equality as
one of its central goals. On its return to South Africa from exile in 1990, the
ANC Women's Section was reconstituted as the Women's League, a structure that had independent power over fund-raising and decision making,
even though it remained under the ultimate political control of the ANC's
National Executive Committee. And yet, the league was unable to translate
this newly won relative autonomy into an opportunity to build a strong
women's organization. I argue that power struggles between feminists and
nationalists within the ANC Women's League, which led to feminists' leaving the organization, were at the heart of the league's failure to shift from a
women's auxiliary into an effective political vehicle for women within the
ANC following the organization's unbanning.

As chapter 4 shows, the importance of autonomy as a variable in the
success of the women's movement was demonstrated by the formation in
1991 of the Women's National Coalition, an alliance of a wide range of
women's organizations with the explicit aim of ensuring that women participated in negotiating the transition from apartheid to democracy. The
coalition, unlike earlier formations of the women's movement, such as the

Federation of South African Women, was constituted from its inception as an independent organization along the lines defined by Molyneux. Independence suggests that the organization "is defined as a self-governing community which recognizes no superior authority, and nor is it subject to the governance of other political agencies."[19] Although its affiliates were linked to political parties, the coalition, as an organization, had no formal alliance with any single movement or party and continually asserted the primacy of women's control over its decision making. At the same time it was able to exploit the political links of its affiliates (most particularly those of ANC women activists) to provide a conduit to decision makers.

External Political Opportunities, Political Discourses, and Their Influence on Women's Political Organizations

This book seeks to locate women's organizations within the broader political landscape of a national struggle against oppression based on race and class. A central question in this regard is the extent to which the external political environment in which women's organizations operated was conducive to the pursuit of the goal of gender equality. Each of the periods and institutional arenas discussed in this book offered different opportunities and constraints for women's organizations, and each demanded a renegotiation of the relationship between women's organizations and other political movements. The importance of the external political environment is supported by numerous case studies of women's movements that suggest that the internal characteristics of women's organizations—their theoretical orientation, strategic choices, and patterns of mobilization—are highly dependent on the balance of political forces in each national and historical context.[20]

This external environment is analyzed by focusing first on the nature of political opportunities for the emergence and development of the women's movement, distinct from the movement for national liberation, and the discursive environment within which the women's movement sought to position its claims.

Looking first at the political opportunity structure, defined as the extent to which developments in the wider field of politics—the nature of the state and other political movements, the conditions in which women mobilized—shape the political opportunities for collective action, the book focuses on two key moments. The first shift in opportunity came in the late 1970s and 1980s, when the political terrain of opposition to apartheid shifted to the local level, and women's participation in community organizations was encouraged as part of the process of expanding resistance at the grassroots level. The emphasis on local organizing and the politicization of community issues relating to resource distribution and access to services, as opposed to national politics against the apartheid state, drew many women with no previous history of collective action into political struggle and subsequently into local women's associations. Furthermore, the shift in opportunity reconfigured the universe of political discourse to include not only universalistic demands for a democratic state but also new gendered concerns. The immediate household struggles of women that derived from their gender roles as mothers and housewives shifted the conception of political onto terrain in which women had a direct and demonstrable interest and in which their political action was legitimated and applauded by the dominant political movements (albeit for their own reasons of political expediency).

The second was the change from apartheid to democracy, which provided new procedural rules and opened space for women's formal political participation. As Jacquette has argued, "The period of transition [from authoritarianism to democracy] is not politics as usual; it offers new opportunities and sets different constraints. . . . Social movements—including the women's movement—have an advantage during the transition because they can mobilize followers and bring people into the streets. Transitions are political 'openings' in the broadest sense; there is a general willingness to rethink the bases of social consensus and revise the rules of the game."[21] The opening up of fundamental questions about the nature of the new political and social order in South Africa offered the opportunity for women to insert their claims for women's rights into the institutional fabric of the new democracy. As in Brazil, Argentina, and Chile the transition to democracy in South Africa propelled women's organizations into alliances across class and party lines that would have been politically unthinkable before political liberalization.[22] The Women's National Coalition lobbied for extended political rights for women—not just the right to vote but the right to participate at the highest levels of decision making. Affirmative action for women was successfully mooted as a mechanism to overcome social and cultural obstacles to women's participation, at least within the dominant political party, and gender representation became a measure of the inclusiveness of the new democracy. In addition, a new set of institutions was created to mediate the implementation of formal commitments of government to gender equality.

Participation in formal political institutions is only one aspect of the conditions for heightened collective action, however. Shifts in political alignments also increase the opportunities available to marginal social movements, as dominant movements and political parties may be uncertain of their support bases or may wish to attract a broader range of constituencies to their side.[23] If social groupings are able to constitute themselves as a constituency, they may be able to negotiate for their demands to be taken up by political parties. In South Africa this opportunity to redefine women as an electoral constituency, and not just a constituency for mass nationalist mobilization, presented itself most clearly in the lead-up to the first democratic elections in 1994. In chapter 5, I explore the ways in which women's organizations lobbied for greater representation, in the numerical sense of ensuring that an increased number of women would be elected to Parliament, as well as in the substantive sense of lobbying for women's interests to be addressed in party electoral manifestos and in the policy priorities of the democratic government.

Another aspect of the political opportunity structure that affects social movements is the relationship of the movement to allies and support groups. Tarrow, for example, draws a strong correlation between the presence of influential allies and social movement success.[24] Studies of the success of the Scandinavian women's movement have shown that alliances between left-wing movements and women are most beneficial for advancing gender equality agendas.[25] Katzenstein, drawing on studies of Italy and France, has argued that the relationship is more accurately characterized as one of both opportunity and constraint: "The dilemma for the feminist movement in these countries is that the Left is at once the movement's most promising ally and its detractor, insisting as it does that the priorities of class politics cannot be sacrificed to gender interests."[26]

Even though evidence suggests that the women's movement is most successful in those political systems where the left is relatively strong,[27] as I showed in the discussion of autonomy, the danger of co-option is always implicit in such an alliance.[28] Women's movements are particularly susceptible to co-option in periods immediately following authoritarian rule, when their political allies assume office in the new democracy. In some cases states led by leftist parties may institutionalize concerns about gender equity on condition that women's organizations relinquish autonomy.[29] In other cases parties in power may co-opt women's issues to serve as political resources for the party's political ends. Thus these parties may use their minimal levels of attention to gender equality as an alibi to show their commitment to democracy while undermining the attempts of the women's movement to offer critical alternatives to state-defined priorities.[30] These concerns require that the trajectory of the relationship between women's organizations and nationalist movements need to be traced into the new state and that the balance sheet of gains and losses of institutionalization of gender into liberal democracies needs to be carefully toted up. As several feminist analyses of the state have pointed out, it is not just the women's movement that has to be analyzed in this relationship but the nature of the state itself.[31]

The second aspect of the external environment relates to the discursive space available to women's organizations to articulate aims and goals that were distinct from those of the dominant resistance movements. Molyneux has referred to this as the problem of authority, and Jane Jenson has suggested the concept of the "universe of political discourse" as a lens through which to explore this problem. Both deal with the ideological space allowed to women's movements to shape their own goals. Molyneux has argued that the authority to define goals, priorities, and actions may not always come from within the women's movement but may derive from external sources, even when there is a separate women's movement.[32] Her emphasis on the issue of authority suggests that the informal power of the national liberation movement, both internal and external, in agenda setting needs to be explored. Did authority—the legitimate power to determine the goals, strategies, and tactics of the women's organizations—lie within the organizations themselves or in the broader male-dominated political organizations either inside the country (the civic organizations and the United Democratic Front, in particular) or outside the country (the ANC)?

Even within the constraints of alliances, the discursive space available to women's movements matters because it denotes the extent to which the movement is able to develop its own goals, priorities, and actions. In her study of the French women's movement Jenson has argued that the prospects of women's movements are affected not only by the context of institutions and alliances in the external political environment but also by the "universe of political discourse" within which the movement acts.[33] She has defined the universe of political discourse as comprising "beliefs about the ways politics should be conducted, and the kinds of conflicts resolvable through political processes."[34] The universe of political discourse delineates what is considered to be "political" as opposed to private, religious, or economic. Furthermore, it sets the boundaries for political action and identifies which actors in society are considered to be legitimate in particular settings.[35]

Jenson has pointed out that the universe of political discourse is a political construct that is determined by ideological struggle and changes in response to "social change, to political action, and to struggles by organisations and individuals seeking to modify the restrictive boundaries of the political imagination."[36] The demands of women's organizations are shaped only in part by internal debates about what is desirable; they are also and sometimes more influentially determined by what can be achieved within the prevailing discourse. Jenson has argued that women's claims are likely to remain marginalized within a private realm of maternal and familial roles unless there is a change in elite consciousness such that dominant political elites come to see women as citizens rather than as representatives of children or the family.

Taken together, the arguments of Molyneux and Jenson suggest that in the South African context the relationship between national liberation movements and women's organizations must be explored not only by examining the structural and institutional aspects of this relationship but also its ideological aspects. In the book I explore the extent to which the authoritative discourse of national liberation imprinted a particular conception of "political" on the women's movement. In chapters 2 and 3, I consider the ways in which women's organizations negotiated within and against this discourse. On the one hand, women activists were able to leverage greater power for women within the nationalist framework through the privileging of motherhood as the central political identity for women—that is, by mobilizing women in ways that were consistent with the gendered role definition on which nationalism is predicated. On the other hand, the emphasis on nationalism marginalized alternative discourses, in particular that of feminism.

As this book shows, the women's movement in South Africa made tremendous gains during the last quarter of the twentieth century. Yet there were also political losses for the women's movement during this period that need to be carefully examined. As Waylen has argued, it is not just the issue of women's participation but the very terms of the transition that have to be uncovered.[37] As Webster and Adler have shown, in South Africa the emphasis on influencing on the negotiations was often pursued at the expense of deep consultation with the allies of the ANC, in particular those at the local level.[38] How did the Women's National Coalition negotiate the twin tasks of building a sustainable democratic structure while exploiting the opportunities offered by the negotiations? In chapter 4, I examine the influence of the exigencies of the lobbying process—within the frameworks defined by political elites—on the articulation of women's demands. There was an inescapable tension between the demands imposed by the national office to develop political positions rapidly and the processes of consulting with regional structures and affiliates to mediate differences between different groups and develop internal democratic mechanisms that would create a sustainable umbrella body for the women's movement.[39] To what extent, then, were the expectations that the coalition could become a long-term vehicle for national political interventions misplaced? Was the coalition merely a child of the transition, doomed to crumble once the incentives of transition were removed and political normalization was set in place? As I have noted, the extent to which a relatively autonomous and sustainable structure could be built has a central effect on the ability of the women's movement to pose fundamental questions about the distribution of power and resources on terms that were independent of those set by the state or by male-dominated political parties.

The emphasis on citizenship in the postapartheid period also opens up new ways to think about women's political participation in the democratic era. On the one hand, citizenship highlights the importance of women's participation in the institutions of democracy—that is, in the formal avenues through which citizens' participation is structured—and, through the exercise of affirmative action, to ensure women's access to decision-making forums. On the other hand, while democracy confers on citizens the right to participate, the conditions for the effective exercise of those rights are set not only by formal institutions but also by the nature of the linkages between state and civil society. Citizenship can often be exercised at least as effectively, if not more so, through participation in social movements outside the state that seek to articulate interests of different groups of citizens outside and independent of political parties. This kind of citizenship participation can challenge the ruling party's definition of policy priorities, offer alternatives, and exert pressure for accountability of governments to citizens.

To be sure, this brings us back to the central question with which this book is concerned: To what extent could the women's movement build autonomous organizations that retained the capacity for the self-definition of goals and strategies while nevertheless building alliances with other progressive forces—and not necessarily with the same allies as those of the antiapartheid era? The heady days of the transitional period, when all things seemed possible and when, as Jacquette put it, it is decidedly not "politics as usual," have given way to a more sobering period of democratic consolidation. What capacity did the women's movement have to ensure that there can be no return to "politics as usual"? Has the movement sufficient influence on the political institutions and culture that the norms and values of feminism are deeply embedded in the conduct of "politics as usual"? Perhaps most important, did the alliances and strategic choices made by the women's movement enable it to pursue its self-defined goals to remove gender inequalities and transform the conditions of life of the most vulnerable groups of women?

Chapter 1

Contesting Ideologies

Feminism and Nationalism

Two broad and overarching sets of debates surround the women's movement in South Africa. In the first part of this chapter I address debates about the relationship between women's struggles and broader political struggles. I begin by locating women's organizations historically, showing how diverse organizations and demands were increasingly drawn into the nationalist struggle against the apartheid state. I argue that in the early part of the twentieth century women mobilized around a wide range of issues—working women's struggles against low wages and poor conditions in the workplace, local states' attempts to regulate women's economic activities, control of women's mobility by the promulgation of laws restricting the free movement of black people into and within urban areas, rural poverty, and so on—and a variety of organizations—from the Communist Party of South Africa to trade unions and local women's organizations—took up women's issues. By the 1950s these struggles had been subsumed and homogenized within a nationalist narrative that emphasized the primacy of the struggle for national liberation—the struggle against white rule.

I argue that rather than seeing this process as inevitable and self-evident, we need to interrogate the opportunities and costs of nationalism for the women's movement. On the one hand, participation in the national liberation struggle enabled women activists to link race, class, and gender oppression and to universalize the demand for gender equality within the vision of national liberation. On the other hand, the increasing embeddedness of the women's movement in the national liberation movement opens questions about whether and in what ways the project of national liberation and that of women's liberation were congruent. What kind of women's movement was possible within the dual constraints of a population of women differentiated by race, class, ideology, and other factors on the one hand and the dominance of nationalist ideological frameworks on the other? To what extent was organizational autonomy desirable, and under what conditions could it be achieved? This historical overview serves also to mark the persistence of the question of autonomy in the course of women's organizing throughout the twentieth century. Concerns about autonomy did not emerge from the theoretical interventions of academic feminism, as some analysts have suggested,[1] but from the practice of women's organizations.

Early Debates about Autonomy: The Historical Roots of the Women's Movement

Women have been politically active, and have mobilized *as* women, throughout South Africa's history. Many of their protests have been sporadic, varied in content, and characterized by an upsurge of political mobilization around a specific campaign, followed by decline. Thus, for example, women mobilized against the extension of passes to women in Bloemfontein in 1913,[2] against the poll tax for Indian people, and in defiance of other anti-Asian laws as part of Gandhi's *satyagraha* (passive resistance) movement in the early years of the twentieth century.[3] Women also mobilized against restrictions on their economic activity in the Beerhall Protests in Natal in the 1920s, among other incidents.[4] Organized by the Communist Party of South Africa, women workers became active in trade unions in the 1920s and sought to expand their rights through nonracial class-based organization. As both Cherryl Walker and Tom Lodge have pointed out, the participation of women in the trade union movement was vital to the development of the women's movement.[5] In the trade unions women developed leadership and began to articulate the linkages between women's class oppression and their gender oppression.[6] The expanded visions of gender equality, and especially women's insistence that gender oppression could not be treated in isolation from that of class, would become part of the ideological resources on which the Federation of South African Women drew in the 1950s.

Demonstrations against restrictions on beer brewing, the extension of passes to women, and protests against food prices—all protests aimed at the state and employers—nevertheless also challenged the perceptions of nationalist organizations regarding the appropriate role for women in society. For the first half of the twentieth century, women had little political space within the African National Congress (ANC). Although women were actively engaged in a range of political struggles—against passes, high rents, the cost of living, and racist legislation—their status within the ANC was that of auxiliary members, with no voting rights. The women members of the ANC comprised "all the wives of members of any affiliated branch or branches and other distinguished African ladies. . . . It shall be the duty of all auxiliary members to provide suitable shelter and entertainment for delegates to the Congress."[7] Ginwala has commented that "men assumed, and women conceded, that defining and achieving the long term goals was men's territory."[8] Likewise, Walker has noted that "the function of the Women's League during this period was to provide the catering and organize the entertainment at meetings and conferences—the community of interests of African men and women did not extend to the kitchen. There was, at that stage, little effort to broaden established views on women's role on the part of either the men or the women of the ANC."[9]

The Bantu Women's League was dominated by welfarist models for women's public activities and restricted its activities to a narrow range associated with the "upliftment and education" of girls. As such, it bore little relation to the localized struggles of women against economic and social exploitation. Although Ginwala has argued that women participated as de facto members of the ANC at all levels of decision making within the organization,[10] before the 1940s the ANC itself was an elitist organization that was barely interested in developing a mass base.[11] While the Communist Party attracted large numbers of women to its ranks around campaigns such as the cost of food and transport, "African politicians were rather slow to recognise this potential new constituency," according to Lodge.[12]

Only in 1943, thirty-one years after the ANC's formation, were women allowed to become full members of the movement with rights to vote and participate in all levels of its deliberations.[13] The labor needs of an expanding secondary industry and the decline of the reserve economy accelerated women's urbanization, and as members of deprived urban communities, women "formed a significant part of the groundswell of discontent and resistance that rumbled through the townships" in the 1940s, according to Walker.[14] Channeling this militancy into the national liberation movement was an important reason for the formation of the ANC Women's League (and the ANC Youth League). Thus women won their new status in part as a consequence of the ANC's efforts to build up a mass membership, with women regarded as potential recruits, and in part in recognition of the need to "upgrade the status of women," part of the new modernizing language of an emerging nationalism in the ANC.[15] Nevertheless, when the ANC Women's League was set up, it retained its auxiliary status. The Women's League was constituted as a substructure of the ANC, "under the political direction and control of the Congress, and it follows the policy and control of the Congress," a status underscored by its being headed by Madie Hall Xuma, the American wife of Dr. Alfred Bitini Xuma, the president of the ANC, as Walker has noted.[16]

Despite these limitations, Walker notes that the establishment of the ANC Women's League was highly significant. "A body aiming to represent the interests of the majority of South African women had been set up within the premier African political organisation—the ANC had finally come to incorporate women, one half of the people it claimed to represent, into its political frame of reference. A structure was created whereby African women could be channeled into the national liberation movement on a footing that was, at least theoretically, equal to that of men."[17] As Walker further noted, "Women were being organized specifically as African women, setting its [the ANC's] mark on the subsequent form that the women's movement would take in the national liberation movement."[18]

Women's Autonomy in the ANC Alliance

Although relatively quiescent during the 1940s, in the 1950s the ANC Women's League became a key driving force behind the Federation of South African Women, the nonracial women's movement that operated within the Congress Alliance, the umbrella group formed by the ANC, the white Congress of Democrats, the South African Indian Congress, and the Coloured People's Organisation to oppose apartheid. Taking on the struggle against passes, and playing a leading role in the Defiance Campaign, the Women's League was galvanized to go beyond its "tea-making" role to "take a more active lead in organising women to promote a greater awareness of their position within society."[19] Debates about the status of the league intensified, "with the women calling for autonomy and the men wanting greater control," according to Ginwala.[20] In 1945 the executive committee of the ANC Women's League passed a resolution asking that it be allowed to "organise autonomous branches wherever they so desire within the ANC."[21] This was not allowed, and in 1946 the ANC *Bulletin* pointed out that allowing women to establish the league "does not mean parallelism but cooperation and mutual assistance in the building up of membership and

funds for both sections."[22] The process of articulating new roles and organizational capacities was interrupted in 1960, when the apartheid government banned the ANC and the Pan Africanist Congress, and the liberation
movements went into exile.

The increased activism of women in the ANC, the South African
Communist Party, and the affiliated congresses opened discussions about
the possibility of a national women's movement. The ANC had decided in
1943 that "it was not prepared to submerge the ANCWL into a general
non-racial women's movement,"[23] as it was committed to the notion of the
"wagon-wheel"—with Africans, Indians, coloreds, and whites forming the
spokes of the wheel, each racial group organized under its own structures.
The ANC Women's League, however, was an organizational vehicle that
drew only African members. It would have to find some other format for
a women's movement that would be consistent with the organizational
style of the Congress Alliance. The league needed a broader alliance that
would include white, colored, and Indian women. The new organization of
women's groups was to be an equal partner in the Congress Alliance.

By the 1940s women of all races had begun to participate to some extent
in the public world of politics. In Natal, Indian women, conventionally
understood as passive and culturally subordinate to men, began to mobilize
as part of the passive resistance campaign inspired by Gandhi. They organized women by language—Tamil, Gujerati, and Hindi—and drew connections between the struggles of Indians and Africans against white domination while raising the issue of women's rights. The Indian women joined
opposition to the Asiatic Land Tenure and Indian Representation Act No.
28 of 1946 (the so-called Ghetto Act), which prohibited Indians from ac-
quiring fixed property except in "exempted areas" and in return gave Indians a franchise that allowed them to elect white representatives to Parliament. Speaking under the auspices of the Natal Indian Congress, the first
Indian woman doctor in South Africa, Dr. Kesaveloo Goonam, declared,
"We Indian women have to fight for our very life now. Our lot is not just to
stay at home and cook."[24] Fatima Meer pointed out that "the Europeans
consider Indian women to be at such a low level and to be so ignorant that
we are not given the vote." The limited franchise rights that allowed Indians
to be represented by whites was "like a wax doll placed in the hands of a
woman who was told it was a real life baby. It would not work. It is merely a
farce."[25] The Natal Indian Congress (NIC) itself was not convinced that
women should have equal rights. When Dr. Goonam approached NIC leaders to seek representation for women within the organization, they told her
that "Indian women were not sufficiently advanced to receive representation."[26] Attempts were made to form an Indian women's association, but it
does not seem to have materialized. In the 1950s many of the Indian women

leaders involved in that effort—Fatima Meer, Zainab Asvat, Amina Pahad—joined the nonracial Federation of South African Women and threw in their lot with the African majority in the struggle for democracy for all, rather than accept crumbs off the apartheid table.

The federation was formed in 1954 at a meeting attended by members of the ANC Women's League, the Communist Party, and trade unions. The federation was a nonracial coordinating body to which different groups affiliated. At the outset the federation had to address the question of why an organization of women separate from the ANC was necessary. "For the proponents of a federation two key and somewhat contradictory motivations dominated: the fear that an autonomous organisation would compete with the ANCWL, and the conviction that an autonomous organisation was not feasible: there would not be the support to sustain it."[27] Hilda Bernstein recalled that the federation reflected "both the idea that women have common interests, and also a strong political attitude."[28] At its inaugural meeting the Federation of South African Women adopted its "Women's Charter," which laid out the political role of women. Although firmly located within the antiapartheid struggle, the charter also sought to address the specifics of women's oppression: "The law has lagged behind the development of society; it no longer corresponds to the actual social and economic position of women. The law has become an obstacle to the progress of the women, and therefore a brake on the whole of society. This intolerable condition would not be allowed to continue were it not for the refusal of a large section of our menfolk to concede to us women the rights and privileges which they demand for themselves. We shall teach men they cannot hope to liberate themselves from the evils of discrimination and prejudice as long as they fail to extend to women complete and unqualified equality in law and in practice."[29] As this excerpt from the charter highlights, the struggle against women's oppression was not simply *parallel* to the struggle for the rights of black people but was also a challenge to the deeply entrenched gender hierarchies within black (and other) communities. The charter reflected the tension between mobilizing women for national liberation and for women's liberation—a tension that Walker's study of the federation shows was resolved by allowing the push for national liberation to dominate. The ANC "remained the ultimate source of authority."[30]

This acceptance of the dominance of the ANC was pragmatic: the federation's membership was primarily drawn from the ANC Women's League, "whose priorities and internal organisational commitments inevitably exerted enormous influence over the new women's organisation."[31] The federation participated in a number of campaigns organized by the Congress Alliance. In 1955 the federation launched an independent militant campaign against the extension of passes to women that would regulate their urban mobility. The heart of the protest was a march of two thousand women from around the country to the Union Buildings in Pretoria. On August 9, 1956, a date that has become symbolic of women's resistance to apartheid, twenty thousand women assembled at the Union Buildings, where they presented a petition against passes to the National Party government headed by J. G. Strijdom. The march provided some of the richest symbolism associated with women's struggles in South Africa: the photograph of four women of different races standing outside the locked government office door with twenty thousand individually signed petitions; the song ("Malibongwe Amakhosikhazi"—We Thank the Women), the slogan ("Strijdom—you have touched the women, you have struck a rock, you will be crushed"), the image of disciplined defiance (twenty thousand women standing silently in the baking sun), and the passion for the cause (women traveling for days from outlying locations to get to Pretoria, in some cases defying their husbands and fathers and even, by some accounts, defying the ANC).[32]

The women's campaigns against the pass laws spread; several more "defiance campaigns" against pass laws led to the arrest of several thousand women during 1957. The Congress Alliance's response to the scale and nature of the protest was not entirely supportive: the federation's position, enthusiastically supported by the defiance campaigners, was "no bail, no fines," but the ANC leadership argued that instead of seeking confrontation with the authorities, the federation should concentrate on educational campaigns.[33] Helen Joseph has commented that "we were disappointed and a little angry at first, but we were also disciplined and we were a part of the whole liberation struggle. There was no room for any rebellious spirit on our part and there was none. Bail and fines were paid and the women returned to their homes."[34] Hilda Bernstein, a Communist Party member and leader of the federation, points out that "women were not bystanders, nor reluctant participants dragged along by the militancy of the men, but were an integral part of the whole development of the campaigns. Without their activities, the campaigns could not have taken place."[35] And yet, despite their proven organizational abilities, women leaders remained unrecognized by the ANC. Nor was the relationship between the ANC Women's League and the federation smooth. Wells comments that leadership tensions in relation to the marches between the ANC Women's League and the federation played a role in undermining the autonomy of the federation: "Amid continuing charges that the Federation drew support away from the ANCWL, Federation leaders bent over backwards to prove their allegiance to the male-dominated ANC leadership. . . . When Federation members proposed a huge march to deliver their half-million signatures [against passes], they agreed to allow the (male) leaders of the ANC to set the date.

No date was ever set and the demonstration never took place, much to the disappointment of many women."[36] By 1963, whether as a result of gradual compliance with the male leadership's views on women's roles[37] or the increasing repression following the Sharpeville massacre in 1960,[38] the federation was "virtually silenced and driven underground."[39] Although its leading members were banned or placed under house arrest, unlike other political organizations the federation itself was not banned, an important factor in the decision to revive it in the 1980s.

Not all women's organized activities can easily be subsumed within the history of the ANC or the federation. In addition to the overt political organization of women, many other forms of associational life provided solidarity networks for newly urbanized women, functioned as women's forums within religious communities, or performed economic support roles (savings clubs — "stokvels" — and burial societies). These organizational forms need to be recognized if we are to use a more fluid understanding of politics than that defined by male-centered political organizations. In their everyday life within these nonpolitical structures women often develop a collective consciousness that can be mobilized when the survival of communities is at stake.[40] Most of these organizations could be regarded as dealing with women's practical needs, that is, offering mechanisms through which to address women's needs that arise from their gendered social responsibilities.[41] As Temma Kaplan has pointed out, such grassroots support groups can be important sources for the emergence of social movements, and their "unspectacular" concerns to "accomplish necessary tasks, to provide services rather than to build power bases" can seem politically insignificant.[42]

In South Africa the everyday organization of women around their roles as mothers and community members by far outweighs the number of women engaged in overt political activities. Yet, a deeper analysis of women's political organizations suggests that the strategic links and cultural affinities between those organizations and the "apolitical" women's groups are more extensive than is generally credited. During the 1950s it was relatively easy to use existing support and communication networks to mobilize urban women to join the antipass campaigns.[43] The uniform of the ANC Women's League draws on women's tradition of wearing distinctive colors and styles of hats to signal their affiliation to particular church and prayer groups. In the 1980s neighborhood associations of women constituted the roots of the revived women's movement, and the notions of popular democracy that shaped the United Democratic Front can, to a significant extent, be traced to the everyday concerns of ordinary women in their communities. In the 1990s, even though the formation of the Women's National Coalition (WNC) was driven by women in political organizations, it was the associations of hairdressers and beauticians, of stokvels and women farmers' groups—not the branch structures of the political organizations—that gave credibility to the notion of a mass base.

Feminism and Nationalism as Discourses of Liberation in South Africa

Despite the tremendous organizational advances of women's groups in the twentieth century, several questions about the authority of the national liberation movement over women's politics remained unresolved. The ideological framework within which women were mobilized was generated by nationalism rather than feminism. Indeed, within the national liberation movement and its allies in the women's movement, the notion of feminism was vilified to the extent that activists joked about "the f-word." The explicit development of feminist ideological and procedural frameworks for politics was constantly circumscribed by the concern that assertions of feminism might be read as anti-ANC. Despite this, as I argue in chapter 2, women activists were engaged on a daily basis in shaping new understandings of the relationship between women's struggles and nationalist struggles, and in making connections between oppression and exploitation in the public sphere and women's subordinate status in the private sphere.

In the 1950s both the ANC Women's League and the federation drew on a deep sense of "female consciousness," which develops from the "cultural experiences of helping families and communities survive."[44] Female consciousness impels women to political action and, while "emphasising roles they accept as wives and mothers [they] also demand the freedom to act as they think their obligations entail."[45] This was the framework within which women were mobilized to confront the pass laws, and in the course of this confrontation the idea of women as a significant political constituency was born. Thus female consciousness clearly has the potential for facilitating women's political agency.

However, as Maxine Molyneux has pointed out, some distinction has to be made between actions that are based on assumptions of "compliance with the existing gender order" and those that embrace "explicit questioning of that order and of the compliance of women within it."[46] In other words, women's movements that seek to transform social power relations have to mobilize feminist consciousness. To what extent were women's organizations, through their choice of issues and strategies and their visions for a future society, and through the ideological interventions of activists, able to transform female consciousness into feminist consciousness—or, in Molyneux's terms, bridge the political gap to build a movement aimed at securing women's strategic gender interests?

The extent to which feminist activists were able to harness and develop feminist consciousness was constrained by the attitude of the nationalist movement toward this project. From at least the 1970s feminism had an uneasy status within the national liberation movement. On the one hand, it was seen as an ideology primarily articulated by white (academic) Western women. Its perceived intellectual roots in the North were seen to limit its applicability to the experiences of black women in the highly exceptional circumstances of apartheid. Although feminism was by no means a homogeneous set of ideas or political prescriptions, and was certainly not articulated as homogeneous within South Africa, it was treated as such by the ANC. These misperceptions were fueled by the narrow and overly prescriptive versions of feminism that dominated debates in the United States and Britain in the late 1970s,[47] and by the problematic decision of some U.S. feminists to ally themselves with the call to keep politics out of discussions at the Nairobi Decade for Women Conference in 1985.[48]

Within South Africa the perception of feminism as divisive was further reinforced by the association of feminism with demands for greater organizational autonomy, for more decentralized and democratic mechanisms for agenda setting and strategic positioning, and a more nuanced view of how power relations were established and maintained. These emphases and demands were antithetical to the male-dominated leadership both inside the country and in exile. The exiled movement, operating under conditions of constant threat (physical and ideological) and increasingly shaped by the concerns and culture of its military wing, could not easily accommodate demands for direct democracy.[49] In the internal movement under the United Democratic Front, centralized decision making increasingly came to be seen as the key to a successful challenge to the apartheid state, and the long-term procedural concerns of women's organizations were marginalized, even while the rhetoric of gender equality was gaining ground.

By the 1980s a counterproductive polarization had developed: most activists in the antiapartheid movement saw "feminist issues" as referring exclusively to sexual and reproductive rights, while they regarded community-based issues (such as better access to services for women, organizing to end political violence, mobilizing support for displaced people) as grassroots, antiapartheid demands. Antiapartheid activists saw feminism as a separatist strategy, promoted by white feminists with little understanding of the conditions of black women's lives.[50] Although some attempts were made to develop a more inclusive and "indigenous" understanding of feminism, with few exceptions[51] these remained for the most part academic.[52]

Yet the academic debates were not without political import. Knowledge production and political activism were intricately intertwined in discussions about power and meaning in the women's movement. The complexity of these debates is reflected in the reception of Cherryl Walker's path-breaking work on the history of women's activism in the first half of the twentieth century.[53] Her book, the first academic work on women's political history, appeared in 1982 at precisely the moment when women's organizations were reemerging and when the revival of the Federation of South African Women was being debated by women activists within the country as an appropriate umbrella body for the fledgling women's organizations. The decade of the 1950s was being portrayed by the civic organizations and the ANC as the "golden age" of resistance. In this context discussions of Walker's book were charged with political significance; it was the catalyst for debates about the nature and role of women's organizations. The apartheid government banned the book, and it received a less-than-kind reception from women political activists in the ANC.

Walker traces the emergence of politicized women's organizations in response to gendered processes of proletarianization and urbanization. A large part of the book focuses on the period between the formation of the federation in 1954 and its decline in 1963. She argues that although the federation did not characterize itself as a feminist organization—it saw itself as a women's organization committed to *both* the national liberation struggle and the struggle for gender equality—it was nonetheless progressive and ahead of popular thinking as well as of views on the role of women in society held by the ANC elite.[54] Walker argues that despite the increasing credibility of the federation within the Congress Alliance as a result of the federation's militant campaigns against pass laws, the "backward attitude of the men acted as a brake on the progress of women's political activity."[55]

That the real issues at the heart of the debate were more political than academic is evident in a review of the book published in the *African Communist,* the official journal of the South African Communist Party. The reviewer, the pseudonymous "Letseme," lauds Walker's book for its "endeavour to recover from history the role and contribution women have made to our liberation struggle."[56] However, the review severely criticizes Walker's analytical framework: "The questions she poses are derived from concerns of the feminist movement in the contemporary period. . . . In assessing the approach of organisations to women's oppression, the feminist perspective begins to reveal its weaknesses. The significance of the ANC and the successive women's structures linked to it, for example, do not lie, first and foremost, in their approach to the women's question, but rather as organisations of the nationally oppressed, in their approach to the national question."[57] In a subsequent review of the book in an academic journal, three prominent internal activists—members of the United Women's Organisation in the Western Cape—adopted a tone rather similar to Letseme's and criticized the book on a number of grounds: the overemphasis on the role of the federation versus that of women in the ANC; Walker's failure to reveal the structural underpinnings of women's class consciousness; a selective reading of the federation's campaigns; and the failure to explicate the relationships between the regional affiliates and the national structures. These criticisms are worth engaging in themselves, and, indeed, Walker responded to the academic queries at some length.[58]

Far more stinging than the academic debate about sources and causative relationships, however, was the criticism of Walker's use of feminist methodology. Her critics argued that the book reveals the problem of "the easy conflation of [the researcher's] own ideology with that of the organisations being studied."[59] They accuse Walker of applying a "feminist teleology" in her study of the federation and, more particularly, of using the lens of Western feminism. "To Walker, women's organisation is feminist organisation, along the lines of mainline Eurocentric women's liberation feminism. . . . We would dispute that the Federation was a feminist organisation, or had feminist ideals, although its concerns were issues that specifically affect women. . . . For the most part, the Federation's members wanted to be freed to fulfil their feminine and familial roles."[60]

Although Walker is at pains to argue that women's consciousness was neither uniform nor consistent, and that women's perceptions of themselves were always overshadowed by their dominant identification with the priorities of the national liberation struggles, the three reviewers accuse her of "imposing" feminist consciousness on women in the federation. In their view Walker's conclusion—that the federation failed to live up to its promise of acting as a political vehicle for advancing women's liberation because of the constraints imposed by the male nationalist leadership and the organizational difficulties related to its federal structure—could only have derived from her feminist analysis. Pointing to the revival in the early 1980s of women's organizations with symbolic political ties to the federation, the three reviewers conclude that the federation was not a failure. According to these three reviewers, criticisms of the federation were therefore not just misplaced but undermined the "root" of women's contemporary organizing.[61]

I would argue that two issues were at stake in the critique of Walker's book: the legitimacy of organizing women to eliminate gender inequalities and the legitimacy of feminism itself as an ideological framework within which to understand and articulate that organization. Criticizing Walker for "Eurocentrism" in her use of feminism was a way of undermining both women's autonomous organization and independent political debate. This process of marginalization by damning feminism as foreign is not without its correlatives in other nationalist movements in the third world.[62] As

Heng has argued, "The ease with which, historically, the 'modern' and the 'western' have been conflated and offered as synonymous, interchangeable counters in both nationalist and Orientalist discourse has meant that a nationalist accusation of modern and/or foreign—that is to say, Western—provenance or influence, when directed at a social movement, has been sufficient for the movement's delegitimization."[63]

In the remainder of this chapter I explore in greater detail the uneasy relationship between feminism and nationalism, and the particular expressions of this relationship.

Locating Women's Struggles within Nationalism: Strategic Implications

Undoubtedly, the issue of the boundaries between nationalist mobilization and feminist mobilization also was closely tied to the issue of the autonomy of women's organizations from male-dominated political organizations. By the mid-1980s debates about the primary focus of women's organizations—that is, was the task to mobilize a greater number of women into the antiapartheid struggle or into a women's movement?—assumed new significance in the context of a resurgence of popular opposition to apartheid under the banner of the United Democratic Front. There was no single feminist position in this debate, nor was there uniformity in the position of nonfeminist women activists. Rather, there were a variety of positions to be discerned, sometimes within a single organization. For heuristic purposes it is possible to identify four broad strands in the South African debate about the relationship between women's liberation and national liberation.[64]

The "Women Question"

The dominant position within the ANC until the late 1980s was that the emancipation of women was secondary to and contingent upon national liberation. The task of women activists was to mobilize women for the broader struggle. There were two tendencies within this position. Nationalism, in and of itself, tended to be the primary emphasis. Frene Ginwala expressed this view when she commented: "In South Africa, the prime issue is apartheid and national liberation. So to argue that African women should concentrate on and form an isolated feminist movement, focusing on issues of women in their narrowest sense, implies African women must fight so that they can be equally oppressed with African men."[65] In other words, women's organizations should take their political leadership from the national liberation movement. The other tendency was that of Marxist feminism, which held that women's liberation would be achieved only under communism, and until that point the national liberation struggle had to take precedence.[66]

The Radical Feminist Position

Radical feminism was a relatively marginal position, although not unimportant in laying the foundation for an expanded understanding of the sources of women's oppression. This position was articulated primarily by white feminists who worked to end violence against women. Many radical feminists were based at university campuses, while others worked in the rape crisis centers established by feminists in the major cities in the 1980s. A few were also involved in antiapartheid organizations such as the Black Sash and the Johannesburg Democratic Action Committee, which was affiliated with the United Democratic Front. In this view the primary source of women's oppression lay in patriarchy. Male-dominated movements could not be trusted to advance women's interests. Women's organizations should be built as exclusively female organizations that would offer a safe organizational space for women, one characterized by the values of teamwork, nurturing, and mutual support.[67]

The "Workerist" Position

Although this position was similar in some respects to the Marxist feminist position, it was distinguished by its rejection of nationalism as an ideological vehicle. In this view there were no general women's interests, only interests determined by women's class positions. Working women's organizations should be autonomous from the national liberation movement because women's demands would never be met by a nationalist movement dominated by the petty bourgeois interests of men. Women activists should associate themselves with the struggles of women workers and with the independent trade union movement, and women's organizations should be of secondary importance. Women's interests would be met only by the overthrow of capitalism.

The Socialist Feminist Position

This position of socialist feminism was articulated most openly by women activists inside the country, many associated with the trade union movement and with the feminist media, as well as by some academics.[68] Interestingly, it was also supported by some women activists in the ANC in exile.[69] In this view women's organizations need relative autonomy from the national liberation movement. That is, they should link women's struggles with national and workers' struggles while maintaining internal control over decision making. Women's organizations need to be informed by feminism but should be cognizant of class and race differences that produce different interests among women.

As these categories suggest, women activists had little consensus about the necessity of or the most appropriate organizational form for gender-based activism. Not surprisingly, given the strong links between women activists, the internal resistance movement, and the ANC, the imperatives of national liberation dominated this debate. As a discursive framework, nationalism had an authoritative status akin to a master narrative, and within it there were distinct and politically upheld boundaries to women's agency. Maud Eduards has suggested that women's political agency is *always* limited within boundaries that are defined by men, arguing that "women are permitted, even welcomed in politics, if they act as gender-neutral individuals/citizens, accept the traditional party structure, cooperate with men and do not discuss women's conditions in power-political terms. But women who say that *my* conditions are signs of oppression, shared by other women, and that these common experiences must be translated into collective action, are regarded as alien—indeed threatening—to the political community."[70] Nationalism, in contrast with many other political movements, does offer the possibility of collective agency for women.[71] Women are mobilized not as gender-neutral individuals but as gendered beings with collective responsibility. Yet Eduards is correct to note that they are restricted from exercising that agency to redress power imbalances between women and men. In this sense feminism is immediately placed in contestatory relationship with nationalism, and attempts to marginalize the mobilizing language and organizational style of feminists are not surprising. Indeed, for some analysts the aim of nationalism was not so much to marginalize feminism as to silence it. Charman, de Swardt, and Simons, for example, have argued that the emphasis on national unity "preclude[d] a gendered analysis of both class and race in South Africa." In a harsh assessment they suggested that this is the result of an active silencing and even subversion of "those women and men who have the language to identify politically the complexity of the subordination of women in South Africa. This absence of a language enabling gender conflicts to be politicized and expressed as resistance to the political, economic and social domination of women by men occurs in a context where the penalties of resistance and the rewards of acquiescence shape women's material existence. Acquiescence is compliance in a conflict situation."[72]

Despite these attempts to delegitimize feminism as a political discourse, undercurrents of feminism seethed beneath the surface of women's political activities. The specific interpretations of women's oppression by organizations and activists contained sophisticated formulations that might be seen as the kernel of an indigenous feminism. In forging an understanding of the nature of women's politics under the conditions of an overriding struggle against apartheid, women activists were posing prescient questions about the ability to maintain social movements of women. Similarly, as the characterization of the different strands of debate about women and politics within the left indicates, the intensity and specificity of the arguments suggest a thriving intellectual engagement with the realities of the bounded nature of feminist political practice. Debates about autonomy, for example, are central to the articulation of socialist feminism, which offered an important alternative to both liberal and Marxist feminism.[73] Attempts to theorize the connections between women's gender oppression and their oppression as members of particular racial and class categories were also debates *within* feminism as much as they were debates *between* feminism and other ideologies.

The analysis of women's political activities in this book goes against the grain of earlier characterizations of women's politics (including my own[74]), which impose sharp distinctions between women who were organizing against national oppression and women who were organizing against gender oppression. This distinction is an important one insofar as it seeks to underscore the extent to which dominant political organizations can influence, even shape, the agendas of smaller movements that are allied with it. However, it does not allow us to understand the complex processes by which gender consciousness emerges in situations where there are sharp inequalities of race and class as well as gender. The social movement theorists Jean Cohen and Andrew Arato argue that a key aspect of the success of any social movement must lie in the extent to which it is able to root its values, norms, and institutions in the broader political culture.[75] Part of this political culture, in their view, must include the development of a specifically feminist consciousness.[76] As Chandra Mohanty[77] and other third world feminists have argued, such a feminist consciousness cannot—should not—be specified a priori according to the abstract definitions of universal theory but should be defined in the context of particular social formations and should have resonance in the historical experience and political culture of specific societies. Feminism is not a coherent ideology, nor is its usage uncontentious among organizations committed to gender equality, as I have argued. However, Cohen and Arato's point remains important: the extent to which feminist norms and values become embedded within both the women's movement and political culture more broadly is an important marker of the long-term success of the movement.

One important reason to avoid posing too sharp a distinction between nationalism and feminism in South Africa is that, as I have argued, women's activism—both feminist and nonfeminist—is deeply rooted in the antiapartheid movement. This is not a unique feature of the South African women's movement. Kumari Jayawardena's comparative survey of nationalism in Asia uncovers a pattern by which feminism in the third world emerges in the context of modernizing nationalist movements, suggesting that it is historically fallacious to present feminism and nationalism as two separate processes.[78] Indeed, Yuval-Davis has gone as far as to suggest that neither the construct of nation nor that of gender can be properly analyzed in abstraction from each other, as their intersections construct "both individuals' subjectivities and social lives, and the social and political projects of nations and states."[79] And yet, as in many other third world women's movements,[80] most women activists in South Africa were at pains to distinguish their struggles from those of feminism and to associate instead with the dominant nationalist movements. National liberation struggles facilitated and legitimated women's politicization—albeit for reasons of mass mobilization rather than a concern with gender equality per se—and provided the context in and against which to elaborate these formulations. Women were mobilized *as women* on the basis of particular constructions of gender identity and interests by antiapartheid movements inside the country and in exile.

A common defense of the dominance of nationalism over women in South Africa is that it is not nationalism per se that is problematic but the type of nationalism that needs to be explored if we are to predict its political effects on women. "Modernizing nationalisms" are beneficial to women because they offer the opportunity for women to expand Enlightenment values of equality and justice to include women. From this perspective the inclusion of women as full members of the ANC in 1943 was significant because it constituted a decisive break from the traditionalist nationalism associated with the first generation of ANC leaders. The modern, forward-looking ANC that replaced the original organization, appealing for the first time to the ideology of nationalism, sought to give the organization a mass base that included the urban African working class and women. This offered the opportunity for women to expand the notion of equality—previously embedded, as Natasha Erlank has shown, in masculinist Africanism[81]—to include gender as well as race.

Understanding the ANC as a modernizing nationalist movement suggests that rather than treating nationalism as uniform in its manner of mobilizing women, a sociological distinction can be crafted between *types* of nationalism, each of which mobilizes women in distinctive ways.[82] Gaitskell and Unterhalter's comparative study of motherist mobilization in Afrikaner and African nationalism is emblematic of this approach. Thus conservative nationalisms such as Afrikaner nationalism construct women as passive,[83] whereas African nationalism affords women an active political role.[84] For these authors the vital distinction lies in the racially defined version of *nation* in Afrikaner nationalism, which mobilized women only in defense of narrow race interests, and the nonracial basis of African nationalism in which women can make their claims within a democratic framework.[85] Such distinctions have been useful even to distinguish between types of nationalism among African political movements. While some ethnically rooted forms of nationalism, such as that proposed by the Inkatha movement, explicitly articulated a traditionalist position on women's roles and responsibilities,[86] the modernist ANC increasingly came to accept the ideal of gender equality as central to liberation.

In feminist debates outside South Africa, an alternative set of discussions about the relationship between women's struggles and nationalism suggests a historical reading of the development of nationalism. These discussions distinguish two phases of nationalist mobilization: the first is open and inclusivist resistance to colonial domination, and the second is the more elitist phase of state building.[87] In the first phase women, if organized, can insert demands for gender equality into the ideological framework of nationalism and make representational gains such as access to positions within the nationalist movement. In the second phase women are either marginalized from politics as a result of their "reprivatization" to meet the employment needs of demobilized guerrillas,[88] or they are co-opted into the nationalist elites within the state and are used as tokens to demonstrate the progressive nature of the state, even while little attempt is made to redress gender inequalities through state policies.[89] The so-called national machinery for women, developed as a consequence of the first United Nations Decade for Women, is often cited as an example of the institutional means through which such co-option takes place.[90] In such cases rebuilding women's organizations offers the only possibility for women to hold governments accountable to their commitments with regard to gender equality.[91] However, the political space to do this might be constrained by factors such as the degree to which civil society is organized, the ability of civil society to operate free of government restrictions, and the strength of women's leadership.[92]

These accounts from other nations show that although nationalism facilitated women's political agency within carefully circumscribed limits, women could breach these limits if other conditions within the nationalist movement—the extent to which it was rooted in an inclusivist understanding of nation, whether it was underpinned by democratic notions of equality, and the extent to which women could develop strong substructures of their own—facilitated women's participation.[93]

It would seem, therefore, that criticisms of nationalism in third world contexts are tempered by focusing either on the type of nationalism under discussion or on the phase of nationalist struggle. All accept that nationalist movements are inevitable in third world societies and that they have progressive potential, to the extent that they facilitate women's agency. Indeed, a cursory reading of the trajectory of women's politics in South Africa would suggest that both sociological and historical approaches can offer useful insights into the relationship between nationalism and women's liberation and, especially, that this relationship is a symbiotic one in many instances.

Interrogating the Claims of Nationalism

Interrogating the claims of nationalism does not relieve us of the responsibility for examining what *kind* of women's liberation can be envisaged within a nationalist framework and in what ways this might conform to feminist standards of liberation, in its broadest interpretation the empowerment of women as agents in all aspects of their lives and the achievement of substantive equality between women and men. In other words, the historical association between nationalism and women's mobilization in South Africa and in other third world contexts should not prevent us from a critical engagement of the constraints as well as the opportunities that this relationship posed for advancing the fundamental aims of the feminist project. Many other national liberation movements that facilitated women's political agency and promised benefits for women in the postcolonial period failed dramatically to live up to these promises, not least in Africa. As Amrita Basu notes, "The legacy of these movements is bittersweet and inevitably includes dashed hopes, broken promises, and unfulfilled commitments."[94] To associate this legacy primarily with the shift in nationalism from a transformative movement to a state-driven and elitist project—in Mamdani's words, from revolutionary agents to "craft unions of professional politicians"[95]—is only a partial answer. Most important, this explanation does not address why women were unable—or in some cases only very minimally able—to successfully insert themselves into the nationalist elite.

A critical approach to nationalism suggests two areas for attention: the discontinuities between feminism and nationalism, and the degree of autonomy of the women's movement. First, although nationalism might have been the crucible in which feminism in South Africa was born, feminism and nationalism are not completely congruent projects. Although both are concerned with mobilizing women into political movements, women's identities are limited within nationalism and contingent on men, and women's political agency is permitted to the extent that it enhances the popular base of the nationalist movement and signals its progressiveness. By contrast, feminism in South Africa, while emphasising the interconnectedness of gender, race, and class oppression, has been concerned with enhancing women's capacity to address sexual and reproductive issues as well as universal political interests. The articulation of concerns about sexual and reproductive rights is particularly illustrative of the tensions between nationalism and feminism. In seeking to place the right to freedom of sexual choice on the political agenda, feminists were not simply reflecting a difference in emphasis from that of the national liberation movement; they were also questioning its normative assumptions about the nature of the family and the primacy of women's roles as wives and mothers.

The inability of nationalism to encompass the range of women's struggles that center on their bodily integrity and autonomy reveals the boundaries of women's agency within this framework. As Elaine Unterhalter has argued in her work on "struggle autobiographies," men's role in South African nationalism has been understood within a construction of "heroic masculinity," which "stresses autonomy, adventure, comradeship and a self-conscious location in history."[96] The public realm of heroism and adventure is contrasted with the supportive, feminized private sphere.[97]

In a perceptive work Inderpal Grewal and Caren Kaplan have underscored the discontinuities between feminism and nationalism, suggesting that the concept of national identity "serves the interests of various patriarchies in multiple locations."[98] This poses rather sharply the question of whether the beneficial association of women's politics with nationalism is limited not just by the type of nationalism or the particular historical phase of the movement under discussion but by inherent constitutive limits to the extent to which nationalism could accommodate the aims of the women's movement. An increasingly large body of scholarship suggests that feminism and nationalism are at their core antagonistic projects.[99] An influential comparative study has shown the very idea of "nation" to be inextricably predicated on a gendered hierarchy of power that corresponds to that within the patriarchal household.[100] For Grewal and Kaplan feminism needs to be "freed from nationalist discourses."[101]

Nor, it would seem, is there automatically an association between nationalism's modernizing impulses and its underlying gender premises. As Anne McClintock has argued, there is a temporal anomaly within nationalism, a constant shifting between the nostalgia of the past and its "forward thrusting" impulse, which has consequences for gender divisions. "Women are represented as the atavistic and authentic body of national tradition (inert, backward-looking, and natural), embodying nationalism's conservative principle of continuity. Men, by contrast, represent the progressive, or revolutionary, principle of discontinuity. Nationalism's anomalous relation to time is thus managed as a natural relation to gender."[102]

As Heng also points out, the acceptance of modernity is often a selective process in which the technological and economic aspects of modernization are accepted, while "the cultural apparatus of modernisation—the alarming detritus of modernity's social effects—[may] be guarded against as contaminating, dangerous, and undesirable."[103] The extent to which the South African women's movement could transcend these deeply embedded hierarchies and anomalies and negotiate a more beneficial relationship between women and nationalism—and, when the limits of mutual benefit are reached, to break away from nationalism—must therefore form a central part of the analysis of the movement.

This leads us to a second area that demands critical consideration— what are the boundaries between the nationalist movement and the women's movement? To what extent were women able to develop a political movement over which they had strategic control—in other words, to what extent did the women's movement have autonomy in decision making vis-à-vis other political movements? This is an important practical question for the women's movement in South Africa, as my earlier historical discussion has shown. It is also a factor that bears on the long-term sustainability of women's organizations. As several studies have shown, the degree of autonomy of women's organizations relative to other mass organizations and the state is a crucial factor in explaining the degree to which women's movements succeed.[104] The hegemony of nationalism as a framework within which women's liberation should be contextualized was itself an outcome of struggle rather than a preordained and rational choice; as I argued in the historical discussion, women's struggles in the first half of the twentieth century occupied varied sites and expressed a diverse range of interests, not all of which were easily encompassed by the idea of a nationalist struggle. Rather than accept national liberation as an uncontested ideological vehicle, as, for example, Lewis and Hendricks[105] do, I find it fruitful to treat the idea of nation as "a territory of struggle between competing subject positions, narratives, and voices where nationalism or nationalisms may win . . . but cannot wipe out the traces of such struggles."[106] Furthermore, while nationalism might in many instances be enabling for women, the unchallenged authority of nationalism is a major barrier to feminism[107]; without a movement that can negotiate the boundaries of the power of male-dominated movements, nationalism imposes its hegemony on the women it mobilizes.

It is important to note that not only women's organizations sought— or were called on—to define their relationship to the national liberation project. Trade unions, student organizations, and indeed all movements that opposed apartheid and/or capitalism were in the same position as women's organizations. While the political imperative to signal a movement's or organization's stance in relation to nationalism was never explicit (particularly as the ANC was a proscribed organization), allegiance to the Freedom Charter was usually the marker of the organization's position. As Peter Hudson has noted, "There seems . . . a de facto obligation on all social movements and political organizations struggling to transform the South African state to define at some point their position vis-à-vis the Charter. This almost seems to be a condition of their being able to establish a political identity in the South African context."[108]

The alliance between the Communist Party and the ANC placed socialism in a similar relationship to feminism. The theory of national-democratic revolution proposed a two-phased revolution in which the first phase would be the establishment of a national democratic state led by the black working class and the second the creation of a socialist state. In this formulation "the struggle for national liberation is, from the point of view of the exploited classes, the inescapable political form of the class struggle."[109] This approach was highly contested on strategic and theoretical grounds, the specifics of which are beyond the scope of this book. What is of interest in this context, however, is that the preeminence of national liberation was by no means preordained or politically self-evident and that alternative political spaces existed within which feminists could locate their claims for some degree of relative autonomy from nationalism and for some degree of skepticism about the ability of national liberation to secure women's liberation.

Defining the Notions of Women's Interests and the Women's Movement in South Africa

What, then, in the context of competing nationalist and socialist conceptions of political struggle, would be the dimensions of the women's movement in South Africa? Debates about how to characterize women's struggles in South Africa have been considerable, and whether and at what point a social movement of women existed is much contested. Although in political practice these were not new problems—witness the struggles over the status of women in the ANC in the first half of the twentieth century and the relationship between the ANC Women's League, the federation, and the ANC in the 1950s—these debates sharpened both analytically and in political tone in the 1980s, when women's activism was resurgent. Definitions of what would or did constitute a women's movement in South Africa varied and were overburdened with prescriptive formulations of progressiveness, which often was used as a marker of affiliation to either the nationalist or the trade union movement instead of any clear principles of ideological direction or organizational form.[110]

Strategic decisions about the primary role of women's organizations— to mobilize women on behalf of national liberation or a broad-based national women's movement—became inescapable in women's politics with the formation of relatively sustained organizations of women in the major cities. Although, for a number of reasons, the leadership of women's organizations did not see the struggle for national liberation as separate from the struggle for women's liberation, there were tensions over how best to encompass both projects within one movement under highly constrained conditions of political mobilization. As women's organizations sought to demarcate a role that was distinct from both the internal resistance movement and conventional women's organizations such as stokvels and burial societies, the definition of what constituted a women's movement was a matter of concern. Does the mere existence of a range of organizations with female membership and addressing issues of interest to women constitute a women's movement, or are feminist consciousness and common purpose prerequisites for claiming the status of women's movement?[111] Is a women's movement a political force distinctly separate from other resistance movements? And if it is separate, should it be read as dividing progressive forces or as expanding the public sphere? Perhaps the overriding factor in this debate was the existence of a virtually hegemonic national liberation movement, which, like nationalist movements in many contexts, sought to bring all popular struggles under its banner. How could women's issues be defined within the context of such a dominant movement?

The task of defining whether there was indeed a coherent set of interests—and therefore a subject for mobilization—that could underpin a women's movement was the first preoccupation. Were "women" a unified category, the potential subjects for feminist mobilization? There was in fact little attempt to suggest that this was the case: the differences between women of different races and classes were starkly apparent. Within the Congress tradition it was argued that differences between women and between races could be transcended through appropriate political forms such as the federation and the Congress Alliance. Yet in both examples the idea of nonracialism was a misnomer, as Neville Alexander has pointed out.[112] In the federation women were organized separately, along racial lines, with their representative structures brought together at the national level. This form of organization might best be characterized as a multiracial alliance to overthrow apartheid rather than a project of building a new and single national identity. In effect, racial distinctions between women were held intact, and what operated was a form of coalition that failed to break—nor, indeed, did it seek to break—what Bernice Reagon Johnson has termed the "barred cages" of difference.[113]

In the 1980s more explicit attempts were made to define the nature of women's interests. The formulation of "triple oppression" sought to capture the relationship between gender, race, and class oppression. In this formulation black women were the most oppressed because of their threefold oppression as blacks, workers, and women.[114] Black—more specifically, African[115]—women should therefore have been the subject of political mobilization because they were the most oppressed. Criticized for treating oppression as merely an accumulation of economic and social disabilities,[116] and for leading to an "unilluminating repetition of formulae,"[117] the term *triple oppression* nevertheless had great currency in activist circles. Despite its seemingly particular application for describing the intersecting systems of patriarchy, capitalism, and apartheid, the term added little to clarify the specific nature of gender oppression in South Africa. Most popular usages tended to treat gender oppression as an intensifying factor in the oppression of black women, rather than as shaping qualitatively different understandings of how different forms of cultural and economic oppression intersect.[118] The primary value of the term was to identify the authentic subject of the women's movement. In particular, for example, the "rural black woman" assumed iconic status within the women's movement, carrying connotations of extreme oppression, voicelessness, and passivity, to be invoked as the moral subject of the women's movement. As a strategic choice, some feminists also criticized the narrow range of activities considered to be political[119] within the triple oppression framework and the failure to build an autonomous women's movement.[120] These critics argued that women's issues were manipulated as ideological and political resources and that contestation around the terms of women's involvement in the nationalist movement was at worst suppressed and at best ignored.[121]

Some feminists have argued that the focus on national liberation weakened the possibilities for the emergence of an assertive women's movement in South Africa.[122] Others have argued that a reluctance to build a women's movement separate from the national liberation movement stemmed from both the inseparable nature of race, class, and gender oppression as well as from "a strategic choice made in the face of opposition from a seemingly invincible white nationalist party-state that was quick to exploit any sign of division in order to subjugate Black people even further."[123] For Cheryl Hendricks, for example, the terms of women's political activities are set by the state: "The nature of the state induces the particular form and content of struggle. In defining themselves, and being discriminated against, as Black women, the Women's Movement focused its attention on nationalist issues and embarked upon 'women's struggles' within the parameters that the context would permit."[124] In her view, as well as that of other commentators such as Desiree Lewis[125] and Kemp and colleagues,[126] attempts to understand the struggles of women as *in any way* separate from that of national liberation stem from white Eurocentric bias toward particular types of women's movements and bear no relation to black women's political identities. Hendricks and Lewis have argued that the contestation about how to articulate the nature of women's struggles lies less in the tension between feminism and nationalism than in black women's struggle to "define and name," independent of white women. "Racial discourse is at the basis of the knowledge/power dialectic in South Africa and the white interpreter has—wittingly or unwittingly—redefined her authority and often dictated the terms of debates, while black subordinacy has been confirmed in self-defining processes of white knowledge production."[127]

Hendricks and Lewis explore the "suppressed feminism" of African women by exploring the centrality of motherhood as identity for black women. They offer an important rationale for the need for more precise renderings of the relationships between race and class and caution against emotional defensiveness in addressing issues of internal power in the women's movement. Given the substantial and systematic inequalities between black and white women, their concerns are highly significant for this study. To what extent can the debates between women activists be read as stemming from racial inequalities? How were racial identities articulated within women's organizations, and did these identities correspond to the stereotypical understandings of feminism as white, nationalism as black? Such questions, often treated at the rhetorical, accusatory, and emotive level, are best explored through a careful tracking of the dynamics of power within the women's movement. In this book I trace precisely which differences became politically salient at different moments in the movement's history and explore the issues of race and power within the women's movement by drawing on archival material and interviews.

As I argued in the introduction, women's interests cannot be read simply from their economic or social position[128]—nor, indeed, from their racial identity. Women are divided by class, race, regional, and other interests that continually undercut the coherence of gender identities. Although Hendricks and Lewis suggest that black and white women were in two opposing camps, I argue that women's interests were articulated in far more complex ways, with no direct correlation between racial identity and political identity. The formulations of Kemp and colleagues and Hendricks and Lewis, as well as the four positions that categorize the relationship between women and national liberation, suggest that in South Africa women activists have deployed a starkly polarized distinction between third world women's

Table 1.1. Categorizing Rights-based and Needs-based Approaches

	Rights (First World)	Needs (Third World)
Ideological Orientation	"Feminist"	"Revolutionary nationalist"
Mobilization	Strategic Feminist	Practical Needs
Desired Outcome	Formal equality	Substantive equality
Associated Paradigm	Human rights	Justice
Formal Political Demand	Descriptive representation	Interest/functional representation

struggles and feminist struggles in the first world. The implication of this distinction is to separate struggles for "gender rights" from struggles about women's needs, with the former associated with feminist consciousness and autonomous women's movements (see table 1.1).

I would argue that the rigid distinctions suggested by rights and needs do not help us to capture the complex formation of political identities of women in South Africa. South African women's struggles suggest that strategies that are conceived around narrow conceptions of feminism may not be more successful in bringing about changes in the lives of women; democracy (or national liberation) as a framework may offer better possibilities in different historical cases. Indeed, broader struggles against oppression may bring into play opportunities for mobilizing women's multiple identities in new ways, for example, by providing a basis for collective mobilization. Conversely, as I will show in chapter 4, rights-based struggles can form the basis for and create the legal framework within which to pursue substantive equality. Rather than using the polarizing "rights" and "needs" of feminist theorizing, gender politics in South Africa suggests ways in which rights-based actions can facilitate and enhance struggles to meet needs.

In this book I have maintained a distinction between women's organizations and the women's movement, retaining the latter term for those formations that sought to build regional and/or national alliances between different women's organizations and leaving open the possibility that in pursuing such alliances progressive and conservative women's organizations can sometimes be brought together around specific issues. Here too, though, a distinction must be made between the narrow set of alliances pursued in the 1980s by the Federation of South African Women (or FEDSAW, as the revived organization was known), which sought to unite only those organizations with ideological affiliations to the ANC, and the alliance generated by the Women's National Coalition, which was nonpartisan and broad based, including avowedly political organizations as well as those that dealt with women's practical gender needs. The aim of FEDSAW was primarily to harness the energies of the resurgent women's organizations to the nationalist cause. The coalition, although constituted around the more narrowly defined interest of inclusion in the multiparty negotiations process to end apartheid, embraced a more diverse set of organizations in the context of the elaboration of new forms of citizenship.

Chapter 2

The Emergence of Women as a Political Constituency

1979–90

In South Africa you don't decide to join politics; politics
decides to join you.
Ruth Mompati, member of the African National Congress

The 1980s marked a watershed in South African politics. The nature and
scope of resistance shifted from the African National Congress (ANC) in
exile to internal and localized forms of resistance to apartheid. The revival
of independent trade unions with the formation of the Federation of
South African Trade Unions in 1979 provided a crucial avenue for the mobilization of working-class women, and struggles in the workplace soon
spread to communities and households. Beginning in the late 1970s the
emergence of civic organizations in black townships that came to be known
as the civics movement drew women into politics in large numbers, a scale
of women's activism unseen since the 1950s. Early forms of local organization fueled the process of reviving women's political organization on a
larger scale, leading to the formation of three key regional women's organizations between 1981 and 1984: the United Women's Organisation in the
Western Cape (UWO), the Federation of Transvaal Women (FEDTRAW),
and the Natal Organisation of Women (NOW). These groups were pivotal

in shaping the ideological content and strategic direction of the women's movement in the 1980s and 1990s. Although women's organizations were tied to struggles against apartheid through a complex network of political aims, activists, and organizational alliances, the women's groups that emerged during this period also sought to articulate new forms of grassroots democracy. Their emphasis on developing strong organizational structures and open and accountable practices, and on building nonracialism among women, reflected a radically different approach to "the women question." In the process women activists sought—ultimately unsuccessfully—to build a women's movement that, while part of a broader movement against oppression, nevertheless retained relative autonomy from the dictates of male-dominated civic organizations and, from 1983, the United Democratic Front (UDF), the umbrella organization of groups opposing the apartheid government's proposed constitutional reforms.

Women's activism in this period reemerged within the ambit of the growing civics movement in the African, Indian, and colored townships. The civics movement sought to "develop loci of grassroots power among ordinary people to promote an ultimately untheorised process of radical, mass-based transformation from below."[1] Although the civic organizations were part of the revival of the "Congress tradition"—the history of political struggle of the ANC and its partners in the Congress Alliance in the 1950s—the movement also aimed to lay the basis for an alternative form of democracy. This form of democracy was inchoately expressed; as Jonny Steinberg has noted, it often emerged in a "silent and unregistered manner."[2] In broad terms democratic visions were understood as emerging from the grassroots, and political organizations were "people driven" as opposed to elite driven, took localized forms, and were intended to lay the basis for reconstruction of political order after apartheid. In particular, the civics movement articulated a political approach to ending apartheid, in contrast to the guerrilla warfare that the ANC preferred during this period. The movement also represented a shift away from the identity politics of the black consciousness movement that had dominated the internal political landscape in the 1970s.

The core books dealing with the UDF explore in some detail the political values and organizational forms of the new civics movement (township community groups), especially the ways in which civics related to the broader goals of the antiapartheid movement.[3] However, apart from some discussion in Ineke van Kessel's book, this literature pays no attention to women's roles in the civics movement or to women's organizations in alliance with the civics movement. In this chapter I aim to provide more than simply a "gender corrective" to these histories.[4] Rather, through the lens of three UDF affiliates, the United Women's Organisation, the Natal

Organisation of Women, and the Federation of Transvaal Women, I seek to explore two key questions: To what extent did the civics movement and the UDF in practice give voice and power to the grassroots; and did the notions of democracy offered by the civics movement encompass the interests articulated by its women's movement affiliates? I argue that the goals of feminists within these women's organizations went beyond the vision of democracy offered by the civics movement and the UDF. Feminists sought not merely a regime change, nor even simply the expansion of democratic forms to encompass "people's power," but also a reconsideration of the ways in which private inequalities shaped the differential public capabilities of women and men.

This chapter draws on archival material and interviews with participants in women's organizations. These organizations were important to the political landscape of the 1980s for several reasons. They had close relationships to the antiapartheid movement. The leaders of women's organizations were bound by numerous social and political ties to the major civic organizations and trade unions. In part because of these links, the ANC, then in exile, regarded UWO, NOW, and FEDTRAW as central locuses for instilling loyalty to the ANC and adopting strategies sympathetic to the ANC. Together with the ANC Women's League, these organizations provided the leadership and the constituency for the Women's National Coalition, the umbrella body for the women's movement during the crucial years of the transition to democracy. The outcome of struggles waged by and within these organizations shaped the ideological content and strategic direction of the women's movement in the 1980s and 1990s.

Early Forms of Organization: Building Grassroots Democracy

The organizational precursors to UWO, NOW, and FEDTRAW were highly localized, neighborhood-based associations that developed into larger, politically oriented organizations. In most cases very small sparks—events or activists—acted as catalysts. On the new terrain of battle within the townships, women's gendered responsibilities for household and community reproduction acquired a broader political significance. Women emerged as a powerful force in community-level politics, organizing around bread-and-butter issues such as high rents, lack of services, and corrupt local councils. Shamim Meer has pointed out that "this was an era when nothing good was expected from government. Where if anything the government's agenda was to create greater hardship for black South Africans. Women realised that they had to find ways of coping in order to meet their basic needs even as they confronted the authorities."[5] The disruptions of family and household as homes were burned down during unrest in the townships, particularly after 1983 in Natal where conflict between the UDF and the Zulu nationalist movement Inkatha reached civil war proportions, created an added and gender-specific burden for women, who had to reconstruct their homes, often in remote locations.

Phoenix, a new Indian township near Durban populated by people who had lost their homes as a result of the floods in the Tin Town settlement in Springfield, is a good example of the dynamics of this period. In 1976 a group of Indian students from the University of Durban–Westville formed the Phoenix Working Committee to work with the displaced people and create networks of organizations in the new township. Key activists included Pravin Gordhan and Yunus Mahomed, credited with the resurgence of underground ANC political activity in Natal.[6] The child welfare officer for Phoenix was Shamim Meer, a feminist social worker who was associated with the Phoenix Working Committee and other antiapartheid organizations. She played a central role in drawing women into organizations. Inspired by Meer, the Phoenix Women's Circle began to organize women around "people's needs" such as nurseries, child care, and preschools.[7] The Women's Circle began as disparate associations of women in particular sections of the township. The founders of the circle had begun by approaching individual women in sections of the township in partnership with Phoenix Child Welfare. These women then recruited neighbors and other women they knew. A member of the organization described the process in the Northcroft precinct of Phoenix for *Speak* magazine: "To get more women involved we decided to have meetings on each street, and to go door to door to invite women to the meetings. Visiting each home was an interesting experience. Most women were very interested. We held street meetings covering more than 500 houses. Many women attended these meetings. Many of us did not know women in the neighbourhood before, so this gave us a chance to meet each other. At each meeting someone offered her home for the next meeting."[8]

In Phoenix, as in other black townships, the "people's needs" that women acted upon were a response to the most visible consequences of social fragmentation, poor social services and economic marginality. For example, the women decided to start a preschool and obtained permission from the local school principal to use classrooms after school let out in the afternoons. Women also met to teach and learn crocheting, knitting, and baking, and these sessions produced a sense of community. In time, "we also spoke of transport problems and of the problem of no clinic," another woman told *Speak*,[9] issues that propelled the women's groups into conflict with the local authorities responsible for providing such services. In confronting the authorities, in many townships the neighborhood-based associations united

to form a single women's group in the township, often retaining the organizational structure of a neighborhood association while becoming a political force.

In Hambanati, an African township outside Tongaat in Natal, a women's
group was begun in 1984 in response to the failure of local authorities to provide adequate burial facilities. Residents faced the choice of cremating their
dead or burying them at a cemetery some distance from the township. "We
went house to house and demanded of all women to come to a meeting to
talk about this problem. Anyone refusing to come had to tell us where she
hoped to bury her dead. Did she have a special place, we asked," a woman told
a *Speak* reporter. "We met with the advisory board but found they had no
power to do anything. We formed the Hambanati Women's Action Group
and took the problem up with the Port Natal Administration Board."[10]

The efforts to arrange for burial sites led to other campaigns, including
one to relocate a rubbish dump that was too close to black people's homes.
The women dumped garbage on a golf course reserved for whites, forcing
the township council to move the dump to a more remote location. The
success of the campaign strengthened the view that collective action could
improve conditions in the township, and more women joined the group.
"Now that the organisation is solid the Port Natal Administration Board
know[s] that we are a force to be reckoned with."[11] The Hambanati women's
group became a branch of NOW.

Although opposition to local councils and agitation for better basic services were widespread, women's struggles were not confined to the public
sphere. Gradually, women began to make connections between their exploitation in the workplace and their subordination within the home. As a
woman member of the National Union of Metal Workers pointed out, "We
are oppressed at work and we are oppressed at our location and in our
houses. We are sick and tired of this. At work we work hard. There is the
machine you have to push. At the same time you must come home and
cook and do this and do that. . . . Now why should I fight at work against
hard labour and [for] maternity leave and not fight at home? If we women
do not fight for ourselves there is nobody who is going to fight for us."[12] Especially within the unions, women formed strong ideas about the relationship between public struggles for democracy and gender relations at home.
In part this was because active involvement in the unions often put women
into direct conflict with their male partners, who resented the time that the
women unionists spent away from home at evening meetings.[13] Women
interviewed by *Speak* during the 1987 strike organized by the Catering and
Commercial Workers' Union at the OK Bazaars and Hyperama supermar-
kets in Durban, for example, complained that their husbands opposed their
actions. One shop steward pointed out that her activism was possible only

because she was a widow: "My husband didn't want me to move at all. Not even to work. Only to go to the church and the market."[14] MamLydia Kompe, a trade unionist and later founder of the Rural Women's Movement, recalled how male coworkers would expect her to buy them lunch, make them tea, and clean up after them during her lunch breaks. At home her husband complained incessantly about her participation in the Transport and General Workers Union. "These men feel threatened when we push to be equal," she told Jane Barrett and colleagues.[15]

This kind of male opposition to women's activism explains why many women found it much easier to be involved in community-based women's organizations, where mobilization took place at church and the market.[16] There women could meet as part of their daily activities, near their homes and often among friends. Yet even in this more conducive environment, women struggled to combine household and political work. Discussions about the unequal burdens of domestic work and child care became increasingly common in women's groups. Shamim Meer has commented that in the early 1980s, "whenever women came together it was . . . personal struggles that held us back. Women in communities talked in their women's groups about difficulties in getting to meetings because of husbands who expected their meals on time."[17]

Discussions about such personal struggles encompassed the workplace experiences of sexual harassment and lack of benefits for pregnant women and new mothers, as well as domestic struggles at home between women and men. In women's community groups and in women's meetings within trade unions, discussions about violence against women and about the extent of rape[18] and battery[19] within marriage became common. When women raised these issues, they received a mixed response from the political leadership. On the one hand, organization leaders were keen to pursue the mobilization of women at the street and district level—women constituted a significant part of the base of the civics movement, a key constituency, along with youth and workers. Thus leaders of these groups encouraged women in their struggles against the local state and validated them politically within the broader strategy of harnessing "people's power." In the process of mobilizing women, the new organizations were also developing their members' understanding of democracy, participation, and accountability. On the other hand, male leaders and nationalist female activists did not define as political those issues that were related to personal autonomy and sexual and reproductive rights and indeed regarded them as divisive. These leaders encouraged grassroots power and women's leadership rhetorically, but a small group of men continued to make the decisions.

These contradictory responses produced a form of political schizophrenia for women activists, who were seeking new and locally relevant

definitions for the goals of women's organizations. For some activists the
lack of serious attention to women's issues and to the potential for women
to emerge as leaders meant that women's organizations were important as
relatively safe spaces within which women could debate the content of their
struggles and determine their strategic goals—they could fly under the
radar. Other activists regarded the emergence of women's organizations
purely as instrumental in encouraging the local development of the antiapartheid movement. The resulting tensions between different conceptions
of women's organizations pushed these groups into an ongoing process of
negotiating their relationship to the national liberation struggle.

The political context for exploring this relationship was heavily
weighted against the women activists. At the early stages of civic organizing, men in the community did not always recognize women's participation
or even welcome it. Several biographies have revealed the extent to which
women encountered resistance from their partners and their community
leaders once the women's activism became evident,[20] but here I will use an
organizational example. Writing about the Crossroads squatter camp in
Cape Town, Josette Cole has argued that tensions between men and women
were increasingly apparent from the late 1970s: "For a long time women had
known that some men were unhappy with their [the women's] political role
in the community. They [the men] had learnt to live with it in the course of
earlier struggles (1975–1978) when women had constantly to battle against
traditional views which saw politics as the realm of men. Women had taken
the lead despite this criticism because, as they so often stated, it was they
who really 'felt the pain.'"[21]

According to Cole, women were removed from positions in the Crossroads Committee in 1979, and the Women's Committee was "effectively
'banned' from having meetings . . . [and] was forced to revert to earlier patterns of mobilisation and organisation—open air meetings."[22] Although
the women did organize, their political activity was difficult to sustain in
the face of both state repression and male hostility, and "the women of
Crossroads were not able to regain the political position they had once
held."[23] But such experiences fed into the increasing desire among women
activists for separate and strong women's organizations that could cross
township boundaries and provide avenues for solidarity and mobilization.

Like the civic organizations,[24] the newly emerging women's groups regarded building grassroots democracy as an important part of their organizational culture. This was reflected in the participatory process of developing the organization and the attempts to reach decisions in an inclusive and
consensual manner. The constitution of the Phoenix Women's Circle, for
example, was drafted by a working committee that included two people
from each street. One member commented that "we feel everyone must

have a say and that our officials alone can't make decisions. This is why our meetings are important. So that we can discuss things and have our say before we decide anything."[25] Grassroots organizations such as the Phoenix Women's Circle were vital for the democratization of South Africa, even though their stated goals and membership might have been diverse and they may not have explicitly articulated political ideologies. As Alvarez has noted in her discussion of such organizations in a similar political context in Brazil, "These grassroots struggles bore witness to women's and men's unyielding resistance to authoritarian policies," exposing the "regime's inherent contradictions."[26] Additionally, and perhaps more important for the long-term prospects of democracy, they also began to open spaces in which to imagine new forms of political culture. Thus the importance of grassroots activism was not simply to expose the illegitimacy of apartheid or to broaden the base of the nationalist movement but to lay the foundation for a sustainable popular movement of women that would define the shape of postapartheid society. Temma Kaplan's comparative study of grassroots movements underscores this radical potential of localized movements. She has argued that grassroots activism in itself poses a particular conception of democracy: "The term suggests being outside the control of any state, church, union or political party. To the women claiming its provenance, being from the grassroots generally means being free from any constraining political affiliations and being responsible to no authority except their own group. Though such women generally recognise their seeming powerlessness against corporate and governmental opponents, they also assert their moral superiority, their right to be responsible citizens, not according to official laws, but on their own terms."[27]

Kaplan identifies an important set of concerns that shapes the emergence of localized movements. To be sure, in South Africa the "grassroots"— whether women's organizations or civic organizations—has been far from independent of unions or political parties. Rather, local struggles have been understood as microcosms of a larger movement against repression and exploitation, and for many activists alliances with unions and the ANC have been rational and necessary. Yet Kaplan does identify a tension between local democracy-building projects and national politics that helps illuminate the difficulties facing South African women's organizations. The desire of women's organizations to build a space outside the control of political movements—a political space in which women would be organized around issues of their own choosing rather than as a sector of the antiapartheid movement—and the attempt to build on the early traditions of direct democracy was always present. UWO and NOW, in particular, sought to build on early and localized forms of organization while drawing women into the larger political landscape. The extent to which they would be able to sustain these goals was shaped by the broadening of highly localized women's groups into regional women's organizations, by their affiliation with the UDF, and by increasing state repression during the 1980s.

Expanding from Local to Regional Organizations: The Role of the Activists

Only three short years after local activism emerged as a political force, women activists began to debate the need for larger and more powerful organizations that linked the local women's groups. In the Western Cape the UWO was formed at the end of 1978 as a loose structure comprised of women who had been involved in a range of activities: civic organizations, trade unions, and detainees' support committees.[28] The formation of UWO was rapidly followed by that of NOW in 1981. The membership base of these women's organizations was primarily African working-class women, a significant number of whom had been active in local community groups.[29] Indian and colored women were also drawn into civic associations to form a visible presence, although their participation in women's organizations appears to have been at a lower rate.

Most activists joined women's organizations after initially becoming involved in community organizations and trade unions. For Gertrude Fester, a UWO activist, her involvement in a women's organization followed the more typical pattern of membership in the Black Consciousness movement while she was in college, frustration with male comrades on the left, and an abusive relationship: "My awakening to sexism was a gradual one. It took me going through marriage to realise that I was oppressed as a woman. I saw that the brunt of the work done in marriage has to be done by women."[30] Amy Thornton, a white member of the Congress of Democrats who had been banned from 1959 to 1973, recalled being "completely involved in my domestic life. . . . I had four small children. Until one day in 1977 there was a knock on my door and there was Oscar Mpetha, who I hadn't seen for years and years. And he said, 'won't you come and help with some typing at the Food and Canning Workers Union office?' So I went along to the office . . . and then in about 1979, '80, Oscar came again one day and said, 'Listen, we're going to start a women's organisation again—come.' And we started the United Women's Organisation with Dorothy Tamana and Mildred Lesia."[31]

For a small minority of women, gender activism came first. For example, Shahieda Issel, an activist in UWO and the UDF, said that "because I feel women are doubly oppressed in South Africa, the first organisation I joined was a women's organisation. Most men still think that women should play a subordinate role."[32] For Veni Soobrayan, executive member of

NOW, the organization provided a vital space: "In other organizations—like the Natal Indian Congress and the civics [organizations]—it was difficult to be heard as a woman. If you wanted a voice and an active role, it was easier in a women's organization. A women's organization was very fulfilling in that regard."[33]

Antiapartheid consciousness did not necessarily mean consciousness of gender inequalities. Connections between local struggles, national political movements, and gender consciousness—the translation of needs into rights-based demands—were made by a small group of activists who moved between different levels of struggles as well as across different organizations. Women activists were bound by a range of networks to organizations within the broader antiapartheid struggle. For example, the Vaal Organisation of Women was formed in 1984 with Connie Mofokeng, who had been a student activist in the late 1970s, as its secretary. Mofokeng was also an activist in the Vaal Civic Association and was its chief representative and area committee chairperson in Zone 7 of Sebokeng Township, where she lived.[34] Shamim Meer was a key figure in the Durban region. Her résumé illustrates more vividly than most the social and political connections between activists in the 1980s. A feminist activist, she was involved in trade union organization and, through family ties, the ANC. She was a social worker–activist in Phoenix at a crucial period when the Durban-based group of underground activists, led by Pravin Gordhan, was beginning to organize at the community level. Meer's parents, Ismail and Fatima Meer, had been prominent ANC activists in the 1940s and 1950s. Her father was banned for long periods, but her mother remained politically active and was a founding member of the Black Women's Federation and is a close personal friend of Nelson Mandela and Winnie Madikizela-Mandela. Shamim Meer's longtime partner is the prominent trade union activist Bobby Marie. Shamim Meer was active in the Durban Housing Action Committee and was a founding member of the Durban Women's Group and of both the *Speak* and *Agenda* collectives. Such connections were important in the cross-fertilization of ideas and the promotion of common political agendas, but they also produced a fragile leadership base, easily identified and undermined by the state through repression and sabotage.

Feminist activists were particularly important in the attempts to build awareness of gender inequalities into broader political struggles. Activists such as Shamim Meer, Connie Mofokeng, and Gertrude Fester belonged to a small number of "catalytic" organizations that sought to link women's activism around everyday concerns and the broader political struggles. Stepping beyond the ambitions of the national liberation movement, such activists and organizations were concerned about developing women's agency to effect changes in gender power relations as well as racial power relations.

One such organization was the Durban Women's Group, a nonracial grouping of feminist academics, students, and union organizers, which, according to Meer, "attempted to link local community struggles with the struggle against the apartheid state. Our aim in setting up a women's group was to ensure women's rights within communities as well as within the broader struggle for a new post-apartheid South Africa."[35]

However, feminist activists were in the minority within the antiapartheid movement. For many women leaders the goal of activating women had less to do with addressing the structural roots of gender inequalities than with linking local struggles to the exiled national liberation movement and with uprooting the apartheid state. Nevertheless, where the connections between economic and cultural forces and women's oppression were made—however they were made—the emphasis shifted, in Molyneux's terms, from "practical gender needs" to "strategic gender interests." This was a process of politicization that facilitated the emergence of a distinctive feminist consciousness that integrated race, class, and gender oppressions as mutually determined.

The role of political activists in forging links between localized struggles to solve immediate problems and the broader political movement was not uncontested. There was often a gap in experience between women residents and activists who had already become politically involved. Many women in the civics movement hoped for tangible, local, and immediate changes in the townships and looked to civic organizations for direct assistance. For activists such as Meer the connection between struggling for basic needs and larger political struggles was crucial as it was a means to expose the structural roots of inequalities, not to provide people with reformist solutions.[36] Ela Ramgobin, granddaughter of Mahatma Gandhi and an activist in the Natal Indian Congress, NOW, and the UDF, also connected her job as a social worker to her political activism, seeing the lack of political and economic power as intertwined with the lack of basic services for poor people: "I tried to get [people] together to demand [basic] facilities and in the process I also tried to educate them to understand why they were in the position they were in."[37] Meer recalls tensions between activists and township residents in Phoenix over the politicization of such issues as high rents. This was exacerbated by the fact that many activists in the Phoenix Working Committee did not actually live in the township. "People from Phoenix would argue that the rent boycott meant that there was no electricity. They would say, 'You guys come from town and push a rent boycott,'" Meer said.[38] Indeed, as Seekings has argued, "The redress of civic issues was not itself the ultimate goal of the civic strategy. . . . In practice . . . the relevant strategic objective was what might be termed an intermediate goal, building a movement of strong, local-level organisations with broad and sustained popular participation."[39] Not surprisingly, given Seekings's assessment, at the grassroots level the tensions in women's organizations were not so much between white or black women, or even feminists and nationalists, as between community-based activists and those, operating at what Meer calls the big political level—that is, in the broad antiapartheid movement—who sought to accelerate the level of protest.[40]

The role of leadership in women's organizations was also central to defining and/or mediating different conceptions of what issues were appropriate and political in the context of the struggle against apartheid. The political outcomes of building women's organizations could not always be contained by the civic leadership or the UDF, and the demands of women's organizations for more expanded understandings of what constituted political issues are one example of this dilemma. Phumelele Ntombela-Nzimande, who was active in NOW as well as *Speak* magazine, points out that there was a distinction between the ways in which *Speak* readers and political activists within NOW defined "women's problems." *Speak*'s coverage of such issues as maternal health, rape, and battery and women's experiences on the shop floor were well received by readers. This reflected the organized working-class constituency from which *Speak* took its direction; some unions were taking these concerns up as part of their demands for a safer workplace and for maternity benefits for women workers. On the other hand, within NOW there were concerns that *Speak* was focusing on nonessential matters or on issues that might hinder the process of politicizing greater numbers of largely conservative women. "NOW comrades were asking, 'Why write about rape all the time?' These were seen as weird issues to focus on. They said people should speak about the state of emergency, not about wife battering. . . . Those debates didn't come from NOW—NOW never dealt with these issues," Phumelele Ntombela-Nzimande recalled. "Even I don't remember once challenging a NOW meeting to speak about these issues. I felt overwhelmed by the fact that it wasn't appropriate."[41]

For activists like Meer and Ntombela-Nzimande, however, "political issues" such as the state of emergency and "private issues" such as wife battery were neither separate nor mutually exclusive as the basis of organizational strategies. But "we were operating in an environment in which there was a male-defined concept of what political issues were," Ntombela-Nzimande stressed. "If women stood up to speak on political platforms, they wouldn't be shouting, 'Down with rape!' but 'Down with the Botha regime!' There just wasn't the space. . . . Issues like termination of pregnancy were really taboo. If you raised it, you got a sense of 'Are you getting too Westernized, being part of a group that has these other [white] women?'"[42]

The definition of what constituted women's issues and how these would be linked to the universal political goals of the antiapartheid movement preoccupied women's organizations. As I argue in the next section, such discussions could not be divorced from the structure and internal culture of the organizations.

New Structures, New Strategies

At the outset all three regional women's organizations surveyed here debated the aims of the new formations. At the launch of UWO in April 1981 its members adopted a constitution that located the organization at the grassroots level with a focus on "activities which involve the day-to-day problems of people in oppressed communities" and on women's agency in "solving all problems and matters affecting them in the community and places of work."[43] In the accompanying policy statement the organization placed itself firmly in the struggle for democracy, stating that "we cannot abstract ourselves from political issues because they are our daily life. . . . Our place must be as part of the struggle for fundamental rights."[44] The organization's demands for equal pay for equal work, a national minimum wage, and an end to unemployment reflected its broad definition of women's issues. UWO demanded full democratic rights for all South Africans and a fundamental transformation of power relations in society. It also demanded "the right to live with our families where we choose and to have equal rights and status to men in marriage and under all laws."[45] Similarly, NOW defined its goals in broad terms, seeking not just a regime change but also "the removal of all laws and customs that act against women."[46]

While the interconnectedness of race, class, and gender oppressions was based on a deep understanding of these linkages in the daily experience of women, particularly African women, it was not strategically easy to reconcile struggles against gender oppression with those against race and class oppressions. The debates that accompanied the formation of NOW in 1981 highlight the difficulty sharply. There were deep differences over the direction of the organization among Durban women activists, with two positions emerging. The first emphasized a bottom-up development, consolidating organization in communities first and building a working-class leadership with clear mandates from women.[47] While proponents of this position wanted to develop links between national political struggles and local community struggles, they did not want to begin with mobilizing women for national political campaigns. This approach favored a less prominent political profile for the organization in its initial stages. A report to the ANC by an anonymous woman activist in Durban summarized the concerns of this group. The report pointed out that the majority of women in Durban were not organized but that their participation was vital if NOW was to be a broad-based organization. It identified the conditions under which activists would work—"fear of police brutality, fear of incarceration, fear for the security of their families, lack of unity and mistrust"—and noted the reality that, as a result of "the feeling of helplessness and powerlessness to change even their immediate environment," women would be afraid to "act openly, identify with or participate in the activities of an organisation that has overt political links and associations."[48] In this context an organization whose membership was based from the outset solely on political activities would "attract too much attention from the wrong sources and [would] never have the chance to develop and serve the purpose for which it was formed."[49]

The second position, supported by the ANC underground in Natal, favored the creation of a mobilizing vehicle for women that would function explicitly within the political arena as a means of drawing women into the national liberation struggle. According to Hursheela Narsee, "We felt there were already women out there who were political and we needed to consolidate. We felt the need to make a clear political statement irrespective of state repression or whether it might push some women away. We wanted to function as women within the political arena."[50] After lengthy and debilitating debate, NOW chose the mobilizing route, and some women activists left NOW and put their energies into other avenues of activism, including union work.

Closely related to these debates about the goals of the new regional women's organizations was the issue of how they were to be structured. An immediate question was whether the new organizations should set out to affiliate with one national movement, ideally, the Federation of South African Women, or indeed whether one organization should be the seed for the formation of the national organization. A longer-term issue related to the extent to which the formation of a sustainable organization with strong local branches would be a priority in the context of both state repression and the expectation that women's organizations would be part of the programs and strategies of the national liberation movement. In the Western Cape there was considerable discussion about whether UWO, as the first of the "new organizations," should be a national organization. Requests by Durban women activists to affiliate with UWO reinforced the argument that there was a gap in organization that UWO could fill. After debate residents of the Western Cape decided that the emphasis should be on a locally based organization as a more constructive and democratic way of building a women's organization.[51] At a workshop on the issue participants agreed that "a national organisation would delay the practical work of the organisation, and that building autonomous regional bodies would be more useful."[52] UWO would support and encourage women in other regions to form local organizations that would in time affiliate with a national structure.

While this would build a genuinely participatory organization, the cell-like structure would also help protect members from state repression.

The formation of a national women's organization was something of a holy grail in women's politics in the 1980s. An earlier attempt to revive the Federation of South African Women in the 1970s had been initiated by the former federation activists Fatima Meer in Natal and Winnie Mandela in the Transvaal, who formed the Black Women's Federation (BWF) in 1975. The BWF brought together forty-one organizations of women "in an attempt to address Black women's unique experience of oppression."[53] The organization was active during the Soweto uprising in 1976 and located itself ideologically in the dominant Black Consciousness movement—a factor that some argue resulted in its failure to develop a broad base.[54] A more direct hindrance to its development was state repression: within five months of its formation, most of its leaders were banned or detained, and the government prohibited it from holding rallies and political gatherings. The organization itself was banned in 1977, after its second conference. Commenting on the period, Jessie Duarte, an activist in the Federation of Transvaal Women, argued that "there was no women's movement. The rise of the Black Women's Federation was affirmation of Black women being upwardly mobile but it did not consist of feminist activists. Women were still activists taking the helmet of the traditional patriarch, the African National Congress, taking the spear of national liberation but not taking up the spear for the struggle of women's emancipation. There was no national women's movement which was feminist in content. For political women's organisation, it was the side by side story, fighting for the liberation of people."[55]

In the 1980s some activists again raised the hope of reviving the Federation of South African Women and establishing it as the mobilizing vehicle for an authoritative political voice of women. That the federation had never been banned was regarded as an opportunity, both to rebuild an organization that had legitimate and deep support and to keep alive the name and symbols of the ANC, particularly in national antiapartheid politics.[56] The ANC supported and, according to at least two informants, even initiated the formation of UWO and NOW, in part because the ANC saw these organizations as the starting point for reviving the federation.[57] Indeed, the political imperative to revive the federation came from the ANC in exile. Members of the ANC Women's Section, the organization of ANC women in exile, met to outline a strategy for "mobilisation, unification and the launch of a National Women's Movement," to be driven internally by ANC women cadres based on their assessment of "progress on the ground."[58]

This strategic directive exerted a powerful influence on discussions in all three provinces. In Natal, Florence Mkhize, a leader of the federation in the 1950s who was living under a banning order, was consulted about the formation of NOW and lent her support, providing credibility and legitimacy to the new organization.[59] Another Natal federation member, Gladys Manzi, broke her banning order "at great risk to her life" to talk to the women activists about the ways in which women had organized in Natal in the 1950s and 1960s.[60] The unwillingness and inability of UWO and NOW to "go national" accounted for the formation of the Federation of Transvaal Women in 1984. FEDTRAW had the explicit goal of drawing a large number of women into the antiapartheid movement. It was no accident that activists began FEDTRAW during the thirtieth anniversary celebration of the founding of the Federation of South African Women. Celebrations of the anniversary and of the federation's antipass march on August 9, 1956, provided important rallying points in the process leading up to the launch of FEDTRAW.[61] Almost three thousand women attended the August 9 anniversary rallies in the Transvaal, celebrated in 1984 for the first time in twenty years.[62] FEDTRAW's aim was to "unite women in common action for the removal of political, legal, social and economic disabilities."[63] The issue of unity was uppermost; the wide range of women's groups in the Transvaal needed to be knitted together into a political force, and the Transvaal organization was to be the foundation of a national organization. Even as FEDTRAW determined to draw women together around such practical issues as rent increases, the high cost of food, and problems in the education system, it also focused on ensuring the "direct participation of women as equal members of a future non-racial, non-sexist and democratic South Africa."[64]

Despite this high level of support, FEDTRAW was unable to revive the federation. The diversity within the women's movement had resulted in competing regional interests and varied organizational capacities among progressive women's organizations. Internal activists warned the ANC Women's Section of these difficulties in a 1987 report, noting that "if this Federation was to be revived, it was going to be politically weak and would definitely not be able to compete with other national bodies that are not political."[65] The report also warned that the emphasis on support for the Freedom Charter was problematic because it posed too narrow a scope of affiliation: "Some said that if it was not adopted, it would seem as if women were reneging, and if they did adopt it, it would be wrong as many women's groups were not ready. . . . Whatever was to be done, had to be carefully thought out so as not to produce factions in the women's movement."[66]

The federation was an important symbolic rallying point for the new women's organizations, but it also strangled strategic thinking. ANC women activists underground assumed that the organizational structure of the federation was appropriate and valid for the 1980s. Discussions of Cherryl Walker's book were important in raising the questions of whether a federal structure would, first, simply reproduce the multiracial (as opposed to nonracial) approach to organization and, second, whether a revived federation would require a more autonomous structure to facilitate an independent approach to women's organizing. Federation stalwarts were themselves divided on this issue. At the launch of NOW Albertina Sisulu, an activist in both the ANC and the federation, was critical of the decision to establish NOW as an independent women's organization rather than as the Natal branch of the federation. On the other hand, in her message to the UWO founding conference, Helen Joseph, former secretary of the federation, belabored the need to take into account historical context. Comparing the 1980s and the 1950s, she said, "Our organisation must be a child of its time, just as the Federation was a child of that time. Our organisation must build from the bottom. It must be a grassroots organisation, not an umbrella organisation. The Federation was as it was because of the circumstances of those times. Times have changed and circumstances have changed. Our organisation today must grow out of the new circumstances. It must be a child of these times."[67] Joseph's comments are particularly noteworthy for the political space they allowed for women's organizations to define new ways of organizing outside the dominant model of the 1950s.

While UWO used this political space to fashion a women's organization with a strong emphasis on democratic culture and consensus building that was influenced by discussions with trade unions, rather than simply adopting the tradition of the Congress Alliance, NOW and FEDTRAW opted for the older "sectoral model." This difference in overall strategic direction shaped the extent to which the three organizations were able to develop effective structures to facilitate mobilization. Rapid mobilization against the state or in order to be part of campaigns developed by other antiapartheid organizations precluded the careful building of branch structures and attention to consensual decision making. Unlike UWO and the United Women's Congress or even NOW, the Federation of Transvaal Women was not successful in developing a strong branch structure. Its leadership attributed this to logistical difficulties relating to transportation because the Inter-Branch Committee meetings, which brought together executive committee members from the different branches, were held in central Pretoria. As a result, "women had difficulties in attending meetings and therefore decisions [were] taken [even] though [the vote was] unrepresentative."[68] From the beginning, however, tensions were building between FEDTRAW as a women's organization that was advancing a feminist program and following the ANC imperative to revive the federation. In an "intelligence report" to the ANC "Maggy" commented that "branches had no autonomy to take independent programmes or to make press statements as FEDTRAW, and this use[d] to bog down even active branches."[69]

Like FEDTRAW, UWO and NOW were unable to escape the tensions between an emphasis on national liberation and an emphasis on building a women's organization. Organizational responses to these tensions were driven by both the nature of their membership bases and by the broader political context in which they were located. More than half the top-ranking UWO officers were union women, a factor that played a formative role in UWO's organizational culture.[70] Jenny Schreiner, former secretary of UWO (and an underground ANC activist), commented that UWO tried to balance "trade union accountability and short-term accountability, democracy and the payment of subscriptions by standing structures."[71] UWO tried to establish a formal relationship with local trade unions, but this was a difficult process.[72]

Despite the difficulties of clarifying the role of UWO, the democratic unions provided an important organizational model for structuring UWO, given the organization's concern with internal democracy. It was a familiar structure for many UWO members. It offered an alternative to the federal model of the federation, which UWO had rejected as inappropriate because the federal model retained the notion of racially distinct affiliates. The union influence also emphasized order and discipline within UWO. Structurally, UWO consisted of an executive council and local branches, each with its own executive committee. Each branch elected representatives to the executive council, which met every month and constituted the main decision-making body of the organization between annual conferences. The executive council communicated with branches through a monthly letter that explained developments and laid out it meeting agendas. In theory, the executive council had to ratify branch projects, and the branches had to send the council monthly reports. In practice, though, branches enjoyed a fair degree of autonomy, running their own projects according to their self-identified needs. For the first few years, until the imposition of the state of emergency, the branches kept meticulous membership records and maintained a strong branch structure with collective decision making in the executive council. Key office bearers of the executive council (president, secretary, treasurer) were elected by members at an annual conference and branch representatives were additional members. Branches held regular meetings, although attendance was uneven. The executive council met every month and acted as a debating chamber, with every issue discussed first at branch level and then at the council.

This rigorous union style of developing branches with proper mandates was important in building a strong organization. In a speech at the 1983 annual conference of UWO, Zora Mehlomakhulu, an organizer for the General Workers Union, cautioned against a vanguardist approach to organizing: "There is no better way of destroying an organisation than that."

Rather, she advised, "It takes time and patience to build solid organisation. We must see to it that decisions are taken by the majority of people."[73] UWO adopted this approach:

> For example, when we are planning National Women's Day, or discussing an important political campaign . . . we start in our branches. Each branch has a chance to discuss the issue with all their members. In this way every UWO member can understand the issue and have their say. The branch takes a decision, called a mandate. This should not only be a yes, or no answer, but should explain to others why the branch felt that way. Then at Council each branch has two representatives to speak for the branch. These women are not speaking their own feelings there. They bring the mandate that their branch gave them. . . . This is democracy, and it is very important if we want a strong organisation.[74]

The union influence also shaped the emphasis of UWO on the interests of working-class women and on linking women's struggles with broader union campaigns.[75] For example, one of the very first campaigns that UWO undertook was a boycott, spearheaded by the African Food and Canning Workers' Union, of the pasta-making firm Fatti's and Moni's. UWO also had representation on the Wilson-Rowntree and Leyland (Boycott) Support Committees. A support group for the boycott started in the townships with the involvement of many women who had been members of the federation in the 1950s. UWO raised money to help the families of the striking workers, organized food hampers, and produced and distributed pamphlets supporting the strike.

In Natal too NOW began with the intention of building a strong grassroots organization but was unable to do so because of its overall emphasis on the immediate political context. Its structure was comprised of branches linked by a general council, which was scheduled to meet every two months to decide on a program of action and to monitor progress and problems. The General Council consisted of two representatives from each branch; its task was to coordinate the daily activities of the organization.[76] The branch structure of NOW was never strong, in part because of the repressive measures of the state and in part the mobilizing style of the organization, which focused on high-profile campaigns from the beginning rather than devoting its energy to branch development. Instead, the broad direction of the organization, such as the program of action for the year, was developed through debate and discussion at irregular workshops and, inevitably, decision making was frequently crisis driven. At the workshops members made strong efforts to develop a democratic culture and to develop leadership and organizational skills such as minute taking. Translations into English and Zulu were provided to ensure that all participants could engage in the debates. While this was often tedious, it was rigorously adhered to, even when it drove away some members. The leadership was committed to building internal democracy. According to Routledge-Madlala, "For us, consciousness raising was important, building leadership from below was important. We consciously inverted the [organizational chart]—we always put membership at the top and leadership at the bottom to remind us all the time to be inclusive and to listen."[77]

Union women did not form the core membership of NOW as they did in UWO. It is not clear whether this was a consequence or a cause of the decision to create an overtly political structure in NOW, instead of taking the slower route of building a grassroots organization, as UWO did in the Western Cape.[78] Whatever the underlying reasons, the composition of NOW's membership affected the nature of the organization. The majority of its members were older African women whose children were active in student organizations such as the Congress of South African Students. NOW became characterized as a *gogo's* organization,[79] and many politically active young women tended to work within the civics movement or trade unions. Older women were wary of the younger women who belonged to NOW, often considering them to be disrespectful and "too westernised."[80] The older women members were by no means apolitical. Many had participated in ANC and federation activities in the 1950s, and almost all supported the UDF and the goals of national liberation. Despite their earlier activism, they represented a socially conservative constituency, perhaps because women's organizations in the 1950s had chosen to limit their political focus to national liberation and steered away from issues relating to the private sphere.

Certain NOW activities—sewing groups, savings clubs, and the like—were remarkably similar to those of the Inkatha Women's Brigade, the women's wing of the traditionalist Zulu Inkatha movement, and suggest that both organizations were mobilizing similar constituencies. The homeland government supported such activities in Inkatha with money and other resources; these activities were unambiguously welfarist, and the membership of the Inkatha Women's Brigade expanded fairly rapidly.[81] By contrast, NOW struggled to sustain such projects.[82] Organizers—usually younger women with a more political orientation—did not have the time, skills, or inclination to provide sewing lessons for members.[83] The NOW leadership regarded these activities as strategic. "They were a way of organising women. . . . We went in for sewing classes because that is what the women wanted—a possibility of a livelihood. If we didn't [have these projects] we would lose members," Veni Soobrayan said.[84] As repression increased and states of emergency were imposed, NOW "went into a more traditional women's organization role of organizing memorials for comrades, supporting the families of detainees, et cetera," she said. "It was unavoidable. For our constituencies these were very important things. Deaths and mourning were a huge cultural procedure."[85]

These everyday branch activities contrasted with the high political profile of the NOW leadership, which was present at all antiapartheid and anti-Bantustan meetings and rallies. As a result the leadership was under constant threat of detention, and debating organizational development became a luxury. State repression decimated NOW's leadership soon after the organization's founding: its first chair, Phumzile Ngcuka, had to flee into exile; her successor, Victoria Mxenge,[86] was assassinated on August 2, 1985; and the next chair, Nozizwe Madlala,[87] was detained later the same month and held for more than a year and subjected to repeated torture. Other executive members were also detained for shorter periods or had to periodically go into hiding. The detention of Madlala was particularly damaging for NOW. A member of the ANC underground, she was an extremely strong and articulate leader. With Madlala's detention "we didn't lose the organization, but we couldn't regain the stature, clarity of thinking, and legitimacy when Nozi was detained," according to Hursheela Narsee.[88]

Women soon were afraid to be openly associated with NOW: "Having actively characterized ourselves as political meant the challenge was greater in attracting women to join—it was dangerous," Madlala said.[89] The office was moved to the central business district in the hope that the greater visibility would afford the organization some protection. Branches were small, although campaigns mobilized larger numbers for meetings and protest actions. Although the name suggested a provincewide organization, power within NOW was always based in Durban. While the executive was formally composed of branch chairs and secretaries, a small active core in the Durban office was responsible for running the organization. Under the leadership of Nozizwe Madlala, however, NOW started to expand and consolidate its structures. Branches were formed outside the core of Durban townships, in the Natal midlands, and in southern and northern Natal.

The presence of Inkatha in the region also acted as a major constraint on organization in the African townships.[90] Inkatha controlled the resources of the Bantustan, including its police force, and used these effectively to repress progressive political organizations, although it was never able to fully suppress opposition. However, neither Inkatha nor the UDF had organizational hegemony in Natal, although some townships and parts of townships could clearly be identified as falling under the political control of one or another of these organizations. Political activists who were not members of Inkatha feared attack, and meetings were not easy to organize because people preferred to appear apolitical. Members of the A-Team, criminal elements associated with the security police, regularly targeted activists who were identified with the UDF.[91] Natal was in a virtual civil war.

The problems in Umlazi, one of the largest townships in Durban,[92] showed the extent of the organizational challenges facing NOW and the high costs attached to organizing women in Natal. In the 1980s Umlazi was wracked by conflict between Inkatha and the UDF. At a memorial vigil for Victoria Mxenge in August 1985, twelve mourners were killed and several people were seriously injured. Following this, a prominent Inkatha Central Committee member, Winnington Sabelo, ordered all UDF supporters to "get out of Umlazi" and said that "people harbouring them should see they leave or should leave with them."[93] Under these circumstances NOW branches found it difficult to sustain any organized activities or to adhere to principles of democratic procedures.[94]

Examining the program and activities of NOW yields the overall impression that it was a fairly conventional women's group, albeit one located within a revolutionary context. The organizers constantly juggled the need to respond to women's self-identified needs—however welfarist in tone—on the one hand, with the mobilization of women as a political constituency on the other. These demands made it difficult to sustain a political education campaign that drew the connections between structural conditions of racial capitalism and women's oppression. Although early campaigns, such as equal pay for equal work, suggest an impetus to raise these structural and systemic dimensions of women's subordination, Soobrayan recalled that "we rarely used the term *feminism*. Rather, we spoke of people's rights and people's power. The term [feminism] had no currency. There was no attitude towards it, it was meaningless."[95]

It is not surprising that activists in NOW hesitated to adopt feminist language to articulate their programs. The problems of finding an ideological framework that would appeal to women with little political experience *and* compete successfully with the conservative gender ideologies peddled by the Inkatha Women's Brigade were exacerbated by the left's attitudes toward the organization of women in Natal. There was tremendous hostility to autonomous organizations within the civics movement in Natal, where the lines of loyalty were being drawn between Inkatha and the UDF. Neither side offered much room for organizational independence. This was compounded by hostility to feminism itself, which was perceived as promoting separatist and divisive politics. The ANC and the UDF leadership in Natal offered little support for the idea that women might have interests that were not fully represented within the liberation movements.[96] Feminist activists were constantly criticized and even personally derided when issues of gender were raised in strategic planning meetings.[97] Attempts to organize women on the University of Durban—Westville campus in 1980 and 1981 were fiercely opposed by the male leaders of the Students' Representative Council, themselves under the political tutelage of leaders outside the student movement. The male leaders accused feminist activists of being divisive, and the men tried unsuccessfully to stop the first meeting of the women's group.[98] In at least one documented instance senior male activists in the UDF disagreed with and disrupted NOW's strategy in order to distribute UDF literature in a commemorative June 16 campaign. At a meeting of the Natal Indian Congress, which was a key affiliate of the UDF in Natal, NOW leaders were accused of failing to develop an overall strategy of organizing women, and women were told they were "not permitted" to build their organization through "piggy-backing" on other campaigns. "The Durban Central branch [of NOW] was angry over this decision but did not raise it formally through NIC structures," according to a report from the ANC Women's Section.[99]

UDF Affiliation

In both UWO and NOW attempts to develop sustainable organizations were greatly affected by the decision to affiliate with the UDF in 1983. Anne Mager has called this a "dramatic turning point." There was no debate about the necessity of joining the new front; rather, it was considered a logical development of both organizations' stance that women's struggles should be integrally connected to struggles for democracy.[100] Only after affiliation did tensions surface in regard to the decision to affiliate, with some women activists questioning the politics of alliance.[101] The two organizations were caught in the familiar tug-of-war between their perceived role as "the women's auxiliary" and their ongoing attempts to retain autonomy over "the choice of issues to be fought and the manner in which they are fought."[102] UDF affiliation undoubtedly privileged the former over the latter. In effect, UWO and NOW became the women's wings of the UDF in the Western Cape and Natal, respectively, and their branches helped the UDF to set up area committees and to broaden its base. Delegates of the two organizations were called upon to represent "the women's voice" at innumerable meetings. Women and youth were lumped together; this was the sectoral approach, which reflected the structures of representation within the ANC. For example, although numerous other women's groups, such as burial societies and stokvels (savings clubs), were affiliated with the UDF in Natal, NOW had the status of being the political voice of women.

Increasingly, NOW and UWO began to take up issues defined in terms of the UDF's priorities rather than those of the branches. The executives of both organizations spent a significant amount of time attending UDF meetings and workshops, often to the detriment of the women's organizations.[103] The minutes of UWO's executive council constantly refer to the "rapid pace" of UDF campaigns and the difficulties this imposed on communications

between branches and executives, with the result that "a number of mis-
takes have been made because of inadequate preparation."[104] Fester has described the UDF as "a fast-paced male-dominated organisation."[105]

Early in the discussions to form the front, UWO expressed concerns that
the process of building the UDF should not be rushed: "The first task
should be with people working door-to-door in their areas, and organising
area meetings."[106] However, it proved difficult to hold on to the branch style
of organization, which was the cornerstone of UWO. It was not always possible for UWO branches to discuss the appropriateness of the UDF's campaigns or how UWO could shape the style of the front. This went against
UWO's culture of decision making. In 1985 the secretary commented that
"when UDF was formed, UWO played the key role in building and directing the programme of action. This we said was an important task. But we
have let our child run away with us and take a direction that we have not always thought was the best road."[107]

Anne Mager said that, ironically, the membership of the UWO grew "in
order to be part of the new fashionable movement of the UDF—it was almost a social thing," but this did not result in a strengthening of the grassroots power of the movement. Rather, where previously there had been
conscious attempts to resist elitism through the participation of branches,
"we became elitist as a result of joining the UDF. . . . There was much less
organizing going on on the ground and more 'politicking.'"[108] This was a
problem for UWO, for which "a strong branch is not just a big branch. The
members must understand why they joined our organisation, and must
participate fully."[109] But there was little space for UWO to resolve these tensions; the organization was swept along on a national tide.

The differences provoked by UDF activities "nearly erupted" into open
conflict between activists within the UWO, and its executive was initially
concerned that they would "paralyse our organisation."[110] For example, the
executive council was divided over whether to support the UDF's Million
Signatures Campaign, launched in September 1983 to declare opposition to
apartheid and to the government's constitutional reforms. Several branches
abstained from ratifying the executive council's decision to participate in
the campaign because they felt the branches had not been given time to discuss its organizational implications.[111] Despite the organization's position
that national liberation and building the women's movement were mutually complementary processes, there were tensions around which issues
were to have priority and which organization should have first claim on
activists' time. "In many areas it was women who initiated civics but men
who were the leaders. . . . In council it was stated that we had not lost members, rather we had broadened 'the struggle.' The reality was that UWO was
weakened as an organisation."[112]

The breakdown of the internal structures and decision-making proce-dures of UWO was a setback to the organization. UWO meetings were banned under the emergency regulations. Contact between the executive council and the branches became increasingly difficult. Branches them-selves did not meet regularly, and when they did, they had to use prayer meetings as cover. By January 1986 the newly elected UWCO executive council believed that "the struggle had developed so dramatically in the last six months that we needed to assess our organisation's direction and pro-gramme of action."[113] The new leadership sought to build "tight discipline and democracy" in a context in which internal tensions had led to the for-mation of factions, which were mostly divided over whether the organiza-tion should emphasize underground activities or strive to maintain its legal status.[114] Campaigns to oppose high prices, identified by the branches as a key women's issue, met limited success. The mass campaigns of the UDF, such as the hunger strike, all imbued with a sense of urgency, deflected at-tention from UWO's own plan of action.[115] Reflecting on the effect of the states of emergency that were declared before the 1986 conference, the exec-utive council of the United Women's Congress (UWCO), formed as a result of the merger of UWO and the Women's Front Organization that year, commented that "we must be honest and critical. As individual women, many of us have been in the [UDF] marches and in the action. But as an or-ganisation we have not provided leadership to these struggles. UWO has not been sufficiently in touch with events in our areas. Even within the UDF, we have not been in touch. In the last six months we were tailing the struggle in many respects. This is a serious criticism to level at UWO. It is more frightening when the UDF says to us that they are relying on us be-cause, of all the affiliates, we are the most active as an organisation."[116]

These problems arose largely because of the breakdown in the relation-ship between UWCO's branches and its leadership. Decisions made in the executive council and strategies planned at workshops were not taken back to the branches. Many branches did not participate in the campaigns. There were some attempts to deal creatively with the restrictions on organizing imposed by the states of emergency. "We have learnt a new style of work. We do not use the telephone. We do not discuss venues openly. We have re-alised the need to set up communication chains through our branches and executive so we can pass messages easily and safely. At times we have felt we were being cowards or over cautious. But it is our political task to find ways to defeat the enemy's tactics, keep out of Botha's jails and continue to or-ganise. The State of Emergency continues and we will never return to the free way we used to organise."[117]

Brave though these attempts to circumvent the state of emergency were, the organization did not recover from the setbacks to its careful and disciplined forms of organizing. Repression demoralized some members, particularly in the white branches.[118] In the African townships there were still signs of a lively organization. In Zwelethemba women marched against the presence of police in the township, and even though the branch could not meet, women participated spontaneously. The increasing violence in the townships opened new areas of struggle around sexual abuse of women (mainly by police) and the torture of women in detention. The presence of troops in townships mobilized many women who had previously been uninterested in politics to act in defense of their children. With the branches collapsing, however, it was difficult for UWCO to attract women into the organization. The educational workshops had ceased and political work was minimal. The UWCO executive council commented that "we must recruit women for our organisation so that they can learn that the struggle is an ongoing fight for our demands, and not just a sporadic response to police brutality."[119]

Differences within its executive council undermined UWCO, as some branches overturned its decisions with the support of some members of the executive. Members complained that "if we work in this way, where every decision that is taken has to be changed because certain people or groups oppose it, we will never be taken seriously as an organisation and we will never be able to move forward in unity and give the lead to our struggle."[120] In 1988 and 1989 the UWCO executive was unable to develop any central organizational campaigns. Much of the group's activity related to high-profile work for the UDF, such as speaking at meetings and funerals.[121] A volunteers group was established to build new branches and activate the organization. Branches reported that their active membership had dwindled, they were unable to develop autonomous campaigns of action, and that they were reliant on the executive for political guidance.[122]

Not all the consequences of affiliating with the UDF were negative. The UWCO secretaries pointed out that women "have developed an understanding of how other organisations work. This has broadened their understanding of the struggle."[123] The former chair of NOW, Nozizwe Madlala, commented that "we took part in the various campaigns that challenged the South African government. We filled the gap that was created when the African National Congress and other organisations were forced into exile. . . . During the State of Emergency, when a large number of organisations were totally incapacitated, NOW carried the banner of the UDF. In fact, we spearheaded a number of campaigns and filled the gap that had been created by the restrictions that had been served on the UDF."[124]

The formation of the UDF enhanced the national political power of community-based organizations and connected women's grassroots activism to national politics. It gave impetus to the organization of women by providing a political home to women activists within the Charterist fold.[125] The presence of women in national campaigns revealed women's capacity for political mobilization, in a very few cases opening up leadership positions to women.[126] The significant involvement of women in the UDF hinted at the political possibilities that might exist when women's political roles were central to the survival of broader national politics. In the new context of intense mobilization and with the significant influence of feminist ideals, the 1980s offered the opportunity for women's organizations to finally break out of the mold of "women's league" that had characterized earlier women's structures within the democratic fold. Yet this centrality was neither acknowledged by the male leadership nor effectively leveraged by women's organizations, and the ironic consequence of the successful mobilization of women's organizations was the weakening of their structures.

Women's participation in the UDF inserted the values of gender equality into the vision for a democratic South Africa. Although feminism was still not an explicit ideological framework, notions of gender equality and women's rights were important in shaping the campaigns of women's organizations as well as the official values of the UDF. However, many feminists felt that the UDF paid little more than lip service to issues of women's participation for women's equality. Despite the crucial importance of women as a sector of the community, and the role of the UDF women's organizations in building a base for the front, women had a second-class status within the organization. Women were not significantly represented in leadership positions. In 1985 a UDF discussion paper noted that

> Our organisation of women remains inadequate. Our attitude to the place of women in the national struggle tends to remain on the level of assertion of its importance. We have not taken the steps to realize our commitments. We need to understand the objective significance of women in the struggle. . . . One thing must be guarded against: the new dangers that we now face cannot be used as a means of submerging these issues. We still have to face up to the problems of women's issues and no amount of repression can absolve us of that responsibility. . . . The extent to which we overcome this weakness, the extent to which women are in fact constructively involved, will determine the progressive content of the struggle.[127]

Still under pressure to form a national women's organization, a UDF Women's Congress was formed in April 1987, attended by one hundred elected delegates representing NOW, FEDTRAW, UWCO, Port Elizabeth Women's Organisation, Port Alfred Women's Organisation, and Gompo Women's Congress (representing the Border region of the Eastern Cape).[128] The UDF Women's Congress was limited to these organizations because they were seen as sharing the basic principles of "non-racialism, non-sexism and democracy. They are also committed to the development of grassroots organisation."[129] All these organizations were affiliated with the regional structures of the UDF and had relatively clearly developed political profiles. Nevertheless, at the launch meeting for the UDF Women's Congress, the great diversity among these organizations was also recognized and seen as the outcome of the different "objective conditions in each region and the needs expressed by the membership (most of whom are working class women)."[130] At the launch conference delegates outlined a number of problems faced by women in the UDF, including the absence of women in leadership positions, the UDF's failure to address issues of gender discrimination, and sexual harassment within the organization.[131] A conference resolution called for political education for men and women within the UDF "about the oppression of women," mechanisms to ensure the full participation of women in all UDF activities, the eradication of sexism from UDF ranks, and the integration of gender into all UDF campaigns.[132] Delegates were acutely attuned to the longer-term consequences of inattention on the part of women activists to organizational strategies and culture. According to Pregs Govender, former NOW and trade union activist and convenor of the UDF Women's Congress, the resolution was "based on the belief that the practices and structures we are developing now are laying the basis for our future."[133]

The UDF Women's Congress was seen in part as a response to the debilitating effects of the state of emergency: the shift away from open organizational strategies; the torture, rape, and killing of many activists, including women; and the fragmentation of organizational structures and processes of decision making. Govender has said that the UDF Women's Congress was founded in the hope that a national structure would help to rejuvenate regional structures by providing coordination for national campaigns, accelerating political education, and by "asserting women's leadership and women's issues in a more forceful way within the UDF."[134] The top-down approach did not work, however, and the UDF Women's Congress was soon disbanded, with both women leaders and the UDF executive acknowledging that the decision to establish the structure had been a mistake. For the first time the internal and exiled political leadership began to consider whether a women's movement that included only "the core democratic organisations" could be feasible.[135]

Despite the soul searching that accompanied the evaluation of the UDF Women's Congress, the issues raised by women when it was established were not addressed within the parent organization. Early in 1990 the UDF held a national meeting about "the women's question." With a weary tone of déjà vu, the head office reported that "while numerous resolutions have been passed relating to the organisation of women, the development of the women's sector, as well as the role of women within the UDF—no affirmative action has been taken within the UDF with regard to the women's question."[136] At the meeting regional women's organizations reported on their level of participation in the regional executive committees of the UDF. The report commented that "male comrades within the UDF did not take women or women's issues seriously enough. . . . The role of women in the reception of our leaders [newly released from Robben Island] has been restricted to the preparation of meals at the rally's [*sic*] and cooking at the leaders' homes."[137] Discussions were also held on the problems within women's organizations themselves. These included lack of internal political education programs and failure to develop women's leadership. The disunity within women's organizations was singled out as a particular problem, and the UDF resolved to "build unity within the women's movement in order to assert the position of women in one unified strong voice."[138]

Yet even at this late stage, the leadership was unable to abandon the idea that the key role of women's organizations was to organize women for the national liberation struggle. A UDF meeting was called to "develop a comprehensive plan for the development of a strong sectoral organisation of women."[139] The meeting was followed by a workshop of UDF women's groups and women from the Congress of South African Trade Unions. Items on the agenda for this meeting were policy regarding organizing women, national women's unity, and a future plan of action. This was a crucial meeting, taking place only weeks after the Malibongwe Conference, organized by the Dutch Anti-Apartheid Movement in Amsterdam and attended by exiled ANC activists as well as representatives of the women's movement inside South Africa, in January 1990, where the UDF had endorsed the importance of building a nonpartisan women's movement. It offered an opportunity to discuss strategies that union activists and women in the UDF had in common—and the conference itself was an unusual development, given past tensions between the union and the UDF.[140] However, the decision by the UDF-affiliated women's organizations to disband abruptly ended this planning process and, as I show in chapter 3, the formation of the Women's National Coalition a year later posed new challenges for the relationship between women activists in political organizations and those in trade unions.

Discourses of Inclusion: Feminism, Motherism, and Nonracialism

Examining the emergence of the women's movement in South Africa in the 1980s, Kemp and colleagues argue that "self-identified feminist writings and debates . . . drew largely on Western-centred feminist thought to analyse the situation of a largely Third World female population in this country. The theoretical position that women's primary struggle is against patriarchy, or against a capitalist patriarchy, has been advanced mainly by well-educated white women and a few black women. . . . Such analysis has served to silence many Black women and alienate them from mainstream feminist discourse."[141] This powerful political charge captures the tensions that emerged during the early 1990s about power within the women's movement to define and articulate interests and strategic agendas. The presentation of two competing forces within the women's movement, one black and nationalist and the other white and (implicitly) radical feminist, is not uncommon in recent writing.[142] Yet, as I have suggested, instead of a clear racial polarization, I found that black and white feminist activists and researchers were indeed concerned about forging an indigenous feminism that accounted for the interplay of race, class, and gender inequalities. Many activists who were concerned with national liberation saw this as a springboard for addressing gender inequalities. Even though feminism as a term was deemed politically problematic, a distinctive "South African feminism" was indeed emerging during the 1980s.

This indigenous feminism was shaped by the twin but not always compatible needs to address the interplay of gender, race, and class identities, on the one hand—that is, the recognition of complex differences among women—and, on the other hand, a moral imperative to base women's organizations on the idea of nonracialism—that is, on the notion of some commonality of women's interests that extended beyond apartheid-defined identities. The link between these goals was provided by the ideology of motherhood and the political language of "motherism": a celebration of women as mothers, a link between women's familial responsibilities and their political work, and an emphasis on this aspect of women's roles as cutting across class and race barriers. "Mother" became a central trope in national liberationist discourses on gender.[143] Motherhood was often used as an emotive appeal to women's natural caring instincts. Ruth Mompati, an ANC leader, for example, has said that "working with women enabled us to realise that there were no differences between us as mothers. We were all women. We all had the same anxieties, the same worries. We all wanted to bring up our children to be happy and to protect them from the brutalities of life. This gave us more commitment to fight for unity in our country. It showed us that people of our country could work together as well."[144]

Albertina Sisulu, copresident of the UDF, also regarded the consciousness of motherhood as an integral part of women's politicization, commenting that "a woman is a mother, and women are the people who are suffering most. If the government continues killing children, the women will become even more angry, and these are the people who will take up our struggle."[145] This politicization of traditional roles was part of a revolutionary nationalism in which woman, mother, and nation were part of a continuous discourse.[146] Several campaigns that included different races of women, such as protests against troops in the townships and against detention of activists, were conducted under the banner of motherism. As Radcliffe and Westwood have pointed out, motherist strategies are "predicated upon overcoming the public/private divide as it impresses upon women's lives . . . [bringing] mothers in their domestic clothes to the centre of the public stage."[147] Fester has argued that "motherism and 'working shoulder to shoulder with our menfolk' can be seen as a form of South African feminism."[148]

Although the emphasis on motherhood was a successful idiom in many ways, not least in opening spaces for women within nationalist movements, it denied the very real differences in the experiences of mothering and motherhood that emerged from different class and race positions. This glossing over of differences had strategic benefits in that it allowed women to exploit gender stereotypes and to draw white women into the women's movement, thereby denting the supposed unity of white support for apartheid. Of greater concern is the extent to which motherism limited the ability of women's organizations to imagine women's political agency in radical ways. For example, discussions about women's limited mobility within the national liberation movement or the UDF were confined to the small inner circles of women's organizations, because debating these issues in public was seen as disloyalty to the national liberation movement. Issues of reproductive rights, bodily autonomy, and sexual choice were deemed apolitical by nationalists within women's organizations, in part because addressing these issues required reconsidering the traditional identities of women and thus posed a serious challenge to the private sphere that could not be easily accommodated by motherist politics. As I argued in chapter 1, the consequence was that the process of developing a truly indigenous feminism, one that would integrate understandings of race and class and culture in the construction of inequalities, was not allowed the space to unfold.

Within the civics movement taking up issues of women's power and agency in an organized fashion was seen as divisive, or at least politically unstrategic. Frene Ginwala has said that issues of women's oppression were also difficult to raise in exile: "In exile I was told these were intellectual questions."[149] Inside the country too "feminism was what we *did*, but not what we *spoke*," noted the gender activist Sheila Meintjes. "In the 'struggle organisations' there was a strong political correctness. We did not speak about feminism. There were people both black and white within the movement who argued that 'ordinary women' would not understand. In the UWO, the Organising Group felt that an overt feminist agenda might divide women."[150] In retrospect, Fester has argued that "even though some of us saw ourselves as feminists we would not raise it when representing the organisation except in our personal capacities."[151]

While *feminism* as a term was out of bounds, and many activists regarded *motherism* as limiting the terrain of struggle, nonracialism was an ideology that most women in UWCO, NOW, and FEDTRAW considered appropriate, progressive, and inclusive. The idea of a powerful nonracial women's movement had considerable sway at the grassroots level too. Women's organizations implicitly challenged the dominant notion that activists should mobilize within their own racially defined communities. The Durban Women's Group, which was not specifically based within a single community, included women from working-class African, Indian, and colored townships, as well as students and professionals. NOW continued this tradition. Similarly, UWCO self-consciously questioned the effect that its strong branch structure would have in producing racially defined branches because of the group areas restrictions. Fester has recalled that although each branch had a "racial or class identity," branches were "partnered" to facilitate closer relations.[152] For example, a middle-class, colored branch in Wynberg was partnered with the informal settlement of KTC in Cape Town, and together they established a nursery. UWCO encouraged regional caucuses and chose themes for discussion that would encourage debate between women of different races and classes.[153] The kind of cross-race and cross-class organization attempted by the Durban Women's Group, NOW, and UWCO was difficult but vital in the context of apartheid geography, in which communities were racially divided. Grassroots activism that did not address the spatial segregation of communities was at risk of developing race-based politics.

The logistics involved in cross-racial organizing were significant and required considerable organization and dedication on the part of voluntary workers. "Because communities lived at considerable distances from each other, we had to overcome immense logistical hurdles of finding a centrally located venue, ensuring communication in a context where most working class areas have no telephones, and arranging transport in the face of a virtually non-existent public transport system. Public transport was designed to get workers from home to work and back and did not cater for travel from one township to another or even from one section to another within a township."[154] During the states of emergency these attempts to host meetings in the townships were even more risky. Susie Nkomo, a student active in FEDTRAW, has pointed out that "meeting in the townships was virtually impossible, so this necessitated that major meetings happen in the cities and even on campus. Predictably, this led to a situation which empowered those women who lived outside the township, and those township women who could afford to travel into town for those meetings."[155]

Despite these tensions, the nonracialism of the women's organizations was a matter of great pride for its members. In Natal NOW was the only organization with a fully nonracial membership, that is, it was the only organization to which members of all races affiliated as equal individuals, with branches across all racial residential areas. Likewise, UWCO was the first completely nonracial structure in the Western Cape. There was no similar organization for men on the left; indeed, there "was great envy on the part of white men," Anne Mager recalled.[156] For white women on the left, "there was a desperate hunger to be involved and useful; it was important for our identities. We wanted to live out our left identities," Mager said.[157] At UWO's founding conference "an old woman said that she 'saw all people at the conference. Now people can see that there are no blacks and whites. We are all one colour.' "[158] Gender identity was articulated as offering the possibility of uniting women across racial and class differences and, in the context of the apartheid state's attempts to regulate relationships between the different races, this unity was regarded as politically progressive.[159]

Organizational structure was considered to be the key to building nonracialism. The Federation of South African Women had been based on a federal model in which women of different races belonged first to their racially distinct organizations and then as affiliates to the broader movement. Both NOW and UWO sought to move away from this format, which was seen as entrenching the notion that race was significant as a marker of identity. Racial *interests* were treated somewhat differently than racial *identity*. Racial interests were seen as intertwined with those of class and gender, a consequence of the patterns of social and economic development of racial capitalism and patriarchy. Meintjes argued that UWO's decision to allow individual membership rather than to form a federation of organizations that were based in racially defined communities was groundbreaking and facilitated the nonracialism of the organization: "The structure of the organization was terribly important in creating a decision-making process that was truly nonracial. The right structure facilitated the notion that we weren't all the same but [that] the organization [could] still speak with a single voice. . . . It allowed for differentiated interests to be expressed, but at the central level it allowed for the development of coherent strategy."[160]

The nonracialism had to be painstakingly built and nurtured. Differences in availability of time among working-class class and middle-class women, and differences of interest between women, led to diversity of activities and discussions. In Natal Indian and African women activists based in Durban comprised the core leadership.[161] "White women were in and out of the process. It required hard work to sit through long and boring NOW workshops. We were not able to maintain their interest," recalled Hursheela Narsee. "They all recognized the need to be there, but nobody could stand it!"[162] In UWO tensions persisted in regard to which interests should form the core of the organization's activities. Despite the attempts to create single nonracial branches across geographical group areas, in some places this was impossible. The Stellenbosch branch, for example, had three groups: in the colored area of Idasvalley, the African township of Kayamandi, and the white dorp (town).[163] The Western Cape had a colored labor-preference policy, with African workers treated as temporary residents who could easily be "endorsed out," or sent back to the rural areas of the Cape. Colored women were not affected by the pass laws and had better access to housing in the Western Cape. These differences led to tense debates about the executive council's prioritizing of the interests of African women.

White members of the organization had to "leap across to identify with issues of black women."[164] They tended to be university-affiliated middle-class women who were predominantly feminist. This offered valuable opportunities for UWO but also raised concerns about power. White women brought a range of skills to the organization: they organized workshops and training sessions, produced slides and posters, and diligently recorded the organization's activities. But some activists saw their participation as threatening. A report to the ANC on "problems in the executive" states that four colored and African activists "have all expressed fears for their positions within the UWO, specifically in terms of the role they see for themselves as supplying intellectual analysis, a role they feel is threatened by the position of white intellectuals in the group."[165] The report expresses the concern that if branches in nonwhite areas did not develop rapidly, "the UWO will be swamped by white intellectuals."[166] At the annual conference in 1983 these problems were discussed openly. Members complained that "the intellectual Branches in our organisation dominate decision-making. This is very bad for our organisation. Our policy tells us that the oppressed and exploited majority must lead. But our organisation has not been making this happen."[167]

"Intellectual dominance" was countered by an emphasis on strong branch participation in decision making and by the socialist tendencies among the white activists themselves. The organization defined campaigns less in ideological or theoretical terms than on the basis of the practical problems encountered by African women in the townships.[168] "We followed the lead of the African women—that's the only way we could make the organisation grow," Anne Mager said. "You can't decide in an abstract way [what women's issues are]. Issues such as who had the right to housing, the pass laws, the endorsing out [of African women out of the Western Cape]—those *were* the women's issues."[169]

This approach tended to marginalize colored women—in fact, the UWO was relatively weak in colored areas. The small core of activists in colored areas was drawn into working in other organizations, and tensions between activists aligned with different ideological factions on the left were deep. UWO's affiliation with the UDF clearly put it in the camp of the Congress Alliance, and the nonracial approach of UWO alienated activists committed to Black Consciousness or the Trotskyite Unity Movement.[170]

In Natal NOW also self-consciously set out to build a nonracial organization of women. Within the Natal UDF, NOW was the only organization with a fully nonracial membership, with branches across all racial residential areas. The second chair of NOW, Nozizwe Madlala, has recalled that "NOW provided a platform for women to unite across colour and other divides. African women joined hands with women in the Indian and Coloured communities who were resisting the high cost of living and co-option into the tricameral system of the apartheid regime. White women had joined hands with black women and through such organisations as the Black Sash . . . had come out in support of the struggle."[171]

By the mid-1980s one observer found that there was "a sense of urgency" to unite women across racial and ideological spheres and that "our identity as women provides us with one common bond that may help us transcend the [barriers and divisions]."[172] Mary Burton, representing the Black Sash in the talks about reviving the federation, offered the following image of "an intricate, many-hued jersey" for what the organization could be: "not a rigid, imposed pattern, but a unique innovative design drawing on a wealth of diverse colours, textures and materials, its inspiration derived from many sources, a rich weave in which one design blends into the next, offering warmth and comfort as well as strength and beauty."[173]

Powerful though the symbolic and political pull of a nonracial national women's movement was, it was much harder to achieve in practice. At a conference to commemorate August 9 in 1986, the feminist theologian Denise Ackermann argued that "apartheid, in its separation of people, has inured white women from black women, so the suffering of black women isn't an existential reality for white women."[174] Mamphele Ramphele warned that "women should first recognise the lines that divide them and the ties that bind them before they embark on any plan."[175] Nevertheless, as a result of the efforts of UWCO, NOW, and FEDTRAW, imagining a women's movement that recognized women's diversity was relatively easy. Although the notion of sisterhood had no currency in South Africa, Fester has written that "despite the very real class and race differences amongst us, UWO succeeded in building a comradeship amongst us as women and mothers."[176]

Conclusions

By the end of the 1980s women's organizations had been through a major learning curve: the experience of organization and mobilization, albeit not successfully sustained, gave women activists new hope that a women's movement could be built. Debates about equality and the nature of women's oppression in South Africa had advanced significantly through a combination of practical struggle and theoretical debate. Progressive civic and political organizations could no longer avoid at least the rhetoric of women's emancipation and the necessity for women's participation. Women activists too felt that they were part of an exhilarating movement.[177] *Speak* editor Karen Hurt captured the sentiments of many activists whom I interviewed when she said, "For me, it was a time of awakening and of understanding power relations in society. I was lucky to be active among people who understood the bigger picture."[178]

Despite the heightened mobilization and the emergence of a cadre of feminists, however, in some respects the picture of women's organizations at the end of the decade was depressingly similar to that at the beginning of the decade: women's organizations were weak and demobilized. Writing in the first issue of the new feminist journal *Agenda* in 1987, the feminist unionist Shamim Marie (Meer) commented that "the organizations that exist at the present time are reliant on a few very committed women who tirelessly give themselves to sustain their organizations. The masses of women remain outside of these organizations. . . . Women's organizations in this country have not yet made their mark as women within broader struggles. We have been too busy taking up general community struggles. Very seldom have issues affecting women been taken up."[179]

A key explanation for this demobilization must surely be the extent of repression that women activists faced, particularly in Natal. The external conditions under which women's organizations worked—of states of emergency and targeting of women leaders for detention by the state—were not always conducive to their attempts to build democratic, accountable structures. This is not a sufficient explanation, however. This study of UWO, NOW, and FEDTRAW suggests that some attention must also be placed on the extent to which the broader politics of mass mobilization shaped the trajectory of women's organizations. Women's organizations needed a measure of autonomy in order to build their structures and articulate their interests on their own terms; such autonomy was barely tolerated within the broader progressive movement.

As the case studies in this chapter show, women's organizations were weakened in many ways by affiliation with the UDF. First, the halting journey toward establishing organizational autonomy and political space vis-à-vis civic associations and trade unions was derailed. Looking back, Pregs Govender of NOW noted that the UDF "didn't allow [women's] organizations to continue on our own path and for organic leadership to emerge. It didn't allow women to determine and shape the way in which they worked."[180] Jenny Schreiner of the UWO commented that the organization's branches "became more focused on mobilization than capacity building."[181] Second, the loss of an experienced cohort of leadership into the UDF structures affected the ability of women's organizations to devise strategies that would respond to the states of emergency in 1985 and 1986 or to new political opportunities offered by engagement with the UDF. Finally, women found it difficult to participate in some of the political tactics employed by the UDF. The focus on public protests such as sit-ins at foreign consulates, large campaigns such as the Million Signatures Campaign, mass rallies, and international mobilization rather than mobilization at a local level favored the political participation of men. Women's dual burden of work and home, and their lack of confidence in public speaking (especially in English), among other factors, made many of these strategies impossible for women to use.[182] This mode of organization also undermined the painstaking bottom-up style of organization favored by UWCO and aspired to by NOW. Ironically, while seeking to mobilize "the masses," broad-based organization suffered drastically as a result of the UDF national campaigns.

By the mid-1980s women's organizations had not yet built up deep levels of leadership in their branches; UDF-style mobilization exposed the top structures of the organization to government retaliation while not allowing time for new leaders to emerge. Seen from a longer-term perspective, it was inevitable that building a women's movement with a democratic culture and shaped by women at the local level would get lost once all women's political energies were directed into the UDF. From women's perspective, the promise of the civics movement—that democracy would be reshaped from below— was broken very much earlier than the existing literature on the UDF suggests. What I have shown in this chapter is that at the grassroots level, women's visions for a new democracy encompassed political as well as social and cultural transformation. Although relatively muted by the priorities of the civics movement, the distinctiveness of feminism in this period lay in the articulation of linkages between gender oppression in the private sphere and race and class oppression. Women's organizations opened new political spaces for women alongside the mainstream of male-dominated union or civic organizations. These spaces, small though they were, represented arenas in which organization could flourish outside the domination of male activists. Each organization studied here forced open, in different ways, an understanding of the scope of politics that went beyond the formal political realm of parties and movements to encompass the daily and intimate forms of oppression and exploitation that characterized women's experiences.[183]

The relative emphasis of each organization on the extent to which the "national question" should dominate agenda setting led to different organizational styles that affected their ability to develop sustainable mobilizational vehicles and, in turn, influenced on their ability to negotiate autonomy vis-à-vis male-dominated political organizations. Although attempts to establish autonomy were undercut by developments in the external political universe, the political values and organizational styles that developed were at the core of subsequent strategies to build women's organizations and to negotiate the boundaries of the relationship between women's organizations and other political movements.

Women activists had to confront not only their immediate comrades in the civic associations and unions—many of whom, both female and male, were either dismissive of the particular character of women's demands or angered by what they termed divisiveness—but also the political canon of the liberation struggle, which had established a hierarchy of struggles in which women's liberation featured only vaguely in a utopian future. Despite the emphasis of political leaders within the UDF on the narrowly *political* aspects of revolutionary change, women's organizations linked women's private household struggles to larger questions of economic marginality and articulated the need for social and cultural transformation as integral to liberation. Although nationalism was not displaced as the overarching ideological framework of struggle, women activists debated the consequences of this emphasis for women's autonomy and for the likely trajectory of postliberation political developments.

Chapter 3

The ANC in Exile

Challenging the Role of Women
in National Liberation

The 1980s were "radical years"[1] not only for the internal resistance movement that I discussed in chapter 2 but also for the African National Congress (ANC) in exile. New debates about women's role in politics took place within the movement, with women activists in the ANC Women's Section and guerrillas in Umkhonto we Sizwe (MK, Spear of the Nation, the ANC's military wing) demanding internal transformations that would recognize their right to an equal role in political struggle. Although the ANC had long acknowledged the desirability of mobilizing women for national liberation, in the 1980s women activists began to raise the issue of what, specifically, national liberation would deliver to women. Influenced by the resurgence of women's organizations inside South Africa, as well as by the international women's movement, they argued not only that the liberation of women could not be separated from national liberation but that it was an integral part of how liberation itself was defined.

This chapter is concerned with when and how these arguments were made, the reception of women's demands by the ANC leadership, and, more broadly, with the relationship between gender equality and national liberation. The ANC, as Raymond Suttner has argued, is an organization with multiple traditions and arenas of operation. This chapter addresses debates within one arena, the ANC in exile, seeking both to expand the understanding of the nature of the movement in exile as well as to explore the organizational changes that made the ANC's extraordinary commitment to gender equality possible. Maxine Molyneux's notion of "directed collective action," defined as the situation in which the "authority and initiative clearly come from outside and stand above the collectivity itself,"[2] provides a framework within which to explore the relationship between struggles for gender equality and national liberation. While directed collective action may successfully draw women into political participation, the goals of the women's organizations "do not specifically concern women other than as instruments for the realisation of the higher authority's goals; and/or even if they do concern women, control and direction of the agenda does not lie with them as an identifiable social force."[3] Nevertheless, Molyneux suggests that there may be "considerable fluidity in a given historical context; in one situation there may be a movement from direction to greater autonomy as the collective actors acquire more political resources and influence over the political process."[4] In the ANC the authority and initiative for women's political activities were formally held by the National Executive Committee (NEC). However, women activists within the movement increasingly challenged this situation. I seek to explore in this chapter the (incomplete) process of movement from directed action toward autonomy. In particular, I am concerned with uncovering how women in the ANC were able to acquire increased resources and influence, and in what ways they sought to use these advantages to enhance both struggles for gender equality and the agenda for substantive democracy.

This chapter outlines three categories of influence on the increasing assertion of women's interests within the ANC. The first relates to internal organizational experiences: internal culture, debates about the power and status of women's structures within the ANC, and changes in the composition of the movement's membership. The second relates to the theoretical debates that flowed from attempts to find a role for women in national liberation, including the extent to which the Women's Section could have autonomy in relation to the ANC. The third influence was ANC women's exposure to and interaction with international feminist debates and with women's organizations in postindependence African countries. These influences intersected to reshape the ANC and lay a basis for new practices and discourses of gender equality and democracy.

The Position of Women's Structures in ANC in Exile

As I argued in chapter 1, for most of the twentieth century women were second-class members of the ANC. Although the organization made significant moves to articulate new political roles for women during the 1950s, these developments were halted by the proscription of political movements in 1960. In the 1960s Ruth Mompati, based in Morogoro, Tanzania, headed "women's affairs" for the ANC External Mission. In exile the ANC Women's League was suspended. Instead, women in the ANC were organized from 1969 (following the recommendations of the Morogoro Conference) as the Women's Section, headed politically by the Women's Secretariat. In 1971, the Secretariat was reorganized, with Florence Mophosho, Magdalene Resha, Edna Mgabaza, Kate Molale, and Theresa Maimane as members. Florence Mophosho headed the structure, having been transferred from her position as a member of the Secretariat of the Women's International Democratic Federation, an international socialist organization of which the ANC had been a member since the late 1940s. From 1981 Gertrude Shope was president of the Women's Section. In 1983 the Women's Secretariat established a substructure called the National Women's Executive Committee, which conducted the day-to-day business of the Women's Section.

Formally defined, the key tasks of the Women's Section were to mobilize women into active membership within the ANC and to mobilize political and material support internationally.[5] Although in part a successor to the Women's League, and with a similar role within the ANC, the Women's Section was organized along different lines. The relative autonomy that the ANC Women's League had begun to delineate in formal terms, if not in practice, was eroded. "The Women's League was an independent body with its own constitution and laws, and it could make its own decisions. But the ANC felt there should only be one organisation in exile, and that we should carry out our work collectively. The constitution of the ANC has been suspended in exile, and new structures like the Women's Section have developed."[6]

As I will show in this chapter, the status and powers of the Women's Section were to become a thorny issue in its relationship with the ANC's National Executive Committee. In addition to the main office in Lusaka, the Women's Section had several regional units, each with at least five members. All women in the ANC in exile were automatically members of the Women's Section (unlike the Women's League before the ANC was banned—women in the ANC had to apply for membership in the league).

Mavivi Manzini has said that during the 1970s it was not clear what concrete policies the ANC should have with regard to women.[7] From its inception in 1969, the primary role of the Women's Section was to act as the movement's social worker. According to Frene Ginwala, its role was "supportive, a social network, rather than political."[8] For almost all of the 1960s and 1970s the Women's Section functioned as a network of solidarity rather than as a mobilizing agency. According to documents in the ANC's archives, a leader of the Women's Section once commented that "we only served as a servicing machinery and we were not directly involved in the mobilisation and organisation of women inside our country."[9] Although young militants later criticized the "apolitical, social work" role of the Women's Section, the support services that the Women's Section undertook—such as establishing child care facilities and processing donations of food and clothing—were important to ANC members in the context of exile. For some younger members the provision of these services allowed feminists in the movement to "take their rightful place in the struggle—it may not have been the most politically advanced, but the Women's Section made women's activism possible," Ntsiki Motumi said.[10]

Conditions in exile were harsh, particularly for those deployed in African countries. Exiled members of the ANC lived for the most part on meager funds raised by the movement abroad. In Africa most did not work for a salary, although all members regardless of rank received a small stipend equivalent to fourteen Zambian kwacha a month, and board and lodging were provided.[11] People were moved around according to the needs of the movement. This produced uncertainty and anxiety and reinforced the power over the rank-and-file of a small elite that controlled resources.[12] Lodge has suggested that daily life in exile was characterized by "frustrations and apparent triviality," which could "promote escapist delusions, mutiny and apathy amongst rank and file."[13] These frustrations were reinforced by the relative failure of the ANC to mount any successful military or political campaigns within the country during its first decade of exile. For some exiles the psychological burdens were almost unbearable, and the Women's Section offered solidarity and a sense of security very similar to the way in which prayer groups and savings clubs offered newly urbanized women support within the country during the early twentieth century.[14] The Women's Section East Africa Region, for example, reported in 1981 that "many [women] are idle and very anxious about being involved in meaningful activity, either work or school. Some are ill and feel insecure, and so on. Others are just going through a difficult stage of readjustment to exile, an abnormal situation that we only fully appreciate when we are already out here. . . . General meetings bring us together to share our views. . . . They also give us a feeling of belonging with one another, which is very essential, especially in exile."[15]

In 1984 the Women's Secretariat reported an increase in the number of women with mental illness.[16] Muff Andersson, an MK cadre, said that the movement had no mechanisms to help members cope with depression and anxiety: "Women felt they could not even talk about it. There was a fear that if you acknowledged these feelings, you might be seen to be weak and less dependable for revolutionary work."[17] But the Women's Section often responded to such social crises, and the necessity of its practical activities shaped its conventional role as a women's auxiliary of the national liberation movement. In this capacity its role was both validated and valuable for the movement; however, this work pushed some women activists to question the extent to which the movement was in practice committed to women's equality and whether in fact women stood to gain equality *automatically* from national liberation. As I will show, such questioning of the theoretical hierarchy of nationalist struggle and the male structures of authority within the ANC was not popular.

The Women's Section was responsible for the well-being and education of children of ANC members in exile. It set up and ran various nursery schools, including the Dora Tamana Crèche in Lusaka, and the Charlotte Maxeke Crèches in Mazimbu in Tanzania. The running of these nurseries was taken very seriously, and numerous training workshops were organized on nutrition and child care, for example, for the nursery workers. Although the ANC had a policy of keeping families together whenever possible, many children were separated from their parents, and members of the ANC Women's Section acted as surrogate mothers—an effort to make the nurseries "a home and not an institution."[18] Mavis Nhlapo, administrative secretary for the Women's Section in the early 1980s, said that "the maternal instinct of protection certainly drove the Women's Section."[19] An MK cadre noted that "I didn't have to choose between motherhood and politics because the Women's Section made it possible for me to do both. I knew I could leave my child in good hands."[20] This was a minority view, though: most women in the movement were very unhappy about being separated from their children.[21]

Despite the emphasis on women's maternal role, motherhood itself limited women's mobility within the movement.[22] Women members of MK were forbidden to become pregnant. Women deployed to the Angolan camps had IUDs inserted as a matter of policy. "Some women became infertile as a result. We were told we had to do it because if we fell pregnant we wouldn't be allowed to be there," Andersson recalled.[23] ANC policy was to send new mothers to Morogoro with their children. Young mothers and babies were sent to the Charlotte Maxexe Mother and Child Centre, which, while it provided a caring environment, was also "regarded by the authorities as a way of isolating those who had behaved in an unacceptable way."[24] For young women "there was a slight horror about having children and being sent to Tanzania," where they would spend long months without any activity, according to Sean Morrow, Brown Maaba, and Loyiso Pulumane.[25]

Women in MK argued that new mothers should "be flung back into the actively fighting ranks so that childbirth does not become the devastating route to demobilisation."[26] At the urging of the Women's Section, the Secretary General's Office agreed in 1981 that "day-care centres should be established in all areas to enable mothers to continue with their tasks after conceiving."[27] To be sure, the ANC was limited by financial constraints in meeting this objective; nevertheless, the Women's Secretariat pointed out that "female comrades have been the victim of this decision while men are let loose and some have got married to other women and abandoned mothers of their children."[28] Financial considerations aside, the National Executive Committee of the ANC did not appear to grasp the political significance of a good child care system. When the issue was raised by the National Women's Executive Committee (NWEC) in 1984, the ANC's treasurer general again "levelled strong criticism over the creation of crèches all over."[29] The issue continued to trouble women members of the ANC. "We seem to travel in a dead end street with marriage and babies being at the end of the street. There is not and can never be a contradiction between marriage and having babies on one hand and fighting on the other. There have been revolutions before, women have married and women have borne children during these, but women have fought. We are not and cannot be exceptions," the Women's Section reported in 1987.[30]

Social welfare problems intensified rapidly after 1976, with the sudden influx of young people into ANC camps in Africa. Most were aged fifteen to twenty, and they brought with them the problems of teenagers everywhere. Inevitably, the Women's Section was left to take care of this group, to be surrogate mothers. Many of these youngsters had gone into exile with youthful idealism, believing that "they would be back [home] with Kalashnikovs within six months."[31] Instead, they found themselves in conditions that were often harsh and with long periods of inactivity while they waited to be transferred to educational institutions in the Eastern bloc, United States, or Britain or to military camps. The number of teenage pregnancies increased, and the Women's Section was frequently drawn into resolving personal and relationship problems. "Torn from their parents, our students, particularly the very young ones, need to be associated with our women as mothers, to guide them particularly in upholding the discipline of the movement. This would go a long way in giving them a sense of belonging and boosting their morale," the ANC Women's Secretariat reported in 1981.[32]

The Women's Section was asked to organize recreational and cultural activities for young girls to keep them occupied.[33] Through skills-training workshops the young women learned crafts such as weaving and producing t-shirts and other items for the movement. The Women's Section also counseled students and monitored their progress; such counseling sometimes included assuming the role of moral regulation. Students studying abroad posed their own set of problems. They sometimes defected from the movement, and some women who married foreigners did not report to ANC headquarters for duty after completing their studies. Tensions between male and female students abroad were numerous, caused by the ubiquitous "relationship" problems. Women students complained that men "were only interested in getting them drunk and getting them into bed," and the Women's Section was called in to mediate, sometimes as far afield as the Soviet Union.[34] Young men in the ANC repeatedly attacked women students who went out with foreigners, despite an ANC ban on marriage between ANC women and foreigners. At a meeting of the Women's Secretariat and the Youth Secretariat, the two groups agreed that "we try very hard to discourage our women getting married to foreigners and positive attitude of male comrades towards female will help alleviate the problem in the socialist countries. Women must be made to understand their allegiance to the country and our people."[35] Andersson pointed out that the sexist attitudes regarding marriage stemmed from "the expectation that a woman would follow her husband into his home so South Africa would lose. If a man marries a foreigner, it will strengthen the South African struggle, but if women married a foreigner it would strengthen the man's struggle."[36]

The control of women also extended to their relationships with South African men who were not members of the ANC.[37] For example, young women who went out with members of the Pan Africanist Congress (PAC) were seen as breaching discipline. In some cases the ANC administered corporal punishment, although the Women's Section advised against it: "Some of the girls have been bitten [*sic*] on their back-sides and some bear scars. But the punishment has not been effective because some of them have gone back to the PAC men."[38] Later, when the young women were questioned, they said they did not know that the differences between the ANC and the PAC were of a serious nature. The Women's Section preferred that young women be warned and then expelled, and protested strongly (but unsuccessfully) against corporal punishment as a mode of discipline.

As a result of the practical work that the Women's Section took on in relation to women and children in exile, it often advocated that the exiled movement adopt more progressive social policies and strategies. In some respects these ideas predated positions that emerged from women's organizations during the 1990s. For example, health facilities in the camps were inadequately staffed and stocked, and the Women's Section, bearing the brunt of the consequences of this for women and children, felt compelled to assume responsibility for making improvements. But members of the NEC sometimes criticized the efforts of the Women's Section: "Health is a charge of the movement. It is not a women's matter."[39] Because of the high pregnancy rate among teenage comrades, the Women's Section took responsibility for sex education and family planning. The Women's Section also recommended that sex education be part of the curriculum at the Solomon Mahlangu Freedom College (Somafco) in Tanzania, although the NEC refused. The Women's Section suggested, somewhat desperately, that "perhaps the word sex education could be changed."[40] As Morrow, Maaba, and Pulumane have noted, "the school did not show a sure touch in its approach to sexuality and pregnancy among students."[41] Another example was the increasing conviction in the Women's Section that abortion should be legalized—again a consequence of the incidence of botched abortions on teenage girls in Lusaka where abortions were illegal.

A significant and widespread problem was violence against women. Women's Section documents carry numerous reports of abuse, with women appealing to the Women's Section for assistance and for discipline to be meted out to abusive men in the movement. This abuse sometimes extended to children. Even worse, in one document the Women's Section notes that "we hear of a number of children who have had to be stitched heavily having been 'punished' by *officials* of the movement."[42] The Women's Section made several unsuccessful attempts to deal with the problem, arguing as late as 1987 that "a long standing practice, that of women abuse and child battering, has now become common in the ANC. The movement should, with proper directives from this conference, come up with a policy on this negative practice. While waiting for the implementation of the code of conduct, we could use and implement measures taken, otherwise our aim of building and producing responsible cadres of this movement will soon be destroyed and defeated."[43]

The Women's Section at Mazimbu adopted a policy that "offending men should be locked up for two weeks, whether or not this was requested by their partners."[44] Most disturbingly, it was not only men who were violent. In one instance, a matron at Mazimbu was accused of beating a child who had been left in her care while the mother was away on a scholarship. "The beating was so severe that subsequently the child could neither sit down nor walk properly."[45] In 1988 a working committee was set up to compile a report because the issue of violence "has now been considered by the high structures of our movement."[46] It was also hoped that the newly established Emancipation Desk in the Women's Section, headed by Zanele Mbeki (wife of Thabo Mbeki), would monitor developments, but the problem of violence against women remained an issue for the entire period of exile.

The Women's Secretariat also had to deal with the constant movement of its members; all were assumed to be in transit and at the behest of the movement might leave to pursue studies, be deployed into MK, or accompany a transferred spouse. The result was that for a long time the Women's

Secretariat was a very unstable structure.[47] It was hard to build up a core team and to develop its own relationships and contacts with underground activists in the internal women's movement. It received very sporadic information about women's activities inside the country and usually relied on intelligence from London, which had a steady stream of internal activists passing through. As a result the Women's Section was not always able to follow the "complex situation" in women's politics inside the country.[48] Under these conditions it was hard for the Women's Secretariat to consolidate—or even conceptualize—a more overtly political role.

The magazine *Voice of Women,* the key propaganda organ of the Women's Section, was intended to provide one of the crucial linkages between internal women's organizations and the exiled movement. It was established in 1971 to mobilize South African women inside and outside the country into ANC structures; to lobby the international community to support the ANC's cause; and to "take up issues which affect women."[49] The publication was never very successful. It was produced under extremely difficult conditions in Lusaka: outdated and barely functioning machinery, poorly trained journalists, and few financial and informational resources. The journal received a boost with the deployment of Mavivi Manzini in 1981 as its editor and head of the subcommittee on information and publicity; she was complemented by a team that included the trained journalist Marion Sparg. This team was analytically skilled and articulate, but even then problems persisted. Staff would acquire skills, only to be redeployed by the NEC to some other position with no provision for replacements. According to the minutes of a 1984 Women's Section meeting, "Comrades were very angry that things should be done in this manner. It showed how our male comrades undermine the work of the Women's Section by simply taking comrades without discussion."[50] In any case, the code of discipline that operated in the ANC in exile made attempts to shift the parameters of responsibility and accountability over decision making difficult, if not anathema.[51]

One key implication of the lack of skills and continuity was the weakness of the *Voice of Women* and the Women's Section in building effective communication with the internal women's movement. The 1981 conference of the Women's Section, for example, decided that the journal should discuss issues from home more fully (although reports from home were very patchy) and take on the task of political education for internal activists.[52] This was consistent with the general ANC emphasis after 1979 on developing an internal political base rather than relying solely on armed struggle to overthrow the apartheid state.[53] However, the magazine (and the Women's Section itself) did not have up-to-date information on internal developments, and the periodical was not widely circulated inside South Africa.[54] "VOW was said not to be giving direction to the problem of organisation of women inside the country which is needed presently. Here it was pointed out . . . that due to the lack of information of what is the level of organisation of women at home, the problems existing and the objective conditions existing it has become very difficult to give such direction. Some time an attempt was made of calling for women to form a national body, and as we were doing it the women at home were calling for the consolidation of regional [sic] and formation of regional women's organisation so we were not at par with the women at home."[55]

In 1983 it was estimated that the press run for each issue (of the four planned per year) of *Voice of Women* was five thousand copies, half of which were for distribution inside South Africa. The Women's Secretariat told the Political Department of the ANC that it was concerned that this number was too small. The response was that "the rise in quantity will depend on the quality since some of the issues do not even find their way into the country due to the quality of the articles."[56] The Women's Section recommended that "permanent representatives be sought in the Forward Areas to collect information, do interviews, write draft stories, etc for VOW."[57] The Zambian Women's Regional Section suggested the formation of an editorial board. This brought in some skilled oversight: the board's role was "to meet to collectively decide on articles to be taken up in VOW, and on the general political line to be followed."[58] The editorial board wrote and edited articles. These were then sent on to Thabo Mbeki, as head of the Political Commission of the NEC, for final editing.[59] The Women's Secretariat noted criticism that VOW had "a weak political content, which makes VOW not to match the revolutionary situation in the women's front inside the country. The machineries concerned with the distribution inside the country have complained that VOW does not always guide the women in their everyday struggles; but only responds spontaneously on issues taken up. Even then, it does not address itself to the tactics used by women at a particular time, and does not help them to assume higher forms of struggle."[60]

A key impediment to the ability of the Women's Section to develop a good intelligence network was the limited power of the structure within the ANC. Communications between internal cadres and the movement were governed by the Revolutionary Council, a structure that, until its dissolution in 1983, had no more than one woman member at any given time.[61] The Women's Section was not allowed to have direct links with women inside the country, as the ANC regarded the decentralizing of communication networks as a weakening of military discipline. In any case, the mobilization of women was not seen as a high priority for the Revolutionary Council[62] or its successor, the Political-Military Council (nor for Military Headquarters—I discuss later in this chapter how few women were deployed inside the country), and consequently very few such linkages developed and even these "were invariably infiltrated," Nhlapo said.[63] Some women (most notably the union organizer Ray Simons) ignored the formal structures and maintained their own contacts "and were sometimes hauled over burning coals as a result," according to Nhlapo.[64]

Beginning in the early 1980s, the Women's Section wanted to take responsibility for preparing fact papers for distribution among women in exile but was limited by resources.[65] In 1984 the NWEC complained to the NEC that the report on the internal situation by the Women's Secretariat "was edited by the Political Headquarters to the extent of not making any comprehension to the members of the NWEC. What was appearing in the report was simply no different from what we all get from news briefings."[66] The NWEC reiterated that "as an executive body of the women, it is necessary for this body to address itself to the question of mobilisation and involvement of women in the struggle. We need to know what the needs of women are, what guidance could be given. It is 1984 and yet the women are not in touch with the women at home."[67]

The Impact of the '76 Generation

Only at the first conference of women in exile, in Luanda in 1981, did a clearly defined political position on women began to emerge within the Women's Section. The first conference provided an important platform for women in the ANC to debate and assess their strength inside the liberation movement. By this stage there had been a significant influx of young women into the exiled movement following the 1976 Soweto uprising. Lodge cites security police estimates that by mid-1978 approximately four thousand refugees were undergoing insurgency training in Angola, Libya, and Tanzania,[68] with the number growing to ten thousand by 1986.[69] With the influx of young people into exile after 1976, the ANC became "predominantly an organisation of young men and women surmounted by senior echelons of soldiers and bureaucrats whose exile had in many cases preceded the births of their new disciples."[70] Not surprisingly, this situation opened many new areas for internal conflicts within the ANC, and here I focus on those relating to gender.

Since its exile the ANC had placed extraordinary emphasis on the role of armed struggle "not only as the primary means by which eventually to overthrow the South African state but also the major means to advance the ANC's cause in each phase of escalation towards that ultimate goal."[71] Umkhonto we Sizwe thus constituted the powerhouse of the exiled movement. After 1976 MK, which had been overwhelmingly male in composition, saw a dramatic increase in the number of women combatants, who by 1991 constituted approximately 20 percent of the army.[72] The women who joined the movement in this period brought new energy and militancy from the townships into the ANC and particularly into MK. The simple fact of their joining the armed wing acted as a destabilizing factor in the most masculine of the ANC substructures. As Mtintso said, "Their very presence began to break down conservative elements within the ANC."[73]

Many women had been local leaders of the student movement and "couldn't be pushed around, they stood their ground."[74] Thandi Modise, part of the '76 Generation and subsequently a commander in Umkhonto we Sizwe in Angola, noted that "the ANC was really caught off guard, didn't know what to do with us—too many young people coming in, some of them too energetic."[75] The MK woman—described by the Women's Section as "an independent personality who can be seen by her detachment from ego; she has good qualities as a person without self-pity and arrogance"[76]— became an icon of the national liberation struggle.

It is difficult to be precise about the political influence of women in MK as this is an underresearched area. Apart from Jacklyn Cock's groundbreaking work in 1991, and Goldblatt and Meintjes's work for the Truth and Reconciliation Commission,[77] sources are thin. In particular, there is little analysis of the political influence on the ANC of women's role in MK. Cock has argued that "there is no doubt that women have played an important and courageous part in MK activities. Undoubtedly the nature of the struggle and the breakdown of normal male-female roles encouraged many women to discover new capacities within themselves. . . . At the same time, the image of the female fighter—the MK guerrilla—has become a popular mass image of the strong, liberated woman."[78]

Yet, it has also been argued that the militarization of the struggle undermined women's organization. Albie Sachs, for example, sees the turn to armed struggle as a setback for women. "The more the struggle focused on armed combat the more it took on a male character and women played an auxiliary role as carriers."[79] Thenjiwe Mtintso, on the other hand, sees the developments within MK as the beginning of a new process of opening opportunities for women within the ANC as the movement began to recognize women's contribution.[80] In part this was because of the status MK itself enjoyed within the ANC. "MK had a rank of its own. [They were seen] to have a tougher commitment. . . . They made tough choices and made comradeship stronger," Mtintso said. "Women members of MK had to be taken seriously. They had to explode the myth of women as inferior on a day to day basis. They did not articulate feminism but had to prove themselves in the field and gain respect. Women as a collective gained respect out of the performances of individual women. Men had to give respect even if it was grudging."[81]

Ironically and unwittingly—and despite the resistance of the military leadership—MK provided an important arena within the movement in which to raise issues of gender equality. Interviewed in the *Voice of Women*, one cadre called MK a "school of equality."[82] Although the language of equality was not common parlance, given the rigid hierarchy and emphasis on military discipline that characterized the armed wing, women combatants drew on other aspects of ANC rhetoric to make their claims. As Thandi Modise has argued, "We said we wanted to be treated like everybody else. . . . They said 'And therefore you will dig like every man does and therefore you will do, whatever.' And we said 'Fine!' So we dug the trenches and the men would sit there and smoke and we dug! It was difficult . . . our hands! . . . Your body would ache because in the mornings the road work . . . they made it extra difficult—going up and down the mountains. We needed to prove we'd keep up. . . . Try to be one of the boys because that is one of the protections you have."[83] The rigorous training was strategic. Jackie Molefe put it bluntly: "What we try and get across is that when the SADF [South African Defence Force] comes the cadres will not be able to choose. You must be able to defend yourself."[84]

Women and men received the same political and military training,[85] although women's training was often not as physically rigorous and their roles were not the same. Even though women were often better shots than men, they were not allowed to participate in sniper training, and women were excluded from traditional combat roles. While men spent long periods in the camps, women tended to leave very shortly after their training.[86] Instead of combat, women were trained to do courier work. This was seen as undermining the commitment to equality, and women in MK demanded that "there should be no *Umkhonto wabafazi* [of women] or *wamadoda* [of men]."[87]

There was no doubt that life in the camps was physically and psychologically grueling. As Lodge has noted, "Placing large numbers of men in holding camps for long periods of inactivity is an almost certain recipe for low morale and indiscipline."[88] While women were demanding equality and respect from their male comrades, they also benefited in some ways from being treated as special cases. On the one hand, the treatment of women as appendages and possessions of men sometimes exposed them to abuse, but on the other hand, special protection mitigated some of the worst effects of camp life and its anomie. Janet Love, a white activist who joined MK after 1976, commented on the contradictory effects of patriarchal attitudes: "I was far more fortunate than a lot of other people, and I think that was [because] of a much more conscious effort within MK to generally pay more attention to the sorts of decisions that would need to be taken around women. . . . There was much more of a conscious effort to make sure that women would be utilized to a greater degree than men. I mean, there were men that stayed in the camps for more than ten years, and I want to tell you that is hideous."[89]

Tensions within MK over the perceived failure to return trained cadres to the country during the early 1980s were enormous.[90] Women cadres were particularly concerned at the low numbers of women sent back to act as underground activists. They argued that "it has been proven that the chances of survival in the underground for women are greater than for men. People at home have actually demanded/recommended that the ANC should send and train more women."[91] Molefe's comments to Cock suggest that accepting equality was almost as difficult for the women as for the men: "Some of the women can't cope with the exercises. It takes some time to convince women; they have hangovers [*sic*] about how a woman should be treated because of their upbringing. In the beginning they expect help or say they can't exercise too much because they will come to have legs like men. . . . In the beginning the boys expected to have their clothes washed, and the girls would do it."[92]

Women's presence in MK was by no means easily accepted. Although the high level of commitment of women within MK and the fact that some women performed better than men in the field and in shooting practice forced men to recognize women's capacities,[93] women were constantly questioned about "what [they] were doing in a man's world," Nhlapo said.[94] There was ambiguity about women's formally equal status on the one hand and the ways in which traditional gender relationships could offer women both emotional comfort and preferential access to scarce resources on the other. Love commented that "things were tough there [in the camps]. You are filled with uncertainty. . . . You know sometimes women were flattered by attention [from male leaders]. Material things then became on offer, you know, sort of the extra trip to town or the extra possibility of going to select items of clothing from jumbles that was sent us by charitable institutions from Europe. . . . And that is also quite undermining. Somehow one asks, 'Why am I doing this? Who am I?' Not so much 'Why am I MK? Why am I politically involved?' but 'Why am I associated with particular people?' You kind of think you got it taped, you think you are doing it for the right reasons, and then you kind of get ambiguous about it."[95]

In a 1987 report women in MK complained that "comrades are in a hurry to 'privatize' women because of the shortage of women in MK."[96] Mtintso commented that "camps could dull your sharp gender mind, but you also dulled it deliberately. You didn't want to look at roles as exploitative, you deliberately didn't want to see it. . . . Life is tough . . . you wanted to make your life as comfortable as possible. . . . I could benefit from having a relationship with commanding personnel. If I don't, life is going to be hell. All of us experience hell, men and women, but men bring things from town, goodies."[97]

Sometimes the unequal power relations between men and women slipped into abuse. Mavis Nhlapo said that women felt they were treated as "second-class citizens. I was appointed a commissar and so I heard all the problems. I fought hard for the rights of the women. Even some of the senior people took advantage of the girls. I felt they should be setting an example."[98] Modise recalled an incident in Tanzania, where there was a fight about the sexual availability of women cadres. "There was this idea that we [women] needed to be superfit. Against the enemy, the South African state, then, and against men who just wanted to take advantage of us. . . . But there had been a fight one night over girls . . . because there had been a feeling among some men that because there are these five, six women there, why should they [the men] be sex starved? and there were others who said, 'No, they are not there to be sex slaves—if they want to have affairs, they will have affairs; if they don't want to, then you are there to protect them.' "[99] This was true in other parts of the movement as well. Albie Sachs said that "the line was 'it's simple, we agree with equality.' But young women wanting scholarships sometimes had to sleep with people or could be given tasks on the assumption that women are available as sexual partners."[100]

Clearly, connecting the expansion of women's roles and women's status was not easy. The "sharp gender mind" nevertheless shifted the conception of women's status within the ANC. However it was defined, if the concept of equality could be accepted within MK—supposedly, the arena in which the most committed members were located—then it could be extended to other parts of the ANC. Mtintso pointed out that the significance of women's involvement in MK was that "women were saying we are full citizens in the ANC."[101]

Not surprisingly, given MK's extremely hierarchical and authoritarian structures, it was also within MK that the limits of rhetorical commitments to equality were most directly experienced. MK was slowest to respond to the demands for the greater representation of women in its leadership and least receptive to the need to mobilize women around issues of women's emancipation. While women were making strides throughout the 1980s in other structures of the movement, Nhlapo said, "the MK side was still a big problem. Post-1981 the leadership of MK did not want the Women's Section involved in the activities of women in MK. This created a lot of bitterness. We felt the women in MK were getting a raw deal—women who were deserving of positions were not getting them. We had several discussions with the NEC, with the Revolutionary Council, with Military Headquarters, we knocked on every door but were told MK is a completely different domain."[102]

This slowness to respond to concerns about gender equality must be linked to the overall undervaluing in MK of the political aspects of the struggle against apartheid. Although a major strategic review within the ANC in 1978–79 shifted the emphasis from military to political means of struggle, armed struggle remained the bedrock of the ANC's vision of revolution.[103] Issues such as greater independence of the Women's Section in defining relationships with internal women's organizations, and the concerns with democratic culture and values that were being slowly articulated by women in the movement, got little attention in MK. Women's frustration with the lack of progress in convincing MK of the need for greater internal democracy translated into dissatisfaction with the structures of women's representation inside the ANC. The difficulties with MK exposed the limited powers of the Women's Section inside the ANC and became the source of tensions between the Women's Section and women soldiers, tensions that pushed debates about organizational autonomy and the role of political mobilization to new heights by 1987.

The claim of women in MK for "full citizenship" had implications for women's position within the movement. In President Oliver Tambo women had a sympathetic, if paternalistic, leader. Tambo was not a feminist, but he was "quite liberated, especially for his age. His international experiences broadened his worldview," Mtintso said. "He was one of those inherently progressive characters, a revolutionary democrat who lived his beliefs in practice. . . . He was able to look at women with respect. They had sacrificed more than men, by leaving home they [women] showed advanced political thinking. He wanted to give everyone the opportunity and ability to play a role."[104] Albie Sachs made a similar argument about Tambo's role: "OR's leadership wasn't so much to promote the cause of women as women. He saw himself as a leader of a broad organization and saw that there was a section of the organization that was held back. His vision was as a democrat rather than as a nonsexist."[105]

During Tambo's presidency women gained significant opportunities within the ANC. For example, Tambo appointed several women as representatives of the movement abroad, including Lindiwe Mabuza, Barbara Masekela, and Ruth Mompati. These postings gave women an opportunity to demonstrate their skills and also exposed women in the ANC to the rising tide of feminism internationally. For the women based in African countries, the mid- to late 1980s was a period in which "the question of gender struggle as distinct began emerging. We see reversals in Mozambique, Zimbabwe, and Namibia. For women comrades 'normality' meant going back to the kitchens," Mtintso said. "We began to be quite worried about what liberation is going to offer."[106]

Debates on Organizational Autonomy

Throughout the 1980s the precise role and status of the Women's Section within the ANC were much debated. The documents of the various conferences of the Women's Section reveal how hard women activists tried to win some measure of control over their programs and some degree of authoritative voice in overall ANC decision making. The 1981 conference of the Women's Section identified the key task as the mobilization of women inside the country as active ANC members. The conference recommended that the head of the Women's Section should automatically become a member of the NEC. This would give women representation in the movement's highest decision-making body for the first time. Although the NEC accepted the proposal, an attempt was made in 1983 to overturn it on the grounds that the NEC was not a federal body and that women on the NEC were elected in their own right rather than as representatives of constituencies. The NEC's position was that the head of the Women's Section, Gertrude Shope, was "in the NEC in her own right . . . but she has every right to raise matters that affect the Women's Section. She has *no obligation* to report to the Women's Section on her work in the NEC."[107]

After the 1981 conference the Women's Section began to pay much greater attention to the importance of political education for members of the Women's Section and of providing more effective leadership to the emerging internal women's organizations. Nhlapo said that "we saw the need to develop a theoretical basis for women's struggle."[108] Inspired by their travels to socialist countries and their exposure to different women's movements in Europe, younger women in the ANC began to think about developing a mobilizing framework appropriate to South African women.[109] They tried to strengthen the *Voice of Women* and to produce shorts on women's issues for the ANC radio station. Several units started internal education projects, broadening the previous focus on literacy and adult education to include education about women's political history and debates about the role of women in the liberation struggle.[110] In 1983 the Women's Secretariat also discussed the need for the movement as a whole to take responsibility for political education about the emancipation of women. At this meeting some women expressed concern at the low number of women deployed as underground agents inside South Africa, with some arguing that this made it more difficult to mobilize women into the ANC and MK. The NEC never adequately addressed the problem. Women "were virtually ignored," Nhlapo said.[111]

The Women's Section worked incredibly hard to raise funds and gather materials for the movement, especially clothing for women and children.

The Women's Section's networks with women's organizations around the world, particularly the affiliates of the Women's International Democratic Federation, produced large amounts of money, clothing, and equipment for the movement.[112] Nevertheless, "when we needed to finance women's projects, the treasurer general would tell us there was no money for women," Nhlapo said.[113] At the same time the treasurer general's office was not always meticulous about recording money that came in and informing the Women's Section of its arrival. At times this put the Women's Section in a difficult position with regard to donors, as the women were unable to account for specific donations.

Despite women's increasing visibility and role within the ANC in the early 1980s, the organization continued to be male dominated. At a 1982 seminar a speaker noted that "men seem to want us to be perpetually in the kitchen. Our relations with them are jeopardised if we attend first to the non-domestic affairs and are late or unable to perform to perfection the domestic work that awaits us. . . . Some men refuse to accept the leadership and authority of women i.e. it would appear they support that the lady comrade is senior to them in authority but in practice they would never take her instructions."[114]

Mtintso said that "in some ways the organization was also closed off. In raising women's issues we were seen as petty. We were called *umzane*—the women,[115] while men were called *the soldiers*. There were already expectations of failure so we have to overperform. Even men overperform in order not to be beaten by women. In that environment you can't raise gender issues—we are all laying down our lives. We only discussed it insofar as there are specific needs for women. We were not talking about politics."[116]

Nhlapo recalled that women were constantly accused of "not understanding, not being sufficiently committed to national liberation, diverting the movement, being difficult."[117] And not only the men or the leadership were resistant to political discussions about women's emancipation. The East Africa Region of the Women's Section, for example, found it difficult to discuss the "women question" in Dar-es-Salaam. "We found that politically it was risky to introduce the concept of a 'revolution within a revolution' to young, politically immature people. . . . It was acknowledged that the majority of our women are more practically than intellectually orientated," the regional section reported in 1981. "Although they are involved in the fight against the fascist regime, we do not necessarily approach it from the same angle. . . . [Women] cannot be forced into political discussion when they are faced with concrete problems like food and clothing for themselves and their children. . . . With this analysis the Committee felt that we had to try our best to attend to the women's problems; we have to be practical and make them feel involved, not being lectured to."[118]

Nonetheless, as mobilization of women inside the country intensified, the Women's Section began to feel the political pressure and urgency to provide political leadership and direction.[119] Increasingly, women within the movement began to develop a feminist voice. In 1983 Ray Simons produced an assessment of the internal situation in which she urged less "ceremonial mobilisation and greater strategic direction."[120] One mechanism for focusing activists' energies on strategic areas of mobilization, and to raise ideological debate on the role of different sectors and agents in the national liberation struggle was to designate special themes to particular years. 1984 was devoted to accelerating the mobilization of women. The Year of the Women Committee, appointed by the National Executive Committee, identified the objectives for 1984 as to pay tribute to "the fighting women of our country and to increase their fighting ranks and make them assume their rightful role in the forefront of the struggle."[121] With regard to the Women's Section's internal mobilization, the goals would be to create a single national women's organization and to broaden women's organization inside the country.[122]

The focus on forming a national women's organization inside the country, preferably under the name of the Federation of South African Women, was paramount. This would consolidate the organization of women and "promote unity in the ranks of women opposed to apartheid and supportive of the ANC, and reactivate women activists at home."[123] The Women's Section reminded women activists that their key task remained that of national liberation and called on activists to "spare no effort in organising women to become underground workers for the ANC, and to take part in the armed struggle to liberate our country from the grip of the fascist warmongers and their puppets."[124] The basis for unity would be the Women's Charter, adopted at the founding conference of the Federation of South African Women in 1954. The thirtieth anniversary would provide the impetus for the revival. The Women's Section Internal Sub-Committee urged underground comrades to set up an ANC caucus in the organization "to ensure that in all this activity the movement should have a direct hand in guiding the formation of a national women's organisation."[125] However, as I showed in chapter 2, a national women's structure could not be imposed by fiat from exile. Internal women's organizations were not ready for unity, and despite numerous efforts well into the late 1980s, the revived Federation of South African Women did not gain a national presence. The gap between the expectations of the exiled movement and the internal movement was starkly revealed in this case: the desire of the Women's Section for a strong *sectoral* representative body of women was out of kilter with the internal direction of the United Women's Organisation in the Western Cape, which was moving toward a strong grassroots organization. The

Women's Section also was out of step with the difficulties that the Natal Organisation of Women was facing in opposition from Inkatha and the state, and with the lack of organizational depth at the Federation of Transvaal Women. Although the Women's Section no doubt gave courage and legitimacy to its underground activists, its role in stimulating and directing the internal women's movement was limited by local concerns and power struggles.

The influence of the Year of the Women on official discourses within the ANC was visible even though—or perhaps because—there was no coherent program of action. The Year of the Women exposed the ANC's weaknesses in integrating gender equality into the core work of the movement. Despite the creation of an organizationwide committee to oversee the program of action for the Year of the Women, it soon became the responsibility of the Women's Section rather than the movement as a whole.[126] Nhlapo said that the Year of the Women failed in its most crucial task, that of "making the women's issue a national issue and not just a women's issue."[127]

In early 1984 the Women's Section began calling for more discussion about the role of women in the ANC. At the first meeting of the National Women's Executive Committee in April 1984, the leadership noted that "the role of the Women's Section in the ANC is often misunderstood by the membership" and called for a sustained program of political education.[128] Concerns were also raised about the degree of control that the Women's Section had over decision making. The Women's Section repeatedly requested greater autonomy, although it was prepared to concede broad policy decisions to the NEC. The Women's Section complained that "sometimes the women feel that some seriousness is not attached to matters raised by women whereas decisions and recommendations are made for the benefit and the enhancement of the work of our struggle as a whole."[129]

The tentative and somewhat oblique language in which these requests and complaints were raised reveals the lack of organizational receptivity in the NEC, which tended to blame the complaints on ignorance and lack of discipline. A report from just one meeting between women representatives and the NEC shows the nature of the reception that women received. Women representatives reported that the NEC member Joe Nhlanhla's concern was that "one of our problems is that we women have become women first then ANC." Women were warned against "sectarianism," with Josiah Jele arguing that there was no need for women to have a special role in decision making "because the leadership considers recommendations made by women." The men again emphasized the "vertical structure" of the ANC. The secretary general, Alfred Nzo, was unhappy that "an impression of gross crime is being committed. The way the ANC regards women in the organisation. It is an ANC he does not [know] of. . . . He shared the views of the other comrades that there is no deliberate discrimination against women."[130] In a heavy-handed response the treasurer general also dismissed the concerns raised by the National Women's Executive Committee, claiming that "there are a lot of sentimental utterances about this and that . . . if this meeting had a real programme of deliberation, he [the treasurer general] would be contributing fully."[131] It was Oliver Tambo who was able to shift the meeting from the haranguing and ridiculing tone adopted by other members of the NEC to an emphasis on the importance of finding out what gave rise to women's unhappiness. Without the space Tambo created, the antagonistic response from the NEC might have ended women's attempts to transform the internal culture of the movement.

Undeterred, women activists continued to raise the "women question" and to push for a sharper understanding of the relationship between national liberation and women's emancipation, with the South African Communist Party journal *African Communist* providing an important forum for these debates. In 1984 an article by the pseudonymous Mosadi wa Sechaba,[132] located the urgency to organize women in the need to "activate the masses" for the revolution and quoted Lenin's comment to Clara Zetkin that "if the women are not with us, the counter-revolutionaries may succeed in setting them against us."[133] Understanding women's oppression as caused primarily by apartheid, the article posits a two-stage struggle in which women's emancipation would follow from national liberation.[134] Sechaba argued that "women should be mobilised by making them realise that our national democratic revolution will free them not only from national oppression and class exploitation, but also from oppression as women. This will give them an extra motivation for joining the struggle. Women should be made aware that they are expected to contribute at every level in every trench of our struggle—in the military as well as the mass political struggle—and not as mere supporters and sympathisers."[135]

In 1985 the Women's Section called for a regional seminar to discuss the role of women in the struggle and within the ANC. The Second ANC National Consultative Conference in Kabwe in June 1985 devoted a special session to women. A discussion paper circulated for the conference raised openly, for the first time, the collusion of men in the ANC with "traditional, conservative and primitive constraints imposed on women by man-dominated structures within our movement. Our movement has the task, as a vanguard of the liberation struggle of minimising these constraints as much as possible."[136] Arguing that "in our beleaguered country the women's place is in the battlefront of struggle,"[137] the discussion paper on women boldly declared that "our task is to prepare men and women for equality; this means that we must fight against male chauvinism, male domination, we must do away with male domination in the home, village, town, factory, workshop, in politics, economics and religion. In particular, we must fight domination even within our movement. No society is free if women are not free."[138] Bravely, considering the kind of reaction the Women's Section had faced in its meeting with the NEC in 1984, the paper again challenged the movement's tendency to belittle the work of the Women's Section and to see women as secondary subjects. It argued that "a women's movement is as decisive as the imperativeness of a working class movement."[139]

These arguments finally began to gain support in the NEC. At Kabwe the NEC departed from its earlier approach of mobilizing women solely for national liberation and formally recognized that women's equality would deepen and enhance the quality of democracy itself. The conference agreed that "the task of organising and mobilising our women into a powerful, united, active force for the most thorough-going democratic revolution falls on men and women alike."[140] For the first time the Women's Section expressed an interest in a more thorough bill of rights, one that would reflect women's demands for equality, "so that women know what they are fighting for."[141]

ANC president Oliver Tambo's closing speech at the conference is regarded as an affirmation of the need to strengthen women's voice within the organization. Tambo advanced the proposition that South Africa should not be seen as free as long as women were oppressed and that women's oppression had to be addressed not just by women but by the movement as a whole. This marked the first of a number of significant declarations and statements by the ANC leadership aimed at providing political support for women's struggles to organize themselves. Tambo emphasized the need for women to be represented at all levels of the movement, including within the NEC. Later in 1985, at a meeting between the South West Africa People's Organisation (the Namibian liberation organization) and the ANC in Kabwe, Sam Nujoma and Oliver Tambo made a joint pledge to the women of Namibia and South Africa that "we would not consider our objectives achieved, our task completed or our struggle at an end until the women of Namibia and South Africa are fully liberated."[142] Tambo's role in supporting women's empowerment within the movement had a significant influence. His speech was quoted countless times in women's meetings inside and outside the country. Many women who returned from exile and are today in leadership positions in government attribute their rise to his encouragement.

Feminism, National Liberation, and the Representation of Women's Interests

The Nairobi Conference of the United Nations Decade for Women in July 1985 was a significant event for women in the ANC. It provided an opportunity for the Women's Section to meet directly with activists from home and to strategize about the strengthening of women's organization. The Women's Section claimed to have secured unity between the United Women's Organisation and the Federation of South African Women in one of these meetings.[143] Ginwala has argued that the right-wing backlash at the conference inadvertently offered an opportunity for ANC women to take a leadership role.[144] The U.S. delegation, led by Ronald Reagan's daughter Maureen, opposed a resolution against apartheid on the ground that this was a political issue rather than a women's issue. Issues like violence against women were posed as genuine women's issues, and the U.S. delegation pushed hard (on the ground of feminism) for the exclusion of geopolitical issues from the conference resolution. The Women's Section had been alerted to this strategy well in advance by the NEC and had begun to prepare a position against it as early as 1984. The Women's Section argued that "there is a move to depoliticise the Nairobi Conference by the Zionist and pro-American element. They argue that if we talk politics, we cannot talk about actual development problems."[145]

The ANC delegation, fresh from a Non-Aligned Movement meeting in Delhi in April at which it had been agreed that growth, development, and equity were intertwined, led the opposition to the U.S. position. The ANC sent all its key women leaders to Nairobi, including Ruth Mompati, Frene Ginwala, and Gertrude Shope, with the male leadership also present because the ANC had heard that P. W. Botha was planning an international "comeback" in Nairobi.[146] Through its participation in the Non-Aligned Movement, the ANC delegation could draw on the support of the Latin American countries and India for a resolution against apartheid. Ginwala has said that this marked a turning point not only in the international struggle against apartheid but also in the debate about the relationship between the liberation of women and national liberation.[147] At Nairobi the struggle was to reassert the ANC's stance that there could be no women's liberation without national liberation; in other words, the ANC fought against an apolitical feminism, which the American women seemed to represent, and asserted a socialist feminist position.[148]

The experiences of women in Africa in the 1980s were especially influential in alerting women in the ANC to the need to formulate more effective strategies to integrate gender equality into the ANC's core principles. The postliberation record of nationalist movements in most African countries was poor: women's position did not significantly improve after independence, despite rhetorical commitments by political leaders. The underlying structural forces that produced unequal relations of gender persisted and were in fact exacerbated by the lack of a systematic approach to the woman question.[149] The pattern that women activists discerned was that the focus during the liberation period of drawing women into active politics was dropped and in its place were allowed to reemerge ideological constructions of women's position as subordinate to men.[150] These issues were highlighted at the First World Conference on Women in Mexico City in 1980, and especially at the UN Decade for Women meeting in Nairobi in 1985 at which the ANC Women's Section was highly vocal. This acute dilemma of nationalism—that women were promised fundamental transformation during the era of opposition struggle but sidelined when liberation movements took power—did not go unnoticed by South African women activists.

The experiences of other African countries also sounded warning bells within women's organizations inside the country. As I argued in the introduction, intense debates had already begun in the mid-1980s on the relevance of feminism to national liberation as women's organizations began to delineate political spaces that were to some extent independent of the ANC. Yet women activists were articulating only in muted tones their growing reservations about the dominance of nationalist frameworks. For many women in the exiled movement, the brand of liberal feminism articulated by the official U.S. delegation to the Nairobi Conference simply underscored their own criticisms of feminism as bourgeois, imperialist, and irrelevant to the South African women's movement. Attitudes against feminism within the ANC and its allies hardened, even as women inside the movement were increasingly demanding a stronger political voice and greater autonomy in strategic decision making related to the direction of the women's movement.

At the second conference of the ANC Women's Section, held in September 1987 in Angola, debates about women's role in the movement between younger and older women, and between MK and the Women's Section, were dominant. The "unity of women" in the ANC was visibly fractured. The struggles described in this chapter for a greater role for women within the ANC and MK, the hankering for closer organizational links between women inside the country and in exile, and the demands for some degree of autonomy for women to define and articulate their interests and express these through a stronger organizational form finally came together at this conference. The relationship between national liberation and women's liberation was put firmly on the agenda of the conference, seemingly against the wishes of older members of the Women's Section. A paper circulated before the conference, "Women's Role in the NDR" (national democratic revolution), urged the movement to build women's emancipation into the project of "people's power" and to accelerate the political participation of women.[151] This position was supported strategically by introducing, through a tape-recording, a paper written by internal activists. The paper challenged the ANC Women's Section to get the ANC to state unequivocally its "long term programme, strategy and tactics . . . in confronting women's oppression and safeguarding women's democratic rights in a free and united South Africa." It raised again the lack of an independent constitution for the Women's Section and suggested that the ANC finally adopt a bill of rights "which will be a document adopted by the ANC as a whole and not by women alone. This act will commit even more all the sectors of the ANC to the eradication of discrimination against women and the safeguarding of their rights in a free South Africa."[152] The Women's Congress of the United Democratic Front encouraged the efforts of the Women's Section in its message of solidarity, which urged the conference "to correctly chart the way forward and prepare not only for the seizure of political power but for the strategic role of the women in a free and democratic and non-sexist South Africa."[153]

The participation and representation of women was seen as vital in ensuring that the conference address that equality. Delegates constantly made reference to the danger that the ANC's commitment to women's emancipation might degenerate into lip service from the president and other leaders, with little attempt to address the need for implementation and action.[154] In a paper entitled "An Understanding of South African Women in Society and Their Role in the Liberation Struggle," one group of delegates pointed out that, while women participated in large numbers in grassroots organizations, "they are glaringly absent at the leadership level. Are the two connected and, if so, how? Why is it that outside of women's organisations, and to some extent the trade unions, over 50% of the oppressed population has scant representation in the leadership of our struggle?"[155] The paper outlined a range of factors that produced this outcome, including reluctance among both men and women to believe that women could be effective leaders. A paper prepared by women in MK suggested that at least some attention needed to be paid to the role and strength of the Women's Section itself.

In its composite report the National Preparatory Committee commented that a gulf seemed to exist between the Women's Section and women in the military, with the Women's Section playing almost no role in providing political direction to women cadres. Visits by the Women's Section to the camps tended to focus on the immediate social welfare needs of women cadres, rather than on the strategic issues of the role that women cadres could play if deployed inside South Africa. The Women's Section "is not a fighting organ. There seems to be a Chinese wall between the Women's Section and the Politico/Military Structures."[156]

Despite formal statements about the need for more women in leadership, women continued to be underrepresented within political ANC structures. Ruth Mompati, a member of the NEC in the 1960s and again in 1985, highlighted the need for women to be organized within the ANC. "Even in an organisation that supports the liberation of women, we have had to work hard to build the confidence of our women, because we are victims of history, victims of our traditions, victims of our role in society."[157]

The debate about the need for greater representation of women, raised initially at the Kabwe conference but not followed through by the NEC, was again hotly debated at the ANC Women's Section conference in Lusaka in 1986. Members of the Women's Section argued that if women were to be effectively organized inside the country, women within the ANC had to have a greater role in identifying women's problems and be "involved in the solutions at all levels including the highest organs of decision-making."[158] They questioned whether even sympathetic men could move beyond an "intellectual perception" of women's oppression to act as effective representatives of women.[159]

The question of what representation would mean evoked different responses. For some activists the absence of women in leadership positions had consequences for the extent to which the norms and values of gender equality were institutionalized within the movement. An unattributed internal document commented that women had always been marginal to the work of the movement and that women's participation had not led to a "challenge to men about women's subordination, within the ANC, and in society in general.[160] From this point of view participation had to be strengthened by greater representation. Others questioned whether representation per se would have an effect on the movement. For example, for Ruth Mompati, one of only three women (out of thirty-five) on the ANC's National Executive Committee in the late 1980s, women's underrepresentation on the ANC's internal structures was not a useful indicator of the organization's attitude toward women. "One of the reasons there are only three women on it is that very few senior women have left the country. But also there are a lot of women leaders *inside* the country who, if we had a free South Africa, would be on the National Executive. So we can't really judge the representation of women in leadership positions by looking at the National Executive of the ANC. Secondly, we have to continue to fight to put our women into leadership positions and to make them more able so that they can lead and articulate their problems."[161]

As Mompati's comment suggests, while calling for greater numerical representation of women on the NEC, the Women's Section was nevertheless

concerned about the quality of representation. At the 1987 Women's Section conference a call for the implementation of the ANC's policy on equality was accompanied by a warning that transformation "cannot be effected
by simply appointing a few women to positions of leadership, or providing
special training courses to help them overcome initial disadvantages."
Rather, what was needed was political education that challenged "traditional patriarchal attitudes [which] not only prevent women joining the
struggle, but affect those women already in the movement and prevent
them contributing to their full potential."[162]

The emphasis on the need for political education for *men* and women
signaled the increasing extent to which women were articulating internal
gender-based tensions within the movement. Male attitudes toward
women—"backward, conservative and chauvinistic"—began to emerge explicitly as a problem in the organization. MK activists described these as "a
cancer that is slowly but surely eating through the ranks of our organisation. . . . The longer we nurse them like a terminal tumour, the deadlier they
become both to ourselves and to the movement."[163] Male resistance to
women's progress, once discussed tentatively, and qualified by statements
reiterating the primacy of national liberation, was discussed openly and
frankly in 1987. As women in MK wrote, "At this moment in time we cannot
afford the luxury of polite niceties."[164]

The concern about gender equality as political rhetoric was well
founded. In 1988 the ANC issued its "Constitutional Guidelines for a Democratic South Africa," "widely regarded as the most important political document since the Freedom Charter," according to Albertyn.[165] In a careful
analysis of the formulation of the guidelines, Dorothy Driver has argued
that they "did not meet the requirements posed by ANC feminists," despite
revisions following a meeting between the Women's Section and the drafting committee.[166] The guidelines acknowledged the need for gender equality in the public and private spheres and supported affirmative action as the
means to effect equality.[167]

However, this clause was the sole reference to gender equality. As Albertyn has pointed out, the guidelines' provisions "refer to material inequality
on the basis of race only."[168] Although the guidelines appear to incorporate
the demands of women, "the wording and location of the clause demonstrate little appreciation of the material and ideological underpinnings of
gender oppression and provide little on which to base political and legal
claims for substantive gender equality."[169] One key area of contention was
the wording of the clause on the family. In its original formulation the
clause provides for the "protection of the family." Driver has noted that the
ANC's National Executive Committee proposed a reconsideration of that
clause, calling instead for "the establishment of women's rights over their

own fertility, and for childcare to be equally shared by fathers and mothers. Furthermore, it proposed the *removal* of patriarchal rights over the family."[170] The revised guidelines did not take these proposals into account. Instead, they were to appear in a separate charter of gender rights, to "be incorporated into the Constitution guaranteeing equal rights between men and women in all spheres of public and private life and requiring the state and social institutions to take affirmative action to eliminate inequalities, discrimination, and abusive behaviour based on gender."[171] Gwagwa has noted that the guidelines' clause on women reveals "flaws in the ANC/ MDM treatment of the family."[172] The ANC's political statements, she suggests, portray the organization as having a static view of this dynamic organization. This flaw originates from the organization's use of the family as a mobilizing tool, as a result of which power relations within the family are not examined. Instead, "The family gets subsumed within the wider struggle against apartheid and capitalism."[173] Despite the enormous leaps in the understanding of equality within the ANC, the movement remained wedded to gendered assumptions about social roles.

The limitations of the guidelines highlighted the hurdles that still existed inside the ANC, particularly the limitations for women of a movement driven primarily by a nationalist struggle and discourse. Writing about this period, Frene Ginwala noted the "failure of the organisation to take its own policy on gender issues seriously." She wrote that the adoption of policies on gender equality "owed more to the persuasive advocacy of some women members than to the level of understanding of either the membership or the entire leadership."[174] The shallowness of the commitment to gender equality had consequences for the extent to which women's demands might be institutionalized in the new democracy. As Driver has pointed out, "A constitution cannot maintain itself without broad-based political support, nor can it in itself guarantee change."[175]

The struggles between women and men in the ANC, and between women within the Women's Section, did ultimately shift the ANC's position on the role of women in the movement. In August 1989 the ANC Women's Section in London held a seminar, "Feminism and National Liberation," at which, for perhaps the first time, feminism was explicitly used as a legitimate language in which to describe women's struggles. Out of this seminar and related discussions in which both women and men participated, the ANC produced the May 2, 1990, document on "the emancipation of women in South Africa." This document recognized the need for the ANC to explicitly address the "question of the emancipation of women," noting that the establishment of principles and the development of practices consistent with gender equality are "long overdue."[176] The statement explicitly advocated affirmative action mechanisms and made responsibility for achieving gender equality one for the organization as a whole, not just for women within the organization. The commitment was an important one. As Jacklyn Cock has noted, "It means we are not some tiny marginalized group working for an eccentric goal. We have the support of a mass-based movement which not only shares our goals but which provides us with the space to formulate demands."[177]

The timing of the statement was also important as it signaled a promise by the ANC to carry its commitments into the democratic era and by implication into government. It opened a larger space for women—indeed, demanded of them—to begin to consider the concrete substance of their demands for equality in relation to key areas of social and legal policy making. As a result lively and open debates on gender issues emerged during a range of conferences in the early 1990s. Most notable among these was the Malibongwe Conference, organized by the ANC and held in Amsterdam early in 1990, which brought together for the first time women in exile and activists inside South Africa—a mere two weeks before the unbanning of the ANC, Pan Africanist Congress, and South African Communist Party. This conference was a watershed event, not only because it brought women together but also because it addressed a range of issues—from the future democratic constitution to the political participation of women in political positions to violence, health care, and customary law—in ways that prefigured gender debates about the constitution and about policy during the transition to democracy. For example, in a keynote address the senior ANC official Frene Ginwala (later co-convenor of the Women's National Coalition), called for a postapartheid constitution to include in its preamble a clause explaining gender oppression and its effect; to include an equality clause and place a constitutional duty on the state to ensure race and gender equality; to protect women from cultural practices that discriminated against them; and to recognize reproductive rights.[178] This speech signaled a decisive break from the argument that demands for gender equality would divide and weaken the struggle against apartheid. The more explicit use of feminist language to frame women's demands was also evident in other papers, including those prepared by women's organizations inside the country. In a paper produced by women activists in the Western Cape, for example, the authors argue that "we also realise that national liberation and socialism do not guarantee the emancipation of women."[179] Although the theoretical formulations of gender remained relatively weak,[180] the Malibongwe Conference reopened the possibility of feminism as an open political, and not merely academic, discourse.

Conclusion

Although there was undoubtedly an incremental change in the access and influence of women in the ANC, women's shift from a political role as "side-by-side"[181] actors to acting as political agents in their own right with their own set of interests was not an easy one. As I have shown in this chapter, it was a slow and often painful process of organizational change and debate, clashing constantly with the hierarchical and militarized organizational mode that characterized the ANC in exile. It is worth emphasizing that the process of democratization was both gradual and incomplete, if only to underscore the point that national liberation movements (and nationalism as an ideology) have been highly resistant to demands for gender equality. Although nationalist politics provided a crucial context for the politicization of women, it did not easily accommodate women's demands for autonomy, articulating their interests, or developing strategies that would advance gender equality. As Dorothy Driver has commented in relation to the development of the ANC's constitutional guidelines, gradualism can "signify masculinist resistance," and it is worth plotting the issues that men in the movement considered challenging.[182] Women's demands for greater organizational space and power cast a sometimes unwelcome spotlight on the limits of nationalism as democratic discourse, and on the exclusionary and hierarchical aspects of exile culture, particularly one in which military mobilization was favored over political organization.

This chapter suggests that women, more often and consistently than any other sector within the liberation organization, opened debates about what a democratic culture might look like. Women's organizational demands—for gender equality, greater control over strategic decision making in the sector, accountability, and a more open style of decision making—and the responses they encountered provide a lens through which to examine the nature of the exiled movement. The internal political culture of the ANC was a contested terrain, where the conduct of internal debate, the determination of what was political, and the accepted hierarchies of voice and authority were disrupted. The process of shifting, disrupting, and reconstructing the organizational culture and objectives laid the basis for a radically new perspective on democracy and gender equality that was to inform the content of the ANC program in the 1990s. As the acting secretary general Tom Nkobi acknowledged in 1990, the debates would "determine the meaning, the content that liberation will hold."[183]

Strong women's organizations even within the ANC, and a well-articulated and precise formulation of women's demands, were to become increasingly important in the transition to democracy. Directed collective action had opened many opportunities for women's political mobilization, but it also had its limits. By the early 1990s the struggles within the exiled movement and the internal women's movement underscored the importance of a relatively autonomous women's movement that could maintain its own agenda while nevertheless retaining its alliance with larger political movements for transformation. The opportunities for this would increase dramatically during the transitional period following the unbanning of the liberation movements.

Chapter 4

The Return of
the ANC Women's League

Autonomy Abrogated

On February 2, 1990, the National Party government lifted the bans on pro-scribed organizations, changing the landscape of politics in South Africa. To some extent the lifting of bans was a surprise to women activists. Al-though it came barely a week after the ANC's Malibongwe Conference in Amsterdam, at which the focus was squarely on women's visions and policy demands in postapartheid South Africa, several interviewees commented on their astonishment when the announcement was made. Pingla Udit, who was in exile in London at the time, said, "It felt like you had been push-ing a wall and suddenly the wall fell."[1]

Partly because of the energy generated at the Malibongwe Conference, women in the ANC immediately debated the implications of the unban-ning for women's organizations. In May 1990 the ANC Women's League met in Lusaka with approximately seventy women from women's organiza-tions inside the country to discuss the "disbanding of current organisations and the possibility of their joining the ANC Women's League."[2] Despite the emphasis on the need for women's emancipation to be recognized as part of ANC policy, reflecting the momentum developed at Malibongwe, the meeting nevertheless resolved that "the initial thrust of the Organisation would be to recruit members into the ANC. Thereafter women would be recruited into the League."[3] Nevertheless, "much discussion revolved around empowering women, increasing their participation at all levels of the movement and especially in decision-making and policy formulation."[4] Those present agreed on a number of amendments to be proposed for the ANC constitution, then under discussion by the movement as a whole. These amendments included the requirement that "the ANC be responsible for the emancipation of women" and the need for developing enforcement mechanisms "relating to gender relations, political rights, women workers' rights, harassment and abuse." The meeting also agreed to recommend an amendment to the ANC constitution that would require that 25 to 30 percent of National Executive Committee members be women. The meeting emphasized that the affirmative action program should be "not only position oriented but also task oriented."[5]

Along with other ANC substructures, the Women's Section returned to the country on a wave of triumphalism. The Women's Section reverted to the name of the ANC Women's League. The strategic emphasis agreed to in Lusaka, on mobilizing women into the ANC rather than the league, was not unanimously supported in the league, with many activists wanting to retain a focus on women's liberation. However, this shift that they desired from "side by side" to feminism, was not easily achievable either. At a press conference in August 1990 in Durban to celebrate the return of the league, the more militant group within the league (Mavivi Manzini, Baleka Kgositsile, and Frene Ginwala) emphasized the need to organize and mobilize women in defense of their rights. At the subsequent rally, however, a reporter found that "it was hard to say what made it a women's rally. There were men speakers encouraging women, some men performers entertaining the crowd, lots of ANC fashion clothes, drum majorettes and women doing their usual thing—cooking. Selling all sorts of delicacies cunningly produced with a minimum of space and equipment at the side of the road. There was little vision for the future role of women—perhaps this was the task of the women delegates who met the day before—but there was lots of good cheer and comraderie [sic]."[6]

The reestablishment of the Women's League was also accompanied by intensive debate about whether organizations such as the Women's Congress of the United Democratic Front, the United Women's Congress, and the Natal Organisation of Women should retain some autonomy from political organizations. As I have argued, although connections between these organizations were strong—they shared a similar history and vision—there were nevertheless areas of autonomy and of different organizational cultures. However, since the mid-1980s women's organizations had been struggling to sustain themselves; maintaining two women's organizations—an ANC Women's League as well as an independent women's organization—in each region with similar aims and led by the same group of activists would be even harder. At the same time women activists needed to feel that they were part of a larger movement on the cusp of victory. The tension, as always, lay in the relationship between women's struggles and national struggles. Opportunistic or not, the dominance of the ANC Women's League was achieved surprisingly easily. At the meeting at which the United Women's Congress decided to dissolve, the MK soldier and trade unionist Lucy Nyembe said bluntly, "The ANC must become the political home of women in this country. Our major task is to go into our communities and to organise in such a way that we draw women nearer to the ANC."[7] Then-jiwe Mtintso characterized the ANC position to integrate all women's organizations as "opportunistic. The ANC wanted women to organize but within the ANC. . . . Women's role within the ANC was to organize other women into the movement."[8]

Very quickly, a power struggle began to emerge between internal activists and exiles. "Some women in leadership worried about whether in the ANCWL they would have the same power. Women, just like men, want power," Phumelele Ntombela-Nzimande said.[9] Tensions were strong around issues of control as well as of political capacity between the former exiles and members of the internal organizations. Some internal activists felt that the returning exile leadership assumed that the exiles were in charge. "We were disappointed with their attitude. . . . We made several approaches, said we were ready to join, to assist. We were excluded, we felt deliberately," Routledge-Madlala said.[10] Whereas internal leaders had strong links to the grassroots and were well known, exiles had yet to prove themselves as individuals. Ntombela-Nzimande said, "We didn't know Baleka [Mbete-Kgositsile], for example, from a bar of soap. Exiled women had their own challenges of getting credibility with those who had been inside and borne the brunt of repression."[11] An ANC cadre commented on her frustration on returning home: "When I went outside, they saw you as part of the inside, and when we came back, we were seen as part of the outside."[12]

Although the exiles had vast international experience and were very aware of the international women's movement, they had had little actual experience of building women's organizations, particularly under the difficult conditions that existed in many parts of the country (e.g., the violence in Natal). One activist commented that this limited their contribution. "I was personally disappointed about the lack of vision of the ANCWL. . . . It was because of their role in exile. They were doing soft support work for the ANC. Inside we had a better, more realistic vision. It was *us* who raised the possibility at Malibongwe of the ANC being unbanned and the need to be prepared. They didn't raise it. The ANCWL put too much emphasis on petty issues, on personalities. They were antagonistic to strong women inside."[13] Jennifer Schreiner also pointed out that exiled members of the Women's League had very little experience in building grassroots organizations and lacked the skills to take the league into the transitional period.[14] Nozizwe Routledge-Madlala noted that one weakness that emerged was "the lack of a program of action emerging from women's own articulation of their needs and agendas. We'd learned the value of this [in NOW]."[15]

While the Women's League was adamant about the political need to draw all women's organizations under its banner, inside the country there was varied response to the issue of disbanding the independent internal women's organizations. The majority of organizations linked to the United Democratic Front (UDF) opted to fold their structures into the ANC Women's League. In the Western Cape and the Transvaal the decision to merge with the league was more easily taken than in Natal; it was seen as a fait accompli, an extension of the process of becoming a UDF structure.[16] In a letter to the UDF, the United Women's Congress outlined its reasons for disbanding: "[The] Western Cape women's organisations followed in the footsteps of the ANC Women's League, and took up the spear when the ANC was in the underground. With the unbanning of the African National Congress, UWCO started a process of discussing our role in the new situation. UWCO decided that the role our organisation has played can now best be taken up again by the ANC Women's League. So UWCO will disband. . . . Our members are joining the ANC and working actively to build the Women's League. We are excited to be reunited with our comrades from exile, and to be part of the one national women's organisation, where our hearts and loyalties belong."[17]

It was, surprisingly, within NOW that the strongest opposition to disbanding was expressed. NOW was divided into two camps on the issue of integration. One camp argued that NOW had existed as a women's formation under the banner of the UDF, itself aligned in vision, if not formally, with the ANC. The integration of NOW and the league was therefore a logical development. Another camp argued strongly for a women's organization that was not politically aligned.[18] For some women this was tied to the demand for a politically autonomous women's movement, in which women's struggles would be in alliance with but not subordinated to the national liberation movement. For many women in this camp, however, the issue was the safety of women activists in Natal townships because of the concern that being identified as a member of the league would be dangerous in the context of ongoing ANC-Inkatha tensions. NOW member Phumelele Ntombela-Nzimande pointed out that "none of these discussions was necessarily based on what would be the best vehicle to raise sharply our interests as women."[19]

While there were some concerns about the need for separate women's organizations, problems of capacity tipped the balance in favor of disbanding—the same thin layer of women activists would have to work within both the league and an independent women's organization. Furthermore, if relationships between exiles and internals were strained, they would be even more problematic if independent organizations continued to exist. Partly for this reason, one activist said, "I felt we should disband because the antagonism shown by women in the ANCWL was too difficult for us to handle. We didn't have the capacity to function side by side. We had to close down because some women were involved in both the ANCWL and [the internal women's organization]. The antagonism to the internals was untenable."[20]

But the dissolution process was not without its costs. A major step backward was the reinforcement of the shift away from the process of building a mass base. Jenny Schreiner, a member of the United Women's Congress, the South African Communist Party (SACP), and the ANC, said, "The decision to relaunch the Women's League was correct. All the UDF women's organizations were clearly ANC aligned. But I'm not sure we should have disbanded organizations as quickly as we did. We lost the mass-based nature of women's organizations. . . . We also lost the nonracialism. The first Women's League executive was very African. We lost the mass base, and I'm not sure we established a good balance between external and internal."[21] Nozizwe Routledge-Madlala concurred: "We pointed out [to the exiles] how hard we'd worked to build an alliance across class and race, and it was lost . . . treated as unimportant. The people brought in from the inside were Winnie Mandela, et cetera—they were not representative of the women."[22] Meer has argued that while the disbanding of women's organizations "strengthened the Women's League, at the same time it demobilised and weakened groups that had built grassroots support and carried out practical projects for many years."[23] The values of internal democracy and accountability that had characterized the UDF-affiliated organizations were underplayed in the power struggles for leadership of the national women's movement. "Leadership had taken on a different meaning," Routledge-Madlala said. "It became a ticket to power, whereas during the 1980s the reward from being a leader was having support, that you were doing what members wanted you to do."[24]

Unbanning and the Reconstitution of the ANC Women's League inside the Country

The unbanning of the liberation movements in February 1990 posed new challenges for the ANC Women's Section—now reconstituted as the ANC Women's League—and for its relationship to both the ANC leadership and the internal women's movement. As I showed in chapter 2, by the end of the 1980s women's organizations inside the country were fragile and vulnerable to the dictates of the male-led internal antiapartheid movement. One consequence was that they were unable to effectively establish autonomy from the ANC Women's Section once it was unbanned, and they were unable to sustain an independent presence. And yet the transitional period demanded active political interventions to ensure that any future political negotiations and their outcomes, as well as future policies, were representative and favorable for women. The challenge was who would lead the women's movement and whether the incipient feminism developed inside the country and in exile could translate into effective political action.

To facilitate the relaunch of the league on August 9, 1990, a task force was assembled, composed of ten women from the former ANC Women's Section and ten activists from inside the country, convened by Albertina Sisulu and Gertrude Shope.[25] The primary role of the task force was to begin a recruitment drive. By December 1990 membership was estimated at 35,845, with 422 branches and 243 potential new branches. Initial problems identified included such logistical difficulties as lack of transportation and office facilities, and the structural difficulties in the relationship between the ANC and the Women's League in individual branches and regions.[26]

Two key debates accompanied the relaunching of the league: the status of the league within the ANC, and the relationship between the league and UDF-affiliated women's organizations. With regard to the ANC's internal structure, the Women's League (and the Youth League) had no formal standing on the National Executive Committee, the movement's key decision-making structure. The ANC's position was that there was no need for the separate representation of women but rather that branches should ensure that their representatives included women. But the league argued that this ignored "the fact that delegates come with mandates from their branches and thus not oblidged [sic] to represent the league. . . . The league has as its major role the task of spearheading the emancipation of women within the ANC and the South African society in general. . . . There is therefore no way the task of the league can be ignored or taken for granted. It can also not be argued that this task can be fulfilled by any women who happen to attend conference. . . . Women members of the ANC will not automatically be members of the League."[27]

The ANC leadership agreed to allow the league fifty-two members to participate as full delegates to the ANC Consultative Conference to be held that year in Durban.[28] Despite this victory, unresolved issues of representation from Kabwe and Lusaka recurred in the league: at a national consultative meeting of the league in Johannesburg in December 1990, members expressed concern about the lack of representation of women in the various working groups and structures of the movement. The conference resolved to call for the "concrete implementation of the programme on affirmative action."[29]

These debates were more than procedural. The league that was reconstituted was significantly different from the structure that had been banned in 1960. By 1990 the old conception of the league as an auxiliary structure was under attack from within the Women's Section itself. Younger members of the new league were seeking greater reassurance that the ANC would indeed commit itself to women's emancipation once it came to power. The status of the reconstituted league would, in their view, symbolize the extent of the ANC's commitment. The Women's League Task Force argued that "the ANCWL is a mass organisation of women within the ANC. It cannot be equated to a department. It has structures and membership which it has to represent and take care of."[30] Justifying the demand for the redefinition of roles and responsibilities of the league, Gertrude Shope, head of the ANC's Women's Section in exile, argued that "we have never fought shy of committing ourselves to the struggle against national domination and racial oppression. Equally, we cannot afford to surrender our rights to end our oppression as women. How we define ourselves will determine how we relate to the ANC as a mother body."[31]

Under pressure to fulfill the promises of the May 2 document on the emancipation of women in South Africa" (see chapter 2), the National Executive Committee agreed to the launch of the league as "an autonomous organisation able to make its own decisions in the struggle, within the overall policy of the ANC."[32] Frene Ginwala commented that "for the first time the Women's League . . . is not a department or sub-section as it has been in the past. . . . It will engage in its own decision-making within overall ANC policy, it will have its own funding, the right to own property, control bank accounts, in other words, the real mechanisms of power. . . . The League is seen and sees itself as an autonomous body. It is not a federation of any kind, so other organisations can't affiliate to it. It is only open to ANC members. Women who are members of the ANC can join or not join, as they choose."[33]

To be effective within the ANC and strengthen its argument for greater autonomy, the league had to be seen to be leading a strong—and identifiable—constituency. However, the process of assuming leadership of the progressive women's movement was neither consistent nor entirely successful. Even at the early stage of unbanning, the Women's League recognized that there might well be a need for a broader alliance of women's organizations, even if all the United Democratic Front women's organizations dissolved into the ANC. Reflecting partly the weaknesses of the Women's Section in building links with and mobilizing women during the 1980s, it was clear that the league did not have hegemony in the women's movement. At a crucial meeting between internal activists and the Women's Section in May 1990, those in attendance agreed that an alliance should be started, perhaps in 1991, in part to build relations with women who supported the United Democratic Front but not necessarily the ANC.[34]

In April 1991 the ANC Women's League held its first national conference after its unbanning; the organization met in Kimberley, where delegates elected the national executive of the Women's League. More than one thousand delegates from ANC Women's League branches and regions attended. Glenda Daniels has argued that the 1991 National Conference of the ANC Women's League "underlined the recent shift towards a more assertive and possibly 'feminist' Women's League which will take the specific oppression of women seriously."[35] The new executive board was a mix of older women activists and young feminists but was dominated by exiles. Gertrude Shope, former leader of the Women's Section, was elected president and UDF member Albertina Sisulu was elected vice president.[36] Both Shope and Sisulu were sensitive to the concerns of younger women activists, recognizing their importance in shaping the new direction of the league. Nevertheless, debates about the role of the league were heated, the options characterized by *Speak* as "mothers club or fighting force." Some members were comfortable with "women's traditional role of bearing children and serving men. Others believe women must be liberated from all forms of exploitation and oppression if they are to be truly liberated."[37]

Media interviews with Shope reveal the extent to which the role of the league was unresolved even at the leadership level. On the one hand, Shope described the tasks in terms that resembled the old Women's Section's language of mobilization. Invoking the discourse of motherhood, she argued that "as women we brought life into this world and I don't see why we cannot do something to protect it."[38] She identified a common set of interests shared by all women, "regardless of whether you are a woman in the northern suburbs or a mother in a township, the death of a child is a feeling that all women can understand. This instinct of a mother and a woman has to be a factor in bringing us together."[39] At the same time, however, Shope argued for the need to "take a stand on women's emancipation."[40] She warned that support for the ANC in the negotiations was not "at all costs," thereby signaling the growing feeling within the league that it would have to mobilize support for women's representation from non-ANC sources. However, Shope described the strategy for organizing women as a gradual process: "I am not saying that tomorrow we will not become radical, but we have to start somewhere. We don't want to start with something that is very drastic. We will ascend, step by step, so that once we have reached that peak, no one will question our action."[41]

The Kimberley conference debated the structure of the league at length. A key concern was to ensure that the leaders of the Women's League would be accountable to the grassroots membership and that branches would have power within the organization. "Women want more than democratic conferences," Speak reported. "They want democracy everyday and they want their leadership to be accountable to them."[42] The problem with taking these commitments further was that the league had yet to establish itself as an organization with members and mandates. As the secretary general, Baleka Kgositsile, wryly pointed out, "What do you structure if you have no membership?"[43] The pace of events internal to the league and in the negotiation process would make building organization even more difficult than the leadership anticipated.

At the conference the Women's League was immediately plunged into a crisis regarding leadership issues. The central problem related to the role of Winnie Mandela, who ran against Gertrude Shope for the position of president. Shope was head of the ANC's Women's Section; Mandela was president of the league's powerful Pretoria-Witwatersrand-Vaal (PWV) region in the Transvaal. Mandela's profile as "mother of the nation" and wife of Nelson Mandela gave her a unique symbolic claim to a leadership position in the Women's League. By this stage, however, she was on trial for kidnapping and assault in relation to the death of Stompie Seipei and the disappearance of Lolo Sono.[44] In the Western Cape a branch of the Women's League threatened to break away if Mandela was elected. The Federation of Transvaal Women, whose core members were in the PWV region, was already divided on the issue of loyalty to Mandela, and some members voiced concerns at the Kimberley conference that she would not be an appropriate choice for president. Her position as the wife of the president of the ANC also worked against her; many feminists were concerned that the league would simply become another "wives' club," like other leagues in Africa, thereby entrenching the auxiliary role. At the same time some members feared that Shope was both too "old school" and "soft" to provide the quality of leadership that would be required to carry the organization through the difficult transition period.

Some considered Mandela's election bid to be part of a broader campaign on her part to strengthen her position in the ANC: as president of the league she would automatically become a member of the ANC's National

Executive Committee.[45] Her reputation as a tough, even ruthless, leader appeared to scare some delegates away from open opposition. One unnamed delegate told the *Star* that "if there is a secret ballot, we hope Mrs. Mandela will be outvoted. But if there is an open ballot, she will certainly be elected."[46] Indeed, electoral procedures were debated for hours at the conference to ensure that the decision would be respected.[47] Shope defeated Mandela, getting 422 votes to Mandela's 196 in a secret ballot.[48] The league proposed to draw up a leadership code for its officers that would give to the members the right to recall leaders guilty of misconduct. While this had overtones of earlier attempts by the United Democratic Front to discipline Winnie Mandela,[49] the proposal for a leadership code also signaled a larger concern with issues of accountability of leadership to membership. This was the first such proposal within the ANC.

For some these debates, while important, had the effect of distracting the league from deeper organizational issues. "We didn't debate how we could become strong in the ANC and how to articulate our issues," Ntombela-Nzimande noted. "We had women with extreme analytical tools and experience under one roof, but they were subsumed by the leadership debate. This weakened the ANCWL so that it has become just a shadow."[50]

The new leadership did in fact identify a set of immediate tasks for the Women's League. These included programs to address social and sexual oppression, the revival of the proposal to set up an ANC commission on emancipation, and initiation of a charter of women's rights. The issue of the charter was an important one; it was a continuation of a process that had begun with the Kabwe discussions on a bill of rights in 1985 and had been identified as a priority during the planning for Kimberley.[51] At this point, although the league sought to accommodate older "motherists" as well as the younger and more assertive feminists who were emerging within the movement, the overall direction of the league confirmed a feminist direction. Young women were determined that there would be no return to the league's role as an auxiliary structure and that the league had the potential to be the strategic base from which to seal the ANC's transformation into a movement that was fully committed to gender equality.

Winnie Mandela's bid for leadership of the league did not end with her defeat at Kimberley. In 1993, at the Second National Conference of the Women's League, she again stood for election to the presidency, this time successfully. Gisela Geisler has articulated the view of many young feminists, that this election "effectively closed the Women's League's short history as a progressive women's voice."[52] Tensions between Mandela and the younger feminists grew as she was criticized for not taking the league or her position as president seriously enough. Some saw her as squandering the hard work that had been put into developing the league as an independent organization. By 1995 she was being accused of using the organization as a stepping-stone to personal power. The *Weekly Mail and Guardian* characterized her leadership style as autocratic and charged that she was using the league "as a platform to launch attacks on the ANC."[53] Finally, in 1997 matters came to a head when eleven members of the executive and many rank-and-file members resigned from the league. Winnie Mandela, however, continued to lead the organization and was reelected at the national conference in 1997, promising to lead members to "the promised land."[54]

Within the ANC more broadly, women found that despite the policy statement of May 2, 1990, there were many obstacles to the implementation of equality within the movement. In Kimberley, Tambo commented that "the position of women within the democratic movement still leaves far too much to be desired. . . . Condemned to menial tasks forever, rarely do they aspire or are seen as potential candidates for high office."[55] The league itself reminded its members that "in the past year we have won many victories, which places us in the process of transition towards the building of a new South Africa. The women's movement has played an important role in making this present process possible. However, we have learnt from many countries that this does not automatically secure our liberation in a future SA."[56]

These organizational roadblocks—and the need for a much stronger *women's* organization—were dramatically revealed at the 48th National Congress of the ANC, held in Durban in July 1991. This congress, the first since the unbanning, adopted a new constitution for the ANC, offering an opportunity for the Women's League to formalize women's representation in the organization's decision-making structures. The Women's League decided before the conference to call for a quota of seats for women on the National Executive Committee—an initial demand of 25 percent was later revised to 30 percent. At a preliminary interregional meeting to prepare for the congress, the Constitutional Committee, the outgoing NEC, and all the regions accepted the proposal over a cumbersome alternative that would have included Women's League chairs and secretaries from each region on the NEC.[57] At the conference, however, the Constitutional Committee proposed that the quota be dropped from the constitution. This provoked one of the most bitter and heated debates within the ANC since its unbanning. Arguments against the quota included that election to the NEC should be on merit, that the system posed too many problems with regard to accountability, and that national liberation was the first priority. Debate was deadlocked. As Horn has pointed out, given that only 17 percent of conference delegates were women, using "the tried and tested method of resolving issues by majority vote was in danger of perpetuating, rather than resolving this problem."[58]

The conference fell apart and, at the suggestion of Nelson Mandela, was adjourned to allow a meeting of the executives of the ANC, Women's League, and Youth League to reach a compromise. The outcome of the process was disappointing: "The following day, the President of the ANCWL apologised to the conference for the ANCWL's disruption of the vote and creating a delay the previous day, before a statement by the ANCWL was read out on the quota issue proposing that the matter be finalised one way or the other. Unfortunately some delegates took this as an apology for having raised the quota issue at all, and one male delegate stood up and patronisingly rapped the women over the knuckles for the indignity which he blamed them for introducing into the conference by their tenacious fight and demonstration for the 30% quota. The 30% quota fell by the wayside."[59]

Women activists were angry at the outcome. Baleka Kgositsile, secretary general of the Women's League, said that women "felt the NEC had abandoned them."[60] Several commentators also noted the strategic errors made by the league itself in the period leading up to the conference. Ginwala has pointed out that "women members, and the ANC Women's League also failed to engage the membership in debate prior to the conference or to promote and project the policies they wanted conference to adopt. In the months following the Women's League Conference to put forward the quota, its own activities focused almost exclusively on campaigns around issues such as the release of political prisoners, and the violence that was unleashed against the people with the connivance of the police and security forces. In practice the League functioned simply as an arm of the ANC, mobilising women into the organisation and the current national struggles. There was little in its approach or activities that was specific to women."[61] The league, she argued further, had "failed its first test" and "lent substance to those critics who have long argued that a woman's [sic] organisation attached to the ANC would inevitably subordinate women's interests."[62]

It was clear from the quota fiasco that the Women's League on its own would not be able to generate sufficient pressure on the ANC, let alone on other political parties, to address gender equality. For many women activists it was a valuable learning experience. "It showed that women have to prepare, educate and organise at a grassroots level to pull off this kind of proposal," one activist told Speak. "It also proved that even when you are promised support from senior leadership, it doesn't mean that you will get it."[63] Kgositsile pointed out: "We've got the future looking at us. We must plan workshops and we must put pressure on the national leadership to make sure that the new constitution ensures the emancipation of women. This is where the ANC Women's League's campaign for a charter for women's rights comes in."[64]

The nature of the defeat, rather than the substance of the quota debate, hardened women's resolve to develop a strong organizational base, even if this meant going outside the ANC. Kgositsile's comments signaled again the need for a national women's movement, a development that, as I show in chapter 5, was to have a major influence on the constitutional negotiations. The forum for this debate was to emerge in the discussions that began in 1991 after the Women's National Coalition was formed.

Within the ANC a long-standing suggestion to form a commission on the emancipation of women,[65] which would address the internal issues of women's representation in leadership and monitor the extent to which women's interests were reflected in policy making, was finally acted on in February 1992. The commission was appointed to follow through on the demand made by women in 1987 and the NEC statement of May 2, 1990, and was perhaps a sop to women after the defeat of the quota proposal. It was headed by Oliver Tambo, with Frene Ginwala as his deputy.[66] The terms of reference included examining, promoting, and monitoring mechanisms for affirmative action within the ANC at all levels, ensuring that "women's experiences and perceptions inform ANC strategy and tactics and its decisions at all levels," including policy, and promoting and undertaking research on gender.[67] In its report to the ANC in December 1994, the Emancipation Commission highlighted the distance that the movement still had to travel before women were full and equal participants. It revealed that most women on the ANC payroll were secretaries with little or no participation in decision making. The adoption of the ANC's policies on gender equality by the branch and provincial structures was erratic and mostly was ignored by members.[68]

While the commission on its own did not make major gains in overcoming these limitations, it provided an organizational space for Ginwala to advance the feminist activists' agenda in the ANC, separate from the troubled Women's League. In particular, it was a base from which Ginwala could participate in, and ultimately lead, the Women's National Coalition. This was an interesting development in that the league was no longer the only space in which women activists within the ANC could find a home. It underscored some of the most notable features of the post-transition government.

Chapter 5

From Mothers of the Nation to Rights-Bearing Citizens

Transition and Its Impact on the South African Women's Movement

> Because transition politics are periods of crisis and thus of intense politicisation, they bring new ideas and institutions into political life. . . . They provide a rare window on how social structures underlie political structures and practices.
>
> Jane S. Jacquette and Sharon L. Wolchik,
> *Women and Democracy*

The "success story" of the South African women's movement in the transition to democracy is by now a familiar one to feminist scholars and activists. Unlike the experience in many other African countries, the transition to democracy after nationalist struggles in South Africa did not lead to the marginalization of women but rather to the insertion of gender equality concerns into the heart of democratic debates. Women's political participation was extended into the realm of representative government, and a range of institutions was created to represent and defend women's interests in decision making. In addition, women's activism ensured that gender equality was protected in the Constitution. Unlike the era of national liberation movement politics, during the transition "women [organized] as women and [entered] the democratic era with new agendas for women."[1]

What accounts for the ability of the South African women's movement to defy the familiar trajectory of postnationalist reconstruction? Analysts have emphasized the role of the women's movement in driving an assertive feminist agenda,[2] while popular rhetoric has treated the existence of the women's movement itself as self-evident rather than a phenomenon that needs explaining. Yet the conventional conditions for social movement success were all but absent in 1990. As I have shown, by the time negotiations for a new democracy began, women's organizations, which had occupied a central role in mass struggles during the early to mid-1980s, were in decline. Their leadership core had been decimated during two states of emergency, and their energies had been diverted from organizing women per se to keeping alive the United Democratic Front (UDF). This leadership weakness was exacerbated when, following the unbanning of liberation movements in 1990, women's organizations collapsed as semiautonomous organizations and merged with the Women's League of the African National Congress (ANC). The merger brought new skills and ideas in debates about gender equality but also imposed enormous costs in terms of the ability of the women's movement to define and articulate a role outside the framework of nationalism. In exile the Women's Section of the ANC had made huge advances in gaining formal recognition within the liberation movement for women's increased participation and representation but still had little power in the movement's decision-making structures. Although women's organizations had made huge strides in winning acceptance for the values of gender equality, feminism remained a contested ideological framework. The conditions for the success of the women's movement in the transitional period were by no means apparent in 1990.

These considerations suggest the need for a more precise explanation for the dramatically transformed fortunes of the women's movement during the transition. Three factors were key: the opportunities offered by the nature of the transition, the creation of an autonomous organization for representing the women's movement, and the context of an earlier struggle for equality within at least one main political organization in the negotiations. First, beginning a process of negotiated transition to democracy offered new possibilities for the women's movement to pursue its claims at a national political level. Feminist debates about the South African transition have neglected to explore the opportunities and costs of the *nature* of the transition. The creation of a liberal democratic state that accorded rights to its citizens regardless of race, gender, or ethnicity unexpectedly allowed feminists to articulate an agenda of equality that unseated nationalist formulations of women's political roles. The unbanning of liberation movements allowed the demands for women's representation and inclusion in decision making that had previously been articulated *within* the ANC to be expanded to the political system as a whole. Furthermore, women's demands were now made on the ground of democracy itself rather than the exigencies or internal consistency of national liberation.

Second, the creation of a national representative structure for the women's movement, the Women's National Coalition (WNC), provided the strategic and organizational vehicle for women activists to articulate these claims independent of the ANC. Although demands for autonomy certainly were not new in the women's movement, the independence of the coalition was a distinctive change from earlier women's organizations. Independence, achieved in part through the bold step of building a coalition that went beyond the organizations sympathetic to the ANC, allowed the Women's National Coalition to exert pressure for accountability in a way that internal mechanisms of party discipline and loyalty could not contain. Its autonomy was therefore a primary source of strength.

However, left to the coalition alone it is unlikely that arguments of progressive feminists for substantive equality, as opposed to formal equality with specific guarantees for women, would have found much of an audience. The Women's National Coalition, driven by women within the ANC, was able to command the support of the ANC at crucial moments in the negotiations. A crucial factor was the existence of a strong political party that favored structural transformation rather than a mere transfer of power and that, as a result of an internal transformation of its decision-making processes and representational structures, had committed itself to eradicating gender inequalities. The formal commitments of the ANC to including women at all levels of decision making and incorporating gender equality concerns in policy frameworks created an ideological basis from which to make women's demands a benchmark of substantive democracy.

Transition: New Opportunities

Analyzing democratization debates from a gender perspective, Georgina Waylen has shown how the focus of what she terms orthodox views of democratization omit women.[3] At a constitutive level this omission stems from a narrow view of politics as an elite-driven process. Phillipe Schmitter has acknowledged that although "women have played a role in every one of these momentous political transformations," nevertheless "women as a socio-political collectivity with distinctive interests and modes of action have not . . . been systematically included in the theories and comparative analyses that have grown up around the topic of democratization."[4] In defense he points out that the emphasis in these studies on the choices and constraints facing elites resulted in the disappearance from the analysis of not only women but also "workers *per se,* capitalists *per se,* landowners *per se* and even the armed forces."[5]

Analyses of the South African transition to democracy, drawing largely on the models developed by the analysts critiqued by Waylen, have likewise tended to focus on the actions and motivations of a narrow range of "key stakeholders,"[6] although some studies have been concerned with the extent to which the masses—workers or activists at grassroots level—were marginalized in the negotiations process.[7] In the main, though, their concern has been more with the diminishing power of socialist activists and trade unionists in the negotiations and less with the effect on women. The view of politics as the business of elites—primarily male—has been common in South Africa and not only within so-called liberal political organizations. As I showed in chapter 2, despite the UDF's pretensions of being a popular movement, its reliance on strategies devised and directed by a small core of male leaders effectively excluded women activists from having an influence on organizational direction and culture. In the ANC too, as I argued in chapter 3, the politics of exile had produced a hierarchical organization that demanded unquestioning loyalty to the leadership. Therefore, to view the process of negotiating democracy only as it took place within high politics in effect values only male-dominated politics—women's role as political agents is downplayed because their spheres of political activity are not seen as significant. This has implications for the way in which democracy itself is conceived, for it is narrowly limited to "an institutional arrangement to generate and legitimate leadership."[8] Issues of social and economic equality—at the heart of women's movement demands in South Africa—are divorced from those of political equality. At the outset of the negotiations the concern with a peaceful transfer of power dominated discussions. The outcomes of democratization were excluded from debate, and as a consequence gender concerns that extended beyond formal equality, such as demands for the redistribution of power, were marginalized or at best deferred to some future political era.

Women's politics in South Africa during 1991–94 can be seen as a constant struggle against that marginalization. In analyzing gender politics during the transition, I have heeded Waylen's advice to use a broader notion of politics, one that encompasses not only processes and institutions among elites but also captures the relationship between popular mobilization and democratization processes—a tension represented in part by the charter campaign of the WNC. As I will show in this chapter, however, women did not entirely succeed in keeping alive questions of power relations and structural transformation throughout the transition, in part because the organizational form of the women's movement—a coalition—was unable to resolve the relative weight of these demands as opposed to the narrower and more easily accommodated focus on political equality. Nevertheless, the modes of organization and politics of interest articulated by women in this period provide a prism through which to refract the particular opportunities and obstacles that were in the way of subordinate groups seeking to enhance substantive democracy.

Transition—the opening of negotiations between political parties about a new democratic order—resulted in an expansion of the political space available to women and, as in Latin America, allowed for the articulation of gender-specific claims.[9] Even so, transitions to democracy should not be regarded as automatically enhancing women's access to power. As several studies have shown, women have often gained less from democratization processes than men—for example, in Eastern and Central Europe democratization has removed many benefits that women enjoyed under the former socialist regimes, and women's labor has been reprivatized into the domestic sphere.[10] Transitional periods and democratization can benefit women only to the extent that they are capable—both ideologically and organizationally—of mobilizing around their particular concerns.

In South Africa, although a negotiated transition fell short of the hopes for revolutionary change that were nurtured by women's organizations in the UDF-ANC fold, it was expected that the ANC would successfully represent the demand for structural, and not merely constitutional, change.[11] This expectation, coupled with ongoing policy debates within the ANC about the content of the Reconstruction and Development Programme, gave women activists a wedge that forced open the negotiations process to allow women a small space. This was facilitated in part by the perception that the national liberation movement had to regard its traditional constituencies as electoral bases for which it was competing with other political parties—in other words, it had to play the new electoral game of democracy. Women could no longer simply be treated as a resource for mass mobilization that could be called on at political will but rather had to be treated as a constituency with electoral power to choose between different political parties. This meant that some concrete response to women's demands was required, and those relating to representation could be accommodated with greater ease than those relating to removing the systemic sources of women's subordination.

Building an Independent National Women's Movement

The idea of a broad nonracial organization of women was not new in South African women's politics. As I discussed in chapter 2, the Federation of South African Women had been a voice for women in the 1950s, and the organization was revived under the same name but using a different acronym, FEDSAW, in the 1980s although with limited success. The idea of a national women's movement was again debated at the Malibongwe Conference convened by the ANC with the support of the Women's Committee of the Dutch Anti-Apartheid Movement in Amsterdam in 1990. Originally planned for October 1989, the conference eventually was held two weeks before F. W. de Klerk's unbanning of the liberation movements. The conference openly brought together the ANC Women's Section with women's organizations inside the country. In a revealing statement the organizers noted "the risk that women's concerns will be subsumed under the national struggle, thus losing out on the opportunity to collectively formulate strategies that will address women-specific oppression and ensure equal participation in the future."[12] At this stage the idea of a national women's movement seemed to still be limited to one that encompassed women's organizations broadly within the progressive fold. There was little explication of the most appropriate structure for the movement, although the conference was sensitive to the debates that had stalled the consolidation of FEDSAW as a national umbrella body in the 1980s.[13]

After the Malibongwe Conference the idea of a national women's organization that would embrace non-ANC members was raised in several forums inside the country. The expectation was that the ANC Women's League would be the driving force behind such a structure and would provide progressive political leadership and content for the program of action. Although the United Women's Organisation (UWO), the Federation of Transvaal Women, and the Natal Organisation of Women united women across race and class lines, none of these was able to provide strong national political leadership for the women's movement for the reasons described in chapter 2. By 1991, in any case, the Women's League encompassed the structures that had existed in the 1980s and was the sole political representative of progressive women's interests at a national level.[14] And yet the conviction that the Women's League was an insufficient vehicle for advancing women's claims was widely held, even among women within the ANC. Justifying the need for a broad movement, Frene Ginwala, the head of the ANC's Emancipation Commission, commented that "if we are going to push for a real challenge to gender oppression and the real emancipation of women, what we need is a strong women's organisation, organised around the issues of concern to women. Therefore, while the League has a particular role to play, we still need a national women's organisation. We need an organisation to which we would bring all women, and women's organisations which do not necessarily subscribe to particular ANC positions. . . . The extent to which we are able to do that and that body is strong, will allow us to empower women. It will allow us to force decisions in our favour when it comes to the either or situation, in a budget debate or anything else. . . . I mean politics is about power and women's liberation is about power. Unless we empower women organisationally, we can't liberate ourselves."[15]

The Malibongwe Conference cleared the political space for women's organizations in the different provinces to explore new forms of alliances, in the process exposing some difficulties that might arise at the national level. In November 1990, for example, a range of organizations in and around Cape Town—including the Women's League, the Congress of South African Trade Unions, Rape Crisis, Black Sash, the National Union of South African Students, and the South African National Students Congress—marched under the FEDSAW banner to protest all forms of violence against women.[16] In November 1991 the Women's Alliance was founded in the Western Cape, "based on the principles of non-racism, non-sexism, democracy and a unitary South Africa," and it included such organizations such as UWO, the Democratic Party, and the South African Domestic Workers Union.[17] The alliance was marked by race and class tensions. Dorothy Ntone and Nomvula Meth have written that in the Western Cape "we have the 'coloured' organisations, and the 'African' organisations—by no conscious design. But don't underestimate the destructive power of the resentments harboured as a result."[18] Nevertheless, Fester has argued that "although power relations were always an issue, many members started to learn the meaning of democracy. Many new affiliates never thought political change was necessary. Through the WA they were politicised and exposed to the lives of oppressed and exploited black women."[19]

The Women's Alliance and other potential regional initiatives were overshadowed by national events. In September 1991 representatives from a wide range of organizations, including political parties, women's organizations, and nongovernmental organizations (NGOs) had met at the invitation of the Women's League to discuss the possibility of a national women's structure that would link women across racial and ideological divisions. This was a significant departure from previous attempts to launch a national women's movement, which had been aimed at drawing together women's organizations that were broadly within the Congress Alliance fold. It was also significant—and important for the sustainability of the organization—that the Women's League was a prime mover behind this process of building an inclusive national structure. "Inclusivity was a strategic thing on the part of women in the ANC. . . . [They] felt it would help to commit to strategic issues. It was about finding common women's issues to make inroads into other political parties," Mtintso recalled. "Frene [Ginwala] argued that the Constitution would not only be drafted by the ANC but would need the support of other women. It was very strategic to win over women by putting them in the same structure. It broadened the mass base—by including women who would support feminism but may not support the ANC—and got support for a progressive women's agenda."[20]

Delegates to the meeting agreed that although women were divided by race and class, there were sufficiently strong grounds for a common struggle,[21] although at this stage the grounds were defined in the broadest possible terms to mean ensuring that women's interests were addressed in postapartheid South Africa. They also agreed that because of the differences, the organizational form should be that of a political coalition based on gender, rather than a single new organization.[22] This culminated in the founding in April 1992 of the Women's National Coalition, comprised of seventy organizations and eight regional coalitions, a remarkable development, considering the faltering attempts to restart FEDSAW in the 1980s. Thus began what Ginwala described as "a conspiracy of women."[23]

The initial mandate of the coalition was for twelve months, from April 1992 to April 1993. This time frame was soon revised, and the mandate was extended until June 1994. The coalition's constitution provided for three categories of participation: national women's organizations, national organizations that included women members, and regional coalitions of women's organizations. The organizations that affiliated differed in size, ideology, and organizational culture, and few could be characterized as feminist in the sense of actively championing issues of gender equality. The initial nonparticipation of the Women's Forum of the Congress of South African Trade Unions, which represented the most organized and numerous women, was cause for great concern. But the trade unions' constitution did not allow for affiliation with coalitions, a problem that the UDF Women's Congress had encountered years earlier. In addition to the constitutional difficulties, there were ideological concerns raised by some trade union activists—again, similar to those that were raised about the UDF Women's Congress—regarding the political value of cross-class coalitions. Some activists in the Women's League were concerned that the Women's Forum, dominated by strong feminists who had not always supported the ANC, might undermine the power of the Women's League within the new coalition.[24] Nevertheless, in February 1993 the trade unions approved in principle a change in their constitution that allowed the Women's Forum to affiliate, and its members were welcomed into the coalition.

The strategic grounds for an alliance between diverse women's organizations were presented by the political parties themselves, in their apparent disdain for women's demands for representation in the multiparty negotiations. In 1991 political parties negotiating South Africa's transition to democracy selected all-male teams for the first round of negotiations. The omission of women fanned a spark that had until then been flickering only faintly. In an unprecedented action some leading members of the Women's League wrote to letters to the editors of various newspapers demanding that the ANC address its failure to include women. At a Women's League workshop in January 1992, delegates demanded that the ANC put more

women on the negotiating commissions at the Convention for a Democratic South Africa (CODESA), which was attended by delegates from nine-
teen political and government organizations. By March 1992 the agitation
had become more widespread, with Helen Suzman, matriarch of the Democratic Party and for thirty years one of a handful of women in the apartheid Parliament, castigating CODESA for excluding women. A diverse
group of organizations and individuals, from the principals of several universities to senior women in political parties, bought newspaper advertise-
ments demanding greater participation of women. Women's marginalization from politics was being challenged as never before. This groundswell of
anger fed into meetings that were held between women from different political parties to discuss the formation of a coalition of women's organizations, and the common interest in women's participation that it highlighted, while minimal in itself, made possible a new political formation.

Yet not everyone was convinced that the transition provided sufficient
political rationale for an alliance that would include women of all political
stripes. Some women's organizations were concerned that the political parties would dominate the coalition at the expense of smaller and less politically astute groupings.[25] Fester has written that some progressive women
had misgivings about the inclusion of the National Party and the Inkatha
Freedom Party in a coalition of women, "what with the killing fields of
Natal," but the ANC Women's League felt that the time was right for a
national multiparty women's organization.[26] Other women activists were
not convinced that the strategy of forming a single national organization
would achieve the specific demands of poor and working-class women[27]
and that these concerns would resurface during the charter campaign. Differences over strategy were particularly marked in Natal, where violent
struggles between the Inkatha and ANC activists were raging in African
townships. The Women's League did not adequately explain to its members
the purpose of the alliance, and many young feminists, in particular, regarded it as an urban, middle-class forum. A young activist in the Durban
Central Branch of the Women's League, for example, asked how an alliance
would help to build the Women's League—"Aren't we simply dissipating
our energies?"[28] For her it was also difficult to envision working with Inkatha members in any capacity, as the decision to invite the Inkatha Women's
Brigade to join the coalition reflected the lack of concern of the national
Women's League for the regional concerns of its members.

Despite these reservations among some women activists in the ANC alliance, the Women's National Coalition was a significant step toward forming
a political movement that was driven by women rather than by the exigencies of male leadership, and the existence of the coalition contributed to the
sense of women as a political force in their own right. For all the differences

among women, not least those of political ideology, the initial exclusion of women from decision making about the shape of the new democracy highlighted an obvious collective interest for all politically active women. More clearly than ever, the initial exclusion of women from the negotiations served to distinguish women as a group and to sharpen the disparities in opportunities for representation in decision making of women and men. In demanding inclusion the Women's National Coalition was using the political opportunity offered by the debate among negotiators on the Bill of Rights and, in particular, the promise that these debates would, as they had in Latin America, provide an "opening for new issues and new ways of doing politics."[29]

An inclusionary strategy was indeed highly rational in the context of the political transition under way in the country. As various studies of transition have shown, the degree of inclusion—who gets a place at the table— shapes both the nature and scope of institutions under negotiation, as well as their long-term legitimacy. Formal processes of negotiation tend to favor political and social groupings that are already organized at the national level or have access to national actors. Poorly organized and supported groupings, such as women and the rural poor, tend to be absent from institutional decision-making processes.[30] In the multiparty negotiations in South Africa, the ANC was seen as representing the poor and the working class as its main constituency. Given the ANC's alliance with the South African Communist Party and the trade unionists, it appeared that the eradication of both racial and class inequalities would be central to the negotiations. Women were less obviously represented as a constituency by the major political actors, despite the ANC's well-developed history of recognizing women's demands. Feminists were worried because powerful forces aligned with the ANC were actively hostile to the notion of gender equality. The Congress of Traditional Leaders of South Africa (CONTRALESA) aimed to exclude customary law from the ambit of the Bill of Rights and to entrench the powers of chiefs.[31] Chiefs sought to protect their traditional powers to allocate land and resources in areas under their control. Organizations such as the Rural Women's Movement, on the other hand, wanted to democratize these decision-making procedures and, in particular, give women control over the land that they worked. As I will show in my discussion of the Women's Charter later in this chapter, women's participation in the constitutional negotiations tempered, if not completely undermined, the power of conservative forces such as the Congress of Traditional Leaders of South Africa. Using moral suasion and multiparty organization, women managed to insert their different notions of democracy and equality into the negotiations process.

The issue of inclusion, however, went beyond the simple demand of one interest group for special consideration and protections. I would argue that it constituted an implicit questioning of the extent to which nonelite groups could expect that democracy per se would increase their access to power. Some analysts of democratic politics have regarded demands for inclusion as symbolic of a fundamental challenge to the legitimacy of democracy. As Iris Marion Young has pointed out, "Calls for inclusion arise from experiences of exclusion—from basic political rights, from opportunities to participate, from the hegemonic terms of debate. Some of the most powerful and successful social movements of [the twentieth] century have mobilized around demands for oppressed and marginalized people to be included as full and equal citizens in their polities."[32]

Indeed, inclusion, framed by the South African women's movement as the right to participate, was the basis from which to launch a broader questioning of the assumptions of political transition and of what Williams has called the "deep structure of inequalities."[33] In this sense feminist activists were conforming to Young's understanding of inclusion as consisting of more than simply "extending already constituted institutions and practices to people not currently benefiting from them enough."[34] In Young's view inclusive politics should mean "a heterogeneous public engaged in transforming institutions to make them more effective in solving shared problems justly."[35] Many activists schooled in the politics of NOW, the United Women's Organisation, and the Congress of South African Trade Unions recognized early that formal representation at the multiparty negotiations would not guarantee effective representation and that inclusion might indeed become a form of co-option into the existing rules and parameters of the political system. Nevertheless, representation, imperfect though it may be for full citizenship, was recognized as an essential precondition for deeper inclusion in debates about the nature of the new democracy.

The Women's National Coalition did not see inclusion in terms of "becoming equal to men."[36] That is, coalition leaders did not assume (although some constituents may have) that the male political world was unproblematic or even coherent in itself. The strategy of inclusion was designed to create the political space in which women could articulate a broader notion of citizenship and to define citizenship in ways that recognized the plurality of interests in society. The strategy of inclusion was meant to broaden the substantive content of citizenship beyond the class and race interests initially represented at the multiparty negotiations.

From the outset the coalition worked with a sophisticated organizational notion of the nature of a women's movement. Apartheid highlighted graphically the distinctions between women; the racial structuring of all social relations meant that the illusion of sisterhood never seriously took hold in South Africa. The white women's suffrage movement, for example, was successful in 1930 precisely because it allowed the Hertzog government to reduce the importance of the few remaining black voters in the Cape Province.[37] By their complicity in this political maneuver, white women placed their racial and class concerns above any solidarity between women. For decades afterward there was little political trust between black and white women, except in organizations such as the federation and the Women's League, where black leadership was established and accepted. Given this fractured history of women's politics in South Africa and, above all, the powerful sense in women's organizations associated with the ANC and the Pan Africanist Congress that women's struggles could not be separated from other political struggles, the coalition never assumed that a sisterhood existed.[38] Indeed, right at the beginning, the coalition argued that it was an organization based on solidarity in pursuit of a narrow agenda. Political differences were acute: there was no common language in which to speak of women's needs, especially because the potentially common discourse of feminism was itself highly contested. At various points the political differences threatened to completely undermine the organization, and while the mandate of the WNC slowly widened to include issues of violence against women, it was always understood that the terrain of common purpose was very narrow.

Perhaps surprisingly in this context, the differences within the ANC that threatened to completely undermine the coalition were not expressed in racial but in ideological terms. Indeed, the concerns with racial identities and with the politics of representation within the women's movement that had dominated gender debates during 1991 and 1992—so completely that one commentator suggested that for feminism it was a "point of no return"[39]—were overshadowed by questions relating to the extent of the demand for equality. As my discussion of the charter campaign will show, the different positions on this demand cannot be categorized along racial lines—participants of all races are to be found on all sides of the debate—but are, rather, a reflection of broader ideological differences. Nor, indeed, can the charter be read as the product of white women's interests, although the drafting team was predominantly white. While racial (and other) differences certainly may affect how political interests are defined, the relationship between racial identity and political interest is by no means axiomatic.[40]

The Charter Campaign

The charter campaign was the glue that held the coalition together. The campaign was intended to be both a mobilizing and educational (consciousness-raising) tool, as well as concrete set of demands to be used at the level of national politics, one that might even be attached as an appendix to the new constitution, as a sort of bill of rights for women. The idea of a charter had enormous symbolic and ideological currency within the Congress tradition, and prominent ANC activists throughout the late 1980s and early 1990s alluded to a women's charter in several speeches and writings. When the UDF Women's Congress was founded in 1987, for example, it adopted the Women's Charter of 1954 "as a source of inspiration to us in the struggle."[41] The May 2, 1990, Statement of the National Executive Committee of the ANC on the emancipation of women in South Africa called on women to begin a debate on a charter of women's rights that "will elaborate and reinforce our new Constitution, so that in their own voice women define the issues of greatest concern to them and establish procedures for ensuring the rights claimed are made effective."[42] As I noted in chapter 3, this call was reiterated at the Malibongwe Conference. An influential article by Albie Sachs in 1990 also argued that "the general principles of the constitution should be enriched by a Charter of Women's Rights focusing on all the concrete areas where the law and public policy play a role in affecting women's lives. . . . The campaigning for and around such a Charter would generate a consciousness which would go a long way to one day making the rights a reality and to reducing the pain and embarrassment with which the subject is suffused."[43]

The location of the charter within this tradition and these debates was important to ensure its legitimacy within the framework of national liberation, even though in practice the coalition was stepping beyond that framework. Conversely, the charterist orientation made some affiliates uneasy as it gave preeminence to the ANC tradition within the Women's National Coalition. During the 1980s the term *charterist* signaled broad affiliation with the goals of the ANC and polarized activists on the left into different ideological factions ("workerist," "black consciousness," etc.).[44] It was therefore by no means an inclusive label, even for progressive women activists. The Women's League was at pains to emphasize that its members envisioned a "women's charter," not an "ANC charter." This was an important distinction for the Inkatha Freedom Party members, who were uneasy about the Women's Brigade's joining a coalition in which the ANC was dominant. Nkosazana Zuma, key facilitator in discussions between the Women's League and the Women's Brigade, pointed out that it was important for all organizations in the coalition to feel comfortable with its key campaign.[45] Inkatha hesitated to join the coalition, refusing to attend a march in Durban to launch the new organization but eventually joined. Initially, the Democratic Party and the National Party also rejected the idea of a women's charter for their organizational associations, whereas the conservative Afrikaner women's organization Kontak and the mainly white, liberal Women's Bureau rejected the political nature of the term.[46] Soon after the coalition was formed, the Democratic Party joined the call for a women's charter as an addendum to the Constitution, reading the significance of a charter within a rights-based approach to the transition.[47]

The adoption of the notion squarely stamped the coalition with the ANC's political dominance, despite the coalition's much-celebrated diversity. The process of drawing up the charter also drew on the ANC's organizational experience with the Freedom Charter. Like the Freedom Charter, the Women's Charter was seen as part of a "rolling campaign," in which women at all levels of society would articulate their interests. In explaining this process, the Pregs Govender, project manager for the coalition, wrote that "many people have said that we should hire a market research company to survey women's needs for a future South Africa. Why go to all the effort and expense of a nation-wide campaign? Those who see our goal as simply drawing up a list of demands in a charter are missing the core of our objective. If women do not get involved and learn to break the culture of silence that binds women across all cultural backgrounds, we will only be further disempowered. Our numbers make us potentially powerful. . . . The very first step in realising this power is to ensure that women 'own' the campaign. . . . Women need to know that this campaign is about South African women seizing the opportunity to begin transforming society and their everyday lives."[48]

In her speech at the founding of the coalition in April 1992, Frene Ginwala, co-convenor of the WNC, also argued for broad consultation with women at the grassroots level, urging the coalition to "grow 'big ears' that reach the farthest corners of our land. Let us encourage women to speak of their problems and how they understand and experience gender oppression in their daily lives."[49] Ginwala, the driving force behind the organization, had an acute sense of the political importance of addressing formal politics. These skills were evident within the ANC-in-exile; she is credited by some for the wording of ANC statements on gender equality in the 1980s.[50] Within the coalition she emphasized the long-term role that a charter could play in protecting women's rights within a democracy. She was able to drive through the idea of a charter with great eloquence in her speech at the founding conference, stressing its potential for uniting women who had been divided by race and class, and its importance in the constitutional process. Sheila Meintjes, a member of the steering committee and later chair of the Research Supervisory Group, said that Ginwala was successful because she understood the significance of the differences between women, and "took the need for inclusion very seriously. . . . She had a vision that both acknowledged differences and transcended them. She gave real leadership."[51]

The charter campaign—dubbed "Operation Big Ears"—was an ambitious proposal. One hundred fieldworkers would begin focus group discussions with women across the country during a period of three months. This process would identify issues that women had in common as well as their divergent interests. It would provide the information for the coalition's strategic mobilization and politicize women about their oppression; it also would link grassroots-level politics to national processes. Most significant was that the charter would be the basis of the demands of the WNC in the constitutional negotiations, lending the organization unquestionable political credibility in a context in which women's demands for representation were constantly denigrated.

In practice, however, the two levels of politics were not easily brought together. Conceived, at least by some within the coalition, as a participatory process,[52] the drafting of the charter represented a form of politics that had a longer-term vision and that required some degree of organizational patience, flexibility, and responsiveness to the sensitivities and constraints of including unorganized and unpoliticized women. On the other hand, interventions in national negotiations required a different form of flexibility— the ability to identify opportunities for lobbying and to respond at short notice, without extensive consultation and education. Indeed, shortly after the coalition was formed, its day-to-day work was reassigned from the National Interim Committee to a small working committee in the head office.

Ironically, while Democratic Party and National Party representatives were persuaded that the charter would be an important statement of intent and addendum to the Constitution, despite its ANC associations, it was harder to convince internal activists that a focus on formal and constitutional politics was appropriate. Reflecting on the reasons for the relative ease with which women from different parties worked together, Meintjes commented that "a lot of women were very good at looking beyond ideological and political differences and slights, for the ultimate recognition that if this didn't work, then South African women would feel the effects in the future. There was a sense of a historical task."[53] Jennifer Kinghorn, cotreasurer of the WNC and a representative of Soroptimists International, observed that even when tensions developed at the national office, "we could stomach it because it was our window of opportunity, and if we didn't get this together, women would never be part of liberation. The cause was much bigger than the individual. And that was what kept us all together."[54]

Certainly, for the women from white political parties and women's groups, staying within the coalition, despite its problems, reflected a political pragmatism. It was clear that without the ANC, a women's movement had little future. To a significant degree the alliance with the ANC women activists allowed white women a space and voice in national politics that they had lacked, given the serious inattention to gender issues, and to women's political capabilities, in their own parties. Interestingly, however, the strength of the ANC-aligned activists did not translate into strengthening the Women's League—indeed, it would seem the Women's League became increasingly peripheral to the daily running of the coalition. As early as 1993 Ginwala complained that "although ANCWL initiated meetings which started WNC, they are now doing nothing about the Women's Charter."[55]

For internal activists, tutored in the participatory politics of the trade union movement and women's organizations of the 1980s, the emphasis on the constitutional negotiations was problematic. Their unease stemmed from the perceived narrowness of a rights-based approach to politics, one that appeared to privilege the achievement of formal equality as the central ambition. As I have shown, there were competing discourses and repertoires of struggle during the 1980s, even within the UDF-affiliated women's organizations. Discourses of rights coexisted with liberation discourses that emphasized radical transformations in social and economic relations. Although many internal UDF-aligned activists had been part of the charterist tradition, with its emphasis on inalienable rights, the ability of rights discourses to provide a vehicle for altering power relations had always been contested. Activists honed in the struggles of United Women's Congress, for example, placed a great emphasis on the value of organizational depth, participatory decision making, and grassroots democracy. By contrast rights discourses, with their emphasis on the state, appeared to ignore the problems of the extent to which women would be able to *exercise* their rights in the context of economic marginalization and cultural subordination. For some women members of the ANC, the very idea of a coalition undermined the radical content of the movement's demands. These concerns were also shared by feminist activists based in the trade unions, who had stayed out of alliance politics in the 1980s, seeing in these struggles only the possibility for limited liberal democratic ideals. Apart from ideological differences, experienced activists were also concerned about building a sustainable organization. Most had been part of the abortive attempts to revive the Federation of South African Women and were acutely attuned to the difficulties of race and class within the women's movement.

For these feminists an equality clause in the Constitution was not so much an achievement as one weapon among many to be used in the struggle against women's subordination. As a result they had no intention of exhausting their strategic energies by engaging the constitutional negotiators. Their primary emphasis was on the mobilization of women through political education and empowerment. The transition to democracy offered a political context for greater mobilization and an opportunity to raise the level of political consciousness among women. Pregs Govender said that in her view, the coalition "started out as more than about the Constitution. I was told [presumably by Ginwala] to conceptualize [the charter] campaign in my office. But that is not how I worked. I wanted to go out and meet women, to hear their views, to build the regions."[56]

The differences between a rights-based struggle focused on influencing the constitutional process on the one hand, and, on the other, the opportunities presented by the transition for the creation of a strong social movement of women with the long-term aim of transforming the gender relations of power echoed many of the debates that took place about the nature and direction of women's organizations established in the 1980s. The debates in the coalition were more muted but nevertheless underlay some of the energy-sapping conflicts that took place in the head office in 1992 and 1993. Debbie Budlender, research coordinator of the WNC, is quoted by Abrams as saying, "I didn't recognise the importance of the Constitution. I didn't think that writing a whole lot of things on paper necessarily meant change. . . . I didn't see the constitutional thing as the goal, I [was focused on] letting people be heard."[57] In part, this comment signified a crucial tension within the coalition—not between ideologically opposed affiliates and certainly not between black and white women but within the democratic tradition and, in some cases, even more narrowly within the ANC, regarding the key objectives of the coalition and its organizational style.

These tensions were heightened by the presence of two highly skilled, confident, and articulate former trade unionists as project manager and research manager. The clashes between Govender and Budlender, on the one hand, and Ginwala, on the other, are well documented in the coalition's archives and are recounted in considerable detail in Abrams's dissertation. Although the personality differences that Abrams explored account for some of these clashes, the differences between these women represented a microcosm of the divergent ambitions for the coalition among key affiliates. Interestingly, Ginwala herself has characterized the tensions as resulting from differences in organizational culture rather than a deeper struggle about the nature of the coalition: "You see, ANC in exile, we were a military unit, and yet, we were a political body with a tremendous amount of consultation. And that always posed a challenge. The United Democratic Front . . . was consultative, but didn't necessarily have the discipline that the military tradition of the ANC had. I think the National Party had an authoritarian tradition . . . and not enough consultation. . . . I do make tremendous demands on people. You find this among a number of the exiles. . . . We come out of this tradition where, our whole lives, we just work, work, work, work."[58] However, far from bringing a consultative model to the coalition, Ginwala was criticized for imposing a hierarchical—even authoritarian—style on the organization. Govender commented that "Frene's whole way of working was not about mass mobilization. But for those of us in the country, mass mobilization was the key, the emphasis was on participation."[59]

The Aims and Purposes of a Women's Charter

Related to these tensions about the nature of the charter campaign was that the precise goal of the charter campaign was continually debated in the coalition. Feminist lawyers, mostly based at the universities of the Witwatersrand and Cape Town, played a key role in these debates, drawing on the expertise of Canadian feminist lawyers who were brought in by the International Development Research Centre, the Canadian organization that was the coalition's major funder. In 1992 the Caucus on Law and Gender at the University of Cape Town summarized four options, from the strongest to the weakest, for a women's charter: an enforceable legal document with the same legal status as a bill of rights; an enforceable legal document that would be subordinate to the Constitution; a statement on gender equality in the Constitution that would guide but not bind government and the courts; and a set of guidelines on gender equality that could be used by government and the courts if they desired.[60]

In 1993 the coalition's Legal Working Group argued strongly that the charter should be seen as part of a package of instruments and strategies that could be used in the struggle for gender equality and designated this as a fifth option.[61] The advocate Francis Bosman, a member of the steering committee who was associated with the National Party, proposed, as a sixth option, a limited document that would be both aspirational and act as a broad political statement. In January 1994 Ginwala argued at the WNC's council meeting that although the negotiators had agreed on the Interim Constitution, debate on the Bill of Rights would begin anew in the Constituent Assembly that would be elected in April to write the permanent constitution and that women "should therefore take a maximalist position and campaign for the option that will provide the best for women, while at the same time preparing for all possible options within the Bill of Rights debate."[62]

This maximalist position (option 7) would entail that the charter be adopted by the Constituent Assembly as part of the process of ratifying the Constitution, that the courts should thereafter be obliged to take the charter into account in interpreting the Bill of Rights, and that Parliament should ensure that all new legislation complied with the charter. However, by 1994, when the charter was being finalized by the Research Supervisory Group, the three strongest options (1, 2, and 7) were moot because the Interim Constitution was already in place and, despite Ginwala's optimism, the Constituent Assembly was reluctant to reopen debate to allow for entirely new additions. Options 3 and 4 were politically weak from the perspective of building the women's movement, as they focused attention primarily on the state. At the conference to ratify the charter, several coalition affiliates disagreed on the route to be taken, especially in regard to whether the charter should be a political inspirational document (the position of the National Party, Democratic Party, National Women's Bureau, Young Women's Christian Association, Soroptimists International, Western Cape Coalition, and Black Sash) or one that was legally binding on the state (the position of the Northern Transvaal Regional Coalition, Transkei Regional Coalition, Natal Midlands, and Northern Natal Regional Coalition).[63] In any event, the halting, hesitant, and interrupted nature of the campaign left the coalition little choice but to understand the charter as a guiding political document (option 5) to be used within a multipronged strategy, and this was indeed the position adopted by the coalition at its conference in February 1994.[64] One observer at the conference at which the coalition adopted the charter suggested that by that stage some activists were concerned that turning the charter into a legal document would be counterproductive because it opened the possibility that its strong demands would have to be tempered to win acceptance by the Constituent Assembly.[65]

Conflicts about the direction, content, and style of the charter campaign threatened to derail Operation Big Ears completely. Budlender resigned in March 1993, criticizing the decision-making process as being "slow, inconclusive, lacking in openness and undemocratic in style" and the mode of operation as "totally disempowering and undermining."[66] In attempting to define a strategy to collect women's demands for the charter, the coalition, and in particular the team led by Govender and Budlender and supported by Anne Letsebe on the steering committee, made strong efforts to develop a participatory strategy that would reach the most marginalized women. In January 1993 the WNC convened a research methodology workshop involving academics and gender activists, at which several researchers outlined the statistical profile of women, problems of access to rural women, and methodological and political problems in claiming representation for demands that would be collected.[67] At this workshop tensions again arose in regard to the slow pace that would be necessary to undertake proper participatory research. Ginwala stressed the importance of producing a credible document quickly so that the coalition could influence the outcome of the negotiations.[68]

After several acrimonious attempts to develop new strategies to produce the charter, and with donors refusing to release money to the coalition, the organization established the Research Supervisory Group to oversee the charter campaign.[69] Even so, tensions over Ginwala's leadership style continued, and in July 1993 she resigned as convenor, as did Anne Letsebe shortly thereafter. Yet Ginwala's emphasis on the constitutional talks was undeniably important, and their resignations were subsequently withdrawn and all attention turned to the charter as the main priority. Each region sent two delegates to the National Strategy Workshop held in June 1993. The delegates identified five key themes as the core around which to build a national campaign: women's legal status; women's access to land, resources, and water; violence against women; health; and work.[70]

The Research Supervisory Committee, chaired by Sheila Meintjes, an academic with a long history of activism, devised a plan of action that incorporated the need for broad participation of women with the urgency to produce a charter that could influence the constitutional negotiations. This reassured donors, and the campaign took off with enthusiastic participation from the regional affiliates of the coalition and a well-developed publicity campaign around the five key themes. Individuals, organizations, and mass meetings of women convened by regional affiliates (some with as many as eight hundred participants) submitted demands around each theme.[71]

The draft charter was put together by a small, mainly white, team working against the clock. Meintjes described the methodology used during "forty-eight sleepless hours" before the final coalition congress in February 1994 this way: "We put together all the information and organized it systematically and thematically into twelve areas. The issues came directly out of the research. Where there were differences and contradictions [in the submissions], they all went in. We saw this as a draft. . . . The draft research report was taken to all the regions, comments were made and taken back to central office for review. . . . The draft was fine-tuned at a steering committee meeting and then went to [the coalition] congress. At congress everyone who wanted to spent the night processing the changes [made suggestions] from the floor. . . . The document was made eloquent and presented again to congress and debated once more. The polished charter emerged from this and was adopted at the next council meeting [in June 1994]."[72]

Differences and Agreements on the Content of the Charter

While recognizing a plurality of interests, the Women's Charter was not pluralist in the sense of assuming all interests were equal. Rather, the charter explicitly prioritized the needs of poor and economically vulnerable women for government attention (see appendix A). This was a significant area of consensus achieved at the national congress to ratify the charter. The Women's Charter demanded a consideration of the socioeconomic needs of women—access to safe water, access to land, housing, and the like. In so doing, the coalition put on the table the need to deal with issues of substantive equality in the initial framing of the Constitution. As well,

there was a strong emphasis in the charter on the historical processes of exclusion and exploitation, which produced differences among women, and
this historical understanding formed the basis for making the needs of
poor, especially rural, women a priority. Not surprisingly, this emphasis on
substantive equality was not supported by all the affiliates of the coalition,
and disagreements emerged in the debates about the precise content of the
charter. As a result the final charter is prefaced with an "Important Note,"
which states that "while the Women's Charter has been adopted by the
WNC, the women's organisations which are part of the WNC retain their
freedom to reserve their position on particular clauses with which they do
not wish to associate themselves."[73]

Existing literature on the coalition is surprisingly silent on the actual
processes of debate about the charter, and yet it is in regard to the content
that the most revealing differences emerged.[74] Ironically, conservative and
religious groupings such as Dames Aktueel did not object to the draft charter despite the inclusion of a number of clauses that conflicted with their
basic organizational principles—for example, the demand that women
have the right to control their bodies and the right to make reproductive decisions, a veiled reference to the right to abortion on demand.[75] In part this
acceptance was the result of skillful strategic work on the part of the ANC
women who, anticipating destructive debate about the issue of sexual and
reproductive rights, agreed to word this clause in the broadest possible
terms. Their view was that as long as the clause was phrased in a way that
would leave open space for political and legislative lobbying in the future,
they would defer the issue until after the 1994 elections. In any case, many
conservative women's groups lacked the capacity and expertise to analyze
the charter and offer cogent alternatives. Article 9 ("Custom, Culture and
Religion"), Clause 1, which calls for custom, culture, and religious practices
to be subject to the equality clause in the proposed bill of rights, was opposed by the religious women's groups. It was subsequently altered to limit
the application of the Bill of Rights to the status of women in marriage,
law, and public life.[76]

The most bitter differences over the charter were those between the
Democratic Party and the ANC. These differences involved the understanding of equality, the value of state intervention in the struggle for gender equality, and the extent to which the charter should address inequalities
in the private sphere—in effect, how the public sphere was to be delineated.
The Democratic Party offered a vision in which political rights to equality
and participation were to be guaranteed and the extent of state intervention in the structural bases of women's disadvantages were to be mini-
mized. In an early discussion document drafted soon after the coalition was
formed, the Democratic Party leaders Dene Smuts and Carole Charlewood

argued that materialist explanations for women's subordination—as presented by the ANC and South African Communist Party—were misguided and that "gender discrimination is primarily cultural and social, part of a patriarchal pattern of behaviour which has not kept pace with changing roles and conditions."[77] In line with this view the Democratic Party's representations to the coalition on the charter argued against proposals that sought to address the economic basis of women's subordination.

The ANC, on the other hand, argued that social rights should underpin the achievement of political equality. This approach was underscored by the parallel demand by the ANC for a constitutional clause protecting citizens' socioeconomic rights. The Democratic Party argued against proposals that sought to address the economic basis of women's subordination and favored limiting the charter to "what a government can do" and omitting the private sphere altogether.[78] The party opposed inclusion of Articles 8 ("Family Life and Partnerships") and 9 ("Custom, Culture and Religion") on the ground that the state should not legislate these areas. The Democratic Party also disagreed in principle with the demand for affirmative action, specifically, the idea of "equal representation" of women in the public sphere, preferring instead to call for equal *access* to representation. The party was concerned that a wide-ranging charter would lose focus if it "simply takes on board problems and policy areas that do not specifically spring from the subordinate status of women. . . . We are then reduced simply to a special interest lobby pushing for various things in the gratuitous name of women. Either we are serious and consistent about equality or we are not. If we aren't, the Coalition will not hold together."[79]

The party wanted the drafters to replace the word *oppression* (in its view this was "terminology largely used by liberation movements") and replace it with the word *subordination.*[80] Underlying the party's comments was a restricted notion of equality, as meaning the removal of restrictions on women's advancement, and of strategies for achieving equality as lying in struggles to ensure equal opportunity. For example, while Article 2 of the draft charter called on the law to "promote and ensure the practical realisation of equality,"[81] the Democratic Party preferred to limit Article 2 to "tak[ing] [equality] into account."[82] In another example the party opposed Article 4's call for women to have the right to education and training at any stage in life, arguing that "the state can't afford it."[83]

The ANC's comments on the draft reflect an understanding of gender equality as linked to broader political, economic, and social inequalities. The bulk of the movement's comments focused on Article 3 ("Economy"). The ANC expressed concern that three items had been dropped from earlier drafts and called for these to be reinstated. These were the demand for full participation in economic decision making, the recognition of unpaid labor and its inclusion in the government's budgeting processes, and gender stereotyping of jobs.[84] These demands stemmed from parallel discussions on a bill of rights that were taking place within the ANC, and women activists' responses to the ANC's constitutional guidelines. Women activists in the Congress alliance rejected the notion of equality as sameness between men and women. The emphasis was rather on how to ensure that women and men experienced both the benefits and the constraints of society equally. Discussions revolved around what kinds of special mechanisms — such as affirmative action and institutions such as the national machinery for women — could be put into place to ensure equality of outcomes for women and men.[85] The ANC's draft bill of rights, issued in 1990, presupposed a state that would proactively implement rights and envisioned an array of interventionist mechanisms — including affirmative action and redistributive welfare programs — that could be used.

These differences between the key political affiliates in the coalition were not easily resolved. The final charter attempted to temper and modify language so that all affiliates could feel comfortable ratifying the document. Thus Article 1 ("Equality") accommodated their differences this way: "The principle of equality shall be embodied at all levels in legislation and government policy. Specific legislation shall be introduced to ensure the practical realisation of equality. Programmes of affirmative action could be a means of achieving equality."[86] In Article 3 on the economy, on the other hand, the charter states that "the full participation of women in economic decision-making should be facilitated."[87] Nevertheless, not all demands could be reduced to the lowest common denominator in this way, and the differences at the national convention threatened to split the coalition. The compromise finally agreed to was that the charter would be prefaced by a statement that it was a collection of all demands submitted to the coalition and that member organizations did not necessarily support the charter in its entirety. Through this mechanism the coalition was able to acknowledge internal differences while producing a broadly legitimate document that could be put before parties negotiating the bill of rights. Specific policy interpretations of women's demands were, in effect, deferred to parliamentary and legislative debates in the new government.

Despite the efforts of the Research Supervisory Group, the early differences within the coalition slowed down the charter process to the extent that it could have little influence on the constitutional drafting process. In any case, Albertyn has argued that "the effective translation of women's claims for equality into constitutional provisions and legal rights was a process that was initially not clearly thought out by the leadership or understood by the majority of the WNC membership."[88] Coming after the Interim Constitution was finalized, the original multiple strategic intentions of the charter were of necessity tempered, the broader political landscape having altered significantly with the agreements on electoral arrangements and the Government of National Unity. Nevertheless, the charter represented the possibility of a national consensus among women about the minimal demands of the women's movement. As Murray and O'Regan suggested in 1991, the charter "could become a powerful political document, providing a standard against which to judge legislation and public action politically, if not legally."[89] Despite its limitations, the charter retained many of the demands for substantive equality described earlier and thereby set an aspirational objective that went beyond limited conceptions of formal equality. In making demands for greater female representation in the legislature, the assumption of ANC women activists was that these demands would be best addressed by women representatives. Indeed, as I show in chapter 6, ANC women activists promised that the charter would form the basis for legislative and policy interventions.

The Constitutional Negotiations

While the coalition was developing the Women's Charter, it also was engaged in lobbying in relation to discussions at the multiparty negotiations. The coalition identified three key areas of intervention: women's inclusion on negotiating teams, the inclusion of nonsexism in the Constitutional Principles, and the inclusion of an equality clause in the Constitution that would supersede the right to custom and tradition.

Responding to the protests of women at their exclusion from negotiating teams, the Management Committee of the Convention for a Democratic South Africa proposed that women should be included as part of the delegations of political parties. The Women's League initially proposed that the convention grant it separate status from the ANC at the talks, hoping that, once admitted, the Women's League could apply party political pressure around gender issues. This would also allow the league a base from which to caucus with women from other political parties. When a Women's League delegation approached the ANC's Negotiations Committee to inform it of the league's plans, the majority of committee members were unhappy. One negotiator argued that the convention was dealing with political issues, and as the Women's League knew little about politics and was not a political organization, its representation was inappropriate. Other members, more sensitive to recent struggles within the ANC, were more supportive and tried to look for compromise solutions. The Women's League delegation argued that the decision to apply separately was not a retaliatory attempt to embarrass the ANC for excluding women from its delegations but was a strategy to make convention structures more representative. The

Women's League noted that the Congress of South African Trade Unions, an ANC ally, had also applied to join separately. However, the trade unionists agreed to rethink their position on separate representation.

The issue was taken up in the Women's League's Strategising Group, made up of key political leaders of the league as well as leading ANC women academics. The group drafted a submission that the league presented to the convention; the document referred to the gender issues that faced each of the working committees and suggested ways of resolving these. The group recommended, and the ANC officially accepted, an alternative proposal to push for a gender advisory committee to monitor and advise on the gender implications of the convention's terms of reference, as well as the decisions of the Management Committee and working groups. After intense lobbying, the proposal was accepted, but there was no requirement that the recommendations of the gender advisory committee had to be followed. This acceptance was significant because "it meant that for the first time the idea that women had specific political interests and concerns had forced its way onto the formal negotiation agenda."[90] Albertyn said that "although the GAC [Gender Advisory Committee] had limited powers, its appointment was a symbolic, but brief, victory for women."[91] Thenjiwe Mtintso, on the other hand, described it as a "toothless dog."[92] Indeed, the negotiators appeared to view the Gender Advisory Committee as a short-term sop to the "women's lobby," a lobby they perceived as relatively weakly organized. Analysts at the Centre for Policy Studies, a Johannesburg think tank, concluded that the convention "was not enthusiastic about giving priority to women's issues, and would have preferred not to address the question if it was able to avoid it."[93] The ANC's key negotiator, its deputy secretary general, Jacob Zuma, argued that the Gender Advisory Committee "did not achieve the desired result of mapping out the position of women in the strategic design of the working committees. Nor did it address the position of women in particular where decisions were made. It became a ghetto for women created by the progressive structures, because we used the existence of the GAC as an excuse and did not address the absence of women among our negotiators. We still have not done so."[94]

The Gender Advisory Committee did not have sufficient time to establish a role or develop positions in relation to key policy issues. The convention was dissolved as a result of the Boipatong and Bisho massacres and was followed in March 1993 by a new round of constitutional negotiations known as the Multi-Party Negotiating Process (MPNP). The aim of this round of talks was to secure agreement on a constitutional framework for a democratic South Africa. A negotiating forum was formed in April 1993, with representation from twenty-six political parties. The Negotiating Council established seven technical committees that would consider submissions and proposals.[95] From the coalition's perspective the most important of these was the Technical Committee on Constitutional Matters, which would come to an agreement on an interim constitution to be eventually finalized and adopted by an elected Constitutional Assembly. The Negotiating Council agreed on April 27, 1994, as the date for the country's first nonracial elections.

As with the constitutional convention, women were markedly under-represented among the negotiators and in the technical committees of the MPNP. Former members of the Gender Advisory Committee reacted quickly, demanding both that the GAC be included as a technical commit-tee in the MPNP and that political parties include women on their nego-tiating teams. A technical committee would enable women activists to draft and prepare reports on the gender implications of different proposals, which would then have to be considered by the Negotiating Council. The Women's National Coalition wrote an open letter to political leaders accus-ing them of turning the Gender Advisory Committee into a "political ghetto" at the convention and questioning their commitment to representa-tion and participation. The ANC Women's League staged a protest outside the World Trade Centre, the venue for the MPNP meetings, at the first meeting of the Negotiating Council, demanding that "a representative voice of women—from all parties—be heard within the inner chambers of the negotiating council," and threatening to boycott the first elections if women's demands for inclusion were not met.[96]

Increasingly, the option of a Gender Advisory Committee was seen as limited and likely merely to further marginalize women. Instead, women in political parties began to demand inclusion on the decision-making teams. A meeting was convened of all women representatives from the parties in the MPNP; at that session women demanded "the establishment of a Women's Caucus, the release of the report of the all-male Negotiating Council's last meeting where the question of women's participation was de-bated, and to attend the last meeting of the Negotiating Council before the Forum on 1 April, to resolve the issue once and for all."[97] Albertyn has de-scribed the process that followed: "The ANC initially called for the delega-tions to be expanded to consist of one negotiator and two advisors (instead of one negotiator and one advisor), one of the three to be a woman. This was jeered at the Negotiating Council when put forward by Cyril Ramapa-hosa of the ANC. The women then caucused among themselves and the IFP [Inkatha] Women's Brigade suggested that all delegations be expanded to include one woman delegate who would have full voting rights. This was accepted by the Negotiating Council."[98]

However, the battle for representation was by no means won. Very few women were on the lists of technical committee members, and a further skirmish ensued, with new and more representative lists being drawn up.

As Albertyn has pointed out, "The subsequent appointment of women to these committees did not mean that gender concerns were considered by them."[99] She argues that the limited abilities of the women delegates to influence the technical committees—because of their lack of political experience and technical expertise, and the constraints of party cultures and of an unsympathetic environment—made it necessary to influence the MPNP from the outside.[100]

Women activists established the Multi-Party Negotiating Process Monitoring Collective in July 1993 with a donation from the Danish government. Elsabe Wessels was appointed as a full-time monitor, charged with relaying discussions at the MPNP to the monitoring collective, which was comprised of feminist lawyers. Cathi Albertyn was seconded from the Centre for Applied Legal Studies to act as "document monitor." The coalition hoped to develop a "close co-operation between women negotiators and the WNC Monitoring Group."[101] An important consideration for the Women's National Coalition at this stage, given that battles over the charter were unresolved, was to ensure that the formulation of constitutional principles and other agreements at the multiparty talks were as broad and inclusive as possible. "We need to prevent formulations from being sewn up so tightly that the ANC or any other body/organisation of women cannot intervene at a later stage. We need to provide the best possible framework for later intervention—we must therefore ensure that formulations are as open as possible," the coalition reported in July 1993.[102]

The first draft of the Constitutional Principles, prepared on the basis of discussions held at the convention and issued in May, omitted all explicit reference to nonsexism despite a recommendation made by the Gender Advisory Committee at the convention. The coalition sent a submission to the MPNP asking for the explicit inclusion of the principle of nonsexism and prohibiting gender discrimination along with racial discrimination. The technical committee incorporated the demand to prohibit gender discrimination but excluded nonsexism from the Constitutional Principles, arguing that this was implied by the general terms of the principles.[103] Even the ANC wavered on the importance of explicitly including nonsexism, although the language of its own party documents had, since the May 2, 1990, declaration, emphasized a "non-racial, non-sexist democracy." Jacob Zuma has acknowledged in other contexts that the inclusion of the qualifier was important. "Why not simply say democracy? Would that not automatically include being non-racial and non sexist? The answer is NO. . . . It is important for us to underline and emphasise that in the new South Africa our democracy will be inclusive. It will not define the concept or participation in the democratic process in terms of race, nor will it exclude any group. It is for similar reasons that we felt it necessary to describe the new South Africa as non-sexist. The truth is that ours is a very sexist society and women have been excluded from full participation."[104] This sentiment finally prevailed. The debate on the nonsexism clause was reopened when the Interim Constitution was presented to the Constitutional Assembly, and this time women Members of Parliament successfully argued for the inclusion of the principle of nonsexism.

The third aim of the coalition with regard to the negotiations—the inclusion of a strong equality clause in the Constitution—was the most challenging and the most revealing of the political and social obstacles that lay in the path of achieving gender equality. The Women's Charter demanded that "culture, custom and religion, insofar as they impact upon the status of women in marriage, in law and in public life, shall be subject to the equality clause in the Bill of Rights."[105] Unlike many demands contained in the Women's Charter, the clause on custom was backed by a strong women's organization that ensured both that the Women's Charter paid detailed attention to the issue of customary law and that the issue was followed through in the constitutional negotiations. The Rural Women's Movement had been formed in 1986 as a forum to challenge the exclusion of women from participation in rural community structures and expanded its vision to include challenges to male authority within the family.[106] The coalition had mobilized a broad consensus on the need to lobby for the reform of customary law and was supported by technical expertise provided by the Transvaal Rural Action Committee and the Centre for Applied Legal Studies. This was backed up politically by educational workshops organized by the Rural Women's Movement and pickets outside the negotiations venue.

The coalition was met head-on by traditional leaders, for whom an equality clause was anathema as it undermined their claims to hereditary powers. The proposals made by traditional leaders at the MPNP included demands for the exclusion of customary law from the Bill of Rights; that customary law, culture, and religion should not be subject to the equality guarantee; and that communities that were subject to customary law and traditional authority should remain exclusively subject to such authority.[107] The coalition commented that the proposals undermined women's right to full citizenship: "If these recommendations were accepted, millions of SA women would have second class status."[108]

At issue was the extent to which the protection of cultural rights should override other values in the Constitution. Pressured by the coalition, the constitutional negotiators appeared to take into account the potential negative implications of entrenching cultural rights and agreed that customary law should be subject to the equality clause. However, the chiefs were not only a vociferous lobby, they also had the potential to incite political disruptions in rural areas and especially in Natal, where high levels of violence continued throughout the negotiations. Negotiators were reluctant in this context to go "too far," and as a result, the relationship between the clause on custom and that on equality was not clearly articulated. Only in the final constitution did the women's movement's demand that equality trump custom gain acceptance—surprisingly, without much debate.

By this stage the ANC had committed itself to the reform of customary law in its 1994 election platform (the Reconstruction and Development Programme[109]), and, according to Goldblatt and Mbatha, "it was simply a matter of implementing it in a less politically volatile environment."[110] When the agreement on equality was made in relation to the Interim Constitution, the negotiators set up two bodies that would have a role in the process of reforming customary law, one to represent the interests of women (the Commission on Gender Equality) and one to represent traditional leaders (Council of Traditional Leaders). This was an unexpected gain for the women's movement as the Commission on Gender Equality was set up as a statutory body entrenched in the Constitution, empowered to monitor and promote the implementation of gender equality. The Council of Traditional Leaders was given narrower advisory powers: the right to have any bill on customary law referred to it by Parliament and the power to delay a bill for up to sixty days.[111] In the final constitution the Council of Traditional Leaders was to be established by national legislation rather than as a statutory body, and its advisory capacities were somewhat diminished to include advising the government on matters pertaining to customary leadership and the right to make submissions (but not delay) legislation affecting customary law. However, the political tensions between traditional leaders and the women's movement were not resolved by these mechanisms. Instead, the contestation between claims for equality and those for cultural rights was in effect delayed, to be resolved by the new government and by the Constitutional Court.

The Constitutional and Legal Legacy of the Transition

Despite the failure to complete the Women's Charter in time for serious consideration by negotiators, the negotiation process produced several favorable formal conditions for women. The South African Constitution provides a positive framework for the achievement of gender equality, with gender equality as a founding provision, fundamental principle, and fundamental value of the new democracy. The entrenchment of a justiciable Bill of Rights that enshrines both individual and collective rights establishes government accountability in terms of several powerful gender rights.[112] These include a broad and substantive equality right, which includes protection against unfair discrimination on sex, gender, pregnancy, marital status, and sexual orientation[113]; a right to security and freedom of the person, which specifically incorporates the right to be free from all forms of violence from either public or private sources[114]; and the right to bodily and psychological integrity, including the right to make decisions concerning reproduction and to security in and control of their bodies.[115] The Constitution also requires that legislation relating to systems of religious or traditional personal and family law, as well as the exercise of cultural and religious rights by communities, must be consistent with the Constitution.[116] Many believe that this means that discriminatory rules and practices based on religion, tradition, or culture can be declared unconstitutional. The framing of the equality clause in the Interim Constitution in 1993 to explicitly assert gender equality provided the enabling framework within which to advance the demand for structures and mechanisms to ensure equality for women.

The provision for social and economic rights in the Constitution—acknowledging social rights as entitlements—also provides a basis for advancing equality and social justice for women.[117] These social and economic rights include environmental rights (§ 24), land rights (§ 25 (5)–(9)), housing (§ 26), and health care, food, water, and social security (§ 27). Liebenberg has argued that this constitutional recognition "removes [socioeconomic rights] from the realm of policy choices by government. Government is legally obliged to give human rights priority consideration in formulating its laws and policies."[118]

Yet it bears restating that neither formal equality nor the law itself can fully provide solutions to the inequalities of gender. While the Constitution may be hailed as a "state of the art human rights instrument,"[119] various limitations to its impact are already being recognized. The enforcement of rights depends to a significant extent on the ability of women's groups to use this avenue for pursuing their claims on government. The Commission on Gender Equality is specifically empowered to challenge government on the implementation of gender rights, but its organizational capacities in this regard have yet to be consolidated. Furthermore, there are early signs that the clause on socioeconomic rights may be difficult to uphold in practice as it allows wide scope for the interpretation of government responsibilities in the context of severe fiscal constraints.[120] It is interesting to note that government cuts in the allocation of child maintenance grants (discussed in chapter 7) were not challenged on constitutional grounds by women's organizations. Finally, it has been pointed out that judges will not automatically interpret the equality clause in ways that recognize the diversity of needs among women but may choose to interpret equality in universalist and formal terms.[121] These concerns highlight the limitations of relying too heavily on the constitutional and legal mechanisms as guarantees for women and the dangers of allowing legalist strategies to delineate the parameters of gender politics.

Assessing the Impact of the Women's National Coalition

Did the coalition succeed in using inclusionary strategies to broaden definitions of citizenship and redefine the terms of politics? And, had the coalition not existed, would these demands have been pursued by other forces, especially feminists within the ANC? In other words, was the organizational vehicle of a coalition more than the sum of its parts?

The coalition has attracted the intense interest of feminist scholars and activists for several reasons. First, South African feminists have been intrigued by the glimpse of a nonracial, politically motivated, and feminist women's movement that the coalition offered. Second, they have been interested in the conditions that would allow women's organizations to influence national and macro-level political decision making. And third, the coalition appears to offer a model for the ways in which a women's movement might recognize diversity/plurality while nevertheless retaining a sense of collective purpose. As I have shown in this chapter, the coalition gave organizational articulation to the need for gender representation and broadened it beyond the liberation movements to include political parties that either did not have democratic ideologies or saw democracy in narrow and formalistic terms. In doing this, it brought gender equality directly into the mainstream of public political discourse.

This was no mean feat. As I showed in chapters 2 and 3, the issue of gender equality was not directly resolved politically within the liberation movement and remained peripheral to the United Democratic Front inside the country, despite numerous declarations of intent. Although the coalition operated on a limited mandate, it exposed the extent to which, despite all the formal commitments made by parties such as the ANC, the parties failed *even in their own limited terms* to acknowledge women's citizenship. The coalition was able to effectively exploit this credibility gap to question the terms on which the new democracy was being negotiated. In this respect the South African transition shared some features of the Latin American transitions to democracy. As Jacquette and Wolchik have found, the commitment to equality was a marker of differentiation of the new democracy from the old authoritarian political model. "In Latin America, women's issues were congruent with and symbolic of a larger political transformation."[122]

In South Africa the choice of a negotiated transition, involving consensus among the major political parties and liberation movements, produced a rights-based discourse that opened a space for women activists to extend

feminist conceptions of democracy. There was an inherent tension in constitutional debates about democracy. On the one hand, the liberal notion of
equality had considerable attraction as a framework within which to supersede apartheid's race-based mechanisms for organizing political representation. Democratic mechanisms needed to be found to ensure that ethnic
mobilization was not carried over (and reinstitutionalized) in a democratic
South Africa. On the other hand, the ANC was an organization with a strong
socialist component; for large elements of its supporters it was synonymous with an anticapitalist, antiliberal struggle. Indeed, some members saw
the process of transition itself as a sellout of the revolutionary ideals of the
movement.[123] Through its alliance with the trade union movement (and in
its role as the political arm of the workers' struggle) the liberation movement
was acutely aware of the class conflicts that shattered racial—and gender—
unity. The use of a liberal discourse—and particularly the stress on rights,
was therefore by no means an easy one. Feminism as legitimate ideology in
this context provided the glue that held together a diversity of claims. The
new universe of political discourse, the emphasis on citizenship and consti-
tutions, enabled the women's movement to adopt feminist language that
went beyond the nationalist framework of collective interests and group
rights by emphasizing women's difference. The approach of feminist lawyers associated with the coalition was important in building a bridge across
the two discourses of transformation and rights. For them, as Kaganas and
Murray have pointed out, while it was important to win a strong set of formal commitments to gender equality, it was also vital to look "beyond law
and formal equality to identify problems and solutions."[124]

The shift away from discourses of nationalism was highly significant
and enabling for feminist activists. Feminist activists and scholars had long
been concerned about the constraints of nationalism on women's political
agency, even within the liberation movement.[125] Within the ANC women's
struggles were treated as subordinate to and defined by the larger national
struggle, women's roles were confined to a narrow spectrum of movement
activities based on stereotypical assumptions about women's interests and
capabilities, and feminism was delegitimized as a model of liberation. The
undermining of nationalism in the transition, however, was prompted less
by feminist interventions than by the recognition among the major negotiating parties of the dangers of right-wing nationalism to the establishment of a stable, democratic, and unitary state.[126] If the idea that the primary mechanism of political mobilization and organization centered on
ethnic affiliation were to be institutionalized, it would open the door to both
right-wing Afrikaner and Zulu claims to some degree of special power in
the new order or perhaps even of special territorial control. In any event,
women delegates to the Multi-Party Negotiating Process, bolstered from

outside by the coalition and the Rural Women's Movement, were successful in ensuring that the constitutional clause on the status of customary law was subject to the clause on gender equality. However, as Mbatha and Goldblatt have pointed out, the nature and extent to which rights to culture would be subject to rights to equality was not clearly spelled out.[127]

Citizenship, broadly conceived, displaced nationalism as the new political ideal and the political language through which the aspirations of subordinate groups were expressed. Within this framework women were able to articulate claims for strong equality. Citizenship offered a more enabling framework because the rights-based discourses that accompanied it allowed for the use of feminist mobilizing language of women's power and autonomy. Unlike nationalism, citizenship as articulated by the ANC during the transition emphasized the individual-in-community rather than only the collective rights of the community as an undifferentiated entity. While some political parties wanted to limit citizenship to formal equality and political rights, the strong ANC tradition of social justice was hard to override.[128] As even women within the National Party and Democratic Party eventually conceded, a strong emphasis on the individual would not allow for the creation of programs and strategies to overcome the historical imbalances of gender relations and of apartheid: the predominance of women among the dispossessed rural populations, and the legacies of inequality of access to education, employment, and control over land. On the other hand, the notion of community had long been criticized in South Africa for its tendency to elevate the concerns of the elite over those of the politically weak.[129] From a feminist perspective, as Yuval-Davis has shown, an emphasis on community (or nation) hides inequalities within the nation, particularly those of gender. Nation, as she points out, is often used in liberation discourse in ways that keep women's role subordinate and private.[130]

Because the ANC itself conceived of citizenship in substantial rather than formalistic terms, the new discourse allowed for women to place themselves at center as the marker of whether the elite-driven negotiated transition would be inclusive of poor and excluded people. By the time the constitutional negotiations began, women's organizations had already debated the nature of mechanisms in the state and processes in civil society that would be conducive to advancing gender equality.[131] Gender activists pushed hard for socioeconomic rights and reproductive rights, establishing a constitutional basis for affirmative action and for a widened notion of social citizenship.

Indeed, the transition was not a revolutionary victory but a carefully worked-out compromise in which the ANC had to balance the need for peace with its commitment to social justice. Within this debate women came to occupy a peculiar status as the proving ground for the extent to which the new order would be inclusive, participatory, and permeable to socially excluded groupings. Responsiveness to this constituency was thus assured, at least in the short term. That many of the demands of women—political inclusion, a strong national machinery, an equality clause, and so on—could be relatively easily accommodated within the crafting of democratic institutions facilitated this political process.

However, it would be wrong to overstate the extent to which the transition was facilitating of women's politics. A close look at the process of decision making during the transition reveals that, as Schmitter has conceded of other contexts, real power was confined to a small group of actors. Much of the decision making in the South African transition took place in bilateral meetings and circles from which women were excluded. Despite this, women were able to make broad gains, largely because attention to women's demands increasingly came to be seen as a marker of commitment to demands "from below." Gains were incremental, often against resistance or indifference, but, once won, male politicians began using them as political collateral against the watering down of earlier claims for radical changes in economic relations (especially nationalization and redistribution). Attention to the feminist agenda, even if only rhetorical, allowed liberation movements in particular to maintain their progressive image while increasingly weakening socialist forces in their midst. Where meeting women's demands would seriously conflict with the interests of other politically organized groupings, or would create the potential for loss of "more important" constituencies—such as the perceived loss of ANC access to and control over rural constituencies as a result of reforms of customary law that might result in backlash from traditional leaders—the negotiators were less keen to concede, and when they did, it was only to defer the conflicts to some future time.

There is no doubt that, thin and fragile as the ANC's commitment to gender equality was, it assumed the moral high ground on issues of gender equality. The success of women in the ANC in persuading the organization's leadership and branch structures to take account of gender in sectoral policy formulation (notably health) had an important "knock-on" effect within the coalition, as it raised the internal stakes for demonstrable gender sensitivity. As I will show in chapter 6, by the first elections in 1994 other political parties—the Inkatha Freedom Party, the Democratic Party, the National Party, and the Pan Africanist Congress—all had issued platforms on the position of women, although none of these had explored the implications of broad principles on gender equality for specific sectoral policies.

The involvement of women's sections of political parties was the key to the success of the coalition, even if it was criticized by many observers.[132] However limited, these structures had access to the negotiators in a way that nonparty women's organizations did not, and these activists had strong career interests in ensuring the inclusion of women in national decision making. They were also more skilled at using the technical expertise of lawyers and academics and at recognizing the need for offering concrete alternatives at the negotiations. The success of the coalition in influencing policies was thus dependent on its link to political parties and not just on the strength of the women's movement. The connection with technical experts and academics was not always welcome within the coalition. Fester has written that the presence of academics "enhanced the quality of the debates but increased tensions about domination and insensitivity. New ways of working were introduced which some of us found difficult. In building new alliances and new organisations, a new culture emerged. There was an air of 'professionalism' and a very fast pace."[133]

However, the professionalizing of women's politics was a central aspect of the success of the coalition in its lobbying role during the transitional negotiations. The successful mobilization of a gender "triple alliance"[134] of activists, academics, and women politicians was key to this process. The goal of mobilizing a grassroots movement soon proved impractical: the pace of political negotiations moved faster than the process of developing the charter.[135] The consultative relationship between regions and the national leadership was difficult to manage when women delegates of political parties requested support at short notice from the coalition. Much of this support was technical—organizations had to be able to develop positions and mobilize expertise to translate these into technical formats virtually instantaneously. Cathi Albertyn, who acted as legal expert for the coalition, has pointed out that the negotiations were "in the end often legalistic and technical, overly dominated by lawyers, inaccessible to the majority of the population and largely forged through a top-down process of negotiation, bilateral meetings and political deals."[136] For some women, such as Asha Moodley, the head of the Azanian People's Organisation's Secretariat for Publicity and Information, the coalition was a failure. She has suggested that "the majority of women never heard of it or the Women's Charter it drew up."[137] In the context of the negotiations the more gradual process of building a women's movement undeniably—if not inevitably—gave way to ensuring that the formal outcomes of the negotiations were as favorable as possible for women.

The coalition was not backed up by a strong mass movement of women. As is evident from chapter 2, its affiliates tended to be legitimate women's organizations with long histories but with weak organizational capacities and resources. Its strongest affiliate, the ANC Women's League, pursued a dual politics: it appealed to the ANC from the independent base of the coalition, and it appealed to the ANC's internal commitments to represent the demand for gender equality. The coalition was able to claim a broad constituency across party lines, and it was able to mobilize women within political parties to exert internal pressure on their party leaderships. This gave it moral clout and made it difficult to dismiss. The independence of the coalition in relation to political parties was not feasible for any single women's organization to develop.

Decline and Demobilization

Despite these achievements, the coalition did not survive once the immediate context of transition changed. The successful interventions in national politics in 1992–93 period had stimulated expectations that the coalition would continue to act as the national umbrella for the women's movement,[138] even though its own stated mandate was limited to the development of the Women's Charter for Effective Equality and a campaign against political violence. After the national conference to ratify the charter in February 1994, the regional alliances discussed the future of the coalition; views were mixed. The Western Cape was keen to continue with the coalition, while in the Orange Free State the steering committee had collapsed. The Eastern Cape had concerns that the coalition was "ANC orientated."[139] At a steering committee meeting in May, the Western Transvaal region representative confessed that the region "was only now beginning to understand the Coalition."[140] The Women's Charter Alliance of Southern Natal argued for the continuation of the coalition on several grounds, including the role it could play in monitoring the progress toward achieving the demands in the charter, mobilizing, educating, and organizing women.[141] The Transkei region wanted the coalition to act as a mechanism for accountability of women in government, suggesting that "women in parliament should consult with women at grass root [sic] level before each parliamentary sitting and same MPs should report."[142] The Western Cape region suggested that the coalition could play a key role in the preparations for the upcoming Fourth World Conference on Women in Beijing in 1995 and in lobbying for and monitoring the implementation of the charter. The Democratic Party felt that while the coalition should continue, its role might "diminish in importance" when the Commission on Gender Equality was set up.[143] With similar reservations the South African Communist Party Gender Department argued strongly that the coalition had outlived its usefulness. It suggested that the Gender Commission should be set up "with urgent effect." The Communist Party representatives felt that the coalition was neither necessary nor suitable for the achievement of a strong women's movement and that this role should be taken on at lower levels such as the regions: "Where regions have opted for, or do opt for continuing with the WNC, time will show the sustainability of the WNC type structure. Should these regional structures sustain themselves, it would indicate that there is a real basis for a women's movement to develop. Should they not sustain themselves, it would show that the WNC is not a basis for a women's movement and that regional organisation of the WNC has been dependent on national funding/stimulus."[144]

Most significantly, the ANC Women's League decided that, having fulfilled its mandate of ensuring greater representation of women in political structures and developing a women's charter, the coalition was no longer needed.[145] Several reasons have been offered for this new position: the league could not stomach an independent women's movement; the league wanted to preserve its traditional support bases among rural women; the league lacked the capacity to sustain a commitment to the women's movement. None is entirely convincing. To suggest that the league would first initiate an independent movement, and then seek to destroy it once it had fulfilled some hidden agenda of getting more women into the ANC, implies a level of Machiavellian planning that is hard to credit—if only because the league has never been that well organized. Changes in leadership that had been occurring within the league, in particular the resignation of several high-profile feminists and the takeover of the league by the Winne Mandela faction—and subsequent disagreements about the relationship between the league and the coalition—played a key part in the new approach to the coalition. Having decided against a continuation of the coalition, the league withdrew its official representatives late in 1994. Women's League headquarters instructed its branches not to work with the coalition. League members who did not agree with this decision—especially those outside Gauteng—continued to be active within the coalition.[146] Their participation was considered to be undisciplined, even though they did so as members of other affiliated organizations. At the 1996 Conference of the Women's League, "undisciplined" participants in coalition activities were branded disloyal and instructed to withdraw from the coalition.

Despite these tensions inside the Women's League—or perhaps in response to the political machinations of the league—the regional affiliates of the coalition highlighted the need for the coalition to continue to function as an autonomous structure, and it was decided that, to this end, women who represented political parties could not hold office in the coalition. As Nozizwe Routledge-Madlala pointed out, "It made sense not to allow women MPs to be leaders [of the coalition], but we missed the opportunity to build an alliance between women in political office and women in civil society."[147]

The role that the coalition envisioned for itself after 1994 was to act as a civil society watchdog, to ensure that the formal commitments to equality would be translated into policy and budgetary commitments. Tumiko

Daima, the media and public relations director of the coalition, argued that "the primary challenge that faces the WNC is how do we take the bread and butter concerns of women, especially grassroots women, be they urban or rural, and begin to qualitatively transform their lives."[148] The coalition planned to continue its national lobbying role. However, since 1994 the coalition has been virtually invisible as a national actor. It has made virtually no suggestions about any of the key policy or legislative processes.[149] Its activities appear to have revolved around attendance at major international conventions of women, including the Beijing Conference and the Beijing+5 review meetings. None of these has been used as an opportunity for networking and lobbying to define and articulate South African women's position on key areas of international gender debate. Nevertheless, the coalition has continued to portray itself as the legitimate representative of the women's movement in South Africa. In this role, for example, it has represented the "women sector" in the Development Chamber of the National Economic Development and Labour Council, a South African organization that promotes social and economic policies and development, although the coalition's efforts to raise the gender implications of key decisions on labor market policy have been desultory at best. This is not to suggest that gender has disappeared from national debates; rather, the space of advocacy for gender equality has been taken by other NGOs and, to a lesser extent, the statutory Commission on Gender Equality.

The decision to exclude women politicians from leadership in the coalition—advocated strongly by the liberal affiliates such as the Women's Bureau, Women for South Africa, and the Democratic Party[150]—deprived the coalition of its driving force and its link to national politics. The immediate decline of the coalition can be attributed to the movement of a significant number of its leaders into government after 1994. The most visible of these were its coconvenor, Frene Ginwala, who became the first Speaker in Parliament; Project Manager Pregs Govender, who became an MP; and Ellen Kornegay, a member of the Research Supervisory Group, who became the first head of the Office on the Status of Women. The coalition's leadership fell onto the shoulders of less experienced women—and on the tier of the coalition that had always been weaker and less able to make connections between national and women's politics.

These changes in leadership were common to all major progressive organizations in civil society and fueled a popular conception that civil society had been demobilized after 1994. To be sure, the establishment of democratic politics fueled new challenges for the civic associations as they faced uncertainty regarding how to operate in the new democratic environment. As Meer has pointed out, "They have had to reposition themselves in relation to the new government—a government elected by the majority of

South Africans and in whose machinery are many former comrades and colleagues. The weapons of the 1980s, honed for use against the apartheid state, are no longer appropriate. The government is no longer the enemy of the people. Struggle NGOs have had to develop different tools for the changed terrain, for their new tasks of lobbying and pressurising government to act in the interests of the majority of South Africans."[151]

For some commentators, engaging the state had led to a demobilization of civil society. Michael Neocosmos has argued that "increasingly depoliticised, the role of the popular movements has been emptied of the vitality that can ensure that 'the people' are able to generate and make autonomous democratic prescriptions on the state."[152] While there are convincing elements in this argument about civil society as a whole after 1994, I would argue that women's organizations followed a somewhat different pattern. There is a danger in reading the decline of the coalition as a sign of the general decline of the women's movement. The coalition was made possible precisely because of the transition. As Frene Ginwala herself acknowledged in her final speech as convenor of the coalition, "the basis on which we were able to unite and maintain our unity was because we had a very specific and a very narrow objective and we need to be very careful that we don't run so fast, try and achieve so much, that we come apart. . . . One of the biggest challenges that we face . . . is to define a new relationship between women, women's organisation, the political processes, political parties and government in our country. Because we are entering a new era and we need to work out those relationships."[153]

The crisis of leadership was exacerbated by the 1994 decision to bar women parliamentarians from holding office in the organization, thus removing the crucial link between formal politics and the women's movement. Ginwala attempted to block this rule, noting the importance of maintaining an autonomous women's movement while also retaining leverage in arenas of power. "There is a danger that we will be co-opted by government; this has happened in so many countries. So let us use government resources, let us lobby government, but let us keep our independence as a women's movement, whatever its formation, so that we are not co-opted," she urged in that final speech. "But we need to find a balance. Let us not say: All politicians out. Our task is to infiltrate the political processes and therefore we have to establish a relationship and we have to find one that will balance and work in our favour."[154] Nevertheless, it was decided that the coalition should be firmly part of civil society.[155] It in unclear whether in fact women politicians would have continued to play any role in the coalition once elected to Parliament.

Loss of leadership alone does not account for the decline of the coalition. The base constituencies of the coalition were always relatively weak

organizations that had small local constituencies with few linkages to national politics. By the mid-1980s this was even true of the more political
women's organizations. This factor would suggest that the weak status of
the coalition may be temporary rather than inherent in the nature of political practice in a postmodern era or indicative of the impossibility of creating sustainable organizational forms for the women's movement. The focus
during the transition period was on high-profile national-level interventions that left little room or energy for bottom-up organizational development. The strength of alliance-based political structures derives from the
strength of its members, and any regeneration of the women's movement
will need to build from the bottom up. Democracy may indeed be more
conducive to such forms of organization. State repression in the 1980s put
enormous pressure on resistance movements to abandon attempts to build
democratic political cultures.

The lack of attention to organization building within the coalition itself,
however, was not linked to such repression. It stemmed in part from poor organizational resources, and in part from unresolved tensions within the coalition about the goals of the charter campaign. Both reasons underpinned
the inability of the coalition to recover from the loss of its first generation of
leaders. As a result the coalition never developed a coherent sense of long-
term purpose on the basis of internal experiences and debates. Transition
provided the glue that held the coalition together; its organizational form
became difficult to sustain once the external rationale was removed.

However, the fate of the coalition should not be seen as archetypal of the
women's movement. Rather than a complete decline—which would suggest
a lack of capacity to "generate and make autonomous democratic prescriptions on the state," as Neocosmos has described—after 1994 there was a process of reconfiguration and repositioning of women's organizations. There
was a shift from a national united women's movement to a more disaggregated movement with activism occurring at a number of different points in
the political system. While the idea of a national constituency of women
with a clear set of demands may no longer exist, a disaggregated women's
movement appears to have taken its place. Three main lines of fracture are
discernible. The national level has seen a proliferation of sectoral or issue-
based networks that are highly articulate about policy and have relatively
good access to the policy-making process. Examples of these are the National Network Against Violence Against Women, the Reproductive Rights
Alliance, and the Anti-Poverty Coalition. A different example at this level is
the coordinating and facilitating role played by the Commission on Gender
Equality in the first two years of its existence (although this role was not
sustained). The organizations and networks operating at this level do not
have any clearly defined constituency with whom they have an ongoing

relationship of mandate building and accountability, although they may indeed have broad moral accountability. The issue-based networks take a "critical engagement" approach to the state, rather than an adversarial one, while reserving more traditional forms of protest such as strikes and marches for moments when they seek to break negotiation deadlocks. Klugman has characterized this as "policy activism," a situation in which political action takes the form of advocacy.[156] A second level is the level of policy advocacy, relatively well supported by donor agencies and informed about the technical and research needs of the policy environment. Examples of such organizations are the Women's Development Foundation and the Gender Advocacy Programme. Here too, while constituencies are not always clear, there is a progressive commitment to marginalized communities. Finally, there is a mass of women's organizations at the local level that, while closest to women's constituencies, have neither the resources nor the technical expertise to influence policy making through the conventional institutional mechanisms and procedures. These organizations may continue to use social movement political tactics such as protest marches and boycotts, which may be able to connect them with either of the other two levels. An example here is the New Women's Movement and Black Sash protests against the reform of the child maintenance grant, which I discuss in chapter 7.

The question that remained for feminist activists was whether such a disaggregated movement can maintain a collective consciousness that would be available for national mobilization. To what extent could women in the political parties be effective in advocating women's interests if they were disconnected from the broader women's movement? As I show in the chapters that follow, the gains described in this chapter became highly vulnerable in the absence of a strong, independent, and united movement that could pose fundamental questions about policy priorities and hold the new government accountable for commitments made before its election.

Chapter 6

Political Parties, Quotas, and Representation in the New Democracy

Let us . . . say: I am woman; my concerns, my problems, my difficulties, my achievements are an integral part of our new society. No-one will succeed in marginalizing them or me. I am woman, I am South African, I am me. I go to Parliament but I am woman.

Frene Ginwala, comments upon leaving
the Women's National Coalition

Frene Ginwala's stirring words, uttered as she stepped down from leading the Women's National Coalition to take up her position as the Speaker in South Africa's first democratic Parliament, captured the optimistic mood of that phenomenal moment in the country's transition to democracy. For Ginwala, as for the many other women activists who moved from civil society into the state, entering Parliament was not a break with the women's movement but a continuation of women's struggles to break into a male-dominated domain. Ginwala's speech, however, promised more than continuity—she also promised to retain accountability to women, to act politically *as* a woman, and to refuse marginalization or dominance by political interests hostile to women's demands.

As could be expected, the inception of democracy in 1994 once again reshaped the terms under which women engaged in politics in South Africa. As in other new democracies, women's organizations turned to electoral strategies to achieve at least some of their goals.[1] The attention to political parties and electoral politics shifted the emphasis of women activists from the cross-party alliance-based approach of the transitional era to intraparty activity as the parties competed for voters. Although the value of women's cross-party mobilization, as expressed in the Women's National Coalition, continued to be asserted, the impetus and momentum provided by the drafting of the Women's Charter and by the constitutional debates was no longer present. The coalition leaders shifted their concern to the intraparty imperatives of ensuring that party platforms recognized gender and that women were represented on party lists in the proportional representation system. If the period from 1991 to 1994, which I discussed in chapter 5, can be characterized as an unfolding of interest-based women's politics, after 1994 we see a shift to electoral and bureaucratic politics. This has been a common pattern in postauthoritarian transitions and opened new sets of issues for South African feminists, as it did in other contexts. As Jacquette and Wolchik have shown, in Latin American countries "the return to democratic politics created unexpected problems for the women's movements and for social movements in general. The politics of the transition had been intense, with a strong emphasis on rhetoric and mass mobilization. Democracy meant that brave concepts had to be turned into workable legislation, that sustained organizational effort would be needed to ensure that women's issues would be taken up by the political parties, and that legislation would be implemented and monitored."[2]

Comparative literature suggests that all too often the shift from opposition to engaging the state from within is accompanied by the jettisoning of earlier concerns with the achievement of substantive equality.[3] In this and the next chapter I explore the extent to which South African women activists succeeded in ensuring that the demands made in the Women's Charter for Effective Equality and those represented in a range of political documents in the 1980s and early 1990s were articulated through state institutions. In this chapter I explore how women's organizations and the leadership of the women's movement sought to insert themselves and their concerns into electoral politics and what the implications of this engagement were for retaining the relatively autonomous voice of women vis-à-vis political parties. I also examine the debates about the representation of women as a constituency in the new democracy and explore the extent to which political parties were open to the presence and interests of women members.

Women's organizations' demands for greater participation and representation in liberation movements, political parties, and politics in general came into sharp relief with the advent of representative democracy. As I showed in chapter 4, women activists were suspicious of the notion that the formal right to vote would necessarily lead to better policy outcomes for women. Formal membership in political parties and liberation movements had not increased women's political power to any significant degree. However, the women's movement saw as strategically necessary the increased representation of women in elected offices and the greater visibility of "women's concerns" in national political debates. Initially, this led to an intense focus on numbers—that is, measuring the extent of women's participation and a concern about the nature and quality of representation and participation. By the 1999 elections, however, the *quality* of women's participation had emerged as a central area of debate. By then the interventions of women's organizations in electoral politics reflected a concern with specific policy issues and party platforms, and with the relationship between elected women representatives and women voters.

While these shifts suggest a maturing of women's electoral politics in this period and a consolidation of women as an electoral constituency, the extent to which women's policy leverage has increased as a result of representation remains the key question. By the June 1999 election the conception of constituency among women's organizations—the perception, so successfully advanced during the negotiations period, that women shared a set of political concerns regardless of race and class position or party ideology—advanced significantly beyond broad formulations. While representation and participation remained key concerns, there was a much deeper consideration of the strategic uses of political leverage. This was facilitated by a dense network of organizational initiatives to pressure political parties to consider both the quality and the extent of women's representation on their party lists, to challenge parties on the gender implications of their platforms, and to engage in interest group politics around specific policy initiatives. The process of constituency building among women intensified during both electoral periods although, as this chapter will show, electoral outcomes were not solely (or perhaps even primarily) responsible for increasing women's political leverage in the representative sphere.

In this chapter I argue that limitations on women's political effectiveness in South Africa are set by two factors, both relating to the political universe within which women act. The first is the rules and procedures of institutional engagement within which parties operate and over which women have had little influence. These rules and procedures are not only the formal characteristics of the political system (some of which are relatively easily changed) but also the subtle yet deeply entrenched patterns of power and authority within male-dominated institutions. The second limitation on addressing the agenda of substantive equality outlined in the Women's Charter is the tendency within the women's movement to privilege the leadership of women within the African National Congress (ANC) at the expense of developing relatively autonomous leadership. The leadership of the ANC women activists was, as the previous chapters have outlined, a prime reason for the successes of the women's movement in the transitional period and drove the feminist agenda within Parliament. However, by the end of the first democratic Parliament, it was evident that representation, even within a majority party committed to the principles of gender equality, offered no guarantees for women. A broadening of democratic commitment in the political system as a whole and the strengthening of the women's movement outside the state are also needed if women are to be effective in the formal representative realm.

Playing the Numbers Game

As I showed in chapter 5, the idea that women, as a group, constituted an electoral constituency entered South African politics in the early 1990s.[4] The interests that were seen to hold this constituency together, however, were narrowly defined in terms of a common exclusion from the processes and forums of public decision making. Indeed, the prime focus of the Women's National Coalition had been inclusivity. The focus on "getting women in"— that is, onto party lists, to a large extent regardless of political ideology— held together a diverse range of women's organizations and gender ideologies in the period before the 1994 elections. Debate focused on mechanisms to achieve women's representation—most notably, the quota—rather than on the particular interests of different groups of women.

Accompanying the drive to "get women in" was a concurrent emphasis on "getting women's vote out."[5] Women's organizations (and, to a lesser extent, political parties) were concerned that the higher levels of illiteracy, poverty, and spatial marginality would prejudice women's right to exercise their vote. In addition, it was feared that a combination of political violence and patriarchal control would keep women out of the electoral process. Women's organizations therefore devoted a significant percentage of their efforts to voter education campaigns directed at women. These two broad formulations of women's interests—ensuring the representation and participation of women in the electoral process—constituted the ambit of gender politics in the April 1994 election. Demands made by the coalition for women's representation in decision-making structures finally found support among political parties, especially within the ANC. Within these terms the strategic approach of the women's movement was successful. The Transitional Executive Council formed the Sub-Council on the Status of Women and charged it with the specific task of removing any obstacles to the participation of women in the election, both as voters and as candidates. As table

Table 6.1. Representation of Women in Parliament, 1994 to 2004

Party	1994 Total reps.	No. of women	Percent women	1999 Total reps.	No. of women	Percent women	2004 Total reps.	No. of women	Percent women
African National Congress	252	90	35.7	266	95	35.7	279	104	37
Democratic Party/Democratic Alliance	7	1	14	38	6	15.7	50	13	26
Inkatha Freedom Party	43	10	23	33	9	27.2	28	5	18.5
National Party/New National Party	82	9	10	28	4	14.2	7	0	0
United Democratic Movement				14	1	7	9	4	44.4
Independent Democrats							7	3	43
African Christian Democratic Party	2	0	0	6	2	33	6	2	33.3
Freedom Front				3	0	0	4	0	0
United Christian Democratic Party				3	1	33	3	0	0
Pan Africanist Congress	5	1	20	3	0	0	3	0	0
Other				5	2	40	4	0	0
Total	**400**	**111**	**27.7**	**400**	**120**	**30**	**400**	**131**	**32.75**

Source: Unpublished data compiled by Colleen Lowe-Morna, Gender Links, Johannesburg, 2004.

6.1 shows, women increased their representation in Parliament in the course of the three national elections. As a result of the first democratic election in 1994, women constituted a record 27.7 percent of all parliamentarians elected, placing South Africa in the ranks of the top ten democracies—seventh highest—in the world on this indicator.[6] This statistic was widely used locally and internationally to signal the extent to which the new democracy was inclusive and enhanced the image of South Africa as a "good citizen" in the eyes of the world. Although not all parties used a quota for women, for reasons that I will outline shortly, the extent of women's representation emboldened women activists and engendered a sense of optimism about the possibilities for shaping legislative and policy priorities. Furthermore, for the 1999 election slightly more than 1.5 million more women than men registered to vote. This figure suggests that women were informed citizens with regard to the mechanics of voting and that, at least at the procedural level, women were not disadvantaged.

Representation: A Good in Itself?

It is not surprising that women's organizations pursued a strong representational strategy in advance of the 1994 election. An obvious reason is that the liberal democracy crafted by negotiators demanded that feminists devise a strategy appropriate within the context of a multiparty electoral system; that is, the political context required that feminists interrogate the possibilities for increasing women's representation in the conventional institutional sites. The electoral strategy can also be seen as a continuation of women's struggles for representation and participation in the decision-making bodies of both the ANC in exile and the United Democratic Front. In relation to the new democracy women activists sought to hold representative democracy—or government by elected leaders—to the promise that it offered citizens the opportunity to select the representatives they preferred and to remove them from office if they failed to perform. In pursuing representation women activists were equally concerned that it should offer the opportunity for enforcing accountability to constituencies of women through proper institutional mechanisms.

An extensive body of feminist literature has been concerned with the ways in which representative democracy might be designed to ensure women's political participation. This literature shows that women citizens in most democracies face a problem of both representation and accountability. The possession of formal political equality, the vote, does not necessarily translate into representation, even in the broadest sense of the presence of women in representative institutions. Even if representation is significantly increased, some analysts argue, representative democracies fail to deliver accountability.[7] Elections that are free and fair in the procedural sense do not necessarily produce outcomes that reflect the diversity of either interests or identities in societies. Anne Phillips has pointed out that the notable absence of women in legislatures points to a fundamental weakness in democracies and constitutes a political problem for democrats committed to substantial and not merely procedural democracy.

Transitions to democracy offer unique opportunities for women to influence how democracy is broadly conceived. The restructuring of a more inclusive political system provides an important context in which women can advance their particular representational claims. An important factor is the extent to which the new democracy retains group-based notions of representation. Although women's movement demands for special representation of women are a form of group-based claim, the very idea of institutionalizing group representation can be disadvantageous to women.[8] Paradoxically for women, group-based representation can lead to the entrenchment of the power of conservative elites (e.g., traditional leaders, other religious and cultural elites) that find gender equality threatening to their status. While representation of such groups may provide short-term stability in postconflict situations, it does not adequately address the need for redistribution of power to economically and socially marginal groupings.

Despite these tensions between women's claims and those of other groups, the broader political context of a multiparty competitive electoral system required that feminists interrogate the possibilities for increasing women's representation in the conventional institutional sites. As Phillips has argued, within representative democracies political parties offer the most substantial vehicles for advancing group claims to representation, and feminists therefore cannot ignore parties.[9] This strategy derived also from earlier struggles within the ANC, in which women pursued representation in its highest decision-making structures. In relation to the new democracy women activists sought to hold representative democracy—or government by elected leaders—to the promise that it offered citizens the opportunity to select the representatives they preferred and to remove representatives from office should they fail to perform. However, it is important to note, as I showed in earlier chapters, that in pursuing representation, women activists allied to the ANC were equally concerned that representation would offer the opportunity to enforce accountability to constituencies of women through proper institutional mechanisms.

Rianne Mahon and Jane Jenson have pointed to two forms of representation. The first is the "representation of self to others via the creation of a collective identity."[10] The second form is interest representation through parties and civil society organizations. Both forms are important because they involve "the power to give meaning and visibility to social relations, and thereby the power to represent and dispute interests."[11] Quota demands tend to emphasize the creation of collective identity; they rest on the successful articulation of women's group-based interest in entering arenas of power. This strategy derives from the marginal status that most women occupy in society and entails a collective demand for recognition that can win support across class, race, and ideological lines. Interest group representation, on the other hand, may shatter the notion of women as a homogeneous group as the resource claims of some women, based on their class and/or race disadvantages, may come into conflict with the interests of other women or require privileging the building of alliances with other social actors. In the South African experience these forms of representation have not been seen as contradictory but rather as being in creative tension.

Although women activists in South Africa did not explicitly draw on such theoretical frameworks, their demands for representation were seen as a necessary step in creating accountable and responsive government. There was, furthermore, an explicit view that increasing women's representation in Parliament would improve policy outcomes for women. This view was all the stronger among women activists in the ANC who could present the policy proposals developed after the Malibongwe Conference and in the course of formulating the Reconstruction and Development Programme as the basis of policy reforms in the new state. The idea that participation would lead to increased representation and hence to shifts in the allocation of public resources to address women's needs can be understood in terms of a virtuous political circle. The concern that traditional electoral processes will not improve women's chances of representation has led to demands for quotas, which are seen as a means of fast-tracking women's representation and hence kick-starting a virtual political circle.

Debates on Representation and Quotas

Women activists have used the formal commitment to equality, embodied in both the Interim Constitution of 1994 and the final Constitution ratified in 1996, to argue that the underrepresentation of women in Parliament is undesirable. However, in the first years of the new democracy South African feminists could reach no consensus about how to achieve greater representation and were especially undecided about whether quotas were the appropriate mechanism to adopt.

Two broad approaches to the problem of representation for women may be discerned in South African debates. The first focuses on nonstate social and economic forces rather than on the institutions of democracy, whereas the second offers a radical questioning of the institutional underpinnings of representative democracy. In political debates those on both sides are not always logical or consistent. Rather, the shifting positions on representation, both *between* and *within* political parties, reflect an inherent tension between liberal and social democratic versions of democracy, elements of both of which are to be found in the Constitution.[12] The first perspective, which may be broadly characterized as liberal, presents the most common opposition to special mechanisms for increasing women's representation using democratic arguments. It is the perspective held by the Zulu-nationalist Inkatha Freedom Party and the liberal Democratic Party, the official opposition to the majority ANC in the South African Parliament. This perspective is shared, paradoxically, by the radical Pan Africanist Congress. It may also be found in commonsense reactions against group representation. The second perspective is social democratic and articulates strong arguments for the need to create mechanisms for women's representation. Taking the creation of substantive democracy as its cue, the ANC articulates this position. As I showed in chapter 5, this position is by no means uncontested within the ANC.[13]

Liberals may argue that the problems of representative democracy for women stem from inequalities in civil society. That is, formal institutions cannot be held to account for injustices and imbalances in power among citizens, whether these are of class, race, or gender in their origin. As Williams has pointed out, representation within this framework is seen in procedural and individualistic terms: "As long as all citizens have an equal opportunity to influence the electoral process, the outcome of that process is fair, whatever it happens to be."[14] From this perspective institutions are neutral reproducers of external relations. Possession of the franchise has not resulted in the political representation of women as a group for reasons *external* to political institutions. These include the relative weight given to issues of gender equality in national politics, the internal processes of mobility and influence within political parties, and socioeconomic constraints on women's political participation. The solution to women's underrepresentation lies in the removal of these blockages over the longer term through the economic and social empowerment of women that accompanies modernization. This gradualist argument assumes that as more women enter the workforce (the economic realm), and as discriminatory practices such as job stereotyping are removed and educational opportunities are spread evenly between the genders, women will move into the public political realm in greater numbers. The implication of this approach is that issues of gender equality in public policy and government are deferred, either until a sufficient number of women representatives are elected through traditional electoral processes or/and until women voters organize as an electoral constituency. Alternatively, liberals might argue—as the Democratic Party did in the debates about the Women's Charter that I outlined in chapter 5— that the persistent underrepresentation of women is a signal that gender is simply not a significant marker of electoral preferences and behavior.

Opposition to affirmative action strategies by feminists within the Democratic Party and National Party was consistent with their broader party ideologies. From a liberal point of view, the fixing of identity politics, and of group as opposed to individual interests, results in an undesirable expansion of regulatory mechanisms. Indeed, a common argument made in South Africa is that there are more than enough formal enabling mechanisms for women at the moment, including the Constitution, the Office on the Status of Women, and the Commission on Gender Equality.[15] These expand the scope and responsibilities of the state beyond the classical liberal definition, and their use therefore has to be limited if individual autonomy is to be protected. Embedded in the gradualist position is a wariness of the granting of special status to specific groups, stemming from a concern that it reduces the choices of individual voters. Specifying groups and group interests in the formal mechanisms of representation runs counter to liberal individualism, and to the extent that representative democracy is embedded in liberalism, reshaping its institutions to account for inequalities is seen as an assault on individual freedom.

The Democratic Party's leading feminist, Dene Smuts, has argued that quotas are unnecessary—"It's automatic. If there is a good candidate, she will be elected. People do not think twice about it now."[16] MP Kate Prinsloo of the Democratic Party has argued that the quota system in fact "lets political parties off the hook with regard to women's empowerment. It creates the impression that the issue has been dealt with and leads to the view that those who are elected say everything's OK, we come from grassroots organizations and therefore we [are] equipped to speak for women."[17]

By contrast, the New National Party has tended to be more reactive to the way in which gender issues are articulated by the ANC, which has allowed some room for gender activists within the NNP to make inroads into leadership despite the absence of a clear policy on gender equality. While the NNP also officially rejects quotas, some women activists within the party do support for quotas. Tersia Wessels, a member of the Gauteng Executive Council for the party, has acknowledged that the ANC's use of a quota had a positive influence on the party list of the New National Party, and as a result the party made more active efforts to include women in leadership positions.[18] Anna van Wyk, a member of Parliament and executive member of the National Party's Women's Action Group, has argued that "gender should ultimately be eliminated as a criterion for choosing MPs, but in the meanwhile we need affirmative action." She also has argued for "gender parity in party executives."[19] The United Democratic Movement is also opposed to quotas, arguing that quotas are "an insult to women."[20]

However, arguments against emphasizing institutional reform are not confined to liberalism. Radical populist arguments have also been advanced in South African debates, this time to show the dangers of representation deriving from hierarchical mechanisms of decision making. Special representation produces tokenism from this point of view, articulated most clearly by Patricia de Lille, the most senior woman in the Pan Africanist Congress and now leader of the Independent Democrats. In practice, the PAC has not paid much attention to developing strong internal democracy within the party, despite the creation in April 1986 of a women's wing known as the African Women's Organisation. Similarly, the Azanian Peoples Organisation (AZAPO) has argued that, rather than applying a quota, women need to be "empowered from the bottom up."[21] AZAPO's women's wing, Imbeleko, seeks to encourage women's self-reliance, although this appears to be understood within a more conventional "self-help" framework rather than one that is explicitly political.[22] Furthermore, AZAPO is poorly established as an electoral party, did not even contest the 1994 elections, and in 1999 won only one seat. Given these limitations, the ability of radical populist parties to shape the debate on representation has been minimal.

A more consistent and politically influential position has been offered by the Congress of South African Trade Unions, a member of the "triple alliance" and an important influence at ANC congresses. In 1996 trade unionists established the September Commission, chaired by Connie September, their former deputy vice president, to investigate the challenges facing the labor movement. The September Commission's report, completed in 1997, included a chapter on building a movement of women workers, which examined how women could be empowered within the union federation. Noting the underrepresentation of women (15 percent of regional leadership and 8 percent of national leadership), the commission recommended the adoption of a number of mechanisms to accelerate the empowerment of women, including a quota of women for elected positions.[23] The commission proposed a target of 50 percent representation of women in all structures by 2000.[24] Since 1985 the trade unionists' Women's Forum has argued vigorously for affirmative action to increase the number of women at leadership level in the organization. Several unions with predominantly female membership had in fact implemented some form of quota and reported relative progress at the 1997 Congress of the Congress of South African Trade Unions, where the membership discussed the September Commission report.[25] The ANC's adoption of a quota for national elections provided an influential example, with the ANC Women's League and the South African Communist Party supporting the September Commission's proposal.

However, opposition to the quota was widespread among delegates to the trade unions' congress. Their opposition was based on a number of reasons, including "that the quota is insulting to women, as it assumes they need special treatment . . . that women's empowerment should start at the factory floor . . . that they do not want 'comrade mamas' sitting up there unable to argue positions."[26] The congress decided to "develop a programme on building women's leadership within a broad political programme, with measurable targets to be finalised by the Central Executive Committee."[27] Connie September said that "the mere fact that the issue [of representation] was put robustly on the agenda, and we robustly articulated the struggle as for nonracialism *and* nonsexism, and we can't put nonsexism on the back burner—that changed things. In unions, where you didn't think women would be elected, you are seeing changes. We have made exciting strides regarding representation at the level of leadership."[28]

The trade unions' debate is interesting in this context because it offers a view of women's representation that is located within a progressive political framework and is shaped within a context of a strong emphasis on democratic accountability. In the view of trade unionists opposed to the use of quotas, representatives elected through such mechanisms are less likely to act on the basis of mandates from the people and are more likely to seek favor with political elites. Such mechanisms as quotas are open to manipulation by party elites and act as barriers to direct accountability of party leaders to members. The solution is to ensure that women have popular support from the bottom of political structures rather than from the top and that a change in consciousness among members results in their freely choosing women representatives. From this point of view incremental changes that take place within a culture of internal democracy are preferable to "quick fixes." There are two caveats to be made here, however. First, the demand for a quota came from women activists within the union federation who argued that the culture of participation was limited by patriarchal norms that thrived within the male-dominated movement.[29] Second, as the South African Communist Party pointed out in its message to the 1997 trade union congress, such arguments can be glibly used to avoid interim mechanisms that can be used to rapidly advance women's representation. "The SACP believes that the debate on the quota should be located in the context of an understanding of the relationship between apartheid, patriarchy and capitalism. The quota system deals with the structural inequalities and barriers that exist, creating the space for women to take up leadership. The irony is that the unions support affirmative action in the workplace but not in the unions."

Nevertheless, debates on the quota within the Congress of South African Trade Unions raise the important question of whether representative democracy can deliver on what it promises: representative and accountable government. Paul Hirst has argued that "modern representative democracy has predominantly functioned as a means of legitimating governmental power, rather than of making government effectively accountable and open to public influence. . . . While mass democracy gives the electorate a real power to choose some of the major ruling personnel, it also routinizes and minimizes political participation."[30] This analysis would suggest that the nature of representation—in particular, the relationship between electoral constituencies and representatives—needs to be examined at least as closely as the right to representation per se. These concerns have been consistently raised in South African debates about representation. For example, at a 1992 workshop on women in democratic government, delegates grappled with "exactly whose interests they would represent if they were elected to Parliament."[31] As I will discuss later in this chapter, these arguments have implications for accountability within representative democracies.

As I showed in earlier chapters, attempts to address gender gaps in representation have a long history in South Africa. Yet, despite differences over the use of quotas, neither women's organizations nor feminist writers have argued that women form an undifferentiated political constituency. On the contrary, a central feature of women's politics in the 1990s was the notion of difference—of class, race, age, location, and ethnicity.[32] Even accounting for such differences, it is relatively easy to show the salience of women as a category in electoral politics because of the glaring disparities between the population of women voters and the numbers of women in elected bodies, even in contexts where formal equality is an established norm.[33] Furthermore, it is not difficult to argue that a pragmatic interest in representation per se *is* common to all women, regardless of class, race, and ideological differences. The demand for greater representation in its broadest formulation does not prejudge the ways in which gender inequalities will be taken up by representatives once in the legislature. The issue is, rather, one of access to arenas of public decision making so that the various interests of women can be debated and acted upon. As Jane Mansbridge has pointed out, without broad representation it is unlikely that the complexities of social inequalities (including those of gender) can be fully appreciated in policy terms.[34] One significant result of the widespread debate about the quota in 1994 is that virtually all political parties in South Africa have formally accepted the need for greater women's representation.[35]

Representation: Electoral Outcomes

Women's electoral politics has benefited from the creation of a range of mechanisms, including a constitutional provision, to advance gender equality in the democratic state. These mechanisms, agreed to by the Constitutional Assembly in 1996, provided a legitimizing framework and facilitated the advancement of gender claims. The constitutional clause on equality establishes gender equality as the core principle and value of South African democracy. This provision has had far-reaching formal influence, in that both political parties and the Independent Electoral Commission have to ensure that women's participation is not prejudiced in any way by the nature of electoral campaigns or by the procedural aspects of the elections.[36] In addition, the presence of gender activists among members of the Independent Electoral Commission facilitated attention to gender issues in the work of the commission.

The increase in women MPs resulted from the electoral system that South Africa chose—proportional representation on a list basis—as it has been shown to significantly advance women's representation in a number of countries.[37] This choice was dictated in the first instance by nongender considerations such as providing incentives to smaller parties to pursue political mobilization within the formal political system and encouraging larger parties to seek support outside their traditional constituencies. At any rate, the outcome for women's representation was dramatic. A key reason is that the proportional representation list allows considerable latitude to party leaders to determine the candidate slates and, from the perspective of women candidates, to use the list mechanism to override traditional sentiments against women in politics.

This advantage for the women's movement also has a number of inherent disadvantages that may undermine other feminist concerns. Proportional representation systems contain a built-in bias toward a centralist form of internal politics that may be antithetical to the emphasis of the women's movement on democratic culture, thereby reinforcing the range of obstacles to women's power within parties, which I discuss later in this chapter. A related consequence is the possibility that party leaders will choose women candidates who are token representatives, least likely to upset the political applecart, rather than those candidates with strong links to autonomous women's organizations. In addition, the proportional representation system favors accountability of representatives to political parties in the first instance, rather than to electoral constituencies. It places primary stress on intraparty lobbying, rather than constituency preference, as the route to electoral success. The power of party elites mitigates against building strong branch-level structures, and the system undercuts the ability to develop constituencies that can articulate interests from the bottom up, if need be, against the official position of party leadership. Again, this runs counter to notions of accountability that were emphasized within the women's organizations discussed in chapter 2. I will return to these concerns later.

Although the proportional representation system facilitated the use of a quota to ensure representation of women in Parliament, the ANC was the only political party to use the mechanism. The adoption of a quota in 1993 appears to have been a response by ANC leaders to the failed quota proposal for party positions at the ANC's 1992 conference. Following this failure, gender activists within the ANC continued to lobby for a quota. When the internal procedure for deciding on electoral lists was discussed, women activists successfully included the following clause: "Affirmative action for women will be a central part of being representative and we need to ensure that no less than one third of the lists are women. (They are 50 percent of the electorate.) The ANC policy has been consistent in supporting the need for affirmative action and gender equality. The people we elect to represent us in government will be responsible for representing the people of South Africa, not the ANC, and this makes it even more important that we ensure that no less than one third of the lists are made up of women."[38] The ANC's adoption of the quota is widely believed to have had a domino effect for other political parties, resulting in the election of a relatively high number of women to Parliament in 1994.[39] The outcome was similar in the 1999 elections, enhanced by the large majority of votes won by the ANC.

Increasing Women's Leverage within Parliament

Getting women into Parliament in large numbers was only one part of the task of representation. Another was ensuring that women MPs had some leverage in relation to policy decisions. In the South African parliamentary system, decisions are made at two crucial sites, the cabinet and the portfolio committees. Women's participation in these sites in crucial to exercising leverage. Equally important is women's standing within the ruling party. Yet comparative research on women who have entered the representational sphere suggests that entry does not usually translate into upward mobility within the hierarchy of a parliament. In a wide-ranging comparison of women parliamentarians in European democracies, Joni Lovenduski found that women are kept at the bottom of legislative hierarchies and that the proportion of women in legislatures and their representation in executive bodies are not balanced.[40] This was found to be true even for Scandinavian countries, which have a long history of using quotas for women in various forms. Vicky Randall reached a similar conclusion, noting that "at the apex of the representational hierarchy within national governments, women often virtually disappear."[41] When women do break into higher levels of Parliament, a distinct gender pattern in the allocation of ministerial portfolios emerges.[42] Women are generally appointed to "soft" ministries—family, welfare, and culture, a pattern that Lovenduski regards as a further aspect of gatekeeping, whereby the few women who are appointed to the ministerial level are relegated to less important posts.

Interestingly, South Africa does not easily fit this pattern. Following the 1994 election, women accounted for 15 percent of ministers (four of twenty-seven) and 56 percent of deputy ministers (eight out of fourteen) in the cabinet. This suggests that women were significantly represented at the highest levels compared to the proportion of women in Parliament. Although the "social" portfolios (health, welfare, housing) were assigned to women, these are key areas of social services that formed the cornerstone of the ANC's electoral platforms in both elections. Moreover, the deputy ministers of "hard" portfolios—finance and trade and industry—in the 1994–98 Parliament were also women. A more significant gender pattern can be found in examining the membership of portfolio committees in Parliament during this period. Women's representation ranged from zero (public accounts) to 73 percent (health).[43] Committees that women dominated included welfare (60 percent) and communications (66 percent). Women were notably underrepresented in land affairs (18 percent), mineral and energy (12 percent), transportation (12 percent), foreign affairs (12 percent), and labor (19 percent).[44] After the 1999 election the new president, Thabo Mbeki, consolidated women's position in the cabinet, with eight women ministers (of twenty-nine) and eight deputy ministers (of thirteen). This was maintained in the 2004 cabinet. In 2005, following the sacking of Jacob Zuma by President Mbeki, former NOW chairperson Phumzile Mlambo-Ngcuka was appointed deputy president.

The South African case therefore contrasts with the European pattern. Women are significantly represented at the highest levels compared to the proportion of women in the South African Parliament. A similar situation exists in Australia, where Moon and Fountain have found that "Australian women's political fortunes improve as they move from the party to the parliamentary arena."[45] Their explanation for the countertrend is twofold. First, they argue that, in parties of the left, party "gatekeepers" are responsive to the notion that selection of women is good for the party. They are therefore prepared to circumvent, through the use of the party list, traditional cultural and structural obstacles to women's political mobility. Second, Moon and Fountain argue that once women are in Parliament, they are more likely to be judged on merit rather than on their gender. Given that women have to be twice as good as men to overcome intraparty obstacles to their selection, those who are elected to Parliament are likely to be better qualified than their male counterparts. There are important resonances on both counts in the South African case. The ANC, the majority party in all three democratic Parliaments, was highly responsive to demands for gender representation (if not always to quotas), and this has underpinned many party policies. Furthermore, the women's movement has made some inroads into public debate, contributing to a climate in which gender representation is part of the democratic discourse. This has given some leverage to women's sections within political parties to win support for increased representation. The capacities and inclinations of women's sections to play this role therefore have to be carefully examined, as well as the extent to which women in Parliament can act as the crucial link between women's organizations outside the state and decision-making forums within the state. In a democracy access to and power within representative institutions is an important—although, as other chapters of this book emphasize, by no means the sole—route to the advancement of the policy demands of the women's movement, and the link between women in political parties and the women's movement is vital.

There is no doubt that the influx of a vast number of women to Parliament had a dramatic effect on the culture and tone of the institution. In the South African Parliament, as in other legislatures where women made inroads, the mere presence of women "inevitably change[d] existing arrangements and procedures. . . . Parliamentary timetables, places of meeting, childcare provisions, working hours and travel arrangements may be changed to make these more suitable for women."[46] The long-term effect of even these minimal changes was to make Parliament more accessible to women, thus increasing the possibility that more women will being willing to stand as candidates in future elections, regardless of the implementation of special mechanisms.

The (Im)Permeability of Political Parties

The relationship of women to parties and politics in the transition and post-transition periods, and the conditions under which, in Waylen's terms, "conventional political activity" is reconstituted, remains relatively underexplored in third world feminist literature.[47] Literature on women's relationship to the state has tended to focus on the ways in which states have affected women's social and economic position, with little attention to the internal character of particular states from a gender perspective. Some analysts, such as Naomi Chazan, have argued that African women have played no significant role in statecraft.[48] There is virtually no existing theoretical literature about the experience of women in African political parties.

Two broad reasons can be identified for the lack of attention to a gendered analysis of political parties in newly democratizing countries.[49] First, women's movements have tended to avoid political parties because they are seen as (and often are) bastions of male power from which women are either excluded or, when they are included, co-opted.[50] In many African countries where nationalist movements have transformed themselves into political parties, women's secondary status in the nationalist movement has been replicated in the new political order. Mobilizing styles also can exclude women when they may lead to violent conflict. In many countries, such as Uganda, Zimbabwe, and Malawi, the dominance of a single party and the discouragement of politics outside that party have limited the extent of civil society development. This lack of political space available for civil society organization can reinforce the exclusion of women from the public sphere and enhance perceptions that political parties are for men. Tripp has argued that in authoritarian systems, parties have actively repressed women's autonomous associational life in the interests of co-opting women to the legitimation projects of the single ruling party. These experiences produce a profound mistrust of parties and politics and a tendency to seek disengagement from the state and from politics.[51] The co-opting of women's organizations by nationalist movements and then by the ruling parties further undermines any expectations that association with political parties might lead to better policy outcomes for women.[52] Second, parties in many developing countries are poorly developed as political institutions per se. In many African countries parties are not constituted with the strong rules and procedures that would allow for open and democratic internal debate and for access of rank-and-file members to leadership. As Anne Marie Goetz and I have argued elsewhere, "Parties may be such blatantly hollow vehicles for kleptocratic families or ethnic groups, lacking any but the flimsiest organisational structures, decision-making processes, and ideologies, that there is simply nothing there for women to engage with."[53]

In South Africa parties are comparatively well institutionalized. The ANC had developed strong centralized structures in exile that facilitated the transition to an electoral party although not necessarily to a deeply democratic one. White parties were highly institutionalized because of their participation in the electoral process under apartheid. And yet, at both ends of the political spectrum, women's engagement with political parties has been as subordinate members. Political parties have not been comfortable homes for women activists. As I showed in earlier chapters, internal democracy and responsiveness have been difficult to create in both internal and exile political organizations. Political parties in South Africa, as elsewhere, have been male-dominated institutions, even while their ideological impetus has been provided by liberationist discourses and agendas.[54]

These factors explain why women's ambivalence toward political parties and politics produces what Waylen has called the dilemma of "autonomy versus integration. Should women's movements work with the new institutions and parties and risk being co-opted and losing autonomy, or should they remain outside, preserving their independence but risking marginalization and loss of influence as power shifts toward the political parties? No definitive answer has emerged."[55] But for most women's movements in Africa, there is little choice about whether to work with political parties. Liberation movements—precursors to parties—have been the primary vehicles for women's political participation. In the postliberation period, whether they institutionalize as parties, as in South Africa, or cling to the more amorphous "movement" form, they remain the central mechanism for channeling political demands. Rarely are women activists—or oppositional social movements in general—able to build a successful movement outside the ruling party, and where they do, it is against enormous resistance from the party. As Hope Chigudu and Wilfred Tichagwa have asked, "Do [women] have an alternative power base [to the party]? Would they survive if they relied solely on the alternative power base? To both questions the answer is probably no!!"[56]

Under what conditions, then, can feminists successfully engage political parties? In South Africa at least some favorable conditions exist for making the representative system more responsive to women's demands. A positive outcome of struggles for political representation is that political parties have been forced to consider women as an important voting constituency, and this can offer an important lever for women within political parties. Research conducted by the Commission on Gender Equality before the 1999 election showed that all parties had identified women as "voting populations."[57] Parties emphasized the need to recruit women and to increase women's participation in party structures, not least because women form the majority of supporters of the two largest political parties in the country.[58] The most vociferous opponent of quotas for women, the Democratic Party, conducted an audit of party membership that found that 40 percent of its branch chairs and 33 percent of its local council members were women,[59] although only 18 percent of its MPs were women. Despite its principled opposition to quotas, the party, like most others that have representation in Parliament, constantly reiterates its commitment to increased gender representation.

Although it is true that parties are the key gatekeepers to elected office, certain types of parties—those on the left of the political spectrum—are more likely to accommodate women's representational claims and to incorporate concerns about gender equality into their electoral platforms and policy priorities.[60] As I have shown, in South Africa the ANC and its allies have been more open to women's demands. Nevertheless, even left-wing political parties have to be treated with caution by the women's movement.

As Dahlerup has shown, leftist parties have a tendency to "alter feminist demands and use them for their own purpose."[61] This process of co-opting the objectives of the women's movement may lead to some short-term concessions in areas that are less costly and less contentious — for example, recognizing women's special needs in relation to childbirth and child rearing — while not necessarily shifting the basic gender inequalities in access to the labor market. This can lead to a deradicalization of feminism.[62]

Based on Scandinavian experiences, Dahlerup has suggested that one factor in ensuring that parties support feminist demands — as opposed to narrower demands for an increase in numerical representation — is the strength of activism in the women's committees within the party and of women activists within the party. The success of this is likely to be limited in the South African case. As I argued in chapter 3, while the ANC Women's Section and the ANC Women's League have had some success in winning broad commitments from the ANC, it has been pressure from *outside* the movement, through structures such as the Women's National Coalition, that have forced the ANC to live up to its commitments. The second part of Dahlerup's argument is more pertinent in the South African case: the position of women within the parties needs to be strengthened by a powerful women's movement outside the party.[63] Her research shows the importance of an autonomous women's movement; where women's organizations are too close to political parties, they can simply become stepping-stones to party positions.

Arguments that emphasize the use of internal party mechanisms for the advancement of women therefore need to bear in mind that women in decision-making positions will be effective and accountable only to the extent that there is a strong women's movement in civil society acting as a pressure group and an accountability mechanism. This suggests that the emphasis on internal party reform (such as quotas) has to be supplemented by a focus on conditions external to the political party; that is, we need to look at the broader political context in which parties operate to assess the extent to which they are likely to be responsive to women's demands and the extent to which women's representational and policy demands are likely to be co-opted into projects that are not of their own choosing. The relationship between parties and women's movements may be synergistic rather than purely competitive or antagonistic, but in either case it is an unavoidable relationship for third world feminists. This is particularly true in South Africa, where parties have been the main vehicles through which women have made political advances and where civil society is both relatively weak and relatively conservative on gender issues.

However, both an internal and external focus with regard to political parties raises the issue of how constituencies emerge within and around political parties and, specifically, how constituencies of women emerge. It is not surprising that the commitments of the United Democratic Front and the ANC to the values of equality, participation, and social justice opened spaces for women's activism to take heightened forms. Even so, in both organizations it took a concerted struggle by women over a relatively long period of time to make limited inroads into leadership. It is important to recognize the positive effect of these struggles on those formations: without the kind of internal "party" reforms of the 1980s (the focus that women brought to bear on how decisions were made, by whom, and which issues were taken up first), it is unlikely that the ANC would have been so receptive to demands for representation and participation of women during the multiparty negotiations. The women's movement thus benefited enormously from the alliance with leftist political organizations. Concomitantly, the absence of such a history has affected the ability of women in the New National Party and the Democratic Party to make room in the parties' highest structures, as the discussion in the next section shows.

The Internal Politics of Constituency Building

In 1994 Jenny Schreiner, an activist in the ANC and South African Communist Party and subsequently a member of Parliament from ANC, suggested that women in the ANC should "bargain" with their male colleagues to take up gender issues. "We, women in the ANC, should consider approaching men and women nominees for our national and regional candidates lists on this basis: if you take up the issues of women such as job training, child care, access to permanent jobs for women, as part of what you campaign for in reconstruction during the election campaign, then we will vote for you and mobilize votes for you from branch to national level. This can be done to get women on the national list, as well as to make men on the list more sensitive to gender issues."[64]

Although the idea was not pursued within the ANC, Schreiner's concern about how to concretize the party's broad commitments to gender reflected an important aspect of women's organizations' activism in both the 1994 and 1996 elections. In 1994 the feminist journal *Agenda* published a set of questions for candidates, urging readers to "measure the parties by their responses, and tell them we want action, not answers!"[65] Women's organizations campaigned loudly to ensure that the majority of political parties expressed a commitment to gender equality in their electoral platforms. For the most part, though, the results were rhetorical commitments, thin on policy detail.[66] By the 1999 elections the response of women's organizations was to intensify the demands on parties at public forums, demanding greater policy specificity.[67] This was most evident with regard to the debate about offering HIV/AIDS drugs to pregnant women and to rape survivors, when gender activists pushed women representatives from different parties to declare their position on a key health policy issue. The Commission on Gender Equality, together with the Women's Empowerment Unit in the national Parliament, the NGO Women's Development Foundation, the South Africa Local Government Association, and the Women's National Coalition sent an open letter to all political parties challenging them to put women on their electoral lists. The Commission on Gender Equality also met with all parties, although the commission reported that the discussions were very general and that parties had little to offer by way of substantial policy responses to the commission's questions.[68] In addition, the commission lobbied media organizations on the importance of covering women candidates as well as gender issues. This campaign was relatively successful, as a review of the media for this period reveals.

In addition to the central role played by the Commission on Gender Equality, a number of extraparliamentary initiatives tracked party positions on gender, including the Gender Advocacy Programme in the Western Cape, the Electoral Institute of South Africa, the Women's Development Foundation, and Nisaa in Gauteng. The Women's Development Foundation and Gender Advocacy Programme launched a two-pronged national campaign aimed at increasing women's representation and at ensuring that women voters considered party positions on gender issues when voting. As Barbara Watson, director of the Women's Development Foundation, pointed out, "We have to challenge all parties to have a policy on women. At the moment we are too dependent on the will of the majority party."[69] A considerable media effort was begun. This included articles and opinion pieces in contributions to the mainstream media,[70] as well as the development of the *Elections Bulletin,* produced in both tabloid and electronic form by Women'sNet on behalf of a range of women's organizations (see www.womensnet.org.za; Women'sNet describes itself as a "networking support program" to help South African women use the Internet to engage in social activism). These forums were used to debate how parties were taking up key issues such as violence against women, unemployment, housing, and health care.[71]

Not surprisingly, this shift to concerns about the quality of women's representation and accountability to women's interests resulted in contestation between women in political parties about policy issues. Although women activists in all parties had been united about maintaining the pressure for greater political representation, women's forums painstakingly reiterated the limits of their common interests. Below the surface of collective action simmered discontent about the relative power of certain women's organizations and misgivings about the extent to which particular political parties could be trusted to advance the agendas of the women's movement. Within Parliament early attempts to create a multiparty forum for women MPs, such as the Parliamentary Women's Group, have foundered as a result of tensions between the Democratic Party, the ANC, and the New National Party. The opposition parties have constantly questioned the leadership position in the Parliamentary Women's Group of the MPs from the ANC, despite the track record of these MPs in women's organizations. Anna van Wyk, member of Parliament from the National Party, has suggested that "the small number of women in opposition parties militates against co-operation."[72]

These tensions were exacerbated because Parliament did not recognize the Parliamentary Women's Group as an official structure.[73] It operated without a budget. Parliamentary rules were often used to undermine attempts to convene meetings. In some instances male party leaders were critical of the existence of such a structure. Nozizwe Routledge-Madlala, deputy minister of defense, recalled that "an alliance between women MPs [from different parties] had to be built up outside of government. We agreed that we should agree on certain minimal things. Once inside Parliament, it was not so much that there was no will to work together, but obstacles often came from women being dictated to by their caucuses. Some party caucuses were saying you can't belong to several caucuses. Even the ANC Women's Caucus survived only because of the party's moral and political obligations."[74]

Women are not a homogeneous constituency. Even where women MPs are committed to broad principles of gender equality, their definitions of what this means, their strategies for achieving equality, and their female constituencies may be vastly different. Former MP Mavivi Manzini of the ANC pointed out that attempts to build a common front of women in Parliament will not succeed: "We've tried that. It doesn't work. There are differences [between MPs of different parties] over what is to be transformed. There are only a limited number of areas in which women are able to speak in one voice. [Besides,] party whips keep women MPs accountable to the party, not to women's issues."[75]

It is not surprising that the driving force behind legislative reform to eliminate gender discrimination has been the ANC Women's Caucus, rather than the multiparty forum, reflecting the different weight given to gender equality by different political parties. Individual feminists in other political parties have found it difficult to overcome the ideological resistance and lack of effective internal structures within their parties.

By the 1999 elections women's organizations were much more skeptical of the extent to which women MPs represented women's interests rather than party or even personal political interests. The issue of accountability emerged very forcefully in various electoral forums.[76] Despite the deep concern with the idea of accountability in the women's movement, it remains elusive in practice, in part because the issue of the autonomy of women's organizations was not resolved and in part because of the absence of an organizational center in the women's movement that would field candidates. These factors have muddied understandings of accountability—accountability to parties? to women within parties? to all women?[77] Debates among gender activists have focused on both formal aspects of accountability (to political parties) and moral aspects of accountability (to the cause of gender equality). In both cases, however, ensuring accountability requires the consolidation of women—or even different groups of women—as a key constituency.

Ensuring formal accountability requires that women within political parties are relatively well organized—both to enhance the effectiveness of women MPs within the legislative arena and to create internal party mechanisms for holding them accountable to women members and not just party leadership. A tendency among women's organizations has been to conflate the tasks of building constituencies and representing constituencies. Women's sections of political parties (of which women MPs should ideally be active members) can play a significant role in articulating the interests of women supporters of their parties and in ensuring that these are addressed within the party's broad political platforms. In other words, such structures can be vital in the process of building a constituency of women in the party and of party supporters.

If a representational strategy is to be pursued effectively, the ability of women's structures in parties to claim constituencies is crucial to their success within the party, as the central business of electoral politics is attracting votes. To the extent that women's wings of political parties can escape the role of "catering committee," they would have to take on the tasks of grooming women leaders and supporting them for internal party offices. They would also have to function effectively as one among many conduits between women in Parliament and grassroots women. Without active women's sections within parties, women MPs can be left adrift, overburdened with the multiple tasks of committee work, party responsibilities, and gender activism and with no clear political direction (vis-à-vis gender) to their work. The primary task of women MPs should be to define areas of intervention in the legislature and support and report to women in the party—to *represent*, not to build, constituencies. The failure to separate these tasks has led to tensions between women in political parties and women's organizations in civil society.[78]

There is also an expectation of moral accountability within the women's movement. The first cohort of women in Parliament was very aware of this responsibility, as it was argued that their election was the product of collective struggles. Mavivi Manzini, for example, has argued strongly that "women in Parliament are not an elite; they take their lead from the ordinary mass of women."[79] Many women MPs made enormous efforts to consult with civil society and to share information and build strategies collectively, despite the pressures of being pioneers.[80] The late Joyce Kgoali, a trade unionist who became an MP in 1994, suggested that "it is important that there are women's structures outside parliament. Without any support from outside it is pointless. Women parliamentarians must be part of these structures. During breaks in parliament women must go back and account to these structures."[81]

However, the relative demobilization of the women's movement since 1994 will result in fewer women on party lists who have long and deep connections to women's organizations. Without the moral and political pressure from outside Parliament, there is always the danger that women MPs will be unable (or increasingly unwilling) to adequately represent the various interests of women. Women's gains in and through parliamentary representation are an important facet of the long-term battle to recognize women as agents in political processes and to provide voices for women in the various arenas of public decision making. It is important, however, to maintain a critical tension between MPs and government bureaucrats—male and female—who claim to be speaking on behalf of women and the constituencies in whose name these claims are made. Without strong mechanisms for upholding accountability, the danger always exists that representation carries little power to advance the agenda of gender equality.

Institutionalizing Representation: Political Parties after 1994

Women's entry into representative politics in large numbers opened questions of how electoral politics, institutional restructuring (of Parliament as well as party), and constituency or interest-group mobilization could be made to work in women's interests. As several needs assessment studies commissioned by the Speaker of Parliament and by the European Union (key donor to the Women's Empowerment Unit) showed, women representatives were constrained both by external political conditions and by internal cultural and institutional obstacles to their effectiveness.[82]

Despite the many formal enabling mechanisms for gender equality, South Africa has reached no social consensus about the political significance of women's interests relative to other issues of empowerment (most notably, race). No significant differences between women and men on electoral issues or party preferences have been found by any of the electoral surveys, suggesting that the connections between gender inequalities and the position of women are either not recognized or are considered unimportant by women voters in South Africa.[83] The attempt to mobilize the women's vote separately by the Women's Party during the 1994 election was singularly unsuccessful.[84] Many of the formal gains were won, as I argue in chapter 4, as a result of elite persuasion rather than by a strong mass movement of women. Commitments to the principles of gender equality were in effect negotiated by one sector of the women's movement with the leadership of a progressive party before it came to power. From women's perspective this "negotiated revolution" has not yet developed deep social legitimacy for the values of gender equality and justice—or, at least, this is the conclusion to be drawn from the responses by women and men to the voter surveys of the Institute for a Democratic South Africa and the Human Sciences Research Council.[85] The shallowness of support for gender equality has affected the process of building an electoral constituency, as the broad population of women voters did not appear to be convinced of the need to elect women into positions of power.

Stereotypes of women's (non)abilities as leaders persist among the electorate, despite the greater visibility of women in politics. Anecdotal evidence of this abounds among women in political parties—women are regarded, even by other women, as incompetent weak leaders.[86] Where they do succeed, they are often held up for ridicule. As one newspaper article commented, strong women (and particularly black women) are regarded as a nuisance: "Their refusal to be cowed by disapproval has turned them into threatening objects of derision and even, it may be argued, icons of emasculation—a response that is in stark contrast to powerful black male role models who are seen as unthreatening and forgiving."[87]

Although these systematic and cultural barriers to women's access to political power were dealt with as a cross-party issue in the first election, the inability to sustain a structure such as the multiparty Parliamentary Women's Group after 1994 was a strong indication of the shallowness of common interest among women from different parties. Aside from the ANC, parties lacked a history of internal party struggle around equality. Gender work in the Democratic Party, for example, tended to be focused externally; inside the party the mainstreaming approach led to the effective invisibility of issues of gender equality. In the New National Party the women's structure has not moved beyond its traditional role of tea parties and fund-raising to raise issues of power inside the party. Neither the Democratic Party nor the New National Party, while it still operated, had women's caucuses in Parliament. As a result women in the ANC take the lead on issues of gender equality in Parliament, while other parties are reactive and sometimes resentful of the perceived dominance of the MPs from the ANC.[88] Furthermore, it was difficult to maintain the facade of common interests when women in the National Party and the Democratic Party voted against such legislation as the Employment Equity Act, legislation that had been shaped by ANC women MPs to ensure greater protection for women workers.

But even within the ANC, the form of party institutionalization has not always been conducive to the articulation of feminist claims. Centralist elements within the party have been strengthened as power within the party has increasingly come to be a stepping-stone to power within the government. Increasingly, those in the party leadership who are associated with government positions are considered to be more powerful in agenda setting within the ANC. Thenjiwe Mtintso, deputy secretary general of the ANC, commented on the frequency with which, even within the ANC alliance, critics of government's failure to address inequalities met the response that they did not understand the exigencies of government. This set up a tension between party officials including leaders of the Women's League, based in Shell [Luthuli] House in Johannesburg, and the ANC's elected MPs. "There is a tendency to want to close ranks on particular issues and say you don't have the broader picture. You're in Shell House [ANC headquarters], you don't understand government responsibilities. These matters sometimes divert us. . . . They don't owe us anything, they are elected in their own right. So they are not accountable to 'these women' and 'these feminists.' Who are they, we've got our own political agenda."[89]

The ANC's Deployment Committee makes key decisions on which senior members of the party will be moved into key posts such as provincial premiers, mayors, and heads of parastatal organizations. The leadership of the movement is able to use the proportional representation electoral system to shift MPs around according to party leadership dictates.[90] A widely held view is that this power is sometimes used to sideline or silence critics within the party. An example often cited among feminist activists is the "deployment" of Cheryl Carolus, a prominent leader of the United Women's Organisation in the Western Cape and the United Democratic Front. Carolus was one of only two women in the delegation that met with F. W. de Klerk to begin the negotiations process. In 1994 she was elected deputy secretary general of the ANC[91] and later acting secretary general (reportedly only after other, more favored, candidates had turned down the position). One columnist commented that "she has stepped on too many toes. She attacked party positions, embarrassed ANC ministers and disagreed with influential members of the organisation."[92] Carolus was later appointed high commissioner to London, "out of harm's way," according to a source within the secretary general's office.[93] Stadler has commented that the deployment process suggests "the declining importance of civic associations in relation to the ANC as well as of the relatively lesser importance of the party in central administration compared with the party in office."[94] In this more constrained party context, women MPs and ministers might find it difficult to articulate policy positions that differ sharply from those of the party leadership. The tendency of the proportional representation system to favor accountability to the party rather than to particular constituencies may therefore hamper, rather than facilitate, the development of substantive representation over descriptive representation in the long term.

An overreliance on feminists within the party has many limitations for other reasons. As Vos has pointed out, women MPs are hostage to a hierarchical and male-dominated party, where the gender ticket is not the route to party power. One ANC woman MP commented that "we are there to represent women, but at the same time one has to be careful, because at the next election you could be pushed off the list. You have to take account of party loyalties."[95] In the cabinet women are bound by loyalty and are dependent on the leadership for their ministerial positions. The cabinet is "structured in a hierarchical way, even if this is not openly talked of. There are unspoken rules, including how we sit, which allocates a certain role to juniors. When I spoke at my first *lekgotla* [cabinet meeting], I had the feeling from some remarks that maybe I'd been out of turn, even though what I said had been acknowledged. . . . Maybe we need a caucus of women in cabinet, but there is the problem of space and time to sustain the caucus. But there is an attempt to support one another," Routledge-Madlala said.[96]

These concerns are heightened by indications that the consolidation phase of democratization in South Africa is characterized by the increasing centralization of power within the presidency[97] and by a seeming attack on the role of Parliament and particularly the committee system, which is the key forum through which executive accountability is measured. The degree of robust debate in Parliament and the public sphere suggests that there is no fundamental threat to democracy, but the tendency of central party leadership to reassert control indicates a weakening of the ANC's internal democracy.

One avenue for pursuing internal party accountability to its women supporters might be its women's section—the ANC Women's League.[98] The league has automatic representation on the ANC's highest decision-making body and has the formal responsibility of representing women within the party. However, aside from the brief period of the coalition, when the league articulated a strong feminist position, it has not managed to break free of its tea-making role. Although the league's former president, Winnie Madikizela-Mandela, is an outspoken critic of the ANC's leadership (on issues other than gender), the league has not taken a consistent position on gender issues or assumed any leadership role in the women's movement. The league's long period of exile hindered the development of an organized constituency among women, and after 1994 it put little energy into building branches and consolidating its membership base. As I showed in chapter 4, in 1995 young feminists, some of whom were in key positions, resigned their membership out of frustration with the internal difficulties within the league and put their energies into the party as a whole. The league soon returned to its more familiar role as auxiliary to the party, with little capacity to offer political leadership within the women's movement. The failures of the league, as well as the women's sections within other parties, highlight the vacuum that can be created when parties' institutional channels for representation of women's interests are weak. Without feminist-driven women's sections within parties, women representatives can be overburdened with the multiple tasks of committee work, party responsibilities, and gender activism and may lack a sense of direct accountability to women supporters of the party. Even where women politicians might take their representative roles seriously—as the first cohort of women in the South African Parliament did—the task of building constituencies cannot be done by individuals.

Representation: An Effective Strategy?

The relative success of women in increasing their numerical representation begs the question of how they have used their electoral leverage to address substantive issues of women's inequalities. The stress put on representation as a key response to women's movement demands for democratization in South Africa demands examination of the extent to which women in political office can facilitate changes in gender power relations.

Despite the numerical success, many activists were worried about the difficulties of working in a male-dominated terrain,[99] the extra burdens of committee work on the relatively few women MPs, and a deepening rift between women MPs and women's organizations. In one of the first studies of the experiences of women MPs, Hannah Britton found high levels of stress and suggested that many women MPs might not stand for election again.[100] As MP Thenjiwe Mtintso of the ANC has pointed out, "The quota was seen as a double-edged sword: providing opportunities but also adding burdens for women representatives."[101] Mtintso's own research, conducted in the latter part of the first Parliament in 1996, found that women MPs had overcome some cultural and institutional constraints on their participation. MPs she interviewed reported greater confidence, support, and commitment as a result of experience with the technical processes.[102] She reported that the women "developed excitement and confidence when tracing what could be attributable to their own participation and contribution.

She can proudly say at the end, 'this is mine. I did it for this country, for myself and for the women.'"[103]

Despite the optimistic approach of some women politicians, even they would agree that the cultural and institutional difficulties had a real influence on the effectiveness of women MPs.[104] As Nancy Fraser has pointed out, the removal of formal roadblocks to women's participation in the representative sphere is undercut continuously by patterns of deliberation that uphold particular power relations. Drawing on Mansbridge, she has argued that "deliberation can mask domination" as "social inequalities can infect deliberation, even in the absence of any formal exclusions."[105] While political parties, particularly the ANC, trumpeted the large number of women in Parliament, their underlying ethos was that party loyalty, rather than loyalty to constituencies such as women, was primary. Women MPs were in any case not all committed to feminist ideals, and under party leadership pressure and the belittling of the importance of gender,[106] many did not identify openly with feminist agendas. Suzanne Vos, an Inkatha Freedom Party MP, has commented that male dominance and patronage inhibits the articulation of feminism: "There is no doubt that the PR [proportional representation]/list system ensures that all politicians must remain popular with (mostly male) party bosses to survive. Male leadership also invariably selects which women are promoted within party structures and within Parliament. They decide who sits on what committee and who gets speaking time in the House, on what and when. . . . Survival instincts triumph. . . . Men are the game, they control the game."[107]

The ideological differences between women also emerged very quickly as the "critical mass" of women came to grips with the real differences in legislative and policy priorities between political parties. The establishment of a multiparty women's caucus (the Parliamentary Women's Group) failed to provide either a support structure or a lobbying point for women MPs. The ANC Women's Caucus, with a long history of gender activism, acted as the key pressure point within Parliament, even within the multiparty Joint Monitoring Committee on the Improvement of the Quality of Life and Status of Women. The most notable example of the tension that this engendered was the process of introducing employment equity legislation. ANC women MPs worked extremely hard to ensure that women were recognized as a disadvantaged group in the new laws. However, women MPs from the Democratic Party voted against the legislation because the party as a whole was opposed to the imposition of strong labor-market regulation. The Joint Monitoring Committee, under the chair of the experienced gender activist Pregs Govender,[108] was established in part as a consequence of the new government's signing of the United Nations Convention on the

Elimination of All Forms of Discrimination Against Women and provided
an important institutional forum within which to identify a set of legislative priorities and begin to lobby for policy changes. Indeed, this committee
demonstrated the most significant positive influence on representational
strategies.

Working closely with civil society through a series of public hearings
and expert submissions, the committee arrived at an independent assessment of the nature and scale of the HIV/AIDS crisis, for instance, and
called on Parliament to make eradicating the disease and dealing with its effects the "number one priority." Despite ANC and presidential pressures to
back off this issue, ANC members of this committee, led by Govender,
stood firm on the need for antiretrovirals. The committee was also the only
parliamentary committee to openly oppose the massive purchasing of arms
and refurbishment of military hardware. At the opening of Parliament in
2003, Govender joined the Treatment Action Campaign outside Parliament
rather than take her seat with her ANC colleagues in the public gallery on
the National Assembly. Addressing Mbeki directly, she said, "It is time, my
president, to say no to so much unnecessary death, to so much grief, to so
many wars." This was an important indication of the willingness of a few
MPs to challenge the party in the face of competing interests. It is not insignificant, however, that Govender resigned from Parliament at the end
of the 2002 session. Individual feminists were not supported by a strong
women's structure within the ANC. The ANC Women's League has preferred to work (at least openly) within the ambit of existing party policy
rather than challenge the party leadership or embarrass the leadership in
public debate, unlike feminists in the Swedish Social Democratic Party.

Looking more closely at the legislative gains made in the first five years,
it is important to analyze how changes were introduced and whether the influence of women in Parliament is sustainable and not dependent on exceptional MPs such as Pregs Govender (who would probably have been on
the ANC list without a quota). What is notable about the processes of
introducing new legislation was that the network of gender activists in civil
society and the ANC, and especially but not solely, women MPs from the
ANC, was crucial. In the first years of the new Parliament gender equality
was not a priority for legislative attention, despite the formal commitments.
As a result the "gender equality bills" languished in the South African Law
Commission (the legislative drafting agency) until almost the last session of
the first Parliament. Legislation dealing with women's inequality was placed
on the parliamentary calendar only in 1998, toward the end of the first term
of Parliament and only after high-level lobbying by the ANC Women's Caucus with the support of progressive men MPs, including, by some accounts,
President Mbeki. The legislation then had to be fast-tracked through the

National Assembly so that the first Parliament would be seen as being concerned about gender equality as a substantive issue.

The key advocates for the legislation were women MPs who would in all likelihood have been on the ANC list regardless of the quota and male MPs who had a commitment to gender equality. Pressure to push the legislation through before the end of the first term came from gender activists outside the government. In the case of the Termination of Pregnancy Act, the proposed legislation was consistent with the ANC's health policy and with its campaign platform (the Reconstruction and Development Programme), which included reproductive rights. Gender activists had exerted pressure within the ANC before quotas were introduced, and the measure was sponsored in Parliament by the Health Portfolio Committee rather than the Joint Monitoring Committee. These developments suggest that key interventions were related to processes of democratization within the party, supported by constitutional commitments (notably also achieved through internal party pressure and constituency building rather than a politics of presence). As Albertyn and colleagues argued, "'Gender sensitive' women and men holding diverse positions of power and influence in state institutions were far more important in ensuring that gender issues were placed on the policy agenda."[109] In particular, they found that the ability of feminist politicians to lobby successfully within the ruling party, and their networking capacities outside government, outweighed the role of the critical mass of women MPs in getting gender issues on the agenda.

It is interesting to note the kinds of areas singled out for legislative attention in the first five years of South African democracy (1994–99), a period dominated by the need to elaborate the rules, procedures, and norms of the new institutions, policies, and laws. The first "women's law" to be passed was the Termination of Pregnancy Act of 1996, which provides women with access to abortion under broader and more favorable conditions than previously. The other three key pieces of legislation sponsored by the Joint Committee on Women, a special portfolio committee responsible for legislative oversight with regard to gender equality, were the Domestic Violence Bill, the Maintenance Bill, and the Recognition of Customary Marriages Bill, and these took much longer to process. The Domestic Violence Act of 1998 provides protection against abuse for people who are in domestic relationships, regardless of the specific nature of the relationship (i.e., whether marital, homosexual, or family relationships). It is a highly significant piece of legislation because it recognizes that the private sphere of the family is not insulated from the democratic norms established by the Constitution and that women are entitled to state protection of their rights even in the private sphere. The Maintenance Act of 1998 substantially improves the position of mothers dependent on financial support from former partners. The Recognition of Customary Marriages Act of 1998 abolished the minority status of women married under customary law and legalized customary marriages. Other legislation not directly aimed at improving women's condition, such as the Employment Equity Act, included women among its target groups for redress of apartheid-era inequalities. In addition, a number of policy programs were introduced, such as free health care for pregnant women and children. This period also saw significant gains in embedding gender equality concerns in the broad frameworks of social policy,[110] although several areas of legislative discrimination against women remain intact, and legislation is needed in other areas to enable the freedom of women.

When Representation Is Not Enough: The Case of the Communal Land Rights Bill

The real test of whether the representation model would work is to consider what would happen if women's organizations were to push for legislative changes that would directly challenge entrenched patriarchal interests—that is, if women's organizations were to demand changes on the basis of their strategic gender interests rather than women's needs. To what extent would a critical mass of women MPs be able to shape legislative outcomes in the face of a concerted opposition? The contestations over the Communal Land Rights Bill are an instructive case study in this regard, for a number of reasons. As I argued in chapter 5, one key clash in the Constitution-making period was between traditional leaders and feminists, when some traditional leaders' opposition to gender equality set the stage for a protracted conflict. The Constitution itself validated both equality and cultural autonomy while ensuring that equality will prevail when the two areas are in conflict. In legislation proposed by the ANC in 2003 (the Traditional Leadership and Governance Framework Bill, championed by the Portfolio Committee on Provincial and Local Government, and the Communal Land Rights Bill, supported by the Portfolio Committee on Land and Agriculture), concerns about gender equality once again came up squarely against concerns of traditional leaders. At issue in this particular debate was the extent of traditional leaders' formal authority over land allocation in rural areas. The Communal Land Rights Bill was set to become the biggest test of the extent to which a constituency of (rural) women could successfully defend their policy claims against other powerful interests.

Fairly soon after the first democratic elections, the new minister of land affairs, Derek Hanekom, proposed legislation that would shift control of trust land, including a significant proportion of land in KwaZulu Natal held under the Ingonyama Trust, to the central government. Although the proposed legislation would include a variety of different forms of land and property, traditional leaders treated this as a direct attack on their traditional authority. Inkatha Freedom Party leader Mangosuthu Buthelezi went as far as to call it a "severe provocation" to the Zulu nation.[111] The opposition of traditional leaders was strong enough that the ANC feared an electoral backlash, particularly in KwaZulu Natal, and the proposal was shelved. After the 1999 elections the new minister of land affairs, Thoko Didiza, announced that a land rights bill would be introduced in April 2001. Again, the bill was not published, although Didiza undertook to publish it after discussions at a national conference on land rights in Durban in November 2001.

The discussions of the bill in Durban provoked deep divisions, even within the ANC. The bill recognized "communities" as juridical persons and proposed to transfer state land to communities. MP Lydia Kompe-Ngwenya, a veteran land rights activist in the ANC, rejected this proposal, arguing that the land rights of individual users and occupiers needed to be recognized and protected in law, in accordance with the Freedom Charter. Her party colleague and leader of the Congress of Traditional Leaders of South Africa, Nkosi Patekile Holomisa, on the other hand, argued that legal title to communal land should be bestowed on the traditional authority. For the traditional leaders the bill did not go far enough in securing traditional authority, as "communities" would now have rights. For women, on the other hand, the emphasis on communities reinstated the power of traditional leaders as they became the officially recognized representatives of community interests.

Traditional leaders vociferously opposed the eighth draft of the bill, published in August 2002. This draft proposed the creation of land administration structures comprised of community representatives as well as traditional leaders, although traditional leaders would constitute only 25 percent of the council. Communities would be given discretion as to whether the land would be held by communal title or subdivided and registered in the names of individuals. The anger over this reallocation of land authority was so strong among some traditional leaders that many felt it would lead to an outbreak of violence. The Inkatha Women's Brigade and Youth Brigade threatened "retribution if the bill went through parliament." The *Sunday Times* reported an Ulundi resident as saying, "If the bill is passed it will be understood that any tribe member who applies to own land can be killed or have their house burnt down. Many will be happy to strike the match."[112] Mbeki shifted from his usual friendly tone toward traditional leaders to warn that the government would not tolerate violence.[113]

Despite the president's firm warning, the threats of electoral retaliation and political violence in KwaZulu Natal seemed to have an effect on legislators. In July 2003 an informal group of experts, meeting in Pretoria, warned that the government needed to set priorities for land and agrarian reform to avoid political instability in South Africa.[114] At the same time civil society actors were exerting considerable pressure to move ahead on finalizing the bill. That October a final draft of the bill was published; it contained last-minute alterations that provided that traditional councils, set up according to the Traditional Leadership and Governance Framework Bill, would have powers of land administration, allocation, and ownership in communal areas. The cabinet endorsed the measure and announced that it wanted the bill enacted before the 2004 elections, leaving less than a month for it to pass through the appropriate parliamentary processes.

The issue of women's rights remained unresolved. The Traditional Leadership and Governance Framework Bill provides for 30 percent representation of women on traditional councils. It also provides that while 40 percent of the members of the council are to be elected, the remaining 60 percent "must comprise traditional leaders and members of the traditional community selected by the principal traditional leaders concerned in terms of custom."[115] The bill also gives the minister of agriculture and land affairs discretionary powers to determine the nature and content of land rights, without the consultation or consent of traditional leaders. This was in part a response to the concerns of women's organizations that gender equality issues might not be automatically taken into account or might be overridden by the traditional councils. In these cases, the minister would be able to confer rights of ownership or occupation on women. These changes were far from satisfactory for traditional leaders, who saw them as a further erosion of their authority. Tensions between the Inkatha Freedom Party and the ANC in particular escalated. Zulu chief Buthelezi claimed that the ANC had reneged on its agreements with the Inkatha Freedom Party before and after 1994, commenting that relations between the two parties "have never been worse."[116]

Despite the concessions to women's representation in the amendments to the bill, reactions from women's organizations and NGOs dealing with land redistribution were equally vociferous, albeit without the threats of violence.[117] Because space does not permit me to detail the objections or to delineate the sometimes fine differences between different civil society groups, I will concentrate on the objections relating to women's rights. The key objections related to the failure of the bill to protect the rights of rural women, the undemocratic nature of the traditional councils, and the entrenchment of the control of chiefs over key aspects of women's lives. Both the Programme for Land and Agricultural Studies (PLAAS) and the Commission on Gender Equality, in their submissions in November 2003, argued that the bill's goal to restore so-called old-order rights, which had become legally questionable as a result of apartheid laws, did not adequately address the demands of gender equality. Under customary law, as well as under apartheid law, women's rights to land were derivative and temporary. Women could not own land or occupy property in their own right but were dependent on male spouses or customary partners. They lost these rights upon the death of the male spouse, in part also as a result of the principle of male primogeniture, which required that property be passed to the nearest male relative. This principle was upheld as recently as 2000 by the Supreme Court of Appeal, the highest court for all but constitutional cases.[118] PLAAS researchers found that most traditional leaders continued to refuse to allocate land to women. While earlier versions of the bill had explicitly provided for the right to gender equality in respect of ownership, allocation, use of, or access to land, this provision disappeared from the final version of the bill. There was no longer any provision clearly banning discriminatory practices. Similarly, it did not require that rules devised by communities to govern the administration of communal land comply with the equality clause in the Bill of Rights, although earlier versions of the measure did make such provision.[119] Women's concerns were partially addressed by the portfolio committee, which increased the proportion of women on the councils and gave the minister discretionary powers that would include oversight with regard to gender discrimination.

However, the Commission on Gender Equality and PLAAS opposed the discretionary power of the minister in principle. Their two concerns in this regard were that gender equality, as an entrenched right, should not be subject to discretion, particularly in view of the many documented cases of male officials' turning a blind eye to women's complaints, and that the discretionary power created the conditions for a potential abuse of power. Finally, a wide range of organizations opposed the proposal that traditional councils should be appointive, rather than fully elected, bodies. PLAAS pointed out that the Traditional Leadership and Governance Framework Bill "gives tribal authorities perpetual life and the Communal land Rights Bill gives them powers over land that surpass any that they previously enjoyed."[120] The organization argued that "it is very likely that the 30% quota will come from the royal family and be comprised of female relatives of the chief. Can women handpicked by chiefs really be relied on to represent the interests of ordinary rural women, and to address the legacy of gender discrimination against women practiced under customary law?"[121] The Joint Monitoring Committee pointed out that women would be a permanent minority on traditional councils and requested that 50 percent of seats be set aside for women. The Commission on Gender Equality warned that the creation of nonelected bodies with decision-making power over women's access to key economic resources set up a form of secondary citizenship for black rural women, who would be discriminated against on the basis of both race and gender.

This rather truncated narrative of the debates around the Communal Land Rights Bill raises crucial questions about the power of women's organizations and women's representatives in Parliament to successfully defend women's rights. Rural women have never been strongly organized in South Africa. In many instances rural NGOs with dedicated feminist activists (such as AFRA and the Transvaal Rural Action Committee) spoke on behalf of rural women and attempted to represent their specific concerns in national debates. However, there has been little independent organization of women, and in policy terms there was certainly not the kind of organizational base and resources that the Reproductive Rights Alliance or the Network on Violence Against Women, for example, were able to draw on. In the late 1980s and early 1990s the Rural Women's Movement emerged, supported in the initial stages by the Transvaal Rural Action Committee. The Rural Women's Movement was able to make significant suggestions to the Women's National Coalition, participate in the Constitution-making process, and acted as a national voice for rural women. However, by the time the Traditional Leadership and Governance Framework and Communal Land Rights bills were introduced, the Rural Women's Movement was a virtually defunct organization that had collapsed under the weight of financial and administrative problems. Local rural women's groups therefore lacked any connection to urban-based policy debates. As Claasens and Ngubane have pointed out, "There are vibrant groups of rural women, keen and committed to supporting one another and organizing around these issues. However there are currently no resources available to enable rural women to come together in a regular basis to take these matters forward . . . nor . . . are there provincial or national rural women's organizations that can support and co-ordinate the process of organizing rural women."[122]

Research organizations and NGOs such as the Transvaal Rural Action Committee, PLAAS, and the National Land Committee did consult with rural women about the bills. This process was both enabling and problematic. It made it possible for rural women's concerns to be heard by the legislators in the absence of parliamentary hearings in rural areas. Rural women's concerns were thoroughly represented in the submissions to Parliament prepared by PLAAS and the National Land Committee. The Commission on Gender Equality played a leading role in highlighting rural women's interests and concerns, a testament to the more effective advocacy role that the commission has adopted since 2002. However, the alliance with and representation by urban-based land rights NGOs also had drawbacks. MPs from the ANC labeled some of these NGOs as "ultra-left" critics, and while these NGOs had a strong voice, it was not always an influential one. Various interviewees noted the subtle ways in which some NGO representatives were ignored and even belittled. Also, even with the best of intentions, NGOs did not always highlight issues of gender equality in their strategies. Finally, many urban-based activists were young, and age has emerged as an important issue in debates about customary law. Likhapha Mbatha pointed out to me in a personal communication that "older people, rightly or not, perceived young activists as disrespectful. They didn't think young people had the right to talk to them in an angry way." This view was corroborated by other participants in the process, who pointed out that in pursuing changes in customary practices, strategies have to carefully take into account issues of dress, tone, and discourse.

Finally, what about the alliance with women inside Parliament? ANC women MPs did not appear to recognize the significance of the bill until relatively late in the process. They raised no objections to the bill in the cabinet and, of course, it was sponsored by a woman minister. However, the Commission on Gender Equality and women's rights NGOs approached the women MPs, they did signal their concerns about the bill. Naledi Pandor, chair of the National Council of Provinces, worked with women activists to facilitate debate about the bill. The Joint Monitoring Committee made a submission to the portfolio committee on Land and Agricultural Affairs that laid out its objections to the bill—a rare occurrence of one portfolio committee's opposing another. The ANC Women's Caucus also voiced its objection to the bill. However, when it came to voting on the bill in Parliament, none of the ANC women MPs voted against it or officially abstained. The bill passed unanimously through the portfolio committee, Parliament, and the cabinet. Several explanations have been offered for this degree of public support despite the private reservations of ANC women MPs. The first is that there was little strategizing in relation to the bill early in the process. The ANC Women's Caucus, which had been so effective in getting the controversial Termination of Pregnancy Act passed, did not take up the issue of rural women's rights in the Communal Land Rights Bill. This might also have been a consequence of the poor organization of women outside Parliament. Second, some have argued that women MPs had instructions "from above" not to oppose the bill. The finalization of the bill and its appearance before the National Assembly occurred as the parties were drawing up their electoral lists, and some activists have suggested that women MPs feared that they might be left off or pushed low down on the lists. One MP from the ANC, speaking on condition of anonymity, argued that "it didn't appear to be an opportune time to take on the party." Ironically, some of the very factors that had assisted women activists with regard to the Termination of Pregnancy Act—the role of senior members of the cabinet and the portfolio committees and the "party line" of the ANC—now appeared to have worked against them. This led one prominent feminist activist to question "whether there is a strong anchor for gender activism in Parliament any more. We have lots of women in Parliament, but I wonder how strongly they support women's interests when push comes to shove. Especially at election time, the party is what matters."

Women's organizations are debating whether to take the government to the constitutional court to challenge the legitimacy of the legislation. Legal opinions from the South African Human Rights Commission and the Commission on Gender Equality both argue that the legislation violates the constitutional right to gender equality. Legal struggle is the only remaining avenue for those opposing the bill.

Conclusions

This discussion of the relationship between women and political parties poses a number of dilemmas for women activists in South Africa—and in other African contexts. It was the "critical mass" of *feminist* activists—rather than women as a group—that had the most influence in ensuring that issues of gender equality would be raised. Although the *number* of women in Parliament was significant, reshaping legislative priorities and reform measures was the work of feminists, MPs with a political commitment to gender equality. As Deputy Speaker Baleka Kgositsile pointed out, "Our achievement will be measured not just by getting to Parliament but what we do when we get there."[123] In this context the questions about representation must be redirected to focus on ensuring that a greater number of feminists achieve political power. How can feminists gain access to influential positions within the party and within Parliament? How do feminists within political parties balance the often-competing aims of women's advancement and party loyalty? How can women's movements mitigate the perverse consequences of demands for greater representation of women in elected office, in particular, the emergence of elite women leaders with relations of dependency to parties rather than to constituencies of women?

In part, the answer lies in the extent to which party and state organization (as the next chapter will show) can affect the capacity of the women's movement to sustain a relationship of solidarity with women politicians, which at the same time includes demands for accountability to a female constituency. Equally important is the extent to which women can use these moments of transition to recruit support from *men* who support substantive equality within the party. The extent to which feminists find spaces within political parties, through demands for representation—even merely descriptive representation—is also central. From this point of view the tendency in the literature to consider descriptive and substantive representation of women as different kinds of strategies is misleading[124] Rather, the minimal demand for a numerical increase in women's representation can become the ground upon which a deeper struggle may be fought. However, in order for this to happen, fast-tracking representation through quotas cannot become a substitute for building a strong and vocal constituency outside Parliament. Constituency formation has to translate into an electoral threat for it to be meaningful within representational politics. When that aspect of representation is neglected, and too much reliance is placed on party influence, feminists may lose out to more organized constituencies that are hostile to gender equality.

The apparent paradox in South Africa, between the demands of women as an identifiable constituency in electoral politics and the internal debates about different interests within that constituency, suggests that women's politics is conducted simultaneously at two levels. At an external level of politics a narrow terrain of common purpose is mapped out, articulated, and defended, while at an internal level there is vigorous contestation over specific policies and party political platforms. This tendency in women's politics seems counterproductive: it may be argued that women might do better in terms of increasing their political leverage if their external (in this case, electoral) politics was directed at articulating their interests within the framework of party-political contestation, rather than a nonpartisan "common front" approach. However, this dual politics is the outcome of the need for women to simultaneously build a constituency that will have political leverage—to present the illusion of a united constituency, if you will—*and* to articulate the diverse interests of women arising from the intersections of race, class, and gender inequalities. However, it must also be noted that without some form of autonomous women's movement in civil society, it is unlikely that the policy demands of different groups of women will be addressed. In the next chapter I elaborate this argument by turning to an examination of the consequences of state-centered strategies in the context of a weakening women's movement.

Chapter 7

One Woman, One Desk, One Typist

Moving into the Bureaucracy

> No government or bureaucracy feels it has anything to fear from women. In civil society they rarely represent a tightly mobilized constituency, at the domestic level their interests are often closely bound in with those of men in the family and in politics and public administration they are under-represented and have rarely acted in distinctively feminist ways. . . . As a result, far from having anything to fear from women, many governments can make important political gains at the international and domestic levels by espousing gender equity, without serious risk of being held accountable—of having to operationalize the promises made in top-level rhetoric.
>
> Anne Marie Goetz, "The Politics of Integrating Gender to State Development Processes"

As I showed in chapter 6, among the far-reaching changes wrought by the establishment of democracy was the shift of women's organizations from an oppositional relationship to the state to an approach that treated the state as both permeable to women's interests and influence and, consequently, a desirable locus for gender activism. This chapter examines this shift in strategy and the political assumptions and expectations that underpinned it as they relate to the creation of a national gender machinery and to the implementation of gender equality commitments in policies and service delivery. I describe in some detail the formal enabling conditions that have supported the idea that the South African state is open to the participation of women and that have provided the new framework for interventions and relationships with to the state by women's organizations. These include the constitutional provisions for gender equality, the creation of institutional frameworks to address gender inequalities (the national machinery for women), and policies and programs advanced in the first five years of democracy. In effect, these provisions instituted a "gender pact" in South Africa to the extent that they incorporated women as an interest group into the policy-making process.

A number of critical questions frame these descriptions. What are the new terrains of engagement between the state and civil society around gender inequalities in South Africa, and what has been the effect of institutionalization on the relative ability of women's organizations, and particularly feminist activists within both state and civil society, to mobilize around broad political demands? The representative sphere discussed in chapter 5 constitutes only one arena of women's engagement with the state. This chapter focuses more closely on the bureaucracy and the policy arena. As Anne Phillips has pointed out, increasing the number of women elected to Parliament does not necessarily increase the representation of women's interests. She points out that "it is only when there are mechanisms through which women can formulate their own policies or interests that we can really talk of their 'representation.'"[1] This would suggest that the task facing feminists was not simply to increase women's representation in the state (numerically and qualitatively), even though this was a priority.[2] Feminist analysis also needs to uncover the hidden ways in which institutions, as well as state policies (and counterpolicies advocated by women's organizations), constitute the particular interests of different groups of women. Institutions (even the national machineries) are not neutral vessels through which interests are expressed. How women are constituted as a group, and which women within this group are positioned as claimants for services, goods, and the like is a matter of political debate. As Nancy Fraser has pointed out, "Needs talk functions as a medium for the making and contesting of political claims: it is an idiom in which political conflict is played out and through which inequalities are symbolically elaborated and challenged."[3] I explore these questions through a case study of one of the first major processes of social policy reform, the overhaul of welfare for poor children. Through this example I examine how women's different interests have been constituted by both social policy and women's organizations in the changed political environment and the extent to which representation in either the bureaucratic or the representational sphere has advanced women's struggles for substantive equality. This case study allows me to explore differences (of class, race, and political power) between women as well as between women and men. It also poses a fundamental conundrum for those wishing to implement socioeconomic rights—the extent to which political rights that were so hard won in the transitional period continue to be useful instruments in the struggle to overcome the institutional, macroeconomic, and political constraints on the achievement of gender equality.

The short twelve years of democracy allow only preliminary assessments to be made with regard to the effectiveness of engaging the state. With regard to the bureaucracy, in particular, it would be premature to judge institutions that in some cases have been in place for no more than a few years. Instead, in this chapter I highlight the opportunities and problems that presented themselves during this period.

Creating the National Gender Machinery

Compared to the women's movement in other African countries, the South African movement was relatively better placed to exploit the formal democratic gains won during the transitional period. Through the Women's National Coalition women's organizations had developed a voice in national politics that was stronger than ever before. They could also draw on an international context in which feminism had made tremendous gains and in which South Africa was being lauded for its commitments to gender equality.

International political scrutiny was most evident with regard to the establishment of the national gender machinery. International pressure and transnational human rights movements played an important role in supporting the African National Congress (ANC) in exile, in fostering the development of a strong civil society inside the country, and in ending apartheid. After 1994 international agreements and charters took on a new role in maintaining the moral pressure on the ANC government to enact its human rights commitments. With regard to gender the two most significant forms of international support for local initiatives were the United Nations Fourth World Conference on Women (the Beijing Conference), and the United Nations Convention on the Elimination of All Forms of Discrimination Against Women (CEDAW). At a regional level there have been important developments in the formulation and implementation of a policy of gender equality within the Southern African Development Community, which also encouraged the ANC to maintain its leadership role with regard to gender equality.[4]

The Beijing Conference in 1995 provided the impetus and focus for gender activists within government to lobby for implementing government's commitment to gender equality. The South African government's delegation to Beijing was coordinated by the Ministry of Welfare, under Deputy Minister Geraldine Fraser-Moleketi, and was led by the minister of health,

Nkosazana Zuma. Both ministers had histories of involvement in gender activism. The national political leverage afforded by the Beijing Conference cannot be overstated. Both the preparatory consultation processes and the post-Beijing euphoria energized women activists and provided a sense of global urgency and solidarity on gender issues.[5] As a newly liberated country with constitutional and other provisions to advance human rights and gender equality, South Africa (and its official delegation to Beijing) was highly visible; the world was watching the government's approach to gender equality. Beijing was one of the first international forums in which the new democratic government of South Africa participated, and it was eager to demonstrate its commitment to progressive values and politics.

Another international mechanism that was used as a political lever by the South African women's movement was CEDAW. In December 1994 South Africa signed and ratified CEDAW, a major step in advancing the establishment of the national machinery to guarantee gender equality. CEDAW's effect was twofold. In signing the agreement, the government committed itself to a minimum set of standards to ensure that discrimination would end. This acted as a spur to government to give practical content to its political commitments and to support structures for ensuring that commitments are met. One outcome was that the Joint Standing Committee on Improving the Quality of Life and Status of Women shed its ad hoc status to become a full-fledged parliamentary committee with the specific task of monitoring the implementation of CEDAW. Also, reporting on South Africa's implementation of CEDAW, and putting together their report to Beijing, pushed government departments into thinking about their internal structures and policies with regard to mainstreaming gender (rather than dealing with women's issues as a separate category in social policy).[6] This greater awareness within government occurred more rapidly than it might have in the absence of international pressure.[7] Finally, both CEDAW and Beijing undoubtedly gave international credibility and moral authority to the struggles for gender equality within South Africa. The coincidence of local historical struggles and high-profile international developments with regard to gender produced a synergy that advanced internal struggles for gender equality, including the establishment of the national machinery and gender policies.

New Terrains of Engagement

In line with the rest of progressive civil society, women's organizations had to reorient themselves in the period of transition to democracy to engage the state as a key locus for redress of gender inequalities. As the first democratic government took power, the expectations of radical change were widespread in civil society. Indeed, it has been argued that the ANC and its allies anticipated "a boundless vista of possibilities once it seized power."[8]

Although women's organizations had made considerable gains through the support of the ANC, they nevertheless sought to institutionalize these equality commitments in the formal norms, procedures, and structures of the new democracy and thereby reduce the extent of dependency on political will. They had several models of institutional design to draw on, most of which were developed in the wake of the United Nations Decade for Women (1975–85), when states within the UN system set up "national gender machineries" to channel women's policy demands in the state. These institutions, ranging from gender desks in government departments to full-fledged ministries of women's affairs, seek to open up the state to a consideration of women's interests. In countries with weak civil societies these may indeed be the only mechanisms through which women are able to articulate their interests.

A key weakness of the "national machinery" approach, as activists were well aware, is that such agencies have rarely brought about a reduction in gender inequalities.[9] The usual course is that donor countries have insisted that otherwise conservative and even undemocratic political elites establish these agencies; seldom do they come into being as a result of the efforts of national women's movements. In many cases, as Sonia Alvarez pointed out, progressive "gender ideologies have been co-opted by dominant political and economic interests."[10] Although set up as benevolent institutions, national machineries have revealed themselves as "historically constructed frameworks" that create bureaucratic representation for elite groups of women but fail to act as institutional openings for addressing inequalities in power between women and men.[11] Co-option is a particular danger in countries where women's organizations have been poorly structured, lack autonomy from male-controlled political movements, and the influence of feminists has been weak. This has hampered the ability of the gender machinery to effectively articulate and develop women's interests against other competing interests.

Cognizant of these dangers, South African women activists sought to create a set of mechanisms and procedures that would ensure both women's participation in decision making in the new state and the accountability of state structures to women. This strategy was underpinned by the view that better institutional design, buttressed by the presence of women activists within the state and a strong women's movement outside the state, would shift policy priorities and content to encompass gender equity. Politically, those advancing the idea of the national machinery assumed that real change in a feminist direction was possible through the state.[12] The context of dramatic restructuring of the institutional framework of the state as a whole was particularly conducive to articulating demands for an expansive set of institutions, rather than the typically narrow "machinery" favored within the UN system. Creating several sites of interaction between the state and organized groups of women was a way of guarding against co-option and of ensuring accountability. Accountability would be secured at the horizontal level through the creation of the independent Commission on Gender Equality.[13] The Constitution guarantees the commission's autonomy and empowers it to monitor the implementation of the constitutional commitment to equality in both government and the private sector. Accountability to women citizens was to be guaranteed through the activism of the independent women's movement, represented by the Women's National Coalition.

Discussions about the kind of structures and mechanisms needed to advance gender equality began before the organizations of national liberation were unbanned, although these talks were confined within the ANC at forums such as the Malibongwe Conference and no concrete proposals emerged. In 1992 a workshop hosted by the Institute for a Democratic Alternative in South Africa and the University of Natal's Gender Research Group in Durban focused debate within the country on specifically how nondiscrimination should be institutionalized in a future democratic government. South African women had the advantage of coming to these debates relatively late. By 1992 most developing countries had implemented the resolution of the United Nations Decade for Women that governments should establish national machineries for women. The South African approach to national machinery differed somewhat from other countries', whose national machineries were entirely located inside the state. There was some early discussion within the ANC Women's League of a ministry for women's affairs.[14] However, at both the Durban workshop and at a later conference of the Women's National Coalition in 1993, participants debated at length the limitations of a single structure. Mavivi Myakayaka-Manzini, an activist in the league, argued that a multi-institutional approach, rather than a single government body, was more appropriate in contexts where women were systematically excluded from decision making: "It also recognizes that creating a single structure within government does not assist in addressing effective equality for women."[15]

Although most national machineries center narrowly on the "gender focal points" in government, in the South African case national machinery was designed to include both state and civil society structures, partly to create multiple sites of activism and partly to create mechanisms of accountability to women's organizations. As a 1993 discussion about national machinery concluded, "Politicians who do not agree with a strong role for government in the economy will not want government to be funding opposition. Relying on government means that the [funding] tap can be turned off or it can be manipulated. . . . Women need to know they have rights and be confident to be able to stand up for them."[16]

Women's organizations generally favored a broad proposal that called for structures and mechanisms at different levels of Parliament and government (national, regional, and local) and an independent statutory body. This view was underpinned by the notion of mainstreaming gender, which was expressed most forcefully at the Malibongwe Conference and was also the basis of later interventions in policy debates within the ANC.[17] As Razavi and Miller have summarized, mainstreaming involves making projects, programs, and policies of the state gender neutral, as well as making the entire bureaucracy responsible for paying attention to gender issues, such that it becomes routine.[18]

Women activists, particularly the feminists within the ANC, found such an approach attractive for a number of reasons. They regarded women's subordination and exploitation in South Africa as part of an overall system of capitalist and racial domination. At Malibongwe they argued that the transformation of gender relations should be seen in the context of the democratization of the society as a whole.[19] As an approach, mainstreaming seemed to fit into this analysis better than the creation of a separate ministry for women's affairs. Close contact with Australian feminists, including a study visit by a group of ANC-associated academics and politicians in 1994, reinforced the belief that a broadly social democratic state could provide a favorable context within which to advance the gender struggle.[20] In Australia, as Ann Curthoys has pointed out, feminism has successfully used the state to move the women's movement from a position that was "ineffably marginal and profoundly oppositional" to being "the mainstream, the powerful, the controlling."[21] The experiences of national machineries elsewhere reflected a tendency to create new forms of bureaucracy that entrenched narrow political interests of women inside government without in fact changing women's subordinate position in society. For this reason feminist activists favored a small bureaucracy that would seek to integrate gender equity principles into policy frameworks and implementation.[22] Women in the ANC (as well as the Democratic Party) were concerned that the national machinery could become another large bureaucratic structure, within a large and inefficient bureaucracy inherited from the apartheid state. Finally, women in the ANC, at least, were confident that the women's movement in South Africa was sufficiently strong to ensure that gender issues would not easily be marginalized in government.[23] Indeed, feminists regarded the strengthening of the women's movement as a crucial aspect of the strategy to engage the state.[24]

In sum, feminist activists regarded mainstreaming as a strategy for integrating gender concerns into all government policies, and they looked upon the national machinery as a means to that end, rather than as a permanent structure. Success would therefore be measured by the extent to which the machinery was no longer required to ensure that gender inequalities were being addressed in government policy and delivery. The support for mainstreaming from international donor agencies (most notably, the United Nations and the World Bank) would have facilitated endorsement of this approach by the new government, although there does not appear to have been any opposition to the proposals made by ANC feminists.

Two concerns had dominated debates at the 1992 workshop and the 1993 conference on how to ensure that the democratic government would address issues of gender equality. The first was the question of what were the best mechanisms for integrating women into public political life, including government. The mainstreaming approach still required some elaboration of the actual structures that would accompany the broad framework, and the powers and resources that would be conferred on these. The second concern was how to ensure that the national machinery would remain accountable to different constituencies of women, including rural women. Activists constantly stressed at workshops and conferences in the mid-1990s that the success of the national machinery was dependent on the existence of a strong women's movement. Reflecting these concerns, Baleka Mbete-Kgositsile, deputy Speaker in the first democratic Parliament, argued that a strong and well-coordinated women's movement "is crucial if the desired national machinery is to be driven effectively and if it is to be accountable to an identifiable and organised sector of the population."[25] Both concerns have remained central to debates about the establishment and progress of the national machinery, and indeed the design of the machinery takes into account the need for accountability to and monitoring by civil society in the establishment of the Commission on General Equality. As this chapter will show, while the first concern was partially carried forward in lobbying and activism, the emphasis on accountability rapidly disappeared during the first three years of the new democratic government.

The multiple levels of pressure for establishing national machinery structures also reflected varied understandings of the machinery in the early phase. In the period between the 1994 election and the enactment of the legislation establishing the Commission on General Equality in July 1996, five provincial governments (Eastern Cape, Northern Province, North West, Free State, and Northern Cape) initiated legislation to create gender commissions in the provinces. These structures were to be located within government. This created some confusion regarding the appropriate roles, structures, and locations of gender commissions and the relationship between structures inside and outside the state. The confusion arose largely because inclusion of the Commission on General Equality in the Interim Constitution had not been widely discussed or anticipated by the women's movement. Ironically, the strongest of the institutions in the gender machinery, with the widest-ranging powers and the greatest independence from political decision makers, was not even part of the original demands of the women's movement. Albertyn has suggested that the commission was a sop to the gender lobby by the constitutional negotiators to make up for the concession to traditional leaders in formulating a strong clause on the protection of culture and tradition.[26] Madonsela has argued that the commission was poorly conceptualized, "inserted in the Interim Constitution without much thought by certain 'male' experts during the last few hours of the constitution-making process. Attempts to discourage the structure as it had not been given sufficient thought fell on deaf ears. Interestingly, when the time came to developing a full concept of the [commission] in terms of powers, functions and relationship with other constitutional institutions, the 'father knows best' mindset suddenly gave way to the expectation of women discharging this responsibility."[27]

This confusion led to the proliferation of structures at the provincial level. In July and August 1996 the Ministry of Population and Welfare, the ministry responsible for producing the Beijing report, set up a consultative process to clarify the structures of the national machinery. This process highlighted the differences between national and provincial structures and delineated the functions of structures inside and outside government. The workshops drew on a proposal drafted by the Gender Research Group at the Centre for Applied Legal Studies that had been circulated widely during 1995; it became the guide for government decision makers.[28] The machinery created a set of structures in each of the key areas of the state and established one in civil society (see appendix B).

The ministry sought to find an institutional design that would ensure that there would be sufficient channels through which different women's organizations could leverage their demands. Several "strategic nodes" were identified inside and outside government.[29] Women's concerns are channeled within government through the Office on the Status of Women (OSW). The OSW's role is to "conceptualize a national gender policy and provide guidance on its implementation" by working with line ministries, provinces, and public bodies in mainstreaming gender into all policies and programs.[30] Part of the OSW's brief is to act as the liaison between the nongovernmental organizations that deal with women's issues and the Office of the President, as well as to act as liaison with Parliament. Within the legislature women MPs are formally organized in the Parliamentary Women's

Group and through the Joint Standing Committee for Improving the Quality of Life and Status of Women. Formal roles and responsibilities were carefully parceled out between the OSW, the parliamentary committee, and the Commission on Gender Equality to ensure minimal overlap while compensating for weaknesses in any one sector.[31] A significant gap in this design is the absence of any mechanisms at the local government level.

This package of arrangements "institutionalized" women's politics in the sense of drawing women activists into formalized structures and processes of interacting with key state actors and other interest groups. The attraction for women activists was that institutionalization would ensure that gender concerns are addressed in the everyday work of government— procedures, policy formulation, and service delivery. According to Kathleen Jones's analysis, the South African state could be characterized as "women friendly"—a state that has made an explicit commitment to the principle of gender equality and the direct pursuit of this objective through the development of structures and policies.[32] In theory the effect of institutionalization has been to make the state more permeable to the influence of organized constituencies of women. In formal terms the state is now *required* to consider gender issues both in its internal operation and in policy formulation.

In practice, however, consolidating the new institutions of policy representation and advocacy has been far from smooth, even though the entry of previously excluded groups (black women and men in particular) into the civil service was constitutionally and politically validated. The ANC government prioritized two forms of state-led transformation: ensuring that the workforce of state institutions reflects society in terms of race and gender and reducing social and economic inequalities through public policies. These aims are congruent with a feminist agenda of transformation, which seeks to make the public service more permeable to women's interests as well as to use public policy as a lever to redress gender inequities. Both are aspects of what Goetz has termed "institutional gender responsiveness."[33] The first demands an internal focus on gender equity within the civil service; the second requires that policies and service delivery be examined for their effect on gender relations and the degree to which the government agencies "include women equitably among the 'publics' they ostensibly serve."[34]

The idea of activism at several sites in the original design of the machinery assumed that women in the bureaucracy and in Parliament would be able to work together to make the government responsive to the interests of different groups of women. Indeed, shortly after the 1994 election several women ministers interviewed by the feminist magazine *Speak* outlined ambitious plans to implement new policies and transform the civil service. Stella Sigcau, the minister of public enterprises, promised to make the economic empowerment of women a priority for her department by providing

women with such resources as water and electricity.[35] Nkosazana Zuma, the
new minister of health, saw her role as an extension of her gender activism
within the ANC. "It is a very big responsibility that rests on my shoulders,"
she told *Speak*. "But I am excited because the important role women played
in the struggle was recognized."[36] Like Zuma, many activists viewed the
shift into the state as a natural progression that would take the agenda of
equality into more powerful arenas; they did not see it as an abandonment
of the women's movement. However, the large-scale movement of women
leaders from the women's organizations into the state had politically demo-
bilizing effects.[37] As I showed in chapter 5, the Women's National Coalition
virtually collapsed because its leaders left to go into government, and without national leadership, grassroots women's organizations found it difficult
to reformulate their roles in the changed context of democracy.[38]

Working out the details of the national machinery and getting government commitment for these structures took longer than achieving consensus within the women's movement about the nature of the machinery.
There was little time during the negotiation process to reach agreement on
the details of the national machinery—indeed, it was not even an explicit
demand of the coalition. As late as 1994 Brigitte Mabandla, the ANC constitutional expert and gender activist, was arguing that a ministry of women's
affairs might be a good choice and that "it is possible to negotiate favour-
able budgetary terms for the ministry. It is also possible to negotiate the pri-
oritization of the women's ministry because of the recognition of the centrality of gender consciousness in the reconstruction of the country. . . . A
women's ministry would formulate a national programme of action for a
specified period of time directed towards women's development."[39]

Mabandla's detailed proposals for what the responsibilities of the ministry would be (including driving legislative reform and advising the cabinet) suggest that there were some differences, even within the ANC camp,
about the precise nature of the national machinery. While these differences
were not necessarily conflictual, they reflect some lack of clarity about the
detail of the bureaucratic system being proposed. In any event, implementation of the proposal for national machinery, including detailed elaboration of the powers and resources of government-financed aspects, was
postponed until the new government was set up.

Drawing on the Reconstruction and Development Programme (RDP),
processes of policy formulation within the ANC set up parallel debates and
proposals with regard to mainstreaming gender within specific sectors, such
as health and justice. Some of these proposals were carried through into
government in isolation from the larger proposals for the national machinery. By 1995 some government agencies had begun initiatives to address gender concerns.[40] Some departments—justice, defense, water affairs, welfare,

and population development—developed internal gender policies establishing good practice guidelines within the department and for external service delivery.[41] Implementation of commitments to gender equality was
therefore not a linear process but one in which pressure was being applied
at various points and with different rates of success, depending on the degree of organization of women within the sector external to government.

The health sector reveals the nexus of relationships that made early
interventions by feminist activists in policy formulation successful. As I
showed in chapter 2, in the 1980s women's organizations developed an
understanding of how women's social and economic inequalities affected
their health. Women in trade unions demanded attention to maternity benefits, access to contraception, and education about occupational health issues as part of trade union education and campaigning.[42] Opposing the
apartheid state did not facilitate the development of specific policy demands in relation to state-provided health care. However, as Klugman's
case study on the policy process in this sector has pointed out, the progressive health movement, which operated parallel to the women's movement, began to develop some proposals around the effect of population
control programs on women's reproductive rights.[43] She identified two
parallel streams of debate: a rights-based orientation to women's health issues within the women's movement, and a medical orientation in the health
movement (comprised of researchers, clinicians, and health advocates).
The policy linkage between the two was provided by the attempts to develop concrete frameworks that could be implemented in a democratic system. Internal debate within the ANC about various health proposals offered women activists the opportunity to shift the ANC's orientation away
from a medical model to one of women's empowerment and rights.[44]

Engagement of women activists within the ANC enabled the development of gender aware policy frameworks. However, as Klugman has pointed
out with regard to health, and Meer with regard to land,[45] the absence of
analysis of the effect of women's oppression on their health status or their
access to economic empowerment, and the lack of a plan for how the new
government would address gender equality, hobbled the implementation of
policy. Without this clear direction, and without the allocation of resources
to gender training programs for civil servants, policy implementers and service agencies in government tend to revert to conventional and familiar
ideological and technical frameworks and tools. It was expected that the
gender machinery within government, in consultation with the Commission on Gender Equality and women's movement, would develop such an
overarching gender analysis and plan to address gender equality. However,
as I show in the next section, institutionalization of the national machinery
was slow and uneven, and a national gender policy was finalized only in 2001.

National Machinery: Institutionalizing Accountability

The specific provision for the Commission on Gender Equality in the 1994 Interim Constitution concentrated initial discussions on national machinery on this structure. The commission was established in April 1997. In terms of the Constitution and the Commission on Gender Equality Act (1996), the commission is to have eight to twelve commissioners, only two of whom may be part time. The roles and functions of the commission are wide ranging and include monitoring and evaluating the policies and practices of both government and the private sector, as well as public education, making recommendations to government on particular legislation, and resolving gender-related disputes through mediation and conciliation or litigation. Along with the South African Human Rights Commission and the Public Protector, the Commission on Gender Equality is a statutory body, established by the Constitution and accountable only to Parliament. Commissioners are appointed by the president and may be removed from office only by a special sitting of Parliament. These provisions insulate the commission, at least formally, from unwanted interference by political parties or the government.

The Commission on Gender Equality began its work by convening a series of information gathering and evaluation workshops on organizational responses to gender inequality,[46] with funding from the Commonwealth Secretariat. These workshops had a dual effect. They signaled the commission's commitment to a consultative mode of planning, an important factor given the high expectation that the national machinery would be accountable to constituencies of women. Consultation also allowed the commission to define areas of need in terms of mandated roles. The workshops also reenergized women's organizations, which by 1997 felt somewhat adrift from national processes.[47] The commission was perceived as a national facilitator of campaigns and policy interventions on gender equality. This perception shaped its role under its first chair, the respected gender activist Thenjiwe Mtintso.

As I noted earlier, the Commission on Gender Equality faced immediate financial pressures, some of which were alleviated through donations. Political pressure from both inside and outside the state emerged early in the commission's life. Difficulties experienced by the Human Rights Commission in setting up its structures and establishing its profile led to a debate in government about the effectiveness of commissions. A government task force was appointed to review the efficacy of and resource allocation to statutory commissions. A minority opposition party in Parliament, the Democratic Party, raised political questions about the necessity for the range of commissions, criticizing the need for both a gender and a human rights commission. The Democratic Party recommended the two commissions be merged, sparking an intense media debate about wastefulness in government spending.[48]

The Commission on Gender Equality was thus immediately plunged into defending its right to exist as a separate organization and its track record in the short period of its existence. The statutory status of the commission protected it from short-term political threats and changes of priorities. Unlike the Office on the Status of Women, the commission could not simply be removed as a result of changes in political will within particular Parliaments. Although accountable to Parliament, the commission's budget is allocated by the Ministry of Finance through the Department of Justice.[49] Fiscal pressures on government resulted in the commission's having to compete for funds with other statutory bodies, as well as with government departments. The Ministry of Finance allocates a lump sum to the Department of Justice for the commissions, which the Department of Justice then allocates. A practical implication is that the Commission on Gender Equality has to pursue sources of funding other than the parliamentary grant in order to avoid a slow erosion of its capacity to act as an effective watchdog body. In 1998 the commission was more successful in getting approval for its budget of six million rands. The staff expanded from two in 1997 to thirty-five by 1999, and four departments were created: policy and research; legal; public education and information; and finance, funding, and administration. A forum for public debate, the "gender dialogue," has engaged issues such as reproductive rights, violence against women, and elections, bringing together women's organizations, academic experts, and government representatives. In addition, the commission has made submissions on policy proposals with regard to local government, the child maintenance grant, and the draft white paper on safety. A number of submissions were also made to Parliament in connection with various pieces of legislation, including most recently the Communal Land Rights Bill. In partnership with NGOs such as the African Gender Institute, the Women's Health Project, and the Community Agency for Social Enquiry, the commission has sponsored or supported research into processes of policy formulation, baseline data with regard to women, the position of women on farms, and an evaluation of the effect on women of development in the Maputo Corridor, among other projects. The commission also asked the Centre for Applied Legal Studies to produce a comprehensive audit of legislation that discriminates on the basis of gender.

Commissioners are responsible for different provinces. Because of the financial constraints, and the relatively small number of commissioners, the commission has not been able to set up offices in all nine provinces. Nevertheless, it has held a number of provincial consultation workshops and sponsored several provincial projects. These include a major study of witchcraft in the Northern Province, action around violence against women in partnership with NGOs in all the provinces, and a gender audit of the Maputo Corridor project in the Mpumalanga Province.

In some respects the commission has been successful. Initially, it built partnerships with women's organizations and researchers and actively engaged in media information and awareness campaigns around gender issues. However, a number of leadership changes and racial tensions have affected the effectiveness and political direction of the commission.[50] The departure of the first chair, Thenjiwe Mtintso, who was "redeployed" by the ANC to be its deputy secretary general, was the most damaging of those changes. Mtintso brought an astute strategic vision, widespread political credibility, and uncompromising commitment to independence to the organization. A year later the chief executive officer, Colleen Lowe Morna, who had been responsible for driving the commission's work program and raising money from donors, was ousted in an unpleasant (and, according to some, racist) manner. Her departure was followed by the resignation of a number of skilled staff members, leaving the commission with a vacuum in terms of skills and institutional memory and without strategic direction. The resignations of staff members highlighted a crucial tension in the commission (and in other statutory bodies). On the one hand, commissioners are appointed by the president and have political status at the level of cabinet ministers. On the other hand, staff members tended to be more skilled at understanding the nature of gender inequalities and were often better able to conceptualize a strategic direction for the commission. The clash between the staff and commissioners has left power in the hands of the commissioners but resulted in the loss of the organization's energy and strategic direction.[51]

The key weakness of the commission has been in its slowness to act as a watchdog with regard to government. Gay Seidman has argued that this is because the commission has vacillated between a mobilizing and a representational role, which undermines its efficacy.[52] Many appointments to the commission have been based on party loyalties rather than on experience within the women's movement—indeed, Parliament did not even ratify the recommendation of the parliamentary committee that selected new commissioners in 2001 on the grounds that they were inappropriate, unrepresentative, and biased toward the ANC. The commission has not been successful in challenging the government's backsliding in regard to its commitments to gender equality, especially in regard to funding. At the crucial early stages of consolidating the machinery, lack of resources had severe consequences, which I will discuss as part of my analysis of governmental structures responsible for gender. The role and capacities of the commission in this regard are unique as no women's organization is able to exercise this kind of oversight, for both political reasons and a lack of expertise. Nevertheless, many feminists have viewed the weakness of the commission with great sadness. As Seidman put it, "By mid-2000, many feminist scholars and NGO activists, black and white, openly expressed a sense of alienation from and abandonment by the very institution they had helped design, criticizing the commission publically to journalists and even going so far as to suggest that the government should consider cutting funding for the commission's activities."[53]

Representation without Power: The New Institutions for Policy Access

Transforming the state while retaining effective linkages between elected women leaders, women civil servants, and the women's movement was far from easy. Indeed, the state was revealed to women activists as consisting of multiple arenas, each with different cultures and modes of decision making that did not always coordinate with one another as smoothly as the design of the national machinery assumed. Although the Office on the Status of Women is located in the Office of the President and would seem to be at the locus of government power, its powers to influence policy agendas are relatively weak as it has no direct access to the cabinet or to interministerial committees. The gender focal points, strategic nodes within government departments whose task is to integrate gender equity concerns into policy frameworks and implementation strategies, also lack authority. All appointments of gender focal point staff are at the level of deputy director or below, post levels that carry no authority to force directors general of government departments (those officially charged with implementing policy), let alone ministers, to take account of gender concerns. Gender focal points are not automatically part of any process of policy formulation or critical review.

Formal authority for setting policy priorities and direction resides in the cabinet, the highest decision-making body in government. This makes it imperative that there be effective communication between women ministers in the cabinet and the Office on the Status of Women, as well as a joint process of establishing priorities for policy interventions. This is particularly important, given that taking account of women's interests is often associated with increased spending, a political task that requires convincing government to recognize women as a key constituency. However, there is no formal coordination between women ministers and the civil service structures. This constitutes a major weakness. As Sawer has shown in her comparative study of women's policy machinery in Australia, Canada, and New Zealand, "gender expertise must be backed by routinized access to policy development and Cabinet processes, and institutionalized forms of accountability for gender outcomes. While the policy brokering skills of individual femocrats and ministers might be important, bureaucratic entrenchment gives lasting returns."[54]

The informal and sometimes invisible aspects of institutions also impose constraints on attempts to use institutions strategically. Although activism in the unions, the women's movement, and the antiapartheid struggle gave many of the new, mostly black, women bureaucrats valuable experience in how to change an organization, they have struggled to translate these experiences effectively in their new jobs. For those women activists who entered government service after the 1994 elections in the expectation that they would be able to contribute to building democracy from within, the frustrations of coping with the transition from nonhierarchical and open organizational forms to the bureaucracy have been great.

For many women it seems that the bureaucracy is institutionally unable to accommodate their new interests. The civil service has retained the structure and in many cases the culture of the apartheid civil service, which was organized hierarchically, even militaristically.[55] While the highest levels of government may support gender equity as a key policy goal, at lower levels department officials are resistant, if not openly hostile, to attempts to mainstream gender.[56] The majority of the white apartheid-era staff retained their jobs in the civil service by agreements made in the negotiated settlement. Many now see affirmative action as a threat to their job security. Women in the civil service lack a party to back them up on an ongoing basis or to counter their relative lack of seniority. Black women, in particular, lack institutional political clout.

The difficulties of making commitments to gender equality concrete are exacerbated by the appointment into gender focal points of career bureaucrats with little interest in or knowledge of the principles of gender equality. In some departments interviewees expressed resentment about being placed in a position with little possibility of career mobility, while others were indifferent to the political task of equality, waiting for instructions from the national office of the Office on the Status of Women. Many commented that there was general uncertainty about the role of the gender focal points, even at the highest level of administration. "At the moment everybody knows that *gender* is a buzz word—you have to have something called *gender* in your department, or *gender* in your institution. . . . Why it should be there is not clear," a member of the Gauteng Provincial Legislature said.[57] The mainstreaming approach to policy is a particularly rigorous strategy that requires translating broad gender equity commitments into meaningful programs, each of which has to be interpreted within the specific policy priorities and service delivery plans of twenty-seven different departments.

One frustrated OSW staffer commented that her activist history and understanding of the political dynamic of gender power relations was not enough: "You've got to couple it with discipline, management. Because if you make us gender officers today in this department, what will we do, where do we start, what are the critical problems to address and how?"[58]

The small budget for the national office has made it difficult for the OSW to offer effective policy guidance or training.[59] This has produced tensions between provincial offices and the national office. Apart from a lack of cohesion in the government machinery, several staffers at the provincial level made off-the-record comments about the overemphasis on international conferences and commitments and the little direction they receive about how to deal with issues at the provincial and local level. One person who was prepared to comment on the record said, "You cannot just be engaged in a project which ordinary people would not be able to interpret. . . . [The Beijing platform] is too vague and nebulous, and they don't lend themselves to any kind of scrutiny because we know that they won't happen overnight. Let's be realistic about the things outside that militate against our success and [let's] address those things."[60]

Initially, some government departments—justice, water affairs, welfare, and population development—made important advances in developing internal gender policies that established good practice guidelines within departments and for external service delivery.[61] However, these have not been fully implemented. A major stumbling block is the failure of the OSW in particular and the machinery as a whole to develop a broad framework within which specific policy demands could be politically legitimated and against which internal government advocacy could take place. As both Klugman[62] and Meer[63] have pointed out, the absence of analysis of the effect of women's oppression on their health status or their access to economic empowerment, and the lack of a plan that sets strategic priorities, has resulted in piecemeal rather than effective interventions on the part of gender focal points. Without this clear direction, and without the allocation of resources to gender training programs for civil servants, policy implementers and service agencies in government tended to revert to conventional and familiar ideological and technical frameworks and tools.

As I suggested in chapter 6, discussing gender equity in broad political terms in Parliament was easier than actually implementing policy and program changes at the departmental level, where civil service rules make it fairly easy for those hostile to change to use procedures and rules to stifle creativity. Unlike women MPs, who entered Parliament on a wave of acclaim, women civil servants have had to battle constantly both to legitimate themselves within their departments and to implement gender-equitable policy in the field.

These problems have reinforced the tendency of women bureaucrats to focus inwardly rather than build relationships with women's organizations outside the state. Consequently, although there has been some attention to issues of representation within the public service, little attention has been paid to the strategic concern of ensuring that the gender machinery acts as an effective point of access for women's organizations. These difficulties are endemic to governments that have tried to rapidly integrate women, and women's concerns, into the bureaucracy and policy-making processes. Feminist bureaucrats—sometimes termed *femocrats*—are caught between the resistance of male bureaucrats and the expectations of women's organizations outside government. Anne Summers has shown how conventional bureaucrats in Australia in the early years suspiciously regarded femocrats as missionaries, while women's movement activists criticized femocrats for having been co-opted to become mandarins of the state.[64] Increasingly forced to operate within the rules of the bureaucracy, rather than according to the less hierarchal and consultative norms of the women's movement, femocrats become distanced from the political bases that opened space within the state for them.[65]

There was little space to conceptualize and strategize the strategic tasks that faced the national machinery as a whole, and no sense of an overarching set of goals existed that would guide feminist intervention. Although the Women's Charter for Effective Equality had been envisioned as providing this guide, the document was more or less abandoned as a political tool. Demands for quotas have increasingly been delinked from debates about what interests women would represent once they entered Parliament, even though representation and accountability were explicitly linked in pre-1994 women's politics. Nor has the discussion about equality that the Women's Charter began been followed through effectively in post-1994 politics. In the apartheid era a clear line was drawn between struggles for formal equality and those for substantive equality. Formal equality—the achievement of equal rights and opportunities—was regarded as an inadequate conceptualization of liberation. The achievement of formal political and civil rights, while an important gain in itself, was understood as a weak form of equality that would have little effect on the lives of poor women. What was needed was substantive equality, understood as the transformation of the economic conditions that produce gender equality.[66] The Women's Charter articulates a notion of equality that is closer to the vision of substantive equality, with a very clear emphasis on the structural and systemic underpinnings of women's subordinate status.[67] I would argue that a strong notion of equality, one that would provide some guidance about appropriate policy choices in South Africa, would rest on the extent to which overall poverty is reduced, the extent to which women feel safe in society, the degree to which women are recognized as rights-bearing citizens and are able to make choices free of the constraints of domestic and family responsibilities, and free of the pressure to remain in oppressive and violent relationships.[68] This notion of equality has specific implications for social policy, as it would require that resources be directed in such a way that they only to address the needs of the poorest women but also become part of an incremental process of enhancing women's autonomy and full participation in political and economic processes. In examining the child support grant in the next section, I explore the underlying gendered assumptions that limit the effectiveness of current social policy in redressing inequalities of gender.

One project that sought to underscore the importance of engaging the economic decision-making process as the core to effective mainstreaming was the Women's Budget Initiative. This is a joint project inspired by the Australian Women's Budget and involving government, researchers, and civil society.[69] The South African project seeks to examine "the gendered impact of all parts of government's annual budget on the citizens of the country. It looks at both the efficiency and equity implications of budget allocations and the policies and programmes that lie behind them."[70] With the support of the chair of the Joint Standing Committee on Finance,[71] a working group on gender and economic policy was formed in 1994. The Women's Budget Initiative was developed in 1995 under the aegis of this group, and in 1996 South Africa was chosen by the Commonwealth Secretariat as a pilot country in a project on engendering the national budget and macroeconomic policy. The inclusion of a parliamentary committee in the partnership is particularly significant. As Budlender has noted, "One of the greatest strengths of having a parliamentary voice in initiatives, besides the parliamentarians' legitimated power, lies in agitating for changes before budgets are drawn up so as to influence officials rather than making changes after presentation."[72]

The Women's Budget Initiative has analyzed the budget votes of all twenty-seven government departments, as well as the votes of the overall sectors of taxation, budget reform, public sector employment, and intergovernmental fiscal relations.[73] The research posed a number of questions with regard to the nature and extent of departmental spending, the public-private mix in service provision, and the degree of poor women's access to resources. A significant early achievement of the Women's Budget Initiative has been to highlight the importance of gender analysis within the Ministry of Finance, by mobilizing the expertise of feminist policy analysts outside government in tandem with pressure from Parliament. In his 1996 budget speech the minister of finance committed the ministry to developing a "statistical database which will provide information on the impact of expenditures disaggregated by gender, the implementation of targets and indicators

of gender equality and equity in spending and the development of a performance review mechanism to evaluate progress and report to Parliament,"
according to Govender.[74] In addition, the minister later committed the ministry to ensuring the inclusion of women's unpaid labor in the gross domestic product.[75] The 1998 budget review was the first attempt to implement
this commitment, although the Joint Standing Committee on Improving
the Quality of Life and Status of Women has pointed out that more comprehensive integration of gender in the budget is necessary.[76] However, it
has been difficult to sustain this level of commitment. By 2001 the Ministry
of Finance had withdrawn from the Women's Budget Initiative. The difficulties of integrating gender analysis into the Ministry of Finance are to be
expected. As Gita Sen has suggested, the ministries of finance in many
countries are "singularly untouched by the winds of gender change that are
beginning to blow through other ministries. . . . The reasons . . . lie in the
content of what Finance Ministries do, in their prevailing ethos and attitudes, and in the relatively weak capacity of many women's organizations
to engage in macroeconomic policy debates."[77]

The withdrawal of the Finance Ministry from the Women's Budget Initiative means that its status and effectiveness as a joint civil society–state project
remains uncertain. Conceived primarily as a monitoring and auditing exercise, the Women's Budget Initiative has not achieved significant levels of civil
society activism in support of the project. Although the advocacy of the
NGO involved in the partnership (the Institute for a Democratic Alternative in South Africa) has ensured that the government produces gender-
disaggregated data, this has not been strongly linked with organizations that
are questioning the fundamental assumptions of macroeconomic policy.

Creating Enabling Frameworks for
Advancing Gender Equality

Internal constraints of bureaucratic culture are not the only forces that
shape feminists' engagement with the state. The inadequacy of budgetary
resources and infrastructural capacity in South Africa, as in other developing countries, places an often overwhelming constraint on the extent to
which rights are implemented. This is particularly pertinent because many
legislative advances, especially the Domestic Violence Act and the Maintenance Act, require substantial increases in funding if they are to be effective.[78] Indeed, the mainstreaming approach entails significant levels of
planning, coordination, and policy cohesion. Moreover, effective delivery of
services and welfare benefits requires an extensive and functioning administrative system that can reach the rural areas, where a significant proportion
of South Africa's poor women reside.

These constraints have been increasingly visible in the implementation of gender commitments. Gender activists were hopeful that the Reconstruction and Development Programme (RDP), which had been formulated before the 1994 elections with the intensive participation of feminists within the ANC, would provide the macroeconomic framework that would help to justify to the Ministry of Finance the expenditures necessary for achieving substantive equality. The RDP was a program for the radical transformation of society—one that was highly enabling for women activists who saw piecemeal reforms as stifling fundamental questioning of the structural and cultural bases of women's inequality.[79] Yet the RDP was by no means a perfect document from a feminist perspective. Although women activists had worked hard to integrate gender into the whole document, the final program listed women as a sector to be developed, along with youth, rural, and disabled people. Despite the demands for mainstreaming, gender equity appears as to be tacked onto the final report.[80] As the editorial collective of the feminist journal *Agenda* pointed out in its submission to the minister responsible, the 1994 RDP White Paper did not integrate the gender machinery into the program at any level, failed to spell out the need for monitoring the effects of policy (and particularly economic policy) on women, and did not outline any mechanisms for gender accountability.[81] Even given these flaws, however, the RDP did hold out the promise that substantive equality would be the cornerstone of government's approach to policy development.

Within two years, and before the gender machinery was set up, the RDP was demoted from a full-fledged ministry to a desk within the president's office. In its place, and ostensibly as a set of tools to achieve the RDP's goals, the ANC government adopted the Growth, Employment and Redistribution Strategy (GEAR) in 1996. For many observers GEAR consolidated a rightward shift within the new government.[82] In translating the RDP as a campaign issue into RDP as policy (in the 1994 RDP White Paper), a significant shift was made from the primacy of the goal of transformation to "achieving the RDP within the context of fiscal and monetary stringency."[83] The GEAR strategy, dubbed an "internally-led structural adjustment" by some,[84] commits the government to market-led policies for growth, job creation, and poverty reduction, with fiscal restraint as its key condition for success.[85] This changed context had a dramatic effect on the ability of women's organizations to extract meaningful reforms from the state. While the macroeconomic premises in the RDP White Paper and GEAR might have been similar, the political and discursive effects of GEAR's language and politics were significant—and negative for women's organizations. The ANC defended GEAR, which was drawn up in "somewhat secretive conditions" and presented as nonnegotiable.[86] The ANC's defense went against the notions of participation and accountability—the "people-driven program"—that had characterized the RDP rhetoric. Valodia has pointed out that of the seventeen economists involved in drafting GEAR, only one was a woman and only one was not white.[87] Unlike the process that produced the RDP, no women's organizations or gender experts participated in the formulation of GEAR. Gelb has noted that "this was reform from above with a vengeance, taking to extreme the arguments in favour of insulation and autonomy of policymakers from popular pressures."[88]

Women cabinet ministers did not raise any opposition to the adoption of the strategy or point out the negative implications it might have on gender policies.[89] Valodia commented that "the GEAR strategy as a whole does not adopt any gender perspective on economic policy."[90] Indeed, as Marais has pointed out, GEAR "provides no targets for reducing inequality,"[91] and even though the government sought to reduce the deficit without cutting social spending and committed itself to directing savings effected by the policy toward the poor, there were few guarantees. As I will show, the Department of Welfare, at least, and probably other departments in the social sectors, interpreted the policy shift as an injunction to limit the extent of its high-cost programs. Within a short two years, then, even the "add women and stir" approach to policy of the RDP seemed beyond the reach of women's organizations.

Even more worrying for the long-term prospects of leveraging women's presence in government, by 1995 gender activists already were noting a growing distance between women's organizations in civil society and women in Parliament. Although both sides continually reiterated the importance of strong links, activists outside government criticized women in government for lack of consultation, and women in government blamed the collapse of the Women's National Coalition for a breakdown in formal communications.[92] The multipronged strategy for advancing gender equality— strong institutions buttressed by a strong political movement—was already collapsing under the weight of rightward shifts in economic policy, bureaucratic resistance, and a women's movement weakened, if not completely demobilized, by loss of leadership and lack of political expertise.

In short, the gender machinery, conceived in a period when all things seemed possible, was born with its feet bound. Budgets for all structures were minuscule, despite the repeated assurances of government that it remained committed to gender equality. For women's organizations the ability to leverage the symbolic power and legislative representation of women into policy outcomes was severely undermined. Government's assertion of fiscal restraint introduced a new discourse into policy making: the debate was increasingly less concerned with what was desirable and increasingly more concerned with what was possible. Doubtless, this was a reality that accompanied the hard task of government. However, affordability was often assessed in narrow fiscal terms and by prioritizing gross inequalities rather than a concern with the long-term costs of failing to address pervasive systemic inequalities. The formal provisions of the Constitution proved inappropriate for dealing with the ways in which government prioritizes spending. Although the right to social security is entrenched in the socioeconomic rights clause in Constitution (Section 27) the implementation of this right is by no means automatic, nor does it guarantee that the extent of social security provided will be adequate to ensure a decent standard of living. The important proviso to the right to social security is a qualifying clause in Section 27 of the Bill of Rights, which defines the state's obligations as limited to "available resources."[93]

In South Africa the political discourse has clearly shifted from one of rights to one more closely approximating Fraser's "politics of needs articulation." She has argued that "the interpretation of people's needs is itself a political stake, indeed sometimes *the* political stake."[94] Fraser exposed the contested—and not just the contextual—nature of needs claims, an emphasis that is useful for understanding the political contestation about extending of the child maintenance grant. Fraser regards the politics of needs interpretation as comprised of three interrelated moments: the struggle to establish the status of a need as a political matter; the struggle to interpret the need itself; and the struggle to satisfy the need—or the struggle to secure or deny its satisfaction. Fraser's formulation frames the discussion that follows in which I explore the struggle to extend the child maintenance grant to poor children of all races. Because access to these children is through the mother, the child benefit grant is a useful case study of the ways in which policy proposals deal with women's claims on the state. This case offers a clear example of the difficulty of articulating women's rights and needs in the context of other equity claims, despite the existence of formal commitments to gender equality, and of the difficulty of translating into effective policy the contention of the women's movement that race, class, and gender are interrelated.

Constituting Women's Interests: The Case of the Child Maintenance Grant

In 1996 the Department of Welfare began the process of overhauling the system of child and family benefits. At the time the government was also opening debate on the White Paper on Social Welfare, which provided an overarching policy framework that explicitly prioritized poverty reduction. The changes to the welfare provisions for children began in a transitional context of translating broad policy formulations into concrete programs, and the Lund Committee on Child and Family Support, which spearheaded these, was to become the lightning rod for conflicts about the shift in government's macroeconomic policies.

The White Paper on Social Welfare, published in February 1996 and adopted in 1997, establishes a strong maternalist framework for understanding women's social policy needs. It emphasizes the importance of cultural norms and values, particularly the principles of caring and interdependence. However, the emphasis on the cultural value of domesticity is not accompanied by a recognition of the *work* of domesticity. It is significant that the White Paper does not link domestic work and women's access to the public sphere of political participation or women's access to labor markets. This could be seen as loading the dice against women, who bear the practical burdens of domestic work within families and communities. It has been estimated that urban women spend 207 mean minutes per day on domestic work (household maintenance, care of persons, and community service) compared to the 81 minutes spent by men.[95] In rural households, where young children and older people needing care are most likely to be sent, women spend 34 mean minutes per day caring for people, whereas men spent a mean of 2 minutes. Women's caring burdens have, for example, dramatically increased as the HIV/AIDS infection rates have assumed pandemic proportions.

Although feminist language of rights and entitlements has been included in many legislative frameworks, the key welfare policy document, the White Paper on Social Welfare, is couched within a more traditionalist discourse that understands women's caring roles in terms of their responsibilities to families and communities and not in terms of their class interests as working women. Indeed, caring is conceptualized as a problem arising out of apartheid-based familial breakdown rather than a problem that needs to be resolved so that women may exercise their rights to full economic and political citizenship. The particular (and greater) responsibility of the state in meeting social security needs through the redistribution of public resources is diluted by the emphasis on tapping into communitarian values. This limits the effectiveness of the state in addressing women's caring burdens as well as the effect of social policy expenditures on relations of power between women and men. Since the adoption of the White Paper, moral rather than rights discourses have shaped social security provision. There is an interesting disarticulation between the assumptions of the gendered nature of care work in the White Paper on Social Welfare and the emphasis in the Constitution on women's autonomy. Care work is certainly recognized in the White Paper, but that recognition is not presented as the opportunity to shift the burdens away from women. The caring model, which ostensibly values collective social responsibility, does not value the importance of women's autonomy from the expectations of family and community. Collective social responsibility is, in effect, privatized (by shifting it onto communities and therefore women) rather than made a responsibility of the state, and the opportunities to create the conditions for women to exercise their agency in a variety of social and economic arenas are reduced.

The limitations of this conceptualization of child care are evident in the ways in which state support for poor mothers is allocated. The state maintenance grant was established in the apartheid era as the main grant for child and family care. It was awarded on a means-tested basis to certain categories of women. Poor mothers were paid a total monthly grant of 700 rands for a maximum of two children younger than eighteen. Social security measures during the apartheid era were racially discriminatory in the scope and levels of benefits.[96] The majority of beneficiaries were poor white, colored, and Indian families. Although African families constituted the majority of poor households, most African families did not benefit from the grant; they were largely excluded through a range of administrative measures. For example, the homelands and "independent" states such as the Transkei did not administer the grant, rendering vast swaths of the African population without access to social welfare.

The Lund Committee's brief was to explore, among other things, policy options for the provision of social security for children and families "in the context of anti-poverty, economic empowerment and capacity-building strategies" and to develop approaches for effective targeting of programs.[97] The committee was appointed by the director general of social welfare at the time, Leila Patel, a feminist activist who had been in the forefront of the Federation of Transvaal Women. The committee chair, Frances Lund, was a progressive academic with a record of commitment to gender equality. One key expert on the committee was the feminist economist Debbie Budlender, who had been part of the research team of the Women's National Coalition and led the Women's Budget Initiative. There were high expectations that this committee would begin the process of overhauling the social security framework to make it more responsive to the gendered nature of poverty. Indeed, the committee took as its guide various national and international commitments on gender and poverty made by the South African government. These included the Declaration and Programme of the World Summit for Social Development, Copenhagen; the Beijing Platform for Action; and CEDAW. However, the debates that ensued about the Lund Committee's proposals pitted women in national government and in women's organizations against each other as the Ministry of Welfare, led by a gender-sensitive minister and with a gender-sensitive advisory team, came to represent the unpleasant face of government.

It is beyond the scope of this chapter to outline all the proposals made by the Lund Committee. One far-reaching progressive change that the Lund Committee achieved was to shift the terminology used for the person responsible for child care to the *primary care-giver* rather than the *mother* or even *guardian*. This was a small but important shift. As Sainsbury and others have shown, the basis of welfare entitlements is a crucial aspect of welfare states. Entitlements that privilege the head of household tend to undermine women's independent access to benefits. On the other hand, emphasis on motherhood can equally narrow women's access to benefits by imposing moral regulation on women. In the South African case the emphasis on the primary caregiver recognizes the work of child care, regardless of who performs it—an important factor in a context where aunts and grandparents also provide caregiving.

What is of note, however, is that the committee's recommendations were based on a tight budget scenario in which the already inadequate welfare budget faced further cuts from the central government. Despite the commitments to address poverty, the committee felt constrained by this fiscal environment. "The policy directives have been: do not ask for too much more, save money through more effective management and through downsizing the bureaucracy; and redistribute within the present envelope,"[98] the committee's report noted. Lund commented at a conference on the politics of economic reform in 1998 that, "stated extremely simply, the basic strategy was: 'This is an uncertain climate for social security, and there is a lack of popular and political support for the grants for women. If we devise a plan within the fiscal limits set by GEAR (whose basic message was, come up with a plan within the existing envelope) we are likely to retain the existing budget for family-related social security. If not, we'll lose it.'"

Minister of Welfare Geraldine Fraser-Moleketi argued that "in an ideal world, I too would wish to be able to spend more on social security in the immediate term. However, in a developing country such as ours, we have to balance competing demands and decide how to use scarce resources in the most effective way."[99] The Ministry of Welfare saw the balancing act as upholding the principles of racial equity and poverty reduction of women on the one hand, and a strictly controlled fiscal program on the other. Unexpectedly, however, the aim of racial equity came to compete with that of poverty reduction. The choice that faced the Lund Committee became starkly posed as that between spreading the same amount of money more widely and equitably among all races (deracialize) or raising the allocation to poor women by increasing this part of the overall budget (challenging the government's macroeconomic policy). Even merely deracializing the grant would raise welfare expenditures significantly: Lund, Ardington, and Harber estimated that the cost to the state to extend the grant to all eligible caregivers would be 117 rands (approximately U.S. $10) per child, and this would increase the budget from 1.8 billion rands annually to at least 11.8 billion rands annually.[100] Although both deracialization and poverty reduction can be seen as in women's interests, the specific form in which both should be pursued and the ways in which they were prioritized became a matter of political contestation in which women's organizations were presented with a *choice* between these aims.

The Department of Welfare accepted the committee's initial recommendation of a flat-rate child support benefit (75 rands per month) for each child younger than nine, to reach approximately three million children by 2005.[101] One key effect was to radically cut welfare grants to white, colored, and Indian mothers who had been the main beneficiaries of the state maintenance grant. In addition, the committee recommended that maintenance responsibility should increasingly be shifted away from the state toward parents. Nongovernmental and women's organizations denounced the recommendations as an attack on poor people and especially on women. Women's organizations and advocacy groups marched to Parliament and submitted written arguments to the portfolio committee on welfare. The Community Law Centre argued: "The implication of these proposals is that vulnerable and disadvantaged women and children in South Africa will bear the costs of remedying past injustices."[102] Newspapers reported that some welfare offices were "stormed by angry women."[103] At the heart of the criticisms was the view that the minister of welfare had placed the provisions of the policy outside the domain of public debate. Women's organizations and NGOs had been part of the consultations leading up to the development of the Welfare White Paper, which had set an extremely progressive framework for welfare policy and was published in February 1996.[104] Now, however, they were being excluded from the process of elaborating specific aspects of welfare policy. Parliament, the arena in which women had won the most gains, was criticized by women's organizations for being a hollow shell as women MPs did not oppose the welfare minister. Alison Tilley, a member of the Black Sash, a women's advocacy organization that opposed the new grant policy, commented that "our experience is that opportunities for advancing social justice in the context of Parliament are no longer frequent. Parliament is no longer the only place, and perhaps not even the most important place, at which to target advocacy."[105]

In the Western Cape the New Women's Movement, with a primary constituency of poor colored women who would be severely disadvantaged by the new proposals, led the attack on the Lund proposals. In its critique the New Women's Movement asked, "If the government has to cut spending, why is it always in the areas where women, especially poor women, are most vulnerable?"[106] Interestingly, the New Women's Movement, chaired by Rita

Edwards, was formed in 1994 by women activists who saw the need for an autonomous structure that was sympathetic to the democratic government but was able to represent the interests of poor women somewhat independently of the constraints of party loyalty.[107] Its critique of the minister of welfare led to enormous conflict with members of the ANC's Women's League, who questioned the motives of the New Women's Movement and accused it of representing the racial interests of colored women. The New Women's Movement found an important political niche among "working class, unemployed and rural women"[108] in the Western Cape, who undoubtedly saw the welfare reforms as eroding their meager resources. In the face of these critiques the Women's National Coalition remained a silent onlooker, unwilling to criticize its allies inside the state and unable to define new sets of alliances.

Feminist policy analysts criticized the proposed privatization of maintenance for shifting a greater burden onto women, given women's actual primary responsibility for child care, even though the proposal was couched in terms of parental responsibility.[109] In particular, Naidoo and Bozalek argued that "economic policy is formed around assumptions that women's work will subsidize cuts in social spending."[110] The New Women's Movement accused government of "acting contrary to its commitments to redistribute resources to women."[111] Thus the Lund Committee's proposals were seen as further entrenching women's poverty, rather than alleviating it. Ironically, therefore, the attempt of one government agency, led by a feminist and advised by a team of women-friendly social scientists and bureaucrats, found itself in opposition to women's organizations and accused of being antidemocratic and antiwomen.

Protests by women's organizations led to small changes in policy; the new grant was increased to 100 rands per month per child, to be paid to the primary caregivers of children younger than seven.[112] This cutoff age would be progressively increased to fourteen. However, a number of problems remained with regard to the effective implementation of the grant. First, women's organizations have criticized the two-tiered means test to establish eligibility for the grant. The test requires the primary caregiver to prove that he or she is a member of a household with a combined income of less than 9,600 rands per year for urban households and less than 13,200 rands per year for rural dwellings or those in informal areas. Other elements of the means test include a requirement that the primary caregiver show that she or he is actively seeking employment. The South African NGO Coalition has called for this test to be replaced with one that is based on the income of the primary caregiver, arguing that this will be easier to administer. As Liebenberg has pointed out, "This is particularly important in view of the fact that the child support grant requires a doubling of the capacity of the welfare system to process grants. The present system is already over-burdened with huge backlogs in poverty-stricken areas."[113]

These problems were exacerbated by poor management and delivery systems, and in some cases corrupt practices at the provincial levels, which led to *underspending* of welfare budgets for three consecutive years. The Lund Committee anticipated that a major hurdle in the implementation of the grant would be administrative and recommended "a synergistic relationship with the Department of Health" as well as other departments in the social sectors.[114] The Department of Welfare commissioned an assessment of the effectiveness of the grant that was conducted in 2000; the Community Agency for Social Enquiry (CASE) found that the capacity and competence of the Department of Welfare to administer the grant was limited by a range of problems: insufficient information; outdated application forms; lack of coordination between the departments of welfare, health, and home affairs; poor departmental cooperation with NGOs and community organizations; and by "indifferent and even hostile attitudes on the part of Welfare staff."[115] The provinces with the best resources (Gauteng and Western Cape) were the most successful in reaching delivery targets, whereas those with the greatest need (Eastern Province and Limpopo) also had the least functional delivery systems and were the least successful in reaching their targets.[116] Sadly, "the low monetary value of the grant . . . limits the benefit to the point that many potential beneficiaries do not bother to apply for it."[117] CASE recommended an increase in the amount of the grant but noted that "this would require a political decision involving a trade-off with other grants and budgetary items."[118] However, in debates about the nature of these trade-offs, women in national government cannot be said to have represented the political interests of poor women. Although the greater representation of women in Parliament and the use of feminists in the policy formulation processes offered favorable conditions for gaining a redirection of resources to poor women, the removal of macroeconomic policy decisions from the arena of politics reduced the effectiveness of these actors. Only through interventions by women's organizations and NGOs—institutions outside national government—were questions raised about overall policy orientations and spending priorities.

Detailed examinations of policy processes such as those relating to the child maintenance grant provide opportunities to explore the ways in which state policies are themselves constitutive of identity categories and groups. Women's interests are by no means preordained but are often constructed in the context of the machinery of the state. In the case discussed here, demands by the women's movement for nonracialism and poverty reduction were assumed to be compatible and indeed inseparable. While this may be true in many areas of policy, it was not possible to treat them as congruent with regard to the child support grant, given the fiscal constraints imposed by the government's macroeconomic policies. The effect was to highlight divisions in women's interests, between women who were concerned about retaining social security, even though it was established under the racial preference system of apartheid, and those who wanted simply to gain access to the system. As Lund herself commented at a 1998 conference, "Most of the policy changes going on, in health, and in education, have the same basic pattern: a few people (mostly whites) will have to do with a lot less; a lot of people will get a little bit more. But in the case of this welfare reform, a few already poor people (mostly coloured and Indian) will get a lot less; a lot of people will get a tiny something for the first time."

Although it is important to consider how women's interests can be most accurately represented, this chapter has highlighted the need to examine the processes whereby these interests are constituted. As Pringle and Watson have pointed out, the outcomes of particular policies will depend not purely on the limits placed by structures but also on the range of struggles that define and constitute the state and specific interests.[119] The state does not simply reflect gender inequalities; its practices play a decisive role in constituting them.

Conclusions

This chapter has focused on the institutional conditions and relationships that would make women's formal gains sustainable. Given the extent of the constraints on women's use of the state as instrument, and the paradoxical reliance on the gender machinery for access to state resources, what are the prospects for entrenching gender equality as a marker of democratic consolidation? Phillipe Schmitter has argued that the initial advantages of interest groups and social movements in the transitional phase can be translated into "power advantages" if they are located strategically within production or the administration of the state.[120] From this perspective, pursuing institutionalization was undoubtedly a rational strategy on the part of the women's movement, and the "gender pact" was a major movement achievement. However, three factors need to be considered when assessing why the gender machinery has not, as yet, translated into a "power advantage" for women. First, gender equality claims were "piggy-backed" onto democratic debates, and while they acquired symbolic status as a marker of inclusivity (see chapter 5), the dominant political parties did not see them as intrinsically important for the consolidation of democracy. This may seem a startling claim, given the highly developed rhetoric of equality in South Africa and the spaces it opened for women's claims to be inserted into the broad frameworks of the country's democracy, but it is borne out by the relative insignificance of issues of gender equity in the Reconstruction and Development Programme and its complete absence in the strategy of growth, employment and redistribution. Without this deeper institutionalization of the imperatives of substantive equality, political statements on gender equality remain at the level of rhetoric, albeit highly sophisticated. This is a crippling weakness. As Sawer has shown in her comparative study of women's policy machinery in Australia, Canada, and New Zealand, "Gender expertise must be backed by routinised access to policy development and Cabinet processes, and institutionalised forms of accountability for gender outcomes. While the policy brokering skills of individual femocrats and ministers might be important, bureaucratic entrenchment gives lasting returns."[121]

The second factor highlighted by this chapter is that, regardless of the quality of institutional design, external factors bear heavily on the effectiveness of gender machinery. These include the degree of democratization within the political system as a whole, that is, the extent to which policy priorities are open to negotiation, the extent to which government pursues redistribution, and the degree of openness and transparency of government. Although women activists were located at several important sites within the state, none of these quarters openly opposed the elaboration of welfare benefits that do not address the real needs of poor women. It is not entirely surprising, then, that women activists outside the state might see public office as little more than an avenue for career advancement of a small elite of women tied to the ruling party and less as the institutionalized representation of gender interests of poor women.[122]

Third, the successful consolidation of democracy from a gender perspective is dependent not just on getting it right within the state but also—and this is, perhaps, most important—on the extent to which women's organizations outside the state develop the capacity to make effective demands on behalf of their constituencies. In the case of the child support grant, external activism acted as the key pressure for accountability of women in government to their female constituents. However, this level of activism has not been widespread since 1994, and the New Women's Movement has not broadened its interventions beyond the child support grant. The movement of key activists from the women's movement into government has reshaped and relocated the struggle for gender equality as primarily a state-led project. One consequence is to place an unfair set of expectations on activists within the state, given the kinds of institutional constraints that I have described. Equally important, though, is that it may leave unexamined areas of change that lie beyond the limits of the state. In the area of violence against women, for example, although the state can certainly set a legislative framework for remedies and judicial standards for prosecution and treatment of both offenders and survivors, it remains important to address the social practices and cultural norms that legitimize male violence. This can be done only by an active and feminist voice in civil society. It is unlikely that the formal institutions for women within the state will be effective in the long term, no matter how sophisticated its design or how much more resources it can command, without a stronger women's movement outside the state that questions the very terms on which policy is made. For an inclusionary strategy to be successful, politics needs to be reinstated into democratic discourse: South Africans need to debate who articulates needs and how those needs become integrated into policy choices. This requires an effective feminist movement outside the state that can challenge the very terms on which social policy is made.

Government departments have tended to focus on internal issues of gender representation in the bureaucracy. Furthermore, while the Office on the Status of Women proceeds on the assumption that the state can be used as an instrument to address women's needs, my interviews with female civil servants reveal the extent to which the bureaucracy is resistant to the inclusion of women. Staff appointments of feminists have come at levels too junior to have any authority to influence decision making or command respect in deeply hierarchal institutions. The gendered nature of the bureaucracy has been well analyzed by feminists, and these experiences are unsurprising. Kathy Ferguson has argued that bureaucracies by their nature are masculinist and hierarchical and unlikely to be effective avenues for political action with regard to gender equality.[123] Similarly, Stetson and Mazur's comparative study of national machineries begins from the premise that "bureaucracies are the very essence of inequality; therefore, the politics of bureaucracies cannot produce equitable results. Bureaucratic discourse itself produces clients, not participants."[124] Kathleen Staudt has identified what she calls "gendered bureaucratic resistance" to the need for attention to gender inequalities.[125] Indeed, there is little doubt that women's attempts to use gender machinery worldwide have not been as successful as hoped.[126] In this context it is not surprising that interventions at the political rather than bureaucratic level have been the catalyst for such reforms as have taken place.

Gender transformation within the state requires both redressing skewed patterns of employment in the public service sector and examining the extent to which government institutions promote or reproduce relations of power and privilege through the formulation of policy and in their interactions with citizens. Women's experiences in addressing both aspects of transformation have been mixed. The extent to which representational gains translate into policy leverage must therefore be a key area of assessment. The picture that emerges from an examination of the bureaucratic sphere in South Africa is distinctly—and depressingly—different from the party and legislative arena described in chapter 6. My discussion in this chapter shows the extent to which the absence of a concrete strategy for addressing gender equality through policy implementation, the lack of strong political support for women bureaucrats, and an inadequately structured women's movement in civil society have undermined the effectiveness of the national gender machinery. This difference in outcomes in the two spheres of the state has important implications for the advancement of a feminist agenda that seeks substantive gender equality—the agenda for change outlined in the Women's Charter. At the outset it needs to be acknowledged that the processes of change required to make policy development and implementation effective—the shaping of gender-sensitive frameworks and development of institutional structures and capacities—take longer than the passage of enabling legislation. This accounts in part for the differences between women's interventions in the representative and bureaucratic arenas. However, as I have also pointed out, the particular racial and gendered character of the bureaucracy will influence the effectiveness of the gender machinery, even in the long term.

In this chapter I have shown that women MPs have been relatively more successful than their counterparts in the civil service in driving through an agenda of equity. In the civil service, however, progress has been more difficult to achieve. Parliament is a relatively small elite within which the ANC is a strong majority party with no fear of losing votes if it advances gender equity. In the civil service, however, the majority of the apartheid-era staff were grandfathered into their jobs by the negotiated settlement, and many see affirmative action as a threat to their job security. Women in the civil service lack a party to back them up on an ongoing basis or to counter their relative lack of seniority. Black women, in particular, lack institutional political clout. Discussing gender equity in broad political terms in Parliament has also proved easier than actually implementing policy and program changes at the departmental level, where civil service rules make it fairly easy to use procedures and rules to stifle creativity and change. Women in public administration have had to battle constantly, both to legitimate themselves within their departments and to implement gender-equitable policy in the field.

Despite the difficulties of working within the state, large numbers of women have moved from civil society into government, reshaping and relocating the struggle for gender equality and sometimes creating a leadership vacuum in their wake. The danger (as the case of the child maintenance grant shows) is that gender issues in South Africa may become the domain of academics and technocrats, a new elite that may leave black working-class women behind. For an inclusionary strategy to be successful, politics needs to be reinstated into democracy discourse: we need to debate who articulates needs and how they become integrated into policy choices. This observation is sustained by other case studies. For example, Stetson and Mazur's comparative study of national machineries in developed countries concluded that "women's policy machinery will reach high levels of state feminism, on the one hand, when the state is defined as a site for social justice and has the structural capacity to institutionalize new demands for equality, and on the other hand, when society sustains widely supported feminist organizations that challenge sex hierarchies through both radical politics from outside and reform politics in unions and parties."[127]

Birte Siim's study of women's political participation in Denmark has found that the extent of success of the political elite within government was dependent on the extent of political mobilization outside the political parties.[128] Much more depressing is the conclusion of Linda Geller-Schwartz, reflecting on the history of the Canadian machinery, that "those of us who have served in them usually left totally discouraged about their effectiveness. . . . Without external pressure, these structures have little hope of doing more than holding the fort or maintaining the status quo."[129]

The varied success of women within the state, and the differences in experience of women in the legislative and bureaucratic arenas, reinforces the findings of scholars who argue that the state is both contradictory and complex, rather than a coherent actor that can be directed toward a single strategy.[130] As I have shown, some successes were possible in the legislative arena that were in advance of policy development and implementation in the bureaucracy, and while the Office on the Status of Women tended to be isolated from women's organizations at the national level, its provincial structures were more effective in developing channels of communication with civil society. Furthermore, the debate about the contradictory priorities of racial equalization and poverty reduction show the extent to which state policies constitute categories and groups, rather than responding to preordained and fixed interests. New impetus was given to the need for organizations that specifically represented poor women—in this case, the New Women's Movement and the Black Sash—as opposed to broad representation of women by either women within the state or by the Women's National Coalition.

Compared to the women's movement in other African countries, the South African women's movement was relatively better placed to exploit the formal gains won during the transitional period. The women's movement was better organized than ever and engaged in politics at a national level to an unprecedented extent. To be sure, there was some initial demobilization immediately following the 1994 election, as I argued in chapter 5, and, as I have shown here, the distance between women in and outside the state was growing. Nevertheless, women's organizations regrouped around specific areas of policy, participating in the new inclusive processes of policy formulation and sometimes holding government accountable to its broad commitments to gender equality and poverty reduction. Yet the policy outcomes of institutional choices have not shown patterns significantly different from those to be found elsewhere. In part this is because, despite the resurgence of activism around specific issues (violence against women, poverty reduction, HIV/AIDS, and so on), the absence of a strong voice at the national level reduces the ability of the women's movement to raise fundamental questions about the processes of macroeconomic decision making and about the relative weight of different policy priorities.

After examining the relationship between women activists and the state in South Africa, it is evident that there was no uniform assumption within the women's movement that the state could simply be turned into an instrument for achieving gender equality. This chapter suggests that such skepticism was well founded. However, the institutional logic of the gender machinery—the assumption that in fact women's interests could be advanced by making the state the primary locus of political work—pushed such skepticism aside. Other institutional logics—the tendency to hierarchalism in the bureaucracy, the tendency of policy makers to respond to well-organized and economically powerful groups rather than to the most needy groups—further undermined the extent of women's effectiveness in engaging the state. The changed policy environment, paradoxically more democratic in process yet more constrained in resource terms by the pressures of globalization and macroeconomic choices of the government, also limited the ability of the gender machinery to act effectively to articulate women's policy interests. Although the greater representation of women in Parliament and the use of feminists in the policy formulation stage in the Department of Welfare offered enabling conditions to redirect resources to poor women, the removal of macroeconomic policy decisions from the arena of politics reduced these actors to a limited frame of reference. Only through interventions from outside the state by women's organizations and NGOs were old issues of overall policy orientations and spending priorities raised. It is unlikely that the gender machinery itself will be effective in the long term, no matter how sophisticated its design or how much more resources it can command, without a stronger women's movement outside the state that questions the very terms on which policy is made.

Chapter 8

Autonomy, Engagement, and Democratic Consolidation

In this book I have sought to engage the broader theoretical debates about the relationship between feminism and nationalism through the lens of a detailed historiography of the South African women's movement. Rejecting the Manichean choice of characterizing women's organization in South Africa as either an instrument for nationalist mobilization (and consequently women's subordination) or a vehicle for feminist politics (and consequently the heroic upholder of women's autonomy), I have sought to trace the dynamics of the relationship between women and nationalism through a careful tracking of historical events. In many cases women's organizations did not find it possible to choose one or the other definition of their role but rather sought to uphold both the importance of race and class oppression in shaping gender oppression and the distinctiveness of gender oppression from that of race and class. Even where they grappled with the difficulties of pursuing both aims, women's organizations were constrained, by the political contexts in which they were located, in their ability to represent women and facilitate women's articulation of needs and interests in their own terms. These contexts, to reiterate the argument that I made in chapter 1, were determined not simply by the structures of political opportunity but also by the universe of political discourse, that is, by what was "allowed" within the ideological paradigms of dominant political movements.

In building a narrative of women's political organization and mobilization during the crucial historical period of 1980–99, the book also makes a unique contribution to South African scholarship on the national liberation struggle and on gender historiography. This contribution is more than the addition of the "women's contribution" to the struggle, although in itself such a study has considerable merit in a field that remains dominated by male-centered analyses of resistance politics. A more ambitious emphasis of this study is the ways in which dominant conceptions of liberation in South Africa have been constrained by their failure to engage with the profound cultural demands of the women's movement, the limits of democratic participation within nationalist movements, and the inherent (and perhaps inescapable) tension between autonomy and engagement that social movements of subordinate groups face when seeking to impose their demands on broader progressive politics.

Autonomy and Engagement: A Fine Balancing Act

In the first part of the book I sought to show how feminist activists won leverage within the nationalist movement both internally and in exile. I have drawn attention to the slowness of the process in the exiled movement, pointing out how attempts to develop autonomy were always circumscribed by the location of women's structures within the ANC. Members of the Women's Section of the ANC found themselves dislodged from their conventional roles as caretakers and social workers for the movement as young women cadres sought to articulate new roles within the movement. Young women challenged the women's leadership within the ANC, arguing for a shift from the role of women's auxiliary to a women's organization. Their participation in the movement's armed wing, Umkhonto we Sizwe, accorded a fragile legitimacy to their demands, which opened the door to extensive debates about autonomy within the movement. The affiliations of the ANC Women's Section to international socialist women's movements and to the emerging discourses of gender in the West also opened up new ways of thinking about women's political roles. Most significant was that the ability of internal women's organizations to sustain separate organizations and oppose marginalization imposed a political imperative on the exiled women activists to move apace within the ANC.

During the 1980s women activists developed more assertive political strategies to deal with male resistance to women's power within the movement and had considerable success in laying the groundwork for the ANC to court women as a constituency during the transitional period and in the new democracy—most notably, the ANC committed itself formally to including gender equality as one of the goals of national liberation. However, even the formal rhetoric did not adequately address women's demands; documents such as the Constitutional Guidelines made generalized references to gender equality but avoided considering the ways in which gender shaped all aspects of social life and, most particularly, women's (lack of) power in the private sphere.

Struggles to transform the ANC into an organization that was more responsive to the needs and ambitions of its women members were extremely valuable in making the movement more democratic and accountable, although ultimately the various hierarchies that characterized the movement—men over women, older over younger, militarists over political activists, and exiles over internals—continued to persist. Nevertheless, the ANC feminists' experiences of exile, their interaction with feminism in the West, and with the broken promises of nationalism in Africa all shaped the growing awareness that women had concerns that were distinct from those of men within the movement. In the exiled ANC this awareness was expressed in the more vocal demands for autonomy, a loosely used term that denoted the extent to which the Women's Section was able to gather political information relating to the internal women's movement, use money that it raised for self-defined projects, and have an effective voice within the National Executive Committee.

The notion of autonomy also appears to capture the tone of struggles within the internal women's organizations about their degree of connectedness to the national liberation movement. In particular, the United Women's Organisation in the Western Cape and the Natal Organisation of Women believed that they did have autonomy—they maintained their own sources of funding, elected their own leadership, and were accountable to their membership through branches—and indeed male-led organizations did not directly intervene in the decision-making processes of women's organizations. But autonomy did not have the same meaning or political significance for all the women's organizations or for the duration of the period studied here. There were differing emphases on the extent to which women could or should articulate their political programs outside the framework of nationalism. Despite the formal autonomy of women's organizations,

Figure 8.1. Women's Organizations and Autonomy, 1979 to 2004

Autonomy				
ANC Women's Section/League	FEDTRAW	NOW	UWO	WNC

Weak
Directed collective action

Strong
Independent

their activities were hedged by a range of strategic choices made in the context of external political forces.

Drawing on Molyneux's formulations,[1] it seems more appropriate to characterize the different women's organizations studied here along a continuum of autonomy, with the ANC Women's Section at the least autonomous end of the scale (directed autonomy) and the Women's National Coalition at the most autonomous end (independence) (see figure 8.1). For the Federation of Transvaal Women and the Natal Organisation of Women, the broad terms of campaigns and the pace of campaigning were set externally by the United Democratic Front, a logical consequence of the organization's decision to locate itself first and foremost as an antiapartheid organization. The United Women's Organisation in the Western Cape, which tried from the outset to articulate a different approach to women's organizing, one that built structures from the bottom up rather than focusing on mobilizing campaigns, nevertheless found its autonomy eroding in practice, if not formally, as a result of broader political developments.

Molyneux has correctly pointed out that autonomy should not be viewed as a principled feminist end in itself. Nevertheless, this study of the South African women's movement suggests that struggles for autonomy represented vital demands that women's agency be recognized and valued. Furthermore, when women's organizations were able to establish relatively greater distance from the dictates of nationalism and of male-dominated parties, they were able to articulate their claims within a framework that was more enabling than that of nationalism.

A cursory reading of figure 8.1 may suggest that women's organizations attained autonomy in a linear fashion between the formation of the ANC Women's League (or, indeed, the Bantu Women's League in 1912) and the formation of the Women's National Coalition about eighty years later. From a simplistic reading it may be deduced that there was an incremental shift from the auxiliary approach (1912–43) to the "side-by-side" view (1943–92) to the idea that women's organizations should be independent (1992).

However, this detailed study of the 1980s and 1990s suggests, rather, that autonomy was debated, achieved, and lost in a discontinuous rather than incremental fashion. The imperative to link women's struggles to national liberation produced a kind of relative autonomy in the early 1980s, when women's organizations began developing their own structures and their own formulations of women's interests and needs. It was relatively easier to maintain some degree of independence of decision making because of the changed opportunity structure provided by the civics movement, which accepted that women's organizations represented an important and distinct constituency. The opening of new terrains of political struggle at the local level provided the political opportunity for women to be mobilized as a group separately from black people or the nation in general. Although national liberation provided the overall framework, the expansion of the political sphere to the community level, where women had a particular set of roles and responsibilities, provided the mobilizing force. For a brief period until the mid-1980s these decentralized struggles allowed women to develop a sense of agency that shaped the formation of separate women's organizations.

However, autonomy was undermined by the mid-1980s. Political choices outside the women's movement—especially the decision to form a national front of democratic organizations against the apartheid state—had contradictory effects on the women's movement. On the one hand, involvement in the United Democratic Front offered yet another opportunity to link women's demands to community and human rights demands, and to forge a connection between narrow women's issues and issues of public politics. On the other hand, this universalization of women's demands had unwanted consequences, as women's organizations found it increasingly difficult to keep their identities distinct and to pursue organizational development at a pace that retained their constituencies of women. Attempts to build grassroots women's organizations were undermined, and the development of organizational autonomy was virtually impossible. Although women's organizations were aware of the importance of retaining control over decision making and enhancing participatory and consensual decision-making processes, they were unable to sustain their internal cultural forms and consolidate grassroots democracy. Although women's organizations emerged from distinct and diverse local-level groupings of women, some of which were spontaneous formations of women seeking short-term improvements in their quality of life and others of which were formed through the interventions of activists, the context of national liberation ultimately had a homogenizing effect on all their struggles.

Political issues that fell outside the mobilizing realm of nationalism were pushed to the margins. Although the ideology of the civics movement emphasized grassroots democracy and envisioned new forms of democracy that would entail the fundamental restructuring of society rather than simply a change of regime, this vision had limits. Male leaders were either incapable of or unwilling to respond to women's visions for equality except at the most broad and rhetorical levels. In particular, male leadership was unable to engage with those women's demands that encompassed cultural changes, such as the equalization of domestic power and greater personal autonomy for women. Despite women's increased involvement in national politics, "the struggle" for national liberation remained a male-defined affair.

Once the emphasis shifted to the national level, women's organizations were pushed back into their role as auxiliaries. Decimated by state repression on the one hand, and by the emphasis on carrying out the programs and campaigns of the United Democratic Front on the other, women's organizations were in no position to resist the pressure to disband as separate organizations once the ANC was unbanned. Although literature on the demobilization of civil society emphasizes the moment of disbanding the United Democratic Front and collapsing the civic structures into the ANC as the crucial turning point, from the perspective of the women's movement this turning point was reached in the mid-1980s, when women's organizations effectively became the "women's wing" of the UDF. As I showed in chapter 2, this process did not occur without internal struggle within the women's organizations or without a conception of the losses as well as the opportunities inherent in the alliance between women's organizations and the more powerful male left.

By the 1990s it was also increasingly apparent that the power of representation of black people and the leadership of the women's movement would lie with the former exiles. The relationship between internal struggles and exiled movement was a source of tension throughout the 1980s. Although it has been suggested that internal organization was activated by the ANC in the late 1970s, I have shown that, at least in relation to women's organizations, the ANC *responded* to local developments in the townships. In many respects, as I showed in chapter 3, the ANC Women's Section was caught on the strategic back foot, and its weak affiliations and information-gathering networks limited its ability to control the political direction of women's organizations. In chapter 2, I argued that the exiled activists and internal activists disagreed both about whether a national organization should be created and the priorities of such an organization—whether to build slowly from below or push ahead with rapid mobilization into anti-apartheid struggles. Of course, these tensions should not be overstated. Throughout the 1980s most women activists were in favor of linking up with broader national struggles and accepted that the trade-off was the building of sustainable structures.

Despite some formal advances within both the United Democratic Front and the ANC, there were clear limits to the autonomy of women's structures and, in effect, to the extent to which women could express their interests in ways that went beyond the paradigm of nationalism. The failure of the quota demand at the ANC conference in 1991 was evidence of this— even though the issue was eventually won by feminists, it was a signal at a crucial point that the women's movement could not put all its political eggs into one basket. Although the negotiations opened new possibilities for women to universalize their claims as part of the principles and institutions of the new democracy, the ANC's interest in addressing women's demands was limited. Feminists had to begin to organize outside the framework of the national liberation movement to have any effect on the outcomes of the transition. Only two short years after the beginning of the transition to democracy, feminist activists recognized the need for a movement outside the ANC; indeed, despite many acrimonious exchanges between "internals" and "exiles," this was an issue on which both sides agreed.

The formation of the Women's National Coalition was a significant political step, not least because the many attempts to form a national structure for the women's movement finally came to fruition, but also because this time it encompassed women's organizations outside the ANC fold. Within the coalition the differences of race and class highlighted the tension between the notion of women as a common category underpinned by some distinct experience and the lived experiences of women as diverse, multiple, and shaped by nongendered forces and political ideologies, even competing needs and interests. Without explicit reference to the extended postmodern debate in North American and European feminism about the conceptual underpinning of feminism, the coalition refused to operate on the basis of essentialist categories or assumptions of political homogeneity among women. At the same time there was a clear recognition of the need for a shared coherent strategy to ensure that gender was recognized as a socioeconomic fracture by the party negotiators. There was also a recognition that women in each of the political parties needed to participate equally in decision making within their different ideological frameworks. This bears out Anna Jonasdottir's argument that women's interest in having a political presence can be regarded as an objective interest that can override other stratifications between women.[2]

However, any alliance or coalition built on these limited grounds, no matter how independent from particular party direction, is likely to be short term. Defining the common ground as that of political exclusion rather than of socioeconomic interest was a way for women to shift the alliance of diverse women's organizations into a more manageable frame. The coalition attempted to develop a political practice that incorporated and built supportive coalitions based on difference. This notion of "coalition politics" avoided political fragmentation or the superimposition of a false universalism onto the women's movement. In theory it allowed for both autonomous organization and coordinated programs. In practice, however, tensions between the national office of the WNC and the regional affiliates were ongoing, the only coordinated program was the charter campaign, and the dominance of the ANC Women's League regarding political strategy and in terms of access to negotiators tended to override the ability of other women's organizations to shape the coalition in any substantial way. The charter campaign, intended to weld the coalition together, was a process that threatened to undermine the coalition as it inevitably raised competing socioeconomic and ideological interests. The pursuit of independence from political parties, expressed as an issue of principle in 1995, ironically reduced the effectiveness of the coalition. The decision to exclude the participation of women officials of political parties from the decision-making bodies of the coalition removed the crucial link between the women's movement and elected representatives.

The remarkable aspect of the coalition experience was the success of the organization in creating a visible political constituency of women during the transitional process. Whereas feminists in the north were despairing of the possibilities of political praxis as a result of the increasing dominance of disaggregated identity-based politics, the coalition showed how those disaggregated identities could be creatively woven into an effective strategy around a narrow set of common interests. Although it succeeded for a limited period, the coalition's effects were long term, both in entrenching vital gains in the Constitution and the institutions of state and in providing a tantalizing glimpse into what a strong women's movement could be in South Africa. The coalition managed to position itself strategically as the voice of organized women. The coalition's leadership included women with high political profile and with long experience in how parties and liberation movements worked internally. The uniqueness of the coalition's ability to lobby political organizations and demand a place at the negotiation table gave women a powerful voice at a crucial moment in South Africa's political history. There is little doubt that without the coalition, the constitutional arrangements would have looked bleaker for women.

The example of the coalition highlights the fact that when women's organizations form strategic alliances around specific issues, and are able to use this alliance to assert their claims at the national level, their political leverage tends to increase. Part of this strategic alliance in South Africa included cooperation between researchers, lawyers, and women's organizations to achieve a well-thought-out set of proposals to take to negotiators and constitution drafters. In effect, this strategic think tank, informally constituted, was able to mobilize expertise that was in relatively short supply within women's organizations and to concentrate limited political power behind a very specific strategy. As a result of these factors women's organizations were in a unique position to put on the table a clear set of demands with a relatively strong constituency united behind them. Coupled with this, the coalition had strong political legitimacy and a high profile that it mobilized to avoid being marginalized. If its only lasting gain was, as Routledge-Madlala commented in an interview with me, to ensure that "male leaders will not oppose gender equality issues even if in private they form a male cabal," this surely was an advance on the state of political debates at the beginning of the 1980s.

The Current Shape of the Women's Movement

One of the most notable changes in the landscape of the women's movement in the post-1994 period was the fragmentation and stratification of women's organizations in civil society. The collapse of the Women's National Coalition as the political center of the women's movement led to its disaggregation into a diversity of arenas, some of which—such as those closely tied to policy-making processes—were strengthened by new approaches to civil society within the state, whereas other levels reverted to the more familiar community-based forms of organizations.

I have characterized the postapartheid women's movement as operating within three distinct arenas: policy advocacy at the national level, an intermediary arena of networks and coalitions, and the grassroots level of community-based women's organizations. In addition, women continue to participate in political parties and in the new social movements that have emerged as a result of weaknesses in delivering services to poor people.

National NGOs that act as advocacy agents and are tied in to state policy processes have the expertise and, in a relative sense, the funding, to intervene in legal and policy debates and testify at public hearings. They remain extremely active in public debate and have found spaces in the new governance system. Many feminists who were involved in the Federation of Transvaal Women, the Natal Organisation of Women, and the United Women's Organisation in the Western Cape in the 1980s continue to work in this sector. Their primary role is to ensure the implementation and elaboration of the rights-based democratic framework, in itself an important political task, given the advanced formal rights that were secured in the Constitution. At this level organizations can make effective links with other allies in civil society, such as the gay and lesbian rights movement, to mutually reinforce democratic agendas and share strategies. They are easily accessible to the state as well as external donors and play a strategic, rather than representative, role in civil society. Indeed, there is a tension between the relatively high degree of access such organizations have to decision makers and their relative distance from constituencies of women (and particularly poor rural women).[3]

However, keeping close relationships with constituencies is difficult when funding and gender expertise are thinly spread, making it difficult to listen to how interests are being articulated at the grassroots level. Exacerbating this problem is the insufficient capacity to ensure that information about what is happening at the advocacy level flows down to constituencies of women who are directly affected by particular policies. Although some NGOs in other sectors have developed this relationship to their constituencies (for example, the relationship between the AIDS Law Project and the Treatment Action Campaign), this has not happened within the women's movement. As a result the gap between the high level of access to information and awareness of women's rights among the urban elite and the marginality of poor women has grown wider. Even where victories are scored, for example, in the passage of the Maintenance Act, poor women do not always know about these, or, as the Women's Legal Centre pointed out, government departments do not immediately implement the new rulings.[4]

One of the political costs of working primarily with parties and the state is the emergence of gaps between advocacy groups and those constituencies of poor women that have sought, through direct action, to demand their rights to basic services such as water or electricity. Direct action tactics have tended to bring social movements into conflict with the state in ways that have created new lines of fracture in the political terrain. In certain cases the ANC government has deemed criminal particular forms of direct action (such as electricity reconnections and land invasions). In this context the choice of retaining credibility with state actors may, over time, reinforce the elite bias of this level of politics as access to decision making through party and bureaucratic allies becomes more important than pressure from below. The moderate feminist discourses that characterize this sector and that allow access to political decision making can thus act as limits to the women's movement, by gradually constraining the range of potential strategies (and, perhaps, citizenship claims) that are considered legitimate.

The new issue-based networks (such as the Network Against Violence Against Women and the Reproductive Rights Alliance) that have emerged and coalesced around common issues straddle the advocacy and policy roles of the first category but are more likely to have identifiable constituencies. Like the advocacy organizations, the networks tend to be based in cities, especially Cape Town and Johannesburg. Although they are primarily funded by foreign donors, many have also gained support from the local business sector for specific campaigns, particularly in the area of violence against women (for example, the white ribbon campaign). The remarkable aspect of these networks is that they are characterized by attention to issues that would in the 1980s have been regarded as feminist and problematic— that is, issues of women's sexual and reproductive autonomy. This may be a function of the discursive shift from nationalism to citizenship as exemplified by the Constitution, as a result of which women's organizations feel less constrained in the types of issues that they can take into the national political domain. The new democracy, despite its weaknesses, has opened the possibilities for women's organizations to take up issues that are outside the conventional definitions of political action and to demand attention by the state to issues that states have generally been reluctant to regulate (that is, regulating and mitigating men's power in the private sphere).

These networks struggle to hold together organizations that are in some respects competing for similar resources and operating on the same terrain. While they are most effective when they speak with one voice on issues of critical concern, such as gender-based violence, and are able to articulate and lobby for policy alternatives, they are the hardest type of organization to keep alive. They often lack funding to support the networking office, or, when they are too well funded, their constituents may feel resentful that more funding is not being channeled to the actual work on the ground. As we have seen with the Women's National Coalition, coalitions are by their nature fragile structures, having to constantly negotiate the terms of the relationships between members. Where resources are scarce or where organizations are jockeying to be seen as the representative voice on an issue, coalitions are at their most vulnerable. This problem is exacerbated by the fact that the most experienced activists and organizations in this sector are white women, and black women activists entering the field of violence against women have come up against relatively well-established funding and advocacy networks. As a result there has been considerable racial tension in this sector. Not surprisingly, the networks are the most unstable form of organization in the women's movement.

Least visible but most numerous are the women's organizations at the community level. As this book has shown, women's organizations have always existed at this level but have been weakly tied in to national networks. The period of the early 1980s was exceptional for the extent to which community organizing was incorporated into a national political project, and women's organizations shaped and were shaped by the political visions of feminism. However, by the mid-1980s the United Democratic Front dominated strategic decision making, and women's organizations had lost their capacity for independent political action. Twenty years later women's community organizations appear again to be adrift from any politically cohesive project. Yet community-based organizations are the most numerous type of organization in civil society, according to the 2002 Johns Hopkins study of the size and scope of the nonprofit sector in South Africa.[5] The bulk of the nonprofit sector is made up of agencies concerned with culture and recreation, social services, and development and housing. These areas of work are also gendered, according to the study. Culture and recreation is a sector that includes sport and is, not surprisingly, dominated by men. Education and research, social services, and development and housing are sectors dominated by women. The study notes that "this type of organization, of which there was a substantial number, is involved in supporting and improving the lives of ordinary people through associations, development organizations, and co-operatives. Anecdotally, these types of activities tend more frequently to be carried out by women."[6]

This level of women's organizations has been most distant from the state and even women's NGOs and networks that engage the state. A major part of the work at this level is concerned with women's practical needs, particularly in the face of the HIV crisis. The work of these organizations ranges from welfare work, caring for the ill, and organizing and financing funerals to mobilizing at community level against rapists (and particularly men who rape children). In a number of respects women have been the shock absorbers of high levels of unemployment and of the failure of the state to provide a comprehensive and efficient system of social security and health care. The emphasis on the cultural value of caring in government policy frameworks—such as the White Paper on Social Welfare—in effect shifts the burden of caring for the young, the sick, and the elderly onto women (and increasingly onto children as well), without financial compensation for their time and without effective back-up by the state. Yet these increasing burdens are not without political opportunities. In caring for people dying of AIDS, women often have to cross cultural barriers of privacy and respect. As one caregiver noted, "It is hard to *hlonipha* [respect] your brother-in-law in the old way when you clean his sores and the private parts. He respects me now and I have grown to respect and understand his needs." In her view she has had to renegotiate dignity and respect in everyday actions within the household. These cultural negotiations and redefinitions of social roles challenge that commonplace assumption that women are simply victims of the HIV/AIDS crisis.[7]

At the community level women have also discovered other forms of agency. Many are participants in the emerging social movements that are challenging the cost recovery basis on which basic services are delivered. In the absence of perceived weaknesses in the justice system in dealing with violence against women, they have at times effected "citizen's arrests" of known rapists. Although direct action, such as marching to police stations with rapists in tow, is not widespread, it occurs often enough to remind observers of the enormous degree of agency that vests at this level. Political ideologies in this arena may be characterized as being within the deep maternalist tradition of the South African women's movement. Perhaps ironically, the most vibrant and creative forms of collective solidarity are emerging at this level as women seek to address everyday crises with few resources. Yet community-level women's organizations often do not have the time, expertise, or resources to address decision makers, and women within other social movements do not as yet appear to have inserted a gender analysis into the conceptualization of their struggles.

Looking specifically at the resurgence of women's activism in the new social movements, the conception of these arenas as fundamentally democratic and transformative is in many respects an idealization that feminists have challenged for some time. In the 1980s this idealization pushed to the margins struggles to deal with aspects of and institutions in civil society that are inimical to the values of equality and justice. The narrow understanding of what constituted "political action" within the mainstream left meant that social movements did not engage issues of culture and tradition. Relations of power within social movements can be masked, and questions of who has voice and agency within social movements often remain obscured. The new social movements that have emerged since 1994 have often relied on the mobilization of women on the basis of their practical needs—for example, for electricity, land, and housing—but, unlike feminist activists of the 1980s, have rarely linked these to issues of the pernicious gender division of labor. Internal tensions of race and gender within the social movements have rarely been directly examined. As Dawn Paley has pointed out, more than half the activists in the Anti-Privatisation Forum are women, "yet it [is] men's voices that overwhelmingly dominated" a meeting that she recently attended. She questions "how is it that Black women can make up the bulk of the membership of the movements against neo-liberal policies and be so marginalised in the functioning of these organisations?" One of her informants has boldly suggested that women are being used.[8] Similar comments were made to me in relation to other organizations where women were foot soldiers while men assumed the role of generals (as in the United Democratic Front).

These different and vibrant arenas within the women's movement should ideally add up to a strong and diverse social movement. In a democratically effective state they would work together to ensure that poor and vulnerable people are an important constituency for politicians, that there is accountability in public spending, that the constitutional values of equality and social justice are upheld, and that both the public and private spheres are increasingly governed by democratic norms. This has not yet happened in South Africa. In the next section I offer some explanations for this paradox, based on the historical review of the movement in this book. I argue that the most visible gender politics has focused on issues of representation (that is, equality/inclusionary feminism) rather than on policy outcomes.

Democratic Consolidation: What Are the Prospects for Women?

The movement of key women activists into the democratic state had a significant effect on the capacities of the women's movement and the direction of gender activism. This strategy was informed by a critical approach to the capacity of the state to shift gender inequalities and by an understanding that any emphasis on the state should be supplemented by building a strong women's movement outside the state.

Nevertheless, gender activists found the terrain of the state to be difficult in many respects. On the one hand, the state was not a coherent entity over which the ANC and its women's movement allies could simply impose their will. As scholars are increasingly arguing, institutional arrangements have lasting consequences, even after those arrangements have been altered.[9] The two new "institutional habitats" within the state that are currently occupied by gender activists, the representative sphere and the civil service, may both be deemed uncomfortable for women in terms of the rules by which they operate, the modes of decision making inherent in each, and the internal culture of each sphere, despite the differences between these arenas.

It is clear that in many respects women in particular have benefited from the new institutional and procedural arrangements in the state. Women are treated as a constituency with special interests that need to be represented in policy making. The national gender machinery was designed to provide a bridge between different sectors of the state as well as between state and society. Thus for all its limitations the state has been made more permeable to the influence of organized constituencies of women. In practice, as is the case with national machineries worldwide, the South African institutions are elite driven, underresourced, and dependent to a high degree on donor funding. Expertise within the state to mainstream gender is thin; as a result much of the gains made in relation to gender equality are in those areas where policy addresses women directly as a category (for example, termination of pregnancy and maternal health), whereas those aspects of policy in which the relationships between women and men have to be addressed (for example, customary law, land) have been much harder to define. Despite these limitations, Catherine Albertyn has reminded us that "by 2000, women in South Africa enjoyed unprecedented political and legal equality in the form of political participation and entrenched human and legal rights."[10]

Returning to Nancy Fraser's distinction between the identity politics of recognition and the class politics of redistribution, it can be argued that while women have been recognized as a group that has suffered particular forms of oppression, there has been little redistribution of resources and power in ways that change the structural forces on which that oppression rests. Recognition has, rather, been an avenue for reinforcing elite women's access to the formal political system while not (as yet) translating clearly into policies that address the needs of poor women. The reasons for this are complicated and have their roots in part in the tense relationship between feminism and the nationalist movement and in part in the elite biases of the democratic model adopted during the transition.

This elite bias has been exacerbated to some extent by the extent to which women's politics in the democratic period has been reduced to the strategy of proportional quotas for women in government. The 30 percent quota adopted by the ANC for the first three elections is no longer regarded as adequate; rather, a number of women's NGOs have adopted the fifty-fifty campaign, which demands parity of representation in all Parliaments. The president of the ANC, Thabo Mbeki, has committed himself to meeting this target in the 2009 elections. In itself the demand for parity is not problematic. As I argued in chapter 6, normal processes of electoral competition cannot be seen as fair if they persistently produce the underrepresentation of the same subordinate groups in society. I am therefore *not* making an argument that women cannot make group-based electoral claims, that special rules for disadvantaged groups are unfair, or that liberal democracies should be left intact. Rather, I would argue that this study of the South African women's movement suggests that that the *form* of women's democratic inclusion needs attention—that is, *how* women are included can influence how they aggregate as a political power bloc and the kinds of political and policy outcomes that are possible through increased representation. As the discussion of the Communal Land Rights Bill showed, quotas in themselves are unlikely to produce the outcomes desired by feminist activists.

Increasing women's participation in decision making is undoubtedly important. However, we need to interrogate more closely what we understand democratic participation to mean. The thinnest definition (which is often evident in discussions of quotas) is that the mere presence of women in Parliaments removes the masculinist face of political institutions and forces institutions to recognize women. Anne Marie Goetz and I have distinguished this from effective participation, where the emphasis is on more effective interest articulation and representation—that is, to make the voice of women louder.[11] Yet, as Goetz has pointed out, we should be careful not to assume that amplified voice "will automatically strengthen the moral and social claims of the powerless on the powerful and produce better accountability to that group."[12] As this book has shown repeatedly, institutional norms and procedures and the nature of processes of deliberation can undermine the extent and effect of women's voice in the public sphere.

Gender quotas in Nordic countries have their origins in the 1970s when political parties, responding to the increased mobilization of women, applied quotas for women in decision-making positions. Until then, women had only automatic representation on party executive boards through the women's structures within parties. Dahlerup has argued that this was a radical shift in that "its immediate goal was to secure improved access to power and influence in elite politics for women." Two different types of quotas were used in Nordic countries: quotas for popular elections (candidate quotas) aimed at advancing the political representation of women and internal quotas within parties aimed at integrating women into party machineries. In South Africa attention has focused on candidate quotas rather than party quotas, with some organizations such as the Commission on Gender Equality going so far as to demand that these quotas be legislated. However, recognition through quotas is a deceptively easy strategy. A much more transformative demand for representation is reduced to a simple mechanism, unhinged from the crucial questions of what women representatives will do when in office, and how women's organizations should respond when women representatives fail to live up to their promises to change the lives of poor women.

These are difficult questions to pursue at this stage in South Africa's history, when women's organizations have made so many striking gains by conceding authority to the state. Operating in this relationship of junior partnership with the state, women's organizations have, with few exceptions, tended to use a set of tactics that does not rely on mass mobilization or confrontation. Rather, tactics, demands, and rhetoric tend to be moderated to fit the discourses of the state in order to make incremental gains and to retain hard-won openings into the state. A number of crucial legislative and policy gains have been made as a result of this strategy. A notable example is the success in legalizing abortion, despite the deep opposition to this in civil society and in the rank-and-file membership of political parties. Using a carefully argued strategic approach, feminists were able to frame the demand within the more acceptable terms of health rather than as an overt right to bodily integrity. Even so, only the ANC's strong support for the Termination of Pregnancy Act and its refusal to allow its MPs a free vote made possible the passage of the legislation in 1996. In this case a partnership between women's advocacy organizations and a strong political party ally resulted in a clear victory for women, entrenching women's reproductive rights in ways that are still not politically possible in many older democracies.

The strategy of concentrating on gaining access to arenas of decision making was pursued at some cost to the transformatory agenda that had dominated women's organizations up to 1994. The emphasis on engaging the state had three key unintended and unforeseen consequences for the women's movement. The first lies in the effect on the politics of interest articulation of institutionalizing interests. Creating a set of specialized institutions for the consideration of gender shifted the issues of gender inequality out of the realm of politics and into the technical realm of policy making. As Banaszek, Beckwith, and Rucht have pointed out, this is increasingly a problem with national machineries around the world: "Women's movements have been presented with an increasingly depoliticised and remote set of policy-making agencies at the national level. . . . The relocation of responsibility to nonelected state bodies eventually reduces social movement influence."[13] In the administration gender equality concerns have fallen hostage to a range of institutional hierarchies and systemic obstacles that are hard to deal with from outside the bureaucracy. The second consequence of the dominant focus on reforming the state is that very few women's organizations are dealing with issues of cultural norms and everyday practices, which may indeed limit the implementation and effect of legislative reforms. Finally, most activists who moved into the state assumed that public resources would be directed in a concerted fashion toward the reduction of the massive inequalities inherited from apartheid. Instead, antipoverty policies have been mostly ineffective as a result of a combination of policy vacillation, resource constraints, infrastructural weaknesses, and bureaucratic foot dragging. While quotas for women have been written into state initiatives such as the Community Based Public Works Programme, the racial and gendered biases in the economy remain intact. Black women are still more likely to be unemployed, to be paid less than men when employed, and to perform unpaid labor.[14]

This creates tension for those feminists who entered the state on the assumption that it would be a site of strategic intervention. As Thenjiwe Mtintso, a former MP from the ANC and former chair of the Commission on Gender Equality, put it, "When I visit ANC constituencies I experience a feeling of guilt about my privileged position and about my claim to represent their interests as women. I have grappled with my feminism and have questioned the extent to which it articulates the urgent needs of poor women."[15] For Pregs Govender, also an MP from the ANC and chair of the highly effective Joint Monitoring Committee on Women, the tensions between state constraints and her vision for transformation became untenable, and she resigned her seat in Parliament in 2002.

These comments should not be read as meaning that engaging the state was a misguided strategy for the women's movement, or that alliances with political parties necessarily lead to co-option. Rather, what needs to be considered is *how* the state should be engaged, what kinds of legal and institutional reforms should be promoted, and how to build a women's movement that is sufficiently mobilized to support a critical engagement with the state. Poor women in South Africa would undoubtedly be better served by a strong state with the infrastructural capacities to implement functional health, welfare, and basic service delivery. Removing formal inequalities is also important as it creates the normative and enabling environment in which to pursue women's claims to full citizenship. However, it is self-limiting for the women's movement to pursue inclusion in the state in a piecemeal and depoliticized fashion, seeking to include women into existing policy frameworks without questioning whether the overall policy directions are appropriate for poor women, or how to put new areas of policy or law making on the agenda. For example, Neva Seidman Makgetla, an economist for the Congress of South African Trade Unions, has pointed to the limits of law reform in addressing economic inequalities. She argues that "the laws on equity . . . did not directly address the economic context of high levels of unemployment and women's lack of economic assets. Nor did they engage persistent inequalities in homes, communities and schools." What is needed, she has argued, is structural transformation "rather than just better enforcement of anti-discrimination measures."[16]

Changing inequities in social and economic power will require not just the increased representation of women within the state but also the increased and assertive representation of *poor* women within the state. It requires that those elected to power will pursue redistributive policies and that a vibrant social movement will act to ensure accountability to the interests of marginal and vulnerable groupings. The roles of interest articulation (rather than merely group representation) and accountability require a different form of social movement of women. The reduction of the women's movement to a "development partner" has long-term costs for democracy because it reduces the ability of the movement to debate the norms and values underpinning policy directions as well as within other social movements and in civil society more generally. These cultural inequalities can be dealt with only partially by more equitable and gender-sensitive policies; they often reflect power relations that cannot be remedied by state action. Rather, they demand that state policies be supplemented by a vibrant debate in the public sphere about the nature of society. They require a type of social movement that is not merely seeking to make piecemeal interventions in the policy and legislative processes of the state but is engaged with norm setting at the broadest level. In strategic terms this also requires a movement that will form appropriate alliances and seek to influence the norms and procedures of alliance partners, whether these are political parties or social movements.

Yet the faith in the support of the ANC for open debate and for transformation more generally has also waned to some extent in the past two years. In chapter 6, I highlighted the tendency to strengthen centralized control within the party and to place key areas of public policy formulation outside the processes of internal debate that had previously characterized the ANC. The consequences of this shift have been widely felt. As this study has shown, the abandonment of the path of transformation, exemplified in somewhat imperfect form in the Reconstruction and Development Programme, removed the enabling discursive environment in which claims for gender equality could be pressed. The national machinery, designed to ensure both policy effectiveness and accountability, has been ineffectual and unable to respond to the demands of organized women. The Office on the Status of Women, whose responsibility is to develop the draft Women's National Empowerment Policy into a full-fledged plan for mainstreaming gender, seems resistant to presenting any policy for public comment and has insulated itself from the women's movement to the extent that there is no expectation that this part of the national machinery will act as a strategic lever in policy terms. At the National Gender Summit convened in 2001 by the Commission on Gender Equality, the Office on the Status of Women was heavily criticized for failing to develop any policies and programs, and the minister in charge of the office, Essop Pahad, was booed by the representatives of women's organizations who were present when he commented that, after all, poverty is a relative concept. On the other hand, the Joint Committee on Improving the Quality of Life and Status of Women, dominated by women from the ANC, is the only official body to have publicly opposed the Mbeki government's policies on arms acquisition and the provision of antiretrovirals to pregnant women and rape survivors.

The decline of women's policy effectiveness after the initial upsurge following women's entry into Parliament is not unusual. Anna Harvey has shown how U.S. women had considerable influence on national politics for first four or five years after suffrage was extended in 1920, but the influence diminished rapidly. This diminished efficacy lasted for forty-five years, until the 1970s, when women began to influence national policy debates again. In her study Harvey argued that voters' leverage over policy requires the intermediary action of "policy-seeking interest group activity in electoral politics," that is, there must be a threat of "electoral retaliation."[17] Her study has suggested that the strategic issue that the women's movement needs to confront in the context of liberal democracy has less to do with whether women constitute a distinct group than whether electoral and policy elites *believe* that women constitute a voting bloc. This perception, and women's ability to retaliate electorally, depends on the extent to which there are strong women's organizations outside political parties and Parliament.

This is a distinctly different approach to the specific conditions of liberal democracy than the approach that has been taken by women's organizations in relation to the first and second democratic elections in South Africa, where the emphasis has been on increasing women's representation in the state. As the case of the child maintenance grant showed, the danger of leaving policy formulation and priority setting to women inside the state—the brave example of the Joint Monitoring Committee on Women notwithstanding—is that gender issues in South Africa may become the domain of academics and technocrats, a new elite that may leave behind black working-class women—the "moral subject" of the triple oppression approach to understanding gender inequalities in South Africa. It is thus vital to reinstate "real politics" into democracy discourse: debate about who articulates needs and how they become integrated into policy choices. Such politics, moreover, must be engaged not simply by policy elites but also by the voices from below, whose interest in being heard has never been greater.

Appendixes
Notes
Bibliography
Index

Appendix A

The Women's Charter for Effective Equality

This is the second draft charter drawn up through the Women's National Coalition structures and approved at the national conference on February 27, 1994.

Preamble

As women, citizens of South Africa, we are here to claim our rights. We want recognition and respect for the work we do in the home, in the workplace and in the community. We claim full and equal participation in the creation of a non-sexist, non-racist democratic society.

We cannot march on one leg or clap with one hand. South Africa is poorer politically, economically, and socially for having prevented more than half of its people from fully contributing to its development.

Recognising our shared oppression, women are committed to seizing this historic moment to ensure effective equality in a new South Africa.

For decades, patriarchy, colonialism, racism and apartheid have subordinated and oppressed women within political, economic and social life.

At the heart of women's marginalisation is the patriarchal order that confines women to the domestic arena and reserves for men the arena where political power and authority reside. Conventionally, democracy and human rights have been defined and interpreted in terms of men s experiences. Society has been organised and its institutions structured for the primary benefit of men.

Women want to control their lives. We bear important responsibilities but lack the authority to make decisions in the home and in society.

We want shared responsibility and decision-making in the home and effective equality in politics, the law, and in the economy. For too long women have been marginalised, ignored, exploited and are the poorest and most disadvantaged of South Africans.

If democracy and human rights are to be meaningful for women, they must address our historic subordination and oppression. Women must participate in, and shape the nature and form of our democracy.

As women we have come together in a coalition of organisations and engaged in a campaign that has enabled women to draw on their experience and define what changes are needed within the new political, legal, economic and social system.

The development of the potential of all our people, women and men, will enrich and benefit the whole of society.

We set out here a programme for equality in all spheres of our lives, including the law, the economy, education, development and infrastructure, political and civic life, family life and partnerships, custom, culture and religion, health and the media.

Article 1: Equality

Equality underlies all our claims in this Charter. We recognise that the achievement of social, economic, political and legal equality is indivisible. Our struggle for equality involves the recognition of the disadvantage that women suffer in all spheres of our lives. As a result similar treatment of women and men may not result in true equality. Therefore the promotion of true equality will sometimes require distinctions to be made. No distinction, however, should be made that will disadvantage women. Within this context programmes of affirmative action may be a means of achieving equality.

We demand that equality applies to every aspect of our lives, including the family, the workplace and the state. The right to equality shall not be limited to our relationship with the state.

- The principle of equality shall be embodied at all levels in legislation and government policy. Specific legislation shall be introduced to ensure the practical realisation of equality.
- The state shall establish appropriate institutions to ensure the effective protection and promotion of equality for women. These institutions shall be accessible to all women in south Africa.

Article 2: Law and the Administration of Justice

Women demand equality in the development, application, adjudication, interpretation and enforcement of the law. This can only be achieved if the social, economic and political position of women is taken into account in deciding policy, determining legislative priorities, and in formulating, applying, interpreting, adjudicating and enforcing all laws.

- At all times the law, and its application, interpretation, adjudication and enforcement, shall promote and ensure the practical realisation of equality for women.
- There shall be equality in the treatment of women in all legal and quasi-legal proceedings.
- Women shall have equal legal status and capacity in civil law, including, amongst others, full contractual rights, the right to acquire and hold rights in property, the right to equal inheritance and the right to secure credit.
- All public and private institutions shall enable women to exercise their legal capacity.
- Positive and practical measures shall be taken to ensure equality for women complainants in the criminal justice system.
- There shall be equality for women offenders.
- There shall be equality for women in the legal profession
- Women shall be equally represented on, and participate in the selection of, the constitutional court, the judiciary, the magistracy, all tribunals and commissions, including the Human Rights Commission, and in the Department of Justice.
- There shall be educational programmes to address gender bias and stereotypes and to promote equality for women in the legal system.
- Women shall have equal representation on, and participation in all traditional courts, alternative dispute resolution mechanisms and local community courts.
- There shall be accessible and affordable legal services for women. In particular the position of paralegals in assisting women to claim their rights shall be recognised.

Article 3: Economy

Conventional definitions of the economy do not include a major proportion of the work performed by women. The key sectors of the South African economy are occupied and dominated by men. Women face social, economic and ideological barriers to full and equal participation in the economy. Women are perceived in terms of their domestic and reproductive role. Women participate in large numbers in sectors of the economy which are characterised by low wages and poor working conditions. Low remuneration is worsened by discrimination against women in the receipt of social benefits. As a result, many women are forced to make a living outside the formal economy.

- Gender stereotyping and the categorisation of jobs on the basis of sex and gender, must be eliminated.
- Equal benefits must be provided including housing, pensions and medical aid, amongst others.
- There should be no discriminatory taxation. All dependents supported by women breadwinners should be recognised for tax deductions for women.
- Legal mechanisms are needed to protect women against unfair, monopolistic and other exploitative business practices that affect women's participation in the informal economy.
- Safe and healthy facilities must be provided for women in the informal sector.
- Women must be protected from sexual harassment and violence in all the places where women are working.
- Group benefits are needed for women outside formal employment, such as accident and disability insurance, group housing schemes, sick leave and maternity benefits.
- Women need access to credit which is not based on the need for collateral or linked to their marital status.
- Health and safety for commercial sex workers and their clients are needed. Prostitution should be decriminalised.
- Economic policy must secure a central place for women in the economy.
- The full participation of women in economic decision-making should be facilitated.
- The definition of what constitutes economic activity must include all women's work.
- Unpaid labour should be recognised as contributing to the creation of national wealth and should be included in the national accounts.
- Gender stereotyping of work in the home needs to be combatted.

Article 4: Education and Training

Education and training in South Africa has historically focused on schooling, higher education and vocational training in the workplace. It has been male oriented, inaccessible, inappropriate and racially discriminatory. It has ignored women's needs and experience. Education and training is a continuous lifelong process. Education includes educare, adult basic and continuing education, primary, secondary and tertiary education and vocational training for the formal and informal economy. Education and training must meet the economic, social, cultural and political needs of women in South Africa.

- Every woman shall have the right to education and training at any stage of her life in order to realise her full potential.
- Every person has the right to equality within education irrespective of sex, gender, pregnancy, race, sexual orientation, age, disability, urban or rural location, domestic and child care responsibilities and financial status.
- Accessible and appropriate institutions shall be established to provide education to enable active participation by women, particularly rural women, single mothers, and disabled women.
- There shall be no negative gender stereotyping in both curriculum development and educational practice.
- Women shall be represented at all levels of the policy-making, management and administration of education and training.
- Women shall have special access to funds for education and training.
- Childcare facilities shall be provided at all education and training institutions.
- Human rights education to develop awareness of women's status, to build women's self confidence, and enable them to claim their constitutional and legal rights should be implemented.
- Girls and women in educational institutions must be protected against sexual harassment and abuse.
- Sex education shall be provided for boys and girls at all levels of schooling.

Article 5: Development, Infrastructure, and the Environment

Women are primarily responsible for maintaining the household and the community. The majority of South Africans have been denied access to the full range of basic development resources and services necessary to sustain a healthy and productive life. Rural women and informal settlement residents in particular have been denied vital resources. The gradual destruction of the natural environment soil erosion, deforestation and air pollution increases women's household, agricultural and community work responsibilities.

- Women should participate in designing and implementing development programmes to meet their needs.
- Employment generated from development and infrastructure programmes should benefit women.

- Adequate, accessible and safe water supplies and sanitation should be made available to all communities, including those in rural areas and informal settlements.
- Services such as communications and electricity or other appropriate sources of energy must be extended to all communities as a matter of priority.
- Women need safe transport networks.
- Women need affordable and secure housing with non-discriminatory subsidies and loans.
- Women must have equal access to land and security of tenure, including women living under customary law.
- Accessible health care, recreational, educational and social welfare facilities should be provided to women.
- There shall be protection of natural resources to benefit women.

Article 6: Social Services

- Social services should be a right and not a privilege. Inadequate social services place the burden for providing these on women, since women are primarily responsible for maintaining the household and the community.
- Social welfare services should be provided by both the state and the private sector in accordance with the principles of social justice, equality, appropriateness and accessibility.
- Social services should apply to all areas of women's lives, in particular in the home, the workplace, health and education.
- The system of social services should pay special attention to the needs of rural and disabled women.
- State pensions should be provided to all women on an equal basis.
- Accessible and affordable social services should be provided to women.

Article 7: Political and Civic Life

Women have traditionally been excluded from participation and decision-making in political, civic and community life. Democracy requires that the political playing field between men and women be levelled by acknowledging women's right to participate equally in all political activities.

- Women shall have equal opportunity and access to leadership and decision-making positions at all levels of government.
- Rural women have the right to be part of decision-making structures in traditional communities.
- Women shall have equal access to, and representation on, public bodies.
- Traditional institutions shall be restructured in accordance with the principles of equality and democracy.

- There shall be adequate and appropriate support services to facilitate the full political participation of women.
- Women shall have the right to acquire, change or retain their nationality and to pass it on to their children.
- Women shall be free from political intimidation and threat to her person.

Article 8: Family Life and Partnerships

There are many different types of families which have not enjoyed the same rights, duties and benefits. Women bear an unequal burden in maintaining the family and yet have little power to make decisions.

- All family types shall be recognised and treated equally.
- Women shall have equality within the family and within marriages and intimate relationships.
- Women shall have the right to choose the partner of their choice.
- Women shall have equal rights during, and at the dissolution of, a marriage.
- Women married under customary law shall have the right to inherit from their husbands.
- Women must have the right to decide on the nature and frequency of sexual contact within marriage and intimate relationships.
- Partners and all members of the household should endeavour to share domestic responsibilities.
- Women should have equal access to the financial resources of the household.
- Women should have equal decision-making powers and access to information with regard to the economic management of the household.
- The integrity of the partnership has to be maintained without external and familial interference, except where physical, sexual and emotional abuse occurs.
- Women shall have guardianship over their children.
- Women shall nave adequate, effective and enforceable maintenance and/or social welfare benefits for themselves and their children.

Article 9: Custom, Culture, and Religion

Customary, cultural and religious practice frequently subordinates women. Roles that are defined for women are both stereotypical and restrictive Women are often excluded from full participation, leadership and decision-making in religious and cultural practice.

- Custom, culture and religion shall be subject to the equality clause in the Bill of Rights.
- All women shall have the freedom to practise their own religion, culture or beliefs without fear.

Article 10: Violence against Women

Violence in all its forms is endemic to South African society. Both sexual and domestic violence are pervasive and all women live under the threat of or experience violence. Women experience secondary victimization at all stages of the criminal justice system.

- Women shall be entitled to security and integrity of the person which shall include the right to be free from all forms of violence in the home, in communities, in the workplace and in public spaces.
- The state should be responsible for public education about the dignity and integrity of the person.
- There shall be legal protection for all women against sexual and racial harassment, abuse and assault.
- Facilities staffed by trained personnel where women can report cases of rape, battery and sexual assault, undergo medical examination and receive appropriate treatment and counselling shall be provided.
- Appropriate education and training for police, prosecutors, magistrates, judges, district surgeons and other persons involved in dealing with cases of rape, battery, sexual assault and incest must be provided.
- There shall be accessible and affordable shelters and counselling services for survivors of rape, battery and sexual assault.

Article 11: Health

Health services in South Africa have traditionally been unequal, inaccessible and inappropriate. Women in particular are unaware of their rights in relation to health services. Health Services have not been appropriately oriented to meet women's health needs and priorities. The lack of basic life sustaining services, such as water and sanitation, has denied the majority of South Africans access to the resources necessary to ensure good health.

- Equal, affordable and accessible health care services which meet women's specific health needs shall be provided.
- Women have the right to control over their bodies which includes the right to reproductive decisions.
- Access to Information and knowledge to enable women to make informed choices about their bodies and about health care should be provided.
- Education about family planning and family planning services should be provided free of charge to both men and women.
- Every person shall have access to adequate nutrition.
- Appropriate and accessible mental health care services must be provided to women.

Article 12: Media

In South Africa women do not enjoy equal access to, or coverage in the film, print and electronic media. Very few women own or control media institutions or occupy executive or editorial decision-making positions. Women are marginalised and trivialised in the media. The principles of freedom of speech and the press should not justify the portrayal of women in a manner that is degrading and humiliating or promotes violence against them.

- Women must have equal access to all media and media institutions.
- The contribution of women in all areas of public and private life must be reflected in the media.
- The promotion of equality, including affirmative action, in employment must redress current imbalances in the status of women in the media.
- There is a need to monitor the representation of women in the media.
- Negative or injurious stereotypes of women must be eliminated.

This Charter gives expression to the common experiences, visions and aspirations of South African women. We are breaking our silence. We call for respect and recognition of our human dignity and for a genuine change in our status and material conditions in a future South Africa.

Appendix B

Structure and Components of the National Gender Machinery

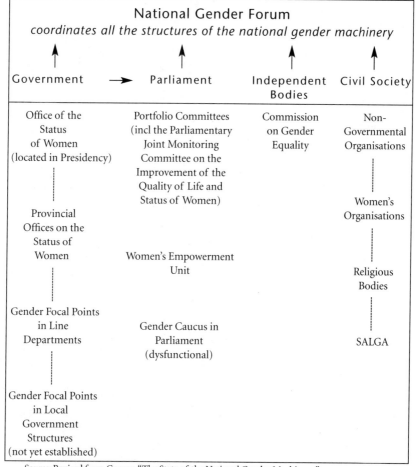

National Gender Forum *coordinates all the structures of the national gender machinery*			
↑ Government →	↑ Parliament	↑ Independent Bodies	↑ Civil Society
Office of the Status of Women (located in Presidency)	Portfolio Committees (incl the Parliamentary Joint Monitoring Committee on the Improvement of the Quality of Life and Status of Women)	Commission on Gender Equality	Non-Governmental Organisations
Provincial Offices on the Status of Women			Women's Organisations
	Women's Empowerment Unit		
Gender Focal Points in Line Departments	Gender Caucus in Parliament (dysfunctional)		Religious Bodies
Gender Focal Points in Local Government Structures (not yet established)			SALGA

Source: Revised from Gouws, "The State of the National Gender Machinery."

Notes

Preface

1. Seidman, "No Freedom without the Women."
2. Meintjes, "Gender, Nationalism and Transformation."
3. Patel, "South African Women's Struggles in the 1980s."
4. Fester, "Women's Organisations in the Western Cape."
5. Routledge-Madlala. "What Price for Freedom?"
6. Meintjes, "Gender, Nationalism and Transformation."

Introduction

1. Mohanty, "Under Western Eyes"; Basu, *The Challenge of Local Feminisms.*
2. Phillips, *The Politics of Presence;* Baldez, *Why Women Protest.*
3. Kaplan, *Crazy for Democracy;* Molyneux, "Analyzing Women's Movements."
4. For example, in the 1980s both the Inkatha Freedom Party and the ANC mobilized women (separately) on the basis of their maternal identities, yet the traditional

Zulu family underpinned the political ideology of the Inkatha Freedom Party, whereas the ANC held to a notion of gender equality.

5. Kaplan, *Crazy for Democracy,* 6.

6. Ibid.

7. Fester, "Women's Organisations in the Western Cape."

8. Baldez, *Why Women Protest,* 5.

9. Ibid., 6.

10. Molyneux, "Analyzing Women's Movements," 225.

11. Tripp, *Women and Politics in Uganda,* chap. 1.

12. Molyneux, "Analyzing Women's Movements," 226.

13. Ibid., 227.

14. Ibid.

15. Ibid., 228.

16. Ibid.

17. Ibid.

18. Ibid., 229.

19. Ibid., 226.

20. See, for example, the case studies in Basu, *The Challenge of Local Feminisms;* Jacquette, *The Women's Movement in Latin America;* and Threlfall, *Mapping Women's Movements.*

21. Jacquette, *The Women's Movement in Latin America,* 13.

22. See Feijoo, "Democratic Participation and Women in Argentina"; Valenzuela, "Women and the Democratization Process in Chile"; and Caldeira, "Justice and Individual Rights," all in Jacquette and Wolchik, *Women and Democracy;* also E. Friedman, *Unfinished Transitions.*

23. Jacquette and Wolchik, *Women and Democracy,* 88.

24. Tarrow, *Power in Movement.*

25. Dahlerup, *The New Women's Movement;* Stetson and Mazur, *Comparative State Feminism.*

26. Katzenstein, introduction, in Katzenstein and Mueller, *The Women's Movements of the United States and Western Europe,* 11.

27. Hellman, "Women's Struggle in a Workers' City"; and Jenson, "Changing Discourse, Changing Agendas."

28. Dahlerup, *The New Women's Movement.*

29. Alvarez, *Engendering Democracy in Brazil.*

30. Goetz and Hassim, "In and against the Party"; Abdullah, "Wifeism and Activism."

31. Pringle and Watson, "Women's Interests and the Post-structuralist State"; Rai and Lievesley, *Women and the State.*

32. Molyneux, "Analyzing Women's Movements," 226; Jenson "Changing Discourses, Changing Agendas."

33. Jenson, "Changing Discourse, Changing Agendas," 65.

34. Ibid.

35. Ibid.

36. Ibid., 67.

37. Waylen, "Gender and Democratic Politics."

38. Webster and Adler, "Towards a Class Compromise in South Africa's 'Double Tradition.'"

39. Goetz and Hassim, "In and against the Party."

Chapter 1. Contesting Ideologies

1. Letseme, "Women's Contribution to the Liberation Struggle"; Budlender, Meintjes, and Schreiner, review of *Women and Resistance;* Hendricks and Lewis, "Voices from the Margins"; Fester, "Women's Organisations in the Western Cape."

2. Wells, *"We Now Demand!"*

3. Beall, "Women under Indentured Labour."

4. Bradford, "We Are Now the Men."

5. Walker, *Women and Resistance in South Africa;* Lodge, *Black Politics in South Africa.*

6. Berger, *Threads of Solidarity.*

7. Ginwala, "Women and the African National Congress," 80.

8. Ibid., 78.

9. Walker, *Women and Resistance,* 33.

10. Ginwala, "Women and the African National Congress," 77.

11. Lodge, *Black Politics in South Africa,* chap. 1.

12. Ibid., 141.

13. Walker, *Women and Resistance,* chaps. 2 and 6.

14. Ibid., 76.

15. Ibid., 89.

16. Ibid., 90.

17. Ibid.

18. Ibid.

19. Ibid., 132.

20. Ginwala, "Women and the African National Congress," 90.

21. Ibid.

22. Ibid.

23. Walker, *Women and Resistance,* 90.

24. Reddy and Meer, *Passive Resistance,* 112.

25. Ibid., 113.

26. *Indian Opinion,* May 6, 1938.

27. Walker, preface to the second edition, *Women and Resistance,* xvii.

28. Bernstein, *For Their Triumphs,* 87.

29. Federation of South African Women, "The Women's Charter" (1954), quoted in J. Barrett et al., *Vukani Makosikhazi,* 240.

30. Walker, *Women and Resistance,* xvii.

31. Ibid.

32. See Walker's 1982 account of the organization of the march. Wells makes similar points in *"We Now Demand!"*

33. Walker, *Women and Resistance,* chap. 17.

34. Joseph, *Side by Side,* 70.

35. Bernstein, *For Their Triumphs,* 82.

36. Wells, *"We Now Demand!"* 117.

37. Walker, *Women and Resistance;* Wells, *"We Now Demand!"*

38. Bernstein, *For Their Triumphs;* Joseph, *Side by Side.*

39. Bernstein, *For Their Triumphs,* 97.

40. Kaplan, "Female consciousness and Collective Action."

41. Molyneux, "Analysing Women's Movements."

42. Kaplan, *Crazy for Democracy,* 6.

43. Joseph, *Side by Side.*

44. Kaplan, *Crazy for Democracy,* 6.

45. Ibid.

46. Molyneux, "Analysing Women's Movements," 235.

47. Basu, *The Challenge of Local Feminisms,* 3.

48. Ginwala interview; ANC, Report of Nairobi Conference, presented at the Second ANC Women's Conference, Luanda, 1987, SAHA Archives.

49. Saul, "Liberation without Democracy?"

50. Lewis, "Theorising about Gender."

51. Horn, "Post-apartheid South Africa."

52. Walker, *Women and Resistance;* Hassim and Walker, "Women's Studies and the Women's Movement."

53. Walker, *Women and Resistance.*

54. Ibid., 279–82.

55. Ibid., 182.

56. Letseme, "Women's Contribution to the Liberation Struggle," 101.

57. Ibid., 103.

58. Cherryl Walker, "Women and Resistance."

59. Budlender, Meintjes, and Schreiner, review of *Women and Resistance,* 24.

60. Ibid., 28.

61. Ibid.

62. Basu, introduction to *The Challenge of Local Feminisms.*

63. Heng, "A Great Way to Fly," 33.

64. It is not possible to offer comprehensive citations for the positions outlined here. Many debates were conducted in activist circles (of which I was a part) and few positions were explicitly stated on paper.

65. Ginwala, "ANC Women," 12.

66. Clara (Jenny Schreiner), "Feminism and the Struggle for National Liberation."

67. Gould, Radloff, and Cuhn, "The Women's Centre, Cape Town"; Van Zyl, "Invitation to Debate"; Mayne, "Discourse on Damage."

68. Hassim, Metelerkamp, and Todes, "A Bit on the Side?"

69. Bernstein, "The Real Challenge of Feminism"; Quincy, "On the Emancipation of Women."

70. Eduards, "Women's Agency and Collective Action," 183.

71. Yuval-Davis and Anthias, *Woman-Nation-State;* Ranchod-Nilsson and Tetreault, *Women, States and Nationalism.*

72. Charman, de Swardt, and Simons, "The Politics of Gender," 64.

73. Kruks, Rapp, and Young, *Promissory Notes;* Briskin, "Socialist Feminism."
74. Hassim, "Where Have All the Women Gone?"
75. Cohen and Arato, *Civil Society and Political Theory,* 562.
76. Ibid., 522.
77. Mohanty, "Under Western Eyes."
78. Jayawardena, *Feminism and Nationalism,* 2.
79. Yuval-Davis, *Gender and Nation,* 22.
80. Saporta Sternbach et al., "Feminisms in Latin America."
81. Erlank, "Gender and Masculinity."
82. Chatterjee, *The Nation and Its Fragments.*
83. This view of Afrikaner women as passive is contradicted by two other significant studies of Afrikaner nationalism: Hofmeyr, "Building a Nation from Words," and Brink, "Man-made Women."
84. Gaitskell and Unterhalter, "Mothers of the Nation."
85. Ibid., 75.
86. Hassim, "Family, Motherhood and Zulu Nationalism."
87. Basu, *The Challenge of Local Feminisms.* See also Reagon, "Coalition Politics."
88. Chigudu and Tichagwa, "Participation of Women."
89. Abdullah, "Wifeism and Activism."
90. Mama, "Women's Studies and Studies of Women."
91. Tripp, *Women and Politics in Uganda.*
92. Goetz and Hassim, "In and against the Party."
93. See also Molyneux, "Analysing Women's Movements," for her assessment of the value of directed action in modernizing nationalist movements.
94. Basu, *The Challenge of Local Feminisms,* 5.
95. Mamdani, "Africa," 88.
96. Unterhalter, "The Work of the Nation," 157.
97. Ibid., 166.
98. Grewal and Kaplan, *Scattered Hegemonies,* 22.
99. See Yuval-Davis and Anthias, *Woman-Nation-State;* Yuval-Davis, *Gender and Nation;* Curthoys, "Identity Crisis"; Parker et al., *Nationalisms and Sexualities;* Brink, "Man-made Women"; Kandiyoti, "Identity and Its Discontents"; McClintock, "Family Feuds"; Boehmer, "Stories of Women and Mothers."
100. Yuval Davis and Anthias, *Woman-Nation-State.*
101. Grewal and Kaplan, *Scattered Hegemonies,* 22.
102. McClintock, "Family Feuds," 2.
103. Heng, "A Great Way to Fly," 33.
104. See, for example, Molyneux, "Mobilization without Emancipation?" in Fagen and Deere, *Transition and Development;* Vargas, "Women's Movements in Peru"; Waylen, "Women and Democratization"; Tripp, *Women and Politics in Uganda.*
105. Hendricks and Lewis, "Voices from the Margins."
106. Liu, "The Female Body and Nationalist Discourse," 37.
107. Heng, "A Great Way to Fly."
108. Hudson, "The Freedom Charter," 7.

109. Alexander, "Approaches to the National Question," 70.

110. Walker, *Women and Gender in Southern Africa;* Hassim, "Gender, Social Location and Feminist Politics."

111. Hassim, "Gender, Social Location and Feminist Politics"; Horn, "Post-apartheid South Africa."

112. Alexander, "Approaches to the National Question."

113. Reagon, "Coalition Politics."

114. Gaitskell et al., "Class, Race and Gender."

115. Racial terminology in South Africa is, needless to say, complicated and constantly shifting. In the 1970s the black consciousness movement defined *black* as including all those who were legally excluded from systems of governing in South Africa: African, Indian, and Coloured. This was the dominant usage of the term *black* until the 1990s, when a new politics of identity demarcated distinctions within the category "black," reinscribing color. The term coloured is used in South Africa to refer to those people who were defined as "mixed-race" in the apartheid population categorization system.

116. Hassim, "Gender, Social Location and Feminist Politics," 68.

117. Walker, *Women and Gender in Southern Africa,* 3.

118. Charman, de Swardt, and Simons, "The Politics of Gender," 42–43.

119. Hassim, "Gender, Social Location and Feminist Politics."

120. Hassim, Metelerkamp, and Todes, "A Bit on the Side."

121. Horn, "Post-apartheid South Africa."

122. Hassim, Metelerkamp, and Todes, "A Bit on the Side"; Charman, de Swardt, and Simons, "The Politics of Gender."

123. Kemp et al., "The Dawn of a New Day," 142.

124. Hendricks, "Gender Politics in a Post-apartheid South Africa," 3.

125. Lewis, "Theorising about Gender."

126. Kemp et al., "Dawn of a New Day."

127. Hendricks and Lewis, "Voices from the Margins," 65.

128. Jonasdottir, "On the Concept of Interest."

Chapter 2. The Emergence of Women as a Political Constituency

1. Adler and Steinberg, *From Comrades to Citizens,* 4.

2. Steinberg, "A Place for Civics," in Adler and Steinberg, *From Comrades to Citizens,* 199.

3. Seekings, *The UDF;* van Kessel, *"Beyond Our Wildest Dreams";* Adler and Steinberg, *From Comrades to Citizens.*

4. There are several studies of women's organizations in this period. See Patel, "South African Women's Struggles"; Hassim, Metelerkamp, and Todes, "A Bit on the Side?"; Meintjes, "Gender, Nationalism and Transformation"; Udit, "Engendering the National Liberation Struggle."

5. Meer, *Women Speak!* 19.

6. Seekings, *The UDF,* 76–79. Seekings also argues that Gordhan and Mahomed were "in close contact throughout with the ANC and SACP [South African Communist Party] in exile, particularly through former Robben Islander Mac Maharaj" (32).

7. "Northcroft Women Organise."
8. Ibid., 13.
9. Ibid.
10. "We Are a Force to Reckon With," 10.
11. Ibid.
12. "We Don't Want to Be Tails," 5.
13. J. Barrett et al, *Vukani Makhosikazi.*
14. "Making Our Voices Heard," 4.
15. J. Barrett et al., *Vukani Makhosikazi,* 106.
16. Ibid.
17. Meer, *Women Speak,* 96.
18. "No to Rape, Say Port Alfred Women."
19. "Rape in Marriage"; "Our Men Must Stop Beating Us"; "Breaking the Silence."
20. Even a cursory reading of the magazine *Speak* will bear this out. See also Russell, *Lives of Courage,* and J. Barrett et al., *Vukani Makhosikazi.*
21. Cole, *Crossroads,* 64.
22. Ibid., 65.
23. Ibid., 67.
24. Cherry, "Traditions and Transitions."
25. "Northcroft Women Organise."
26. Alvarez, *Engendering Democracy in Brazil,* 39.
27. Kaplan, *Crazy for Democracy,* 2.
28. There appeared to be some early opposition to the formation of a separate women's organization. "A member of the organisation said that the women of Gugulethu had long been discussing how to begin such an organisation. Eventually they called a meeting in the civic hall. Some men were against it and tried to break up the meeting but the women were too strong for them" (Minutes of a women's meeting held at Maryland, Hanover Park, August 12, 1979, UWO Papers).
29. Jaffee, "Women in Trade Unions"; Patel, "South African Women's Struggles."
30. Russell, "The United Women's Congress: Gertrude Fester," in *Lives of Courage,* 245.
31. Quoted in Frederikse, *The Unbreakable Thread,* 102.
32. Russell, "Balancing Motherhood and Politics: Shahieda Issel," in *Lives of Courage,* 68.
33. Soobrayan interview.
34. Russell, "From Soweto to Exile: Connie Mofokeng," in *Lives of Courage,* 56.
35. Meer, *Women Speak,* 12.
36. Meer interview.
37. Russell, "An Indian Woman Confronts Apartheid: Ela Ramgobin," in *Lives of Courage,* 137.
38. Meer interview.
39. Seekings, *The UDF,* 54.
40. Meer interview.
41. Ntombela-Nzimande interview.
42. Ibid.
43. Constitution, 1981, UWO Papers.

44. Policy Statement, 1981, UWO Papers.

45. "Policy of UWO for the Fourth Conference, 12 May," 1985, UWO Papers.

46. "Natal Organisation of Women."

47. See Report on Meeting with Durban Visitors, attached to minutes of Executive Committee Meeting, December 20, 1981, UWO Papers.

48. Anonymous activist, undated report to ANC, Ray Simons Papers.

49. Ibid.

50. Narsee interview. In a report of a meeting with activists from Durban, UWO recorded this position in the following terms: "Women in Durban are said to be traditional inclined [sic] so they need a clear platform—they want a home" (Minutes of Executive Committee Meeting, December 20, 1981, UWO Papers).

51. "Workshop: Should the UWO be a National Organisation?" May 30, 1982, UWO Papers. See also Report on UWO, 1985, Ray Simons Papers. Simons also supported the idea of a locally based organization, suggesting as late as 1985 that "Mechanic [UWO] is not a national organisation, nor should it propel to be one, otherwise it would be wrong. . . . We are glad that Mechanic has no intention of being national, and of the decision of disbanding what they called branches [in East London] and allowing their constitution to be used as draft for all areas to change it according to their given conditions" ("Letter to comrades, 21st February, Year of the Cadre," 1985, Ray Simons Papers).

52. "Workshop: Should the UWO be a National Organisation?"

53. Kemp et al., "The Dawn of a New Day," 138.

54. Udit, "Engendering the National Liberation Struggle," 133.

55. Ibid., 132.

56. Dawber, "Transvaal Women Organise," 31.

57. Ginwala and Routledge-Madlala interviews.

58. ANC Women's Section, Report on the Motsepe Meeting, ANC Archives. The meeting was attended by the internal activists Frances Baard and Mildred Lesiea of the United Women's Organisation and Winnie Kgware and Sister Bernard of FEDTRAW.

59. Narsee interview.

60. Routledge-Madlala, "What Price for Freedom?" 67.

61. Report of the Transvaal Interim Committee submitted at the 1st launching conference, December 7–9, 1984, FEDTRAW Papers.

62. Ibid.

63. Jaffee, "Women in Trade Unions," 85.

64. Undated report to the NEC of the UDF, to REC of UDF, to NEC of ANC, FEDTRAW Papers, in a file marked "UDF File," William Cullen Library, Wits University.

65. Anonymous report to ANC Women's Section. Report of the proceedings of the Second National Conference of Women, September, 1987, p. 26, ANC Archives.

66. Ibid., 28.

67. Helen Joseph, "Message from an Ex-secretary of the Federation of South African Women to the UWO for Their First Conference," April 4 and 5, 1981, UWO Papers.

68. "Maggy," "The Critical Evaluation Report on FEDTRAW—Its Progress and the Recommendations on Its Structure and Future Programmes (1984–1986 May)," February 1987, Ray Simons Papers.

69. Ibid.

70. Meintjes (March 3, 2000) and Mager interviews.

71. Udit, "Engendering the National Liberation Struggle," 140.

72. A report of a meeting between the General Workers Union and UWO reveals some of the difficulties in creating a relationship. It was agreed that the two areas of cooperation were that "UWO encourages workers to join the union; GWU encourages women to join the UWO." However, the union representatives were unclear about the role of UWO. One representative said that "people thought the UWO was there to support the struggles of others." Another suggested that UWO "should take up women's issues that would get men to change their attitudes to women." The UWO representatives pointed out that "the UWO did not see the struggle of the women as a confrontation with the men. Experience had shown that the best way to change men's attitudes was for the women to win victories for the community as a whole" (Meeting with General Workers Union, 1983, UWO Papers).

73. Minutes of Third Annual Conference of the UWO held on 26 & 27 March at AW Bauer House, Crawford, 1983, UWO Papers.

74. Democracy in UWO, undated, Ray Simons Papers.

75. UWO proposed two resolutions at the national launch of the UDF, one calling on women "to bring their organisations into the UDF," and another demanding "the right for workers to organise in trade unions and in the communities" (Minutes of the Executive Council, August 17, 1983, UWO Papers.

76. "Organising Women NOW!" 1985, South African Historical Archives.

77. Routledge-Madlala interview.

78. In the early 1980s the democratic trade union movement was wary of the overt emphasis on national liberation, which the trade unionists believed would attract repression by the state and undermine attempts to build long-term sustainable organizations. In Natal the political leadership was dominated by the underground ANC, and the two patterns of organization were considered incompatible. Political leadership in the Western Cape was more divided, and unions had a much stronger influence on women's organization there.

79. *Gogo* is the Zulu word for grandmother.

80. Report of a meeting between ANC Women's Secretariat and "women from home," May 29, 1986, Ray Simons Papers.

81. Hassim, "Family, Motherhood and Zulu Nationalism."

82. One successful project was the production of leather sandals, which were sold to raise money for the organization.

83. Narsee interview.

84. Soobrayan interview.

85. Ibid.

86. Victoria Mxenge was a prominent member of the UDF executive board and the widow of the popular township activist Griffiths Mxenge, who had been hacked to death in Umlazi Stadium in 1981 by members of the security police. Victoria

Mxenge's assassination four years later sparked an escalation of the confrontation between the state, the Inkatha surrogate government in Natal, and UDF-aligned civic organizations. Commemoration services, held around the province, themselves became battlefields. For discussion of these events see Beall et al., "African Women in the Durban Struggle."

87. Nozizwe Madlala became deputy minister of defense in 2001 and in 2004 was named deputy minister of health.

88. Narsee interview.

89. Routledge-Madlala interview.

90. Report on NOW, 1985, Ray Simons Papers.

91. Report of a meeting between the ANC Women's Secretariat and "women from home."

92. Report by the Natal Organisation of Women [to ANC Women's Section], June 1989, Helen Joseph Papers.

93. IBR, *Resistance in the Townships,* 144.

94. Minutes of meeting held between Umlazi branch and executive members of NOW, February 25, 1989, NOW Papers.

95. Soobrayan interview.

96. Report on NOW.

97. Meer and Govender interviews.

98. Govender interview.

99. ANC Women's Section, report "From London," undated, Ray Simons Papers.

100. Mager and Narsee interviews. The ANC endorsed the affiliation of UWO to the UDF and urged that "UWO's voice like all other women's should be active and vocal in UDF. However, UWO must not diminish its activities but should consolidate its gains. UDF's strength will depend on the strengths of its affiliates" (Response to UWO Report of November 18, 1983, Ray Simons Papers).

101. Annual report of the secretaries, June 1984, UWO Papers.

102. Beall, Hassim, and Todes, "'A Bit on the Side?'" 46.

103. UDF Sub-Committee Report, March 1984, UWO Papers.

104. Minutes of a workshop on Strategy and Co-ordination, October 1, 1983, UWO Papers.

105. Fester, "Women's Organisations in the Western Cape," 49.

106. Minutes of the Executive Council meeting, May 7, 1983, UWO Papers.

107. "UWO Secretarial Reports," 1985, UWO Papers.

108. Mager interview.

109. Minutes of workshop on Strategy and Co-ordination, October 1, 1983, UWO Papers.

110. Ibid.

111. Minutes of the Executive Council meeting, October 2, 1983, UWO Papers.

112. Fester, "Women's Organisations in the Western Cape," 49.

113. Report on the Women's Struggle from May 1985–April 1986, ANC Archives.

114. Ibid.

115. Report from UWCO, compiled by Miranda Harare, April 1989, Ray Simons Papers.

116. Report for Conference, February 1986, United Women's Congress Papers.

117. Ibid.

118. Ibid.

119. Ibid.

120. Ibid.

121. Secretarial report covering October 1988 –September 1989, UWCO Papers.

122. Ibid.

123. Annual Report of the Secretaries.

124. Chairperson's report to the Special Conference on the dissolution of the Natal Organisation of Women, September 9, 1990, South African Historical Archives.

125. UDF Women's Congress Position Paper on the Role of Women within the National Liberation Movement, 1987, UDF Archives.

126. Notable examples are Cheryl Carolus and Sister Bernard Ncube.

127. "The Tasks of the Democratic Movement during the State of Emergency," internal discussion paper, October 10, 1985, UDF Archives.

128. Govender, "Launching UDF Women's Congress," 75.

129. Ibid.

130. Ibid.

131. UDF Women's Congress Resolution, April 27, 1987, UDF Archives.

132. Ibid.

133. Govender, "Launching UDF Women's Congress, " 76.

134. Ibid., 75.

135. Undated report. Ray Simons Papers.

136. Minutes of national meeting, March 3 –4, 1990, UDF Archives.

137. Ibid.

138. Ibid.

139. Ibid.

140. COSATU opposed affiliation with the UDF. FEDTRAW and the COSATU Gender Forum had a particularly fractious interaction about the composition of the Transvaal delegation to the Malibongwe Conference. FEDTRAW sought to limit union members to two delegates, and COSATU threatened to withdraw its delegation completely. IOnly high-level intervention and a meeting in Lusaka resolved the dispute. COSATU got five seats for its affiliates. Rachmat Omar, COSATU education officer, recalled that "they didn't want a COSATU bloc, but we were not prepared, so we couldn't even really function as a bloc" (Omar interview). Veni Soobrayan, who was on the planning committee for Malibongwe, explained the committee's view: "We wanted [participation] to be as broad as possible. We wanted to limit COSATU numbers because they were not a women's movement. The ANC-aligned organizations had numerical supremacy, and they wanted to contain [the union] influence within the movement" (Soobrayan interview).

141. Kemp et al., "Dawn of a New Day," 141.

142. See Hendricks and Lewis, "Voices from the Margins," and Lewis, "Theorising about Gender."

143. Gaitskell and Unterhalter, "Mothers of the Nation."

144. Russell, "The Most Powerful Woman in the ANC: Ruth Mompati," in Lives of Courage, 114.

145. Russell, "Co-president of the United Democratic Front: Albertina Sisulu," in *Lives of Courage,* 151.

146. Walker, *Women and Resistance;* Gaitskell and Unterhalter, "Mothers of the Nation"; McClintock, "Family Feuds."

147. Radcliffe and Westwood, "Gender, Racism and the Politics of Identities," 18.

148. Fester, "Women's Organisations in the Western Cape," 46.

149. Daniels, "ANC Women's League," 36.

150. Sheila Meintjes, former member of the UWO, personal communication.

151. Fester, "Women's Organisations in the Western Cape," 46.

152. Ibid., 51.

153. Examples of these themes are "struggles in other third world countries" and "how to build our organization."

154. Meer, *Women Speak,* 13.

155. Nkomo, "Organising Women in SANSCO," 13.

156. Mager interview.

157. Ibid.

158. Report on Conference, 1981, UWO Papers.

159. Govender interview.

160. Meintjes interview (March 3, 2000).

161. White women were more involved in the Pietermaritzburg branch.

162. Narsee interview.

163. Report of Annual Conference, 1983, UWO Papers.

164. Mager interview.

165. Problems in UWO Exec., 1981, Ray Simons Papers.

166. Ibid.

167. Minutes of Third Annual Conference of the UWO.

168. UWO Secretarial Report, 1985. There is some evidence that the ANC was involved at least in ratifying UWO's plan of action. A report in the Ray Simons Papers entitled "Response to UWO Report of 18.11.83" comments positively on the two themes in 1983 (high prices and child care). It also suggests that "committees [of the UWO] should be constituted by ordinary women and intellectuals, as these complement each other. The barrier between the two should be eliminated." Furthermore, the organization should begin to train black women, "who suffer many disabilities imposed by the regime and outmoded traditions which cause them to have no confidence in themselves, hence their hidden talents have to be dug out."

169. Mager interview.

170. UWO Secretarial Report, 1985.

171. Routledge-Madlala, "What Price for Freedom?" 67.

172. Burton, "Women Organise," 15.

173. Ibid.

174. Schwartz, "Liberation–A Feminist Issue?" 6.

175. Ibid.

176. Fester, "Women's Organisations in the Western Cape," 52.

177. Govender interview.

178. Hurt interview, May 17, 2000.

179. Marie, "Women Face the Challenge," 72–73.
180. Govender interview.
181. Schreiner interview, May 20, 2000.
182. Beall et al., "A Bit on the Side."
183. Patel, "South African Women's Struggles"; Fester, "Women's Organisations in the Western Cape"; Routledge-Madlala, "What Price for Freedom?"; Meintjes, "Gender, Nationalism and Transformation."

Chapter 3. The ANC in Exile

1. Mtintso interview.
2. Molyneux, "Analysing Women's Movements," 229.
3. Ibid.
4. Ibid.
5. ANC Women's Secretariat, "Report of the Women's Secretariat of the ANC to the First Conference of ANC Women in the Exile Mission, Luanda, People's Republic of Angola," September 10–14, 1981, ANC Archives.
6. Russell, "Women and the African National Congress: Mavivi Manzini," in *Lives of Courage*, 129.
7. Presentation by Mavivi Myakayaka Manzini to an ANC Women's League workshop, Johannesburg, September 2, 1990. From notes taken by Sheila Meintjes.
8. Ginwala interview.
9. ANC, "Role and Place of Women in Society, the ANC and the Struggle," National Preparatory Committee documents, ANC National Consultative Conference, June 1985, ANC Archives. Muff Andersson said that this was a euphemistic way of saying they made the tea and sang at funerals (Andersson interview).
10. Motumi interview.
11. MK cadres also received a small allowance of twenty Zimbabwean dollars per month, "just enough to buy tampons" (Andersson interview).
12. Lodge, *Black Politics in South Africa*, 296.
13. Ibid.
14. Gaitskell, '"Christian Compounds for Girls.'"
15. ANC Women's Section East Africa Region, Regional report, July 1981, ANC Archives.
16. ANC Women's Section, Report of the National Women's Executive Committee (NWEC) meeting, Lusaka, April 5–8, 1984, ANC Archives.,
17. Andersson interview.
18. ANC Women's Section, Minutes of the Joint Women's Secretariat/RPC meeting, October 15, 1982, ANC Archives.
19. Nhlapo interview.
20. Motumi interview.
21. Andersson interview.
22. ANC Women's Section, Report of the NWEC meeting.
23. Andersson interview.
24. Morrow, Maaba, and Pulumane, *Education in Exile*, 134.

25. Ibid.

26. ANC Women's Section, ANC second Women's Conference national preparatory committee composite report, 1987, South African Historical Archives.

27. ANC Women's Section, Minutes of the meeting of the Secretary General's Office, March 17, 1981, ANC Archives.

28. ANC Women's Section, Minutes of the meeting of the women with the Youth Secretariat, September 23, 1982, ANC Archives.

29. ANC Women's Section, Meeting of the NWEC with members of the NEC, April 8, 1984, Libala Office of the Women's Secretariat, ANC Archives.

30. ANC Women's Section, Women in MK, Paper 3(a), September 1987, National Preparatory Committee Papers, South African Historical Archives.

31. Sechaba and Ellis, *Comrades against Apartheid,* 85.

32. ANC Women's Secretariat, "Report of the Women's Secretariat of the ANC."

33. ANC Women's Section, Women's Secretariat meeting, February 1, 1982, ANC Archives.

34. Nhlapo interview.

35. ANC Women's Section, Minutes of the meeting of the women with the Youth Secretariat.

36. Andersson interview.

37. Morrow, Maaba, and Pulumane, *Education in Exile,* chap. 10.

38. ANC Women's Secretariat, "Report of the Women's Secretariat of the ANC." There are no records to show that young men were disciplined for fraternizing with women members of the PAC, although it is possible that responsibility for men was seen to be the area of the Youth Secretariat.

39. ANC Women's Section, Meeting of the NWEC with members of the NEC.

40. ANC Women's Section, meeting of the Women's Secretariat with representative of the Directorate of Mazimbu, November 8, 1982, Women's Secretariat offices, ANC Archives.

41. Morrow, Maaba, and Pulumane, *Education in Exile,* 134.

42. ANC Women's Section, Letter, Dear Comrade Zanele, January 13, 1988, ANC Archives. Emphasis added.

43. ANC Women's Section, A report of the Secretariat on the state of organisation of the ANC Women's Section since September 1981 for the second conference of the women in the external mission, 1987, ANC Archives.

44. Morrow, Maaba, and Pulumane, *Education in Exile,* 138.

45. Ibid., 141.

46. ANC Women's Section, Letter from G. Shope to the Chairperson of the Regional Women's Committee, Somafco, "Re Child Abuse and Wife/Girlfriend Battering," 1988, ANC Archives.

47. ANC Women's Section, "A Report of the Secretariat . . . since September 1981."

48. Ibid.

49. ANC Women's Section, Report of the ANC (SA) Zambia Regional Women's Section, September 1981–February 1982, ANC Archives.

50. ANC Women's Section, Minutes of the meeting of September 21, 1984, ANC Archives.

51. See Sechaba and Ellis, *Comrades against Apartheid.*

52. ANC Women's Section, Report of the ANC (SA) Zambia Regional Women's Section.

53. Barrell, "The Turn to the Masses."

54. ANC Women's Section, *Voice of Women* (VOW) editorial board meeting, April 5, 1982, ANC Archives.

55. ANC Women's Section, Report of the consultative meeting held with the Maputo political department and representatives of editorial boards of VOW, *Mayibuye*, DAWN, and *Forward*, 1983, ANC Archives.

56. ANC Women's Section, Report on the activities of the ANC Women's Secretariat since 1981, 1983, ANC Archives.

57. ANC Women's Secretariat, Recommendations adopted by the ANC Women's Council meeting, Lusaka, February 22–25, 1983, ANC Archives.

58. ANC Women's Section, Report on the activities of the ANC Women's Secretariat since 1981.

59. In a review of VOW in 1982 Mbeki commented to Florence Mophosho: "Quite frankly, if I were the Women's Secretariat, I would not approve the publication of VOW on the basis of these articles." His reasons included the failure to deal with the internal situation; the absence of central editorial control; the tendency to treat women as a homogeneous group; the failure to balance historical detail with strategic recommendations; and the poor quality of the writing. He commented, "I think that for VOW to become a mobiliser, it needs to devote more space to questions of strategy and tactics rather than to the denunciation of the evils of apartheid. This must mean that we should have a better idea of what the women are doing inside the country, how they are organising themselves, how they are fighting, what issues are agitating them etc." (ANC Women's Section, Dear Sis' Flo, March 4, 1982, ANC Archives).

60. ANC Women's Section, Report on the activities of the ANC Women's Secretariat since 1981.

61. The Revolutionary Council was a structure that brought together the leadership of the revolutionary alliance of the ANC, South African Communist Party, and South African Congress of Trade Unions. Sechaba and Ellis have argued that "the Revolutionary Council had been the means by which the Party had been able to take control of the armed struggle" The Political-Military Council, which replaced it—apparently as a result of criticisms from lower levels of MK—oversaw a decentralized structure "with disparate approaches and resources. Real power lay with the newly established Military Headquarters, consisting of Hani, Modise and Slovo, and the Political Headquarters, comprising Nkadimeng, Mac Maharaj and Josiah Jele" (*Comrades against Apartheid*, 128).

62. As Barrell ("Turn to the Masses," 78) has shown, the role of political mobilization inside the country was seriously undervalued by the Revolutionary Council; only one of eight to ten departments was concerned with political work. The rest dealt with different aspects of military work.

63. Nhlapo interview.

64. Ibid.

65. ANC Women's Section, Report on the activities of the ANC Women's Secretariat since 1981.

66. ANC Women's Section, Meeting of the NWEC with members of the NEC.

67. Ibid.

68. Lodge, *Black Politics in South Africa*, 339.

69. Lodge, "State of Exile."

70. Ibid., 239.

71. Barrell, "Turn to the Masses," 67.

72. Cock, *Colonels and Cadres.*

73. Mtintso interview.

74. Nhlapo interview.

75. Curnow, "Thandi Modise," 37.

76. ANC Women's Section, Women in MK Paper 3(b), National Preparatory Committee Papers, September 1987, South African Historical Archives.

77. Cock, *Colonels and Cadres;* Goldblatt and Meintjes, "South African Women Demand the Truth."

78. Cock, *Colonels and Cadres,* 167.

79. Sachs interview.

80. Mtintso interview.

81. Ibid.

82. "Women in MK," 6.

83. Curnow, "Thandi Modise," 38.

84. Cock, *Colonels and Cadres,* 164.

85. Ibid., 163.

86. Mtintso interview.

87. ANC Women's Section, Report of the proceedings of the second National Women's Conference, p. 39.

88. Lodge, "State of Exile," 235.

89. Love interview.

90. In *Comrades against Apartheid* Sechaba and Ellis recount a mutiny in Angola in 1984, in part over this issue.

91. ANC Women's Section, Report of the proceedings of the second National Women's Conference, p. 42.

92. Cock, *Colonels and Cadres,* 164.

93. Ibid.

94. Nhlapo interview.

95. Love interview.

96. ANC Women's Section, Report of the proceedings of the second National Women's Conference, p. 42.

97. Mtintso interview.

98. Nhlapo interview.

99. Curnow, "Thandi Modise," 37.

100. Sachs interview.

101. Mtintso interview.

102. Nhlapo interview.

103. Barrell, "Turn to the Masses," 89.

104. Mtintso interview.

105. Sachs interview.

106. Mtintso interview.

107. ANC Women's Section, A report of the Secretariat . . . since September 1981. Emphasis added.

108. Nhlapo interview.

109. For example, Mavis Nhlapo spoke passionately about the influence of a 1979 conference in West Germany on August Bebel's *Woman Under Socialism;* Mtintso spoke about the influence of contact with Vietnamese women (an MK delegation visited Vietnam in 1978), and almost all exiled women whom I interviewed spoke about the lessons learnt from the post-independence experiences of women activists in African countries.

110. See, for example, Report of the ANC (SA) Zambia Regional Women's Section.

111. Nhlapo interview.

112. Ibid.

113. Ibid.

114. ANC Women's Section, Seminar of the political participation of women: The Question of Attitudes, 1982, ANC Archives.

115. According to Muff Andersson, *umzane* also means "delicate thing, like a petal."

116. Mtintso interview.

117. Nhlapo interview.

118. ANC Women's Section East Africa Region, Regional Report.

119. ANC Women's Section, Dar es Salaam Zonal Conference: Women's Organisations at Home and Abroad, 1987, ANC Archives.

120. ANC Women's Section, An assessment of the internal situation, with particular reference to the women's struggles and organisations, 1983, ANC Archives.

121. "Year of the Women Programme of Action," 1984, ANC Archives.

122. ANC Women's Section, Report to the Internal Women's Sub-Committee, ANC Women's Section, September 1981–August 1987, ANC Archives. The Women's Section's statement to women inside the country presented the Year of the Women as an opportunity "to enable us to focus our attention upon our women everywhere, in the factories, fields, prisons and ghettoes and to mobilise the greatest number of women, both black and white, *into the struggle for people's power*" (ANC Women's Section, Statement of the ANC Women's Section on the occasion of the 28th Anniversary of International Solidarity with the Struggle of Women of South Africa and Namibia, 1984, ANC Archives; emphasis added).

123. ANC Women's Section, Report to the Internal Women's Sub-Committee, ANC Women's Section.

124. ANC Women's Section, Statement of the African National Congress Women's Section on the occasion of the 28th Anniversary.

125. ANC, Reports from the Island, received January 8, 1985, Ray Simons Papers.

126. ANC Women's Section, Meeting of the NWEC with members of the NEC.

127. Nhlapo interview.

128. ANC Women's Section, Recommendations of the NEC.

129. ANC Women's Section, Meeting of the NWEC with members of the NEC.

130. Ibid.

131. Ibid.

132. A pseudonym meaning "woman of the struggle."

133. Mosadi wa Sechaba, "Women Arise and Fight," 58.

134. Ibid., 56–65.

135. Ibid., 65.

136. ANC, "Role and Place of Women."

137. Ibid.

138. Ibid.

139. Ibid.

140. ANC, Organisational report of the NEC by the Secretary-General, Comrade Alfred Nzo, to the First Legal National Conference of the ANC after 30 years of proscription, Durban, July 2–6, 1991.

141. ANC, "Role and Place of Women."

142. ANC, Joint Statement of President O. R. Tambo and President Sam Nujoma, 1985, Kabwe, ANC Archives.

143. ANC Women's Section, Report to the Internal Women's Sub-Committee.

144. Ginwala interview.

145. ANC Women's Section, Meeting of the Secretariat, July 20, 1984, ANC Archives.

146. According to the Women's Section, "For some weeks before the Conference, several sources of the media revealed that an official South African delegation, led by Mrs Tina Botha, would attend the Conference. We lobbied among all progressive governments and friends to prevent their participation" (ANC Women's Section, Report of Nairobi Conference, Paper prepared for second ANC Women's Conference [Paper 28], 1987, South African Historical Archives).

147. Ginwala interview.

148. "Equality, Development and Peace," *Voice of Women* (1985, 2nd and 3rd quarters).

149. Urdang, *And Still They Dance.*

150. Hassim, "Gender, Social Location and Feminist Politics."

151. ANC, "Women's Role in the NDR," internal discussion paper, 1987, ANC Archives.

152. ANC Women's Section, "Women's Organisation in South Africa," National Preparatory Committee Papers (Paper No. 2), Second ANC Women's Conference, September 1987, South African Historical Archives.

153. ANC Women's Section, UDF message No. 27, Second ANC Women's Conference, September 1987, South African Historical Archives.

154. See also ANC Women's Section, "An Understanding of South African Women in Society and Their Role in the Liberation Struggle," ANC Second National Women's Conference, September 1987, South African Historical Archives.

155. Ibid.

156. ANC Women's Section, Report of the proceedings of the Second National Women's Conference, September 1987, p. 41.

157. Russell, "The Most Powerful Woman in the African National Congress: Ruth Mompati," in *Lives of Courage,* 115.

158. ANC Women's Section, "An Understanding of South African Women."

159. Ibid.

160. Frene Ginwala, "Why Does the ANC Need a Policy on Women?" undated, unpublished paper in the personal files of Jacklyn Cock.

161. Russell, "The Most Powerful Woman," 116.

162. ANC Women's Section, "An Understanding of South African Women."

163. ANC Women's Section, Women in MK, Paper No. 3(a).

164. Ibid.

165. Albertyn, "Women and the Transition to Democracy," 46.

166. Driver, "The ANC Constitutional Guidelines," 89.

167. ANC, "Constitutional Guidelines for a Democratic South Africa," 1988, article W.

168. Albertyn, "Women and the Transition to Democracy," 46.

169. Ibid., 47.

170. Driver, "The ANC Constitutional Guidelines," 89.

171. ANC, "Constitutional Guidelines."

172. Gwagwa, "The Family in South African Politics," 128.

173. Ibid., 127.

174. Ginwala, "Women and the Elephant," 69.

175. Driver, "The ANC Constitutional Guidelines," 89.

176. ANC, statement of the NEC of the ANC on the emancipation of women in South Africa, May 2, 1990, Lusaka, ANC Archives.

177. Cock, "Putting Women on the Agenda," 32.

178. Frene Ginwala, "Formulating National Policy Regarding the Emancipation of Women and the Promotion of Women's Development in Our Country," unpublished keynote address, Malibongwe Conference, Amsterdam, 1990.

179. Western Cape Region, "What Do We Mean by the Emancipation of South African Women?" Paper presented at Malibongwe Conference, Amsterdam, 1990.

180. Charman, de Swardt, and Simons, "The Politics of Gender."

181. The phrase "side-by-side" comes from the final words of the Freedom Charter, "These freedoms we will fight for, side-by side, throughout our lives, until we have won our liberty." In the 1950s "side-by-side" was a phrase used by women in the ANC to connote a role for women that was active rather than supportive. Thus Ida Mtwana, president of the ANC Women's League in 1954, declared: "Gone are the days when the place of women was in the kitchen and looking after the children. Today, they are marching side by side with men in the road to freedom" (ANC Women's League, *ANC Women's League*, 4). Among women activists in the 1980s, the notion of "alongside" men was seen to reflect a nationalist approach to liberation that did not recognize the somewhat autonomous struggle of women for emancipation from patriarchy (Mtintso interview).

182. Driver, "The ANC Constitutional Guidelines"; Bazilli, *Putting Women on the Agenda*.

183. T. T. Nkobi, "We Can Respond to the Challenges of the New Decade," opening address to the workshop of the ANC Women's Section on the rebuilding of the ANC Women's League, 1990, Ray Simons Papers.

Chapter 4. The Return of the ANC Women's League

1. Udit interview.
2. Ramgobin, "The ANC Women's League Returns," 21.
3. Ibid., 22.
4. ANC, Report of the Consultation on Rebuilding a Legal African National Congress Women's Organisation in South Africa, 1990, p. 10, ANC Archives.
5. Ibid.
6. See the report of the press conference by Annecke, "The Launch of the Women's League."
7. ANC, Report of the First General Members meeting of the ANC Women, June 23, 1990, Ray Simons Papers.
8. Mtintso interview.
9. Ntombela-Nzimande interview.
10. Routledge-Madlala interview.
11. Ntombela-Nzimande interview.
12. Udit interview.
13. Interview of senior member of women's organization who wishes to remain anonymous, May 2000.
14. Schreiner interview, May 20, 2000.
15. Routledge-Madlala interview.
16. Mager, and Schreiner (May 20, 2000) interviews.
17. Letter to Comrade Popo Molefe, August 17, 1990, United Women's Congress Papers.
18. Routledge-Madlala and Ntombela-Nzimande interviews.
19. Ntombela-Nzimande interview.
20. Anonymous activist interview.
21. Schreiner interview, May 20, 2000.
22. Routledge-Madlala interview.
23. Meer, *Women Speak,* 120.
24. Routledge-Madlala interview.
25. Exiled activists were represented by Gertrude Shope, Baleka Mbete-Kgositsile, Mavivi Myakayaka-Manzini, Nosiviwe Mapisa-Nqakula, and Nkosazana Dlamini-Zuma. Internal activists were represented by Albertina Sisulu, Sister Bernard Ncube, Dorothy Nyembe, Thandi Modise, and Happy Those. Winnie Madikizela-Mandela was a co-opted member (she was not elected but was invited onto the committee).
26. *ANC Women's League Newsletter,* no. 2 (1991), ANC Archives.
27. Ibid.
28. Conservative elements within the ANC were right to be concerned about the implications of offering the league a formal platform. At the Consultative Conference the league pushed the more radical demand that a certain number of seats on the NEC be reserved for women.
29. *ANC Women's League Newsletter.*
30. "Political and Structural Relationship between the ANCWL and the ANC," paper prepared by the National Women's League Task Force, 1990, p. 4, Ray Simons Papers.

31. Sechaba, "Towards the Emancipation of Women."

32. Ibid.

33. Ginwala, "Picking up the Gauntlet," 2.

34. Report of the consultation on rebuilding a legal African National Congress women's organisation in South Africa, 1990, p. 12, ANC Archives.

35. Daniels, "ANC Women's League," 35.

36. The full executive was comprised of Gertrude Shope (exile, president), Albertina Sisulu (internal, vice president), Baleka Kgositsile (exile, secretary general), Mako Njobe (exile, treasurer), Nosiviwe Maphisa (exile, national organizer), Mavivi Manzini (exile), Hilda Ndude (internal), Thandi Modise (exile), Ruth Mompati (exile), Ivy Gcina (internal), and Winnie Mandela (internal).

37. "The Women's League," 5.

38. Rantao, "Much for Women to Do."

39. Bulbring, "The Battle against Winnie Is Over."

40. Rantao, "Much for Women to Do."

41. Bulbring, "The Battle against Winnie Is Over."

42. "The Women's League," 5.

43. "Restructuring the National Office," 5.

44. She was subsequently found guilty of kidnapping but acquitted on the assault charge.

45. Van der Merwe, "Winnie's Future Hangs on Vote."

46. Ibid. The anxieties about challenging Winnie were well founded. Her appointment to head the ANC's Department of Welfare was opposed by both welfare NGOs and the ANC's executive board. However, Nelson Mandela intervened and blocked her opponents. For a detailed discussion of Winnie Mandela see Meintjes, "Winnie Madikizela Mandela."

47. Van der Merwe, "Winnie's Future."

48. In 1992 Winnie Mandela was accused of misappropriating funds from the ANC's Department of Welfare. In April 1992 Nelson Mandela announced the end of his marriage to Winnie Mandela. Subsequently, Winnie Mandela resigned all her positions in the ANC. Her comeback within the organization occurred with her election as of president of the ANC Women's League in 1993.

49. Seekings, *The UDF.*

50. Ntombela-Nzimande interview.

51. ANC National Women's Secretariat, Circular to ANC Regional Women's Committees on discussions held with the ILC–Women's League, Johannesburg, August 29, 1990, ANC Archives.

52. Geisler, *Women and the Remaking of Politics in Southern Africa,* 82.

53. *Weekly Mail and Guardian,* September 13–19, 1996.

54. ANC Women's League, National Conference report, April 23–27, 1997, ANC Archives.

55. Statement of the President of the ANC, Comrade Oliver R. Tambo, to the National Conference of the ANC Women's League, Kimberley, April 1991, South African Historical Archives.

56. ANC Women's League, Draft document for discussion in regions—Programme of Action, 1990, Ray Simons Papers.

57. Horn, "ANC 48th National Conference," 15. See also Serote, "National Liberation Equals Women's Liberation," 5; Turok, "The Women's Quota Debate," 9.

58. Horn, "ANC's 48th National Conference," 16.

59. Ibid., 17. Horn goes on to point out that the very next proposal was for MK commanders to have automatic seats on the NEC. "This time nobody objected on the basis of merit or democracy." The proposal was accepted.

60. "We've Got the Future Looking at Us."

61. Ginwala, "Women and the Elephant," 69.

62. Ibid.

63. "We've Got the Future Looking at Us."

64. Ibid.

65. The decision to have such a body was first made by the Second National Conference of the ANC Women's Section in Luanda in 1987. At the conference of the ANC Women's League in April 1991, the decision was endorsed.

66. The first commissioners were Uriel Abrahamse, Kader Asmal (ANC exile activist), Jacklyn Cock (professor of sociology and Black Sash activist), Baleka Kgositsile (ANC Women's Section and ANC Women's League), Thenjiwe Mtintso (Umkhonto we Sizwe and SACP), Bongiwe Njobe (ANC Women's League), Thutukile Radebe, Wally Serote (ANC writer), Bangumzi Sifingo, and Arnold (Mankenkhosi) Stofile (UDF).

67. ANC, *Bulletin of the National Commission for the Emancipation of Women*, April 1992.

68. ANC Commission on the Emancipation of Women, Report to the 49th National ANC Conference, December 1994.

Chapter 5. From Mothers of the Nation to Rights-Bearing Citizens

1. Jacquette and Wolchik, *Women and Democracy*, 7.

2. Seidman, "'No Freedom without The Women'"; Meintjes, "The Women's Struggle for Equality"; Cock, "Women in South Africa's Transition to Democracy."

3. Waylen, "Women and Democratization."

4. Schmitter, "Contemporary Democratization," 222.

5. Ibid., 223.

6. Ebrahim, *The Soul of a Nation*; S. Friedman, *The Long Journey*.

7. Marais, *South Africa, Limits to Change*; Webster and Adler, "Towards a Class Compromise"; Saul, "Liberation without Democracy?"

8. Waylen, "Women and Democratization," 332.

9. Alvarez, *Engendering Democracy in Brazil*; Jacquette, *The Women's Movement in Latin America*; Waylen, "Gender and Democratic Politics."

10. Matynia, "Finding a Voice"; Aulette, "New Roads to Resistance."

11. Saul, "South Africa between Barbarism and Structural Reform."

12. Amsterdam Women's Conference Proposal, Lusaka, November 10, 1988, ANC Archives.

13. Malibongwe Programme of Action, January 18, 1990, ANC Archives.

14. It is clear from various interviews that the legitimation of the idea of a

national structure by the ANC Women's League was crucial to the successful pursuit of this strategy.

15. Ginwala, "Picking up the Gauntlet."

16. Holland-Muter, "Women Breaking the Silence!" On December 1, 1990, the Federation of South African Women (Cape Town), decided to disband. "In its place, women agreed on the process of working towards the building of an alliance of women's organisations. A working group was established with the task of drawing in other organisations who believed in a united, non-racial, non-sexist South Africa" (14).

17. Fester, "Women's Organisations in the Western Cape," 57.

18. Ntone and Meth, "New Forms of Racism," 71.

19. Fester, "Women's Organisations in the Western Cape," 55.

20. Mtintso interview.

21. For a detailed organizational history of the WNC, see Abrams, "Fighting for Women's Liberation."

22. Meintjes, "The Women's Struggle for Equality," 48.

23. Minutes of the second council meeting of the WNC, p. 2, Karos Johannesburger Hotel, Johannesburg, July 11, 1993, Women's National Coalition Archives.

24. Omar interview.

25. Meintjes, "The Women's Struggle for Equality," 58.

26. Fester, "Women's Organisations in the Western Cape," 55.

27. Abrams, "Fighting for Women's Liberation."

28. I based this account on notes that I took during discussions within the Durban Central Branch of the ANC Women's League, of which I was a member. See also Hassim, "The Gender Agenda."

29. Jacquette and Wolchik, *Women and Democracy*, 5. See also Albertyn, "National Machinery for Ensuring Gender Equality"; Schneider, "The Dialectic of Rights and Politics."

30. Waylen, "Women and Democratization."

31. Meintjes, "Gender, Nationalism and Transformation," 80.

32. Young, *Inclusion and Democracy*, 6.

33. Williams, *Voice, Trust, and Memory*, 4.

34. Young, *Inclusion and Democracy*, 12.

35. Ibid.

36. Meintjes, "Women's Struggle for Equality," 53.

37. Walker, "The White Women's Suffrage Movement."

38. Meintjes, "Women's Struggle for Equality."

39. Bonnin, "Women's Studies in South Africa," 384.

40. This is not to suggest that concerns about *racism* in the women's movement are illegitimate or unfounded but rather that the evidence for it must come from a more detailed exploration of hidden dynamics of communication and modes of interaction within organizations. For an excellent study in this vein see Seidman, "Institutional Dilemmas."

41. United Democratic Front, Resolutions of the UDF Women's Congress, 1987, UDF Archives.

42. ANC, Statement of the National Executive Committee, May 2, 1990, ANC Archives.

43. Sachs, "Judges and Gender," 11.

44. Hudson, "The Freedom Charter."

45. Zuma interview.

46. Meintjes interview, March 10, 2000.

47. Democratic Party, "Discussion Document on Women's Status Prepared by Ms Dene Smuts MP and Mrs Carole Charlewood MP," October 1991, WNC Archives.

48. Govender, "Breaking the Silence," 42.

49. Frene Ginwala, "Non-racial Democracy—Soon; Non-sexism—How?" Speech to WNC National Workshop, April 25–26, 1992, Johannesburg, WNC Archives.

50. Udit interview; Meintjes, "Women's Struggle for Equality," 57.

51. Meintjes interview, March 10, 2000.

52. Meintjes, "Women's Struggle for Equality," 51.

53. Meintjes interview, March 10, 2000.

54. Quoted in Abrams, "Fighting for Women's Liberation," 35.

55. WNC, Minutes of the second council meeting, p. 2.

56. Govender interview.

57. Abrams, "Fighting for Women's Liberation," 11.

58. Ibid., 32.

59. Govender interview.

60. Caucus on Law and Gender, "What Could a Women's Charter Be," 1.

61. C. Albertyn et al., "The Status of the Charter: Option Five," unpublished WNC discussion paper, July 1993, Albertyn personal files. See also Frene Ginwala, "The Charter for Women's Equality: Discussion Document," unpublished WNC paper, January 1994, WNC Archives.

62. Ginwala, "The Charter for Women's Equality," 4.

63. WNC, Women's National Coalition National Conference, full report, 1994, p. 7, personal files of Sheila Meintjes.

64. Albertyn, "Women and the Transition to Democracy," 53.

65. Baker, "Charting Our Future," 98.

66. Quoted in Abrams, "Fighting for Women's Liberation," 50.

67. The discussion papers presented included "Profile of the WNC" and "Statistical Profile of South African Women" by Debbie Budlender; "Talking with Rural Women" by Beauty Mkhize and Janet Small; "Gaining Access to Women for the WNC Research Project" by Shireen Motala; "How to Get Women to Speak" by Pethu Serote; "Facts Do Not Speak for Themselves" by Laurine Platzky; "How Do the WNC 'Charter' Campaign and the Constitution Intersect?" by Sheila Meintjes; and "Organisational Formations amongst African Women" by Fikile Mazibuko, Papers from the WNC Research Methodology Workshop, Milpark Holiday Inn, Johannesburg, January 23–24, 1993, Meintjes personal files.

68. WNC, Transcript of research methodology workshop, Johannesburg, 1993, WNC Archives.

69. Meintjes interview, March 10, 2000.

70. WNC, Progress report for funders of the WNC, July 1993, WNC Archives.

71. WNC, Commentary of demands submitted, undated, Meintjes personal files.

72. Meintjes interview, March 10, 2000.

73. WNC, Women's charter for effective equality: Working document adopted in principle at the national convention convened by the Women's National Coalition, Johannesburg, February 25–27, 1994, WNC Archives.

74. The only exception in the literature is Albertyn, "Women and the Transition to Democracy." However she too gives only a sketchy outline of the differences.

75. Dames Aktueel Letter of Support for Charter, dated March 4, 1994, and signed by Ester Wessels in her capacity as president, Meintjes personal files.

76. WNC, Explanation of the changes made to the draft Charter of February 28, 1994, Meintjes personal files.

77. Democratic Party, "Discussion document on women's status," p. 4.

78. Ibid., 5.

79. WNC, *Women's Charter for Effective Equality.*

80. Democratic Party, "Discussion document on women's status."

81. WNC, Women's Charter for effective equality: Working document, p. 3.

82. WNC, Democratic Party comment on draft Women's Charter, 1994, p. 5, Meintjes personal files.

83. Ibid., 8.

84. WNC, Comments on draft Charter, fax from Frene Ginwala on behalf of ANC Research Department, April 19, 1994, Meintjes personal files.

85. See Cock, "Promoting Gender Equality."

86. WNC, Women's Charter for Effective Equality, final version, 1994, p. 3, WNC Archives.

87. Ibid., 4.

88. Albertyn, "Women and the Transition to Democracy," 52.

89. Murray and O'Regan, "Putting Women into the Constitution." O'Regan was subsequently appointed a judge of the Constitutional Court.

90. S. Friedman, "The Missing 53 Percent," in *The Long Journey,* 129.

91. Albertyn, "Women and the Transition to Democracy," 55.

92. S. Friedman, "The Missing 53 Percent," 134.

93. Ibid., 130.

94. Speech by Comrade Jacob Zuma, Deputy Secretary-General, Opening the National Workshop of the Commission for [*sic*] the Emancipation of Women, March 12, 1993, ANC Archives.

95. These committees dealt with constitutional issues, violence, fundamental rights during the transition, the independent media commission and independent broadcasting authority, the independent electoral commission, repeal of discriminatory legislation, and transitional executive authority.

96. ANC Women's League, untitled pamphlet, March.1993, Meintjes personal files.

97. Abrams, "Fighting for Women's Liberation," 63.

98. Albertyn, "Women and the Transition to Democracy," 54–55.

99. Ibid., 55.

100. Ibid., 56.

101. WNC, Report on the Monitoring Project of the WNC, August 9, 1993, WNC Archives.

102. WNC, Progress report for funders, p. 8.

103. See Centre for Applied Legal Studies, Second supplementary report on the Constitutional Principles from the Technical Committee on Constitutional Issues to the Negotiating Council, June 23, 1993, WNC Archives.

104. ANC, Speech by Comrade Jacob Zuma.

105. WNC, Women's Charter for effective equality: Working document.

106. Goldblatt and Mbatha, "Gender, Culture and Equality."

107. WNC, WNC progress report, March 1994, p. 2, WNC Archives.

108. Ibid.

109. The Reconstruction and Development Programme explicitly called for the principle of equality to override customary law (ANC, *Reconstruction and Development Programme*, paragraph 5.3.20).

110. Goldblatt and Mbatha, "Gender, Culture and Equality," 104.

111. Ibid., 102.

112. Albertyn, *Engendering the State.*

113. The wording of Section 9 of the Constitution allows a claim based on complex and multiple forms of discrimination; for example, black women would be able to approach the judiciary to seek relief from discrimination on the basis of both race and gender.

114. Constitution of the Republic of South Africa, sec. 12(1)(c).

115. Ibid., sec. 12(2)(a) and (b).

116. Ibid., sec. 15(3) and 31.

117. Liebenberg, "Social Citizenship"; Hassim, "From Presence to Power."

118. Liebenberg, "Social Citizenship," 61.

119. Ibid., 60.

120. For example, in *Soobramoney vs. Minister of Health, KwaZulu-Natal* the Constitutional Court ruled against Soobramoney's claim for dialysis treatment on the ground that scarce resources forced the Department of Health to offer selective access to treatment and equipment (1998 [1] SA 765 [CC]).

121. Albertyn and Goldblatt, "Facing the Challenge of Transformation."

122. Jacquette and Wolchik, *Women and Democracy*, 8.

123. Webster and Adler, "Towards a Class Compromise."

124. Kaganas and Murray, "Law and Women's Rights in South Africa,": 15.

125. McClintock, "Family Feuds"; Walker, *Women and Gender in Southern Africa;* Hassim, "Family, Motherhood and Zulu Nationalism"; Horn, "Post-apartheid South Africa"; Charman, de Swardt, and Simons, "The Politics of Gender."

126. Although nationalism was not completely abandoned, it appears to have taken a benign form. The new constitution is promoted through the slogan "One Law for One Nation," for example.

127. Goldblatt and Mbatha, "Gender, Culture and Equality," 102. Thus interpretation of the clause remains a contested issue. Traditional leaders have organized against a local government framework that reduces the extent of their powers in

traditional areas. The Constitution accords the Council of Traditional Leaders strong advisory powers relating to reform of customary laws.

128. The male leadership of these parties nevertheless held to more minimal definitions of democracy. The tension between these two conceptions remains within all political parties in South Africa.

129. Thornton and Ramphele, "The Search for Community."

130. Yuval-Davis, *Gender and Nation.*

131. A range of conferences were held in the early 1990s, including the Malibongwe Conference in Amsterdam, where policy alternatives were developed; the "Putting Women on the Agenda" Conference in Johannesburg, where issues of equality and the Constitution were debated; and the Institute for Democracy in South Africa Conference in Durban in 1991, which debated the nature and type of national machinery. At all these conferences, participants debated the experiences of other African and of socialist countries. Presentations by Ugandan, Zimbabwean, and Bangladeshi guests were influential in pushing for the national machinery to extend beyond state structures and strengthen the capacity of civil society to hold the national machinery accountable.

132. Anne Marie Nutt, member of the WNC's national executive board, for example, felt that "the WNC organised in a top-down way, taking on too much of the character of the political parties which dominated it" ("Should the Sisters Do It for Themselves," 10).

133. Fester, "Women's Organisations in the Western Cape," 55.

134. This description is Nozizwe Routledge-Madlala's, given in an address to the Conference on Transformation for Gender Justice and Organisational Change, African Gender Institute, 1998. It is a play on the triple alliance of the ANC, South African Communist Party, and Congress of South African Trade Unions.

135. Albertyn, "Women and the Transition to Democracy," 52.

136. Ibid., 39.

137. "Should the Sisters Do It for Themselves," 11.

138. Dames Aktueel, arguing for a continuation of the coalition, commented that "as an umbrella body, it represents almost all women's organisations in South Africa and should continue speaking on their behalf" (Letter from Dames Aktueel, June 3, 1994, WNC Archives).

139. Minutes of WNC steering committee meeting, May 7, 1994, p. 7, WNC Archives.

140. Ibid., 8.

141. WNC, Report from Women's Charter Alliance, 1994, Meintjes personal files.

142. WNC, "WNC Transkei Region: Resolution on the Future of the ANC," 1994, Meintjes personal files.

143. Letter from Dene Smuts, MP, June 3, 1994, WNC Archives.

144. SACP Gender Department submission on the future of the WNC, June 5, 1994, WNC Archives.

145. WNC national conference: Full report, p. 9.

146. Routledge-Madlala interview.

147. Ibid.

148. Daima, "The Forward March of the Women's National Coalition," 6.
149. Albertyn, *Engendering the State.*
150. WNC national conference: Full report, p. 10.
151. Meer, "The Demobilisation of Civil Society," 111.
152. Neocosmos. "From People's Politics to State Politics," 16.
153. Frene Ginwala, Closing speech, Women's National Coalition Conference, Johannesburg, February 25–27, 1994, WNC Archives.
154. Ibid.
155. Horn, "Whither the WNC?"
156. Klugman, "Mainstreaming Gender Equality in Health Policy," 48.

Chapter 6. Political Parties, Quotas, and Representation in the New Democracy

1. Jacquette and Wolchik, *Women and Democracy.*
2. Ibid., 6.
3. See Alvarez, *Engendering Democracy in Brazil,* and Jacquette and Wolchik, *Women and Democracy.*
4. The ANC Women's League took an especially strong stance over women's representation in constitutional negotiations, threatening to boycott the first nonracial elections with the slogan "No Women, No Vote." Although it is unlikely that the league would have been able to pull off a women's boycott of the elections, the threat exposed the limitations of claims to democracy by progressive political organizations.
5. See Zondo, "Women and the Vote."
6. Ballington, "Women's Parliamentary Representation," 82.
7. Hirst, *Representative Democracy and Its Limits,* 2.
8. Okin, *Is Multiculturalism Bad for Women?;* Tripp, "Women and the Politics of Diversity in Uganda."
9. Phillips, *Engendering Democracy.*
10. Mahon and Jenson, "Representing Solidarity," 78.
11. Ibid.
12. Albertyn, *Engendering the Political Agenda.*
13. For example, the ANC has accepted the proposal for a quota for women on its electoral lists but rejects the idea of a quota for internal party office.
14. Williams, *Voice, Trust, and Memory,* 4.
15. These institutions and mechanisms are described in chapter 7.
16. *Redefining Politics,* 102.
17. Comments at EISA (Electoral Institute of South Africa) Roundtable, Putting Women into Power, Johannesburg, February 23, 1999, author's notes.
18. Comments at Commission on Gender Equality's Gender Dialogue, June 29, 1998, author's notes.
19. Comments at conference sponsored by GAP and WDF (Gender Advocacy Project and Women's Development Foundation), Women at the Crossroads: Women and Governance, Cape Town, October 21–23, 1998, author's notes.
20. GAP, "Gender Politics at Local Level," 16.

21. Comment made by Kedibone Molema, AZAPO representative at EISA Roundtable, author's notes.

22. According to the president of Imbeleko, Rose Ngwenya, "We provide training in brick-laying, carpentry and upholstery. We run a health project. Another project is the *Adopt to educate* project. Bursaries are given to high school and college students" ("AZAPO and Women").

23. Other recommendations included devising new organizational strategies to increase women's participation in the union movement, a program of education and training for women, a parental rights and child care campaign, and a leadership role in building a national women's movement. All these proposals were accepted (COSATU, "September Commission Report," 160–65).

24. Ibid., 159.

25. Orr, Daphne, and Horton, "COSATU Congress: Did Women Reject the Quota?" 26.

26. Ibid., 28.

27. Ibid., 29.

28. September interview.

29. Ibid.

30. Hirst, *Representative Democracy and Its Limits*, 3–4.

31. Schefer, "Women Talk Votes and Power," *Democracy in Action*, 8.

32. See Meintjes, "The Women's Struggle for Equality"; Cock, "Women in South Africa's Transition to Democracy"; Fester, "Women's Organisations in the Western Cape"; Hassim and Gouws, "Redefining the Public Space."

33. Phillips, *Engendering Democracy*.

34. Mansbridge, "An Anti-essentialist Argument."

35. A notable exception is the African Christian Democratic Party, whose representative argued against gender equality at the Nisaa Forum on Women and the Elections in May 1999.

36. The Electoral Act requires that all registered political parties and candidates subscribe to the Electoral Code of Conduct, which is designed to promote conditions that are conducive to free and fair elections. These include the tolerance of democratic political activity, free political campaigning, and open public debate. Item 6 of the code specifically requires political parties to put into place mechanisms that will enable women to access their rights.

37. Matland and Taylor, "Electoral Systems Effect on Women's Representation"; Reynolds, "Women in African Legislatures and Executives."

38. "ANC List Process Document," 1993, ANC Archives, 4.

39. Ballington, "Women's Parliamentary Representation"; Hassim, "Gendering Parliament."

40. Lovenduski, *Women and European Politics*, 241.

41. Randall, *Women and Politics*, 109.

42. Lovenduski, *Women and European Politics*; Randall, *Women and Politics*.

43. Mtintso, *The Contribution of Women Parliamentarians*, 64.

44. Ibid.

45. Moon and Fountain, "Keeping the Gates?" 458.

46. Karam and Lovenduski, "Women in Parliament," 146.

47. Waylen, "Women and Democratization," 340.
48. Chazan, "Gender Perspectives on African States," 186.
49. Goetz and Hassim, "In and against the Party."
50. Lovenduski and Norris, *Gender and Party Politics.*
51. Tripp, *Women and Politics in Uganda.*
52. Abdullah, "Transition Politics"; E. Tsikata, "Women's Political Organizations."
53. Goetz and Hassim, "In and against the Party," 3.
54. Tamale, *When Hens Begin to Crow.*
55. Waylen, "Women and Democratization," 339 –40.
56. Chigudu and Tichagwa, "Participation of Women in Party Politics," 2.
57. Seedat and Kimani, "Gender Profile of Parties," 40.
58. *Redefining Politics,* 177.
59. Ibid.
60. Lovenduski and Norris, *Gender and Party Politics.*
61. Dahlerup, *The New Women's Movement,* 17.
62. Sainsbury, *Gender Equality and Welfare States.*
63. Dahlerup, *The New Women's Movement,* 18.
64. "Mobilise for Women," 101.
65. "Key Questions for Election Candidates," 7. The questions related to the valuing of women's unpaid labor; provision of child care facilities and welfare support; greater representation of women in party structures; policies on maternity leave and violence against women; educational and literacy policies; support for women's human rights; women's access to land, housing, and pension; pay equity, and differential taxation.
66. Ballington, "Political Parties and Gender Equality."
67. In a notable example the Commission on Gender Equality expressed its discontent with the quality of party presentations at its Gender Dialogue on the Election in June 1998. Echoing this, Lindiwe Zulu, deputy speaker of the Gauteng legislature, commented that "there was nothing earth shattering about the presentations—this is not acceptable. It is an insult and disservice to women." The report was sent to all political parties ("Women, Politics and Elections").
68. Mihloti Mathye, research director, Commission on Gender Equality, personal communication, May 5, 2000.
69. Comments at AWEPA/GAP conference, Women at the Crossroads, author's notes.
70. The culmination of this effort was the lead story on the front page of the *Star,* the Johannesburg daily, headlined "One Woman, One Vote Is the Key to Power: Majority of Voters Are Female—and They Mean Business" (May 5, 1999).
71. However, a similar exercise during the 2004 election campaign produced a depressing debate for which the political parties had not prepared. See www .womensnet.org/elections2004/index.shtml, accessed August 24, 2005.
72. Comment at the AWEPA/GAP conference, Women at the Crossroads, author's notes.
73. Parliamentary Women's Group, "Rationalising Gender Structures in National Parliament," workshop report, March 26, 1997. Women's Empowerment Unit, Parliament of South Africa, Cape Town.

74. Routledge-Madlala interview.

75. Comments at EISA roundtable, Putting Women into Power, author's notes.

76. These included the Commission on Gender Equality's Gender Dialogue in June 1998, the AWEPA/GAP conference, Women at the Crossroads, in October 1998, and the EISA roundtable, Putting Women into Power, in February 1999.

77. For example, the question of whether women MPs who were members of COSATU represented the union or working-class women was not clarified by candidates interviewed by Dove in "Questions of Accountability," 53.

78. Comments by Barbara Watson, director of the Women's Development Foundation, at Women at the Crossroads, author's notes.

79. Comments at Putting Women into Power, author's notes.

80. Comments by Baleka Mbete-Kgositsile, deputy speaker in the National Assembly, at Women at the Crossroads, author's notes. See also Govender, foreword to Budlender, *The Third Women's Budget.*

81. "Women in Power," 16.

82. European Union Parliamentary Support Programme, "Report of the Provincial Legislatures Needs Assessment Studies"; MBM Change Agents and Ruby Marks Associates, *Needs Assessment of Women MPs and MPLs;* Serote et al., "What the South African Parliament Has Done to Date"; Women's Empowerment Unit, Annual Progress Report"; CASE, *Synthesis Report.*

83. Gouws, "The Gender Dimension."

84. The Women's Party, led by the feminist artist Nina Romm, was unable to secure a single seat in Parliament, despite the relatively low cut-off threshold.

85. Gouws, "The Gender Dimension."

86. Comments made by women representatives of political parties at the Commission on Gender Equality's Gender Dialogue.

87. Taitz, "Dragon or Dragon Slayer?" After she proposed stringent antismoking legislation, Health Minister Nkosazana Zuma was the subject of a *Hustler* magazine article that portrayed her as "the underpaid domestic worker who sadly escaped degradation and became a medical doctor." Readers were advised to cut out the picture of Zuma that accompanied the article and place it on their toilet seat.

88. Camerer interview.

89. Comments at panel discussion on the state of the women's movement, Wits University, May 22, 2001, author's notes. See also Hassim, "From Presence to Power."

90. In a recent example MP Andrew Feinstein, ANC representative on the parliamentary committee on public accounts, was removed from his position as head of the ANC's study group after pushing for an investigation into the government's three billion rand arms deal against the wishes of the president. Justifying this "redeployment," the ANC's parliamentary whip said the study group was being "strengthened so that the ANC, from the President downwards, could exercise political control" (*Sunday Times,* February 4, 2001). The *Sunday Times* reporter noted that "nothing would go from the committee to the plenary of the National Assembly without first going through the caucus and any leaks would be investigated."

91. Several interviewees laughingly referred to the post of deputy secretary general as the burial ground for militant feminist activists, citing as evidence the subsequent redeployment to this post of Thenjiwe Mtintso from the Commission on

Gender Equality, where she had been establishing an independent and forceful organization.

92. Quoted in Stadler, "The Rise and Decline of Party Activism," 7.

93. In July 2001 Carolus announced that she was taking the top position at Tourism South Africa, a nonpolitical job.

94. Stadler, "The Rise and Decline of Party Activism," 7.

95. Informal comment made in October 1998, author's notes.

96. Routledge-Madlala interview.

97. Marais, *South Africa, Limits to Change.*

98. Kemp et al., "The Dawn of a New Day."

99. Many male MPs, even within the ANC, saw women's presence as a token gesture to equality. One male MP commented to Thenjiwe Mtintso: "[Men] don't think that this woman comrade is there because in her own name and right she deserves to be there. What also happens is that because of the quotas even in delegations abroad some women comrades go ten times more even before some male comrades have ever had a single chance to go. Some of these women comrades are almost like flowers that must decorate every delegation" (Mtintso, "The Contribution of Women Parliamentarians," 52).

100. Britton, "Preliminary Report of Participation." "Linda," a woman MP interviewed by Mtintso, commented in 1995 that "this place gives me the creeps. It is unfriendly and unwelcoming. It was meant to make the people feel the power, even in the building itself. I feel overwhelmed and completely disempowered. I cannot see myself making any input never mind impact here. I feel lost. I do not think I will even finish my term of office" (Mtintso, "The Contribution of Women Parliamentarians," 56)

101. Mtintso, "The Contribution of Women Parliamentarians," 53.

102. Ibid., 56.

103. Ibid., 57.

104. CASE, *Synthesis Report on the Participation of Women.*

105. Fraser, *Justice Interruptus,* 79.

106. Feminists who spoke up in the National Assembly were laughingly called "that lot who went to Beijing" (Vos, "Women in Parliament," 108).

107. Ibid., 108–9.

108. Govender was the project manager of the Women's National Coalition and a leading union and women's organizer.

109. Albertyn, *Engendering the Political Agenda,* 149.

110. Gouws *(Un)thinking Citizenship;* Hassim, "The Gender Pact and Democratic Consolidation"; Albertyn, *Engendering the Political Agenda.*

111. *Mail and Guardian,* October 13, 1995.

112. "Tensions Rise over Land Rights Bill," *Sunday Times,* January 22, 2003.

113. Ibid.

114. "Leaders in Land Reform," *Mail and Guardian,* July 31, 2003.

115. Traditional Leadership and Governance Framework Bill (3)(2)(b).

116. "IFP Anger at Traditional Role," *Mail and Guardian,* November 15, 2003.

117. The Landless People's Movement warned that it would encourage voters to boycott the 1994 elections if land redistribution processes were not speeded up.

118. Geoff Budlender, Expert Opinion on Communal Land Rights Bill for Commission on Gender Equality, 2003, Commission on Gender Equality document.

119. Programme for Land and Agrarian Studies, Submission to Portfolio Committee on Land Affairs, 2003, Cape Town.

120. Ibid., 3.

121. Ibid., 4.

122. Claassens and Ngubane, "Rural Women, Land Rights and the Communal Land Rights Bill," 3.

123. Comments at AWEPA/GAP conference, Women at the Crossroads, author's notes.

124. Although I would agree with Anne Phillips that these strategies may be based on vastly different and contradictory assumptions about the nature of the political system, and the roles and capacities of women to impact on the underlying values and institutions of democracies may be limited. Phillips, *The Politics of Presence.*

Chapter 7. One Woman, One Desk, One Typist

1. Phillips, *Engendering Democracy,* 5.

2. Liatto-Katundo, "The Women's Lobby."

3. Fraser, *Unruly Practices,* 161.

4. The Southern African Development Community includes South Africa, Botswana, Madagascar, Malawi, Mauritius, Mozambique, Namibia, Lesotho, Swaziland, Tanzania, Zambia, and Zimbabwe.

5. Budlender, "Women, Gender and Policy-making."

6. Mathye interview.

7. See, for example, reports of the departments of foreign affairs, justice, and land affairs to Commission on Gender Equality Information and Evaluation Workshops (CGE, *Reports on Consultative Workshops,* 114, 118, 186).

8. Marais, *South Africa, Limits to Change,* 160.

9. Mama, "Women's Studies."

10. Alvarez, *Engendering Democracy in Brazil,* 21.

11. Razavi and Miller, "Gender Mainstreaming"; Goetz, "The Politics of Intergrating Gender"; Kabeer, *Reversed Realities.*

12. Albertyn, "National Machinery for Ensuring Gender Equality"; Mbete-Kgositsile, "National Machinery for Promoting the Status of Women."

13. Seidman, "Institutional Dilemmas."

14. Mabandla, "Choices for South African Women."

15. Myakayaka-Manzini, "Past and Present Debates," 2.

16. WNC and Lawyers for Human Rights, "Report on Conference," 10–11.

17. Most papers presented at the Malibongwe Conference were unattributed. For a selection of these views, see the papers entitled "Women in South Africa Today" and "Formulating National Policy Regarding Emancipation of Women and Promotion of Women's Development," Malibongwe Conference Papers.

18. Razavi and Miller, "Gender Mainstreaming," ii.

19. Charman, de Swardt, and Simons, "The Politics of Gender." Also interview with Jackie Cock, member of the ANC Emancipation Commission, April 12, 1999.

20. Contact between Australian, Canadian, and South African feminists was extremely influential. In 1993 Quentin Bryce of Australia and Glenda Simms of Canada attended a key conference debating the nature of the national machinery in South Africa. Canadian legal academics frequently advised the ANC women activists and the WNC. In 1995 Susanne Tongue of the Australian Law Reform Commission was in South Africa and speaking at events aimed at explaining the importance of the Commission on Gender Equality.

21. Curthoys, "The World Upside Down," x.

22. See also Albertyn, "National Machinery."

23. Mabandla, "Choices," 25.

24. Neophytou, "Developing the Commission for Gender Equality."

25. Kgositsile-Mbete, "National Machinery," 24.

26. Cathi Albertyn, personal communication, September 1999. Debbie Budlender also suggests that the commission was a trade-off, agreed to in a context in which there was no sense of budget constraints on institutional forms (personal communication, July 1997).

27. Madonsela, "Beyond Putting Women on the Agenda," 34.

28. The Centre for Applied Legal Studies presented this framework as part of the consultative process in 1996, which led to clarity with regard to the structures.

29. Albertyn, "National Machinery."

30. Commission on Gender Equality, *Annual Report,* 53–54.

31. It was anticipated from the beginning that the weakest sector was likely to be that within the bureaucracy.

32. Jones, "Citizenship in a Women-friendly Polity."

33. Goetz, "Gender and Administration," 8.

34. Ibid., 6.

35. "Women in Power."

36. Ibid., 16.

37. Meer, "The Demobilisation of Civil Society."

38. Daima, "The Forward March."

39. Mabandla, "Choices," 26.

40. See Klugman, "Mainstreaming Gender Equality in Health Policy"; James, "Energy"; and Meer, "Constraints to Land Reform."

41. Government of South Africa, *CEDAW Report.*

42. *No Turning Back.*

43. Klugman, "Mainstreaming Gender Equality in Health Policy."

44. Ibid., 53–54.

45. Ibid.; Meer, "Constraints to Land Reform."

46. CGE, *Reports on Consultative Workshops.*

47. I base this statement on informal comments made to me by workshop participants in July 1997.

48. The Democratic Party's election platform in 1999 included the proposal to significantly reduce the number of statutory commissions and their budgets as party members saw these commissions as wasteful and unproductive demands on public revenue. The party proposed to redirect these funds to programs to reduce unemployment.

49. Unlike government departments, the statutory commissions do not participate in discussions with the Ministry of Finance about their budgets.

50. The first chair, Thenjiwe Mtintso, resigned after being elected deputy secretary general of the ANC. Her replacement, Joyce Seroke, was appointed a year later. In the interim Phumelele Ntombela-Nzimande acted as chair.

51. Seidman, "Institutional Dilemmas."

52. Ibid.

53. Ibid., 559.

54. Sawer, "Femocrats and Ecorats,": 24.

55. Mathews interview.

56. Nchita interview.

57. Jacobus interview.

58. Van Wyk interview.

59. Kornegay interview.

60. Dawson interview.

61. Government of South Africa, *CEDAW Report.*

62. Klugman, "Mainstreaming Gender Equality."

63. Meer, "Constraints to Land Reform."

64. Summers, "Mandarins or Missionaries."

65. Eisenstein, "Femocrats."

66. Elsewhere, Catherine Albertyn and I have argued that even this conceptualization of freedom is limited, as it fails to address the social and cultural dimensions of inequality. See Albertyn and Hassim, "The Boundaries of Democracy."

67. WNC, *Women's Charter for Effective Equality.*

68. Ann Orloff takes this argument much further in suggesting that social policies should aim at decommodification of gender relations by enabling women to form and maintain autonomous households. I am hesitant to apply this notion to women in the South African context, given the particular cultural attachments and support systems that women value within family and communities. It could also be argued that the high number of women-headed households in South Africa suggests that women are indeed free to form autonomous households, but this has patently not empowered women to become full and equal citizens (Orloff, "Gender and the Social of Citizenship," 319).

69. Budlender, "The Political Economy of Women's Budgets."

70. Budlender, *The Third Women's Budget,* 14.

71. The chair at the time was Gill Marcus, who is committed to gender equality. She was later deputy minister of finance and in July 1999 became the deputy governor of the Reserve Bank.

72. Budlender, "The Political Economy of Women's Budgets," 1377.

73. Budlender, *Third Women's Budget.*

74. Govender, Foreword, 4.

75. Ibid.

76. JSCIQLSW, *Annual Report.*

77. Sen, "Gender Mainstreaming in Finance Ministries," 1379.

78. Vetten, "'The Budget Appears to Be Less Than Required."

79. The Reconstruction and Development Programme's six basic principles

were an integrated and sustainable program, a people-driven process, peace and security for all, nation building, linking reconstruction and development, and democratization of South Africa (ANC, *Reconstruction and Development Programme*, 4–6).

80. MP Pregs Govender pointed out that ANC women MPs were given no role in developing the RDP White Paper until the "eleventh hour," when they were asked to "gender edit" the document: "To be asked to edit any white paper from merely a gender perspective is highly inappropriate—any analysis pertaining to women should be done from a race, class and gender perspective so as to ensure that the concerns of poor, black and rural women are not isolated from the women's struggle" (quoted in Kathree, "Where Have All the Women Gone?" 25).

81. Agenda Collective, "Gender Flaws in the RDP."

82. Taylor, "Economic Gender Injustice."

83. Marais, *South Africa, Limits to Change*, 30–31

84. Taylor, "Economic Gender Injustice," 10.

85. Marais, "All GEAR-ed Up."

86. Gelb, "The Politics of Macroeconomic Policy Reforms," 16–17.

87. Valodia, "Finance," 93.

88. Gelb, "The Politics of Macroeconomic Policy Reforms," 16–17.

89. Nor, to be fair, did the more powerful Congress of South African Trade Unions (COSATU) or the South African Communist Party (SACP), both in formal alliance with the ANC. Their opposition to the GEAR policy, like that of women ministers, was silenced by the dictates of party loyalty and discipline.

90. Valodia, "Finance," 93.

91. Marais, *South Africa, Limits to Change*, 34.

92. Kathree, "Where Have All the Women Gone?"

93. Constitution of South Africa, 1996.

94. Fraser, *Unruly Practices*, 162.

95. Budlender, "Women and Poverty," 15.

96. It is noteworthy that the apartheid state had a system of social assistance in place, albeit one that was racially discriminatory. As Seekings has noted, this was unusual in Africa. It provided an important basis for retaining and expanding the system to include "new citizens" (Seekings, "The Broader Importance of Welfare Reform").

97. Lund Committee, *Report of the Lund Committee*, 2.

98. Ibid., 24.

99. *Mail and Guardian*, May 9, 1997.

100. Lund, Ardington, and Harber, "Welfare."

101. It is estimated that 14.3 million children younger than fourteen live with caregivers who earn less than 800 rands per month. Other recommendations of the Lund Committee included payment of the grant to the caregiver rather than the parent, the application of a means test, the registration of children's births, and regular health care for children.

102. *Mail and Guardian*, February 16, 1997.

103. *Citizen*, January 24, 1998.

104. Lund, Ardington, and Harber, "Welfare."

105. Tilley, "Is Parliamentary Advocacy All It's Cracked Up To Be?" 1.

106. Edwards, "New Women's Movement," 35.

107. Marks interview.

108. Edwards, "New Women's Movement," 33.

109. Naidoo and Bozalek, "Maintenance Grant Parity," 30.

110. Ibid., 31.

111. Edwards, "New Women's Movement," 35.

112. Sainsbury, *Gender Equality and Welfare States*. See also Fraser and Gordon, "A Genealogy of Dependency."

113. Liebenberg, "Social Security and Human Rights," 11.

114. Government of South Africa, *CEDAW Report*, 99.

115. CASE, "A Social Impact Study," 120.

116. Guthrie, "Family and Social Security Benefits."

117. CASE, "A Social Impact Study," 120.

118. Ibid.

119. Pringle and Watson, "Women's Interests and the Post-structuralist State." 63.

120. Schmitter, "The Consolidation of Democracy," 430.

121. Sawer, "Femocrats and Ecorats," 24.

122. Chile provides a useful lesson for South African feminists. Chilean feminists working within the state have increasingly represented middle-class professional women's concerns, while popular women's organizations have argued that their interests were not being represented by parliamentarians (Waylen, "Women and Democratization," 108).

123. Ferguson, *The Feminist Case against Bureaucracy.*

124. Stetson and Mazur, *Comparative State Feminism*, 9.

125. Staudt, *Women, Foreign Assistance and Advocacy Administration.*

126. Stetson and Mazur, *Comparative State Feminism.*

127. Ibid., 290.

128. Siim, "Welfare States," 188.

129. Geller-Schwartz, "An Array of Agencies," 57.

130. Pringle and Watson, "Women's Interests."

Chapter 8. Autonomy, Engagement, and Democratic Consolidation

1. Molyneux, "Analysing Women's Movements.

2. Jonasdottir, "On the Concept of Interest."

3. Serote interview.

4. Ndatshe interview.

5. Russell and Swilling, "The Size and Scope of the Non-Profit Sector."

6. Ibid., 26.

7. Albertyn and Hassim, "The Boundaries of Democracy."

8. Paley, "Women Pushed Aside as Men Seek Power."

9. North, *Institutions.*

10. Albertyn, "Contesting Democracy," 604.

11. Goetz and Hassim, *No Shortcuts to Power.*

12. Anne Marie Goetz, "Women's Political Effectiveness," in Goetz and Hassim, *No Shortcuts to Power,* 604.

13. Banaszak, Beckwith, and Rucht, *Women's Movements Facing the Reconfigured State,* 6.

14. Seidman-Makgetla, "Women and the Economy."

15. Mtintso, "Representivity," 573.

16. Seidman-Makgetla, "Women and the Economy," 1.

17. Harvey, *Votes without Leverage,* 11.

Bibliography

Archival Sources

African National Congress Archives, Mayibuye Centre, University of the Western Cape, and William Cullen Library, Wits University.

Commission on Gender Equality, CGE offices, Johannesburg.

Federation of South African Women Papers, William Cullen Library, Wits University.

Helen Joseph Papers, William Cullen Library, Wits University.

Malibongwe Conference Papers, Mayibuye Centre, University of the Western Cape.

Natal Organisation of Women Papers, Killie Campbell Library, University of Natal, Durban.

Ray (Alexander) Simons Papers, University of Cape Town.

South African Historical Archives, William Cullen Library, Wits University.

United Democratic Front Archives, William Cullen Library, Wits University.

United Women's Organisation–United Women's Congress Papers, University of Cape Town.

Women's National Coalition Archives, WNC offices, Braamfontein, Johannesburg.

Unofficial Sources

Catherine Albertyn, personal files.
Jacklyn Cock, personal files.
Sheila Meintjes, personal files.

Interviews

Albertyn, Cathi. Member, Women's National Coalition Monitoring Group, Johannesburg, September 1999.
Andersson, Muff. MK cadre, Johannesburg, September 22, 2000.
Budlender, Debbie. Research manager, Women's National Coalition, telephone, July 1997.
Camerer, Sheila. MP (New National Party), Johannesburg, April 20, 1999.
Cock, Jackie. Member, ANC Emancipation Commission, Johannesburg, April 12, 1999.
Dawson, Celia. Former chair, Steering Committee for Gender Equality, KwaZulu-Natal Provincial Government, Durban, June 18, 1997 (interviewed by S. Naiker).
Ginwala, Frene. Former coordinator, Women's National Coalition, and Speaker in the House of Assembly, Cape Town, July 6, 2000.
Govender, Pregs. MP and chair of the Joint Standing Committee on the Improvement of the Quality of Life and Status of Women, Cape Town, January 19, 2000.
Gwagwa, Lulu. Former ANC member in exile, August 30, 2000.
Hurt, Karen. *Speak* editor, Johannesburg, May 16 and 17, 2000.
Jacobus, Loretta. Member, Gauteng Provincial Legislature and Convenor for the Steering Committee on Gender, Johannesburg, July 16, 1997 (interviewed by S. Naiker).
Kornegay, Ellen. Head of Office on the Status of Women, Pretoria, October 6, 1998.
Love, Janet. MK activist and member of Parliament, Johannesburg, July 8, 1998.
Mager, Anne. United Women's Organisation secretary, telephone, May 16, 2000.
Mahomed, Sekina. Former staff member, Office on the Status of Women, Johannesburg, March 18, 1999.
Marks, Ruby. Executive member, New Women's Movement, Brighton (Sussex), November 8, 1998.
Mathye, Mihloti. Former deputy director, Department of Land Affairs, Johannesburg, March 17, 1999.
Matthews, Matlakala. Head of the Office on the Status of Women, North West Provincial Government, Klerksdorp, July 30, 1997 (interviewed by O. Nkoenyane).
Meer, Shamim. Feminist activist, Johannesburg, March 22, 2000.
Meintjes, Sheila. Former executive member, United Women's Organisation, and research director of the Women's National Coalition charter campaign, Johannesburg, March 3 and 10, 2000.
Motumi, Ntsiki. Member, ANC in exile, telephone, August 28, 2000.
Mtintso, Thenjiwe. MK commander and first chair of the Commission on Gender Equality, Johannesburg, March 23, 2000.

Narsee, Hursheela. Secretary of Natal Organisation of Women, Johannesburg, May 19, 2000.

Nchita, Mrs Z. Head of the Office on the Status of Women, Eastern Cape Government, East London, May 2, 1997 (interviewed by M. Claassen).

Ndatshe, Sibongile. Lawyer, Women's Legal Centre, Cape Town. April 6, 2004.

Nhlapo, Mavis. Administrative secretary for the ANC Women's Section, Johannesburg, September 6, 2000.

Ntombela-Nzimande, Phumelele. Member of the Natal Organisation of Women, *Speak* collective, and commissioner in the Commission on Gender Equality, Pretoria, March 16, 2000.

Omar, Rachmat. Chair, Women's Forum, Congress of South African Trade Unions, Johannesburg, May 3, 2000.

Reinecke, Annette. Member of Parliament from the National Party and delegate to the Beijing Conference, East London, May 30, 1997 (interviewed by M. Claassen).

Routledge-Madlala, Nozizwe. Former chair of Natal Organisation of Women and deputy minister of defense, Pretoria, September 7, 2000.

Sachs, Albie. Judge of the Constitutional Court and member of the ANC in exile, Johannesburg, March 14, 2000.

Schreiner, Jenny. United Women's Organisation secretary and underground ANC activist, Pretoria, May 20 and 21, 2000.

September, Connie. Former deputy vice president, Congress of South African Trade Unions, and chair of the September Commission, Johannesburg, August 6, 2001.

Serote, Pethu. Independent gender consultant, Cape Town meeting, November 2003.

Soobrayan, Veni. Executive member, Natal Organisation of Women, Pretoria, May 21, 2000.

Udit, Pingla. Member of the ANC underground, Johannesburg, September 23, 2000.

van Wyk, Julie. Director for auxiliary services and gender focal point, Department of Education, North West Provincial Government, Klerksdorp, July 29, 1997 (interviewed by O. Nkoenyane).

Zuma, Nkosazana. Chair of the Durban Central Branch of the ANC Women's League, Durban, May 1992.

Secondary Sources

Abdullah, Hussaina. "Transition Politics and the Challenge of Gender in Nigeria." *Review of African Political Economy* 56 (1993): 27–41.

———. "Picking up the Gauntlet: Women Discuss ANC Statement." *Agenda*, no. 8 (1990): 5–18.

———. "Wifeism and Activism: The Nigerian Women's Movement." In Amrita Basu, ed., *The Challenge of Local Feminisms: The Women's Movement in Comparative Perspective,* Boulder, Colo.: Westview, 1995.

Abrams, S. Kristine. "Fighting for Women's Liberation during the Liberation of South Africa: The Women's National Coalition." Master's thesis, Wadham College, Oxford, 2000.

Adler, Glenn, and Jonny Steinberg. *From Comrades to Citizens: The South African Civics Movement and the Transition to Democracy.* Basingstoke, U.K.: Macmillan, 2000.

Agenda Collective. "Gender Flaws in the RDP." *Agenda,* no. 24 (1995): 40–44.

Albertyn, Catherine. "Contesting Democracy: HIV/AIDS and the Achievement of Gender Equality in South Africa." *Feminist Studies* 29, no. 3 (2003): 595–615.

——, ed. *Engendering the Political Agenda: A South African Case Study.* Johannesburg: Centre for Applied Legal Studies, 1999.

——. "Mainstreaming Gender: National Machinery for Women in South Africa." Occasional paper, Centre for Applied Legal Studies, Johannesburg, 1995.

——. "National Machinery for Ensuring Gender Equality." In Sandra Liebenberg, ed., *The Constitution of South Africa from a Gender Perspective.* Cape Town: David Philip, 1995.

——. "Women and the Transition to Democracy in South Africa." In Felicity Kaganas and Christina Murray, eds., *Gender and the New South African Legal Order.* Cape Town: Juta, 1994.

Albertyn, Catherine, and B. Goldblatt. "Facing the Challenge of Transformation: Difficulties in the Development of an Indigenous Jurisprudence of Equality." *South African Journal of Human Rights* 14 (1998): 260–72.

Albertyn, Catherine, and S. Hassim. "The Boundaries of Democracy: Gender, HIV/AIDS and Culture." In D. Everatt and V. Maphai, *The Real State of the Nation: South Africa since 1990.* Johannesburg: INTERFUND, 2003.

Albertyn, Catherine, R. Murphy, N. Pillay, and L. Zondo. "The Status of the Charter: Option Five." Unpublished discussion paper, Women's National Coalition, 1993.

Alexander, Neville. "Approaches to the National Question in South Africa." *Transformation* 1 (1986): 63–95.

"A Long and Difficult Road—Building the ANC Women's League." *Speak* 33 (1991): 12.

Alvarez, Sonia. *Engendering Democracy in Brazil: Women's Movements in Transition Politics.* Princeton, N.J.: Princeton University Press, 1990.

ANC (African National Congress). *Reconstruction and Development Programme: A Policy Framework.* Johannesburg: Umanyano, 1994.

ANC Women's League. *ANC Women's League: Fifty Years of Struggle.* Johannesburg: ANC, 1993.

Annecke, Wendy. "The Launch of the Women's League." *Agenda,* no. 8 (1990): 1–3.

Anonymous. "The Emancipation of Women." Letter to the editor. *African Communist* 97 (1984): 104–6.

Aulette, Judy Root. "New Roads to Resistance: Polish Feminists in the Transition to Democracy." In Jill M. Bystydzienski and Joti Sekhon, eds., *Democratization and Women's Grassroots Movements.* Bloomington: Indiana University Press, 1999.

"AZAPO and Women." *Speak* 36 (1991): 22–24.

Baer, Denise. "Political Parties: The Missing Variable in Women and Politics Research." *Political Research Quarterly* 46, no. 3 (1999): 547–76.

Baker, Carolyn. "Charting Our Future." *Agenda,* no. 21 (1994): 97–100.

Baldez, Lisa. *Why Women Protest: Women's Movements in Chile.* Cambridge: Cambridge University Press, 2002.

Ballington, Julie. "Political Parties and Gender Equality: What Do the Manifestos Say?" *Election Update* 14 (1999): 3 –6.

———. "Women's Parliamentary Representation: The Effects of List PR." *Politikon* 25, no. 2 (1998): 72–93.

Banaszak, Lee Ann, Karen Beckwith, and Dieter Rucht. *Women's Movements Facing the Reconfigured State.* Cambridge: Cambridge University Press, 2003.

Barrell, Howard. "The Turn to the Masses: The African National Congress' Strategic Review of 1978 –79." *Journal of Southern African Studies* 18, no. 1 (1992): 64 –92.

Barrett, Jane, A. Dawber, B. Klugman, I. Obery, J. Shindler, and J. Yawitch. *Vukani Makhosikazi: South African Women Speak.* London: CIIR, 1985.

Barrett, Michele, and Anne Phillips, eds. *Destabilizing Theory: Contemporary Feminist Debates.* Cambridge: Polity Press, 1992.

Basu, Amrita, ed. *The Challenge of Local Feminisms: Women's Movements in Global Perspective.* Boulder, Colo.: Westview, 1995.

Bazilli, Susan, ed. *Putting Women on the Agenda.* Johannesburg: Ravan Press, 1991.

Beall, Jo. "Women under Indentured Labour in Colonial Natal." In Cherryl Walker, ed., *Women and Resistance in Southern Africa to 1945.* Cape Town: David Philip, 1990.

Beall, Jo, Michelle Friedman, Shireen Hassim, Ros Posel, Lindy Stiebel, and Alison Todes. "African Women in the Durban Struggle, 1985 –1986: Towards a Transformation of Roles?" In G. Moss and I. Obery, eds., *South African Review.* Vol. 4. Johannesburg: Ravan Press, 1987.

Beall, Jo, Shireen Hassim, and Alison Todes. " 'A Bit on the Side?' Gender Struggles in the Politics of Transformation in South Africa." *Feminist Review* 33 (1989): 3 –32.

Bebel, August. *Women Under Socialism.* New York: Schocken Books, 1971.

Berger, Iris. *Threads of Solidarity: Women in South African Industry, 1900–1980.* Bloomington: Indiana University Press, 1992.

Bernstein, Hilda. *For Their Triumphs and for Their Tears: Women in Apartheid South Africa.* London: IDAF, 1985.

———. "The Real Challenge of Feminism." *African Communist* 121 (1990): 96 –100.

Boehmer, Elleke. "Stories of Women and Mothers: Gender and Nationalism in the Early Fiction of Flora Nwapa." In S. Nasta, ed., *Motherlands: Black Women's Writing from Africa, the Caribbean and South Asia.* London: Women's Press, 1991.

Bonnin, Debby. "Women's Studies in South Africa." *Women's Studies Quarterly* 1–2 (1996): 378 –99.

Bradford, Helen. "We Are Now the Men: Women's Beer Protests in the Natal Countryside, 1929." In Belinda Bozzoli, ed., *Class, Community and Conflict.* Johannesburg: Ravan Press, 1988.

"Breaking the Silence." *Speak* 20 (1988): 8.

Brink, Elsabe. "Man-made Women: Gender, Class and the Ideology of the Volksmoeder." In Cherryl Walker, ed., *Women and Gender in Southern Africa to 1945.* Cape Town: David Philip, 1990.

Briskin, Linda. "Socialist Feminism: From the Standpoint of Practice." *Studies in Political Economy* 30 (1989): 87 –114.

Britton, Hannah. "Preliminary Report of Participation: Challenges and Strategies." Unpublished report, Syracuse University, 1997.

Budlender, Debbie. "The Political Economy of Women's Budgets in the South." *World Development* 28, no. 7 (2000): 1365–78.

———, ed. *The Second Women's Budget.* Cape Town: Institute for Democracy in South Africa (IDASA), 1996.

———, ed. *The Third Women's Budget.* Cape Town: Institute for Democracy in South Africa (IDASA), 1998.

———. "Women and Poverty." www.genderstats.org.za/poverty.html, accessed August 30, 2005.

———. "Women, Gender and Policy-making in the South African Context." *Development Update* 14, no. 4 (1997): 513–30.

Budlender, Debbie, Sheila Meintjes, and Jenny Schreiner. Review of *Women and Resistance. Work in Progress* 34 (1984): 24–29.

Bulbring, Edyth. "The Battle against Winnie Is Over; The Fight for Peace Begins." *Sunday Times* (Johannesburg), May 5, 1991.

Burton, Mary. "Women Organise." *Sash,* August 1987.

Butler, J., and J. W. Scott. *Feminists Theorize the Political.* New York: Routledge, 1992.

Bystydzienski, Jill M., and Joti Sekhon, eds. *Democratization and Women's Grassroots Movements.* Bloomington: Indiana University Press, 1999.

Caldeira, Teresa P. R. "Justice and Individual Rights: Challenges for Women's Movements and Democratization in Brazil." In Jane S. Jacquette and Sharon L. Wolchik, eds., *Women and Democracy: Latin America and Central and Eastern Europe.* Baltimore: Johns Hopkins University Press, 1998.

CALS (Centre for Applied Legal Studies). "Second Supplementary Report on the Constitutional Principles from the Technical Committee on Constitutional Issues to the Negotiating Council." June 23, 1993.

CASE (Community Agency for Social Enquiry). "A Social Impact Study on the Phasing-in of the Child Support Grant." Johannesburg, 2000.

———. *Synthesis Report on the Participation of Women in Parliament Researched for the European Union.* Braamfontein: Community Agency for Social Enquiry, 1999.

Caucus on Law and Gender. "What Could a Women's Charter Be and What Could It Be Used to Achieve?" Institute on Criminology, University of Cape Town, 1992.

Charman, Andrew, Cobus de Swardt, and Mary Simons. "The Politics of Gender: Negotiating Liberation." *Transformation* 15 (1991): 40–64.

Chatterjee, Partha. *The Nation and Its Fragments: Colonial and Postcolonial Histories.* Princeton, N.J.: Princeton University Press, 1993.

Chazan, Naomi. "Gender Perspectives on African States." In J. L. Parpart and K. A. Staudt, eds., *Women and the State in Africa.* Boulder, Colo.: Lynne Rienner, 1989.

Cherry, Janet. "Traditions and Transitions: African Political Participation in Port Elizabeth." In Jonathan Hyslop, ed., *African Democracy in the Era of Globalisation.* Johannesburg: Wits University Press, 1999.

Chigudu, Hope, and Wilfred Tichagwa. "Participation of Women in Party Politics." Zimbabwe Women's Resource Centre and Network Discussion Paper 9, 1995.

Chubb, Karin. "Fedsaw Relations." *Sash,* May 1989.

Claassens, A., and S. Ngubane. "Rural Women, Land Rights and the Communal Land Rights Bill." Draft paper presented at the Women's Legal Centre Conference on Advancing Women's Rights, Cape Town, October 2003.

Clara (Jenny Schreiner). "Feminism and the Struggle for National Liberation." *African Communist* 118 (1989): 38 –43.

Cock, Jacklyn. *Colonels and Cadres: War and Gender in South Africa.* Cape Town: Oxford University Press, 1991.

———. "Promoting Gender Equality in South Africa." In Susan Bazilli, ed., *Putting Women on the Agenda.* Johannesburg: Ravan Press, 1991.

———. "Putting Women on the Agenda." In Susan Bazilli, ed., *Putting Women on the Agenda.* Johannesburg: Ravan Press, 1991.

———. "Women in South Africa's Transition to Democracy." In J. Scott, C. Kaplan, and D. Keates, eds., *Transitions, Environments, Translations: Feminism in International Politics.* New York: Routledge, 1997.

Cohen, J. L., and A. Arato. *Civil Society and Political Theory.* Cambridge, Mass.: MIT Press, 1992.

Cole, Josette. *Crossroads: The Politics of Reform and Repression, 1976–1986.* Johannesburg: Ravan Press, 1987.

Commission on Gender Equality. *Annual Report of the Commission on Gender Equality.* Braamfontein: Commission on Gender Equality, 1997.

———. *Reports on Consultative Workshops.* Braamfontein: Commission on Gender Equality, 1997.

COSATU (Congress of South African Trade Unions). "September Commission Report." Johannesburg, 1997.

Curnow, Robyn. "Thandi Modise: A Woman in War." *Agenda,* no. 43 (2000): 36 –40.

Curthoys, Ann. "Identity Crisis: Colonialism, Nation and Gender in Australian History." *Gender and History* 5, no. 2 (1993): 165 –76.

———. "The World Upside Down: Feminisms in the Antipodes." *Feminist Review* 52 (1996): v–x.

Dahlerup, Drude. *The New Women's Movement: Feminism and Political Power in Europe and the USA.* London: Sage, 1986.

Daima, Tumika. "The Forward March of the Women's National Coalition." *Towards Democracy* 6, no. 1 (1997): 5 –7.

Daniels, Glenda. "ANC Women's League: Breaking Out of the Mould?" *Work in Progress* 75 (1991): 34 –36.

Dawber, Aneene. "Transvaal Women Organise." *Work in Progress* 34 (1984): 30 –31.

Democratic Party. "Discussion Document on Women's Status Prepared by Ms Dene Smuts MP and Mrs Carole Charlewood MP." 1991.

Dove, Fiona. "Questions of Accountability." *Agenda,* no. 20 (1994): 53 –56.

Driver, Dorothy. "The ANC Constitutional Guidelines in Process: A Feminist Reading." In Susan Bazilli, ed., *Putting Women on the Agenda.* Johannesburg: Ravan Press, 1991.

Ebrahim, Hassen. *The Soul of a Nation.* Oxford: Oxford University Press, 1999.

Eduards, Maud. "Women's Agency and Collective Action." In *Women's Studies International Forum* 17, no. 2–3 (1994): 181–86.

Edwards, Rita. "New Women's Movement: Pap and Bread Are Not Enough." *Agenda,* no. 33 (1997): 33 –36.

Eisenstein, Hester. "Femocrats, Official Feminism and the Uses of Power." In Sophie Watson, ed., *Playing the State.* Sydney: Allen and Unwin, 1990.

"Equality, Development and Peace." *Voice of Women* (1985).

Erlank, Natasha. "Gender and Masculinity in South African Nationalist Discourse, 1912–1950." *Feminist Studies* 29, no. 3 (2003): 653–72.

———. "Masculinity and Nationalism in ANC Discourse in the Twentieth Century." Unpublished paper presented at the Wits Gender Studies Seminar Series, Johannesburg, 2001.

European Union Parliamentary Support Programme. "Report of the Provincial Legislatures Needs Assessment Studies." University of the Western Cape and University of Fort Hare, 1997.

"FEDTRAW's Still Flying." *JODAC News,* Winter 1987.

Feijoo, Maria del Carmen. "Democratic Participation and Women in Argentina." In Jane S. Jacquette and Sharon L. Wolchik, eds., *Women and Democracy: Latin America and Central and Eastern Europe.* Baltimore: Johns Hopkins University Press, 1998.

Ferguson, Kathy. *The Feminist Case against Bureaucracy.* Philadelphia: Temple University Press, 1984.

Fester, G. "Women's Organisations in the Western Cape: Vehicles for Gender Struggle or Instruments of Subordination?" *Agenda,* no. 34 (1997): 45–61.

Frankel, Philip, Noam Pines, and Mark Swilling, eds. *State, Resistance and Change in South Africa.* Johannesburg: Southern Book Publishers, 1988.

Fraser, Nancy. *Justice Interruptus: Reflections on the "Postsocialist" Condition.* New York: Routledge, 1997.

———. *Unruly Practices: Power, Discourse and Gender in Contemporary Social Theory.* Minneapolis: University of Minnesota Press, 1989.

Fraser, Nancy, and Linda Gordon. "A Genealogy of Dependency: Tracing a Keyword of the U.S. Welfare State." *Signs: Journal of Women in Culture and Society* 19, no. 2 (1994): 309–36.

Frederikse, Julie. *The Unbreakable Thread: Nonracialism in South Africa.* Johannesburg: Ravan Press, 1990.

Friedman, Elizabeth. *Unfinished Transitions: Women and the Gendered Development of Democracy in Venezuela, 1936–1996.* University Park: Pennsylvania State University Press, 2000.

Friedman, Steven, ed. *The Long Journey: South Africa's Quest for a Negotiated Settlement.* Johannesburg: Ravan Press, 1993.

Gaitskell, Deborah. "'Christian Compounds for Girls': Church Hostels for African Women in Johannesburg, 1907–1970." *Journal of Southern Africa Studies* 6, no. 1 (1979): 44–69.

Gaitskell, Deborah, J. Kimble, M. Maconachie, and E. Unterhalter. "Class, Race and Gender: Domestic Workers in South Africa." *Review of African Political Economy* 27–28 (1984): 86–108.

Gaitskell, Deborah, and Elaine Unterhalter. "Mothers of the Nation: A Comparative Analysis of Nation, Race and Motherhood in Afrikaner Nationalism and the African National Congress." In Floya Anthias and Nira Yuval-Davis, eds., *Women-Nation-State.* London: Macmillan, 1989.

GAP (Gender Advocacy Programme). "Gender Politics at Local Level." *Agenda,* no. 45 (2000): 13–16.

Geisler, Gisela. *Women and the Remaking of Politics in Southern Africa.* Uppsala: Nordic Afrika Institute, 2004.

Gelb, Stephen. "The Politics of Macroeconomic Policy Reforms in South Africa." Paper presented to History Workshop, University of the Witwatersrand, Johannesburg, 1999.

Geller-Schwartz, Linda. "An Array of Agencies: Feminism and State Institutions in Canada." In Dorothy McBride Stetson and Amy G. Mazur, eds., *Comparative State Feminism.* London: Sage, 1996.

Ginwala, Frene. "ANC Women: Their Strength in the Struggle." *Work in Progress* 8 (1986): 12–15.

———. "Formulating National Policy Regarding the Emancipation of Women and the Promotion of Women's Development in Our Country." Unpublished paper, delivered at the Malibongwe Conference, Amsterdam, 1990.

———. "Women and the African National Congress, 1912–1943." *Agenda,* no. 8 (1991): 77–93.

———. "Women and the Elephant." In Susan Bazilli, ed., *Putting Women on the Agenda.* Johannesburg: Ravan Press.1991.

Glaser, Daryl. "Changing Discourses of Democracy and Socialism in South Africa." In David Howarth and Aletta Norval, eds., *South Africa in Transition: New Theoretical Perspectives.* Basingstoke, U.K.: Macmillan. 1998.

Goetz, Anne Marie. "Gender and Administration." *IDS Bulletin* 23, no. 4 (1992): 6–17.

———, ed. *Getting Institutions Right for Women in Development.* London: Zed Press, 1998.

———. "The Politics of Integrating Gender to State Development Processes: Trends, Opportunities and Constraints in Bangladesh, Chile, Jamaica, Mail, Morocco and Uganda." UN Research Institute for Social Development Occasional Paper 2, Geneva, 1995.

Goetz, Anne Marie, and Shireen Hassim. "In and against the Party: Women and Constituency Building in Uganda and South Africa." In Maxine Molyneux and Shahra Razavi, eds., *Gender Justice, Development and Rights.* Oxford: Oxford University Press, 2002.

———, eds. *No Shortcuts to Power: African Women in Politics and Policy Making.* London: Zed, 2003.

Goldblatt, Beth, and Likhapha Mbatha. "Gender, Culture and Equality: Reforming Customary Law." In Catherine Albertyn, ed., *Engendering the State: A South African Case Study.* Johannesburg: Centre for Applied Legal Studies, 1999.

Goldblatt, Beth, and Sheila Meintjes. "South African Women Demand the Truth." In Meredith Turshen and Clothilde Twagiramariya, eds., *What Women Do in Wartime: Gender and Conflict in Africa.* London: Zed, 1998.

Gould, Debbie, Jenny Radloff, and Cally Cuhn. "The Women's Centre, Cape Town." *Agenda,* no. 10 (1991): 28–30.

Gouws, Amanda. "The Gender Dimension of the 1999 Election." In A. Reynolds, ed., *Election '99 South Africa: From Mandela to Mbeki.* Cape Town: David Phillip, 1999.

———. "The Rise of the Femocrat?" *Agenda,* no. 30 (1996): 31–43.

———. "The State of the National Gender Machinery: Structural Problems and Personalised Politics." *State of the Nation: South Africa* (2005): 143–66.

———, ed. *(Un)thinking Citizenship: Feminist Debates in Contemporary South Africa.* Cape Town: UCT Press, 2005.

Govender, Pregs. "Breaking the Silence." *Agenda,* no. 16 (1993): 42–43.

———. Foreword to Debbie Budlender, *The Third Women's Budget.* Cape Town: Institute for Democracy in South Africa (IDASA), 1998.

———. "Launching UDF Women's Congress." *Agenda,* no. 1 (1987): 79–80.

Government of South Africa. *CEDAW Report.* Pretoria: Government Printers, 1997.

Grewal, Inderpal, and Caren Kaplan, eds. Introduction to Inderpal Grewal and Caren Kaplan, eds., *Scattered Hegemonies: Postmodernity and Transnational Feminist Practices.* Minneapolis: University of Minnesota Press, 1994.

Guthrie, Teresa. "Family and Social Security Benefits in South Africa." *Social Dynamics* 28, no. 2 (2002): 122–45.

Gwagwa, Lulu. "The Family in South African Politics." In Susan Bazilli, ed., *Putting Women on the Agenda.* Johannesburg: Ravan Press, 1991.

Harvey, Anna. *Votes without Leverage: Women in American Electoral Politics, 1920–1970.* Cambridge: Cambridge University Press, 1998.

Hassim, Shireen. "The Dual Politics of Representation: Women and Electoral Politics in South Africa." *Politikon* 26, no. 2 (1999): 201–12.

———. "Family, Motherhood and Zulu Nationalism: The Politics of the Inkatha Women's Brigade." *Feminist Review* 43 (1993): 1–25.

———. "From Presence to Power: Women's Citizenship in a New Democracy." *Agenda,* no. 40 (1999): 6–16.

———. "The Gender Agenda: Transforming the ANC." *Southern Africa Report* (April 1992): 4–10.

———. "The Gender Pact and Democratic Consolidation: Institutionalizing Gender Equality in the South African State." *Feminist Studies* 29, no. 3 (2003): 505–28.

———. "Gender, Social Location, and Feminist Politics in South Africa." *Transformation* 15 (1991): 65–82.

———. "Gendering Parliament." *Southern Africa Report* 14, no. 3 (1999): 5–8.

———. "State-led Strategies for the Achievement of Gender Equality." Paper prepared for DAWN Network meeting, Cape Town, November 1999.

———. "Where Have All the Women Gone? Gender and Politics in South African Debates." Paper presented at the Conference on Women and Gender in South Africa, Durban, 1991.

Hassim, Shireen, and Amanda Gouws. "Redefining the Public Space: Women's Organisations, Gender Consciousness and Civil Society in South Africa." *Politikon* 25, no. 2 (1998): 53–76.

Hassim, Shireen, Jo Metelerkamp, and Alison Todes. "A Bit on the Side? Gender Struggles and the Politics of Transformation in South Africa." *Transformation* 5 (1987): 3–32.

Hassim, Shireen, O. Nkoenyane, and S. Naiker. "Audit of National Machinery." Research Report, Human Sciences Research Council, Pretoria, 1998.

Hassim, Shireen, and Cherryl Walker. "Women's Studies and the Women's Movement in South Africa: Defining a Relationship." *Women's Studies International Forum* 16, no. 5 (1992): 533–60.

Hellman, Judith Adler. "Women's Struggle in a Workers' City: Feminist Movements in Turin." In Mary Fainsod Katzenstein and Carol McClurg Mueller, eds., *The Women's Movements of the United States and Western Europe: Consciousness, Political Opportunity, and Public Policy.* Philadelphia: Temple University Press, 1987.

Hendricks, Cheryl. "Gender Politics in a Post-apartheid South Africa." *SAFERE: South African Feminist Review* 2, no. 1 (1996): 2–18.

Hendricks, Cheryl, and Desiree Lewis. "Voices from the Margins." *Agenda,* no. 20 (1994): 61–75.

Heng, Geraldine. "A Great Way to Fly: Nationalism, the State and the Varieties of Third World Feminism." In M. Jacqui Alexander and Chandra Talpade Mohanty, eds., *Feminist Genealogies, Colonial Legacies, Democratic Futures.* London: Routledge, 1997.

Hirst, Paul. *Representative Democracy and Its Limits.* London: Polity Press, 1990.

Hofmeyr, Isabel. "Building a Nation from Words: Afrikaans Language, Literature and Ethnic Identity, 1902–1924." In Shula Marks and Stanley Trapido, eds., *The Politics of Race, Class and Nationalism in Twentieth Century South Africa.* New York: Longman, 1987.

Holland-Muter, Sue. "Women Breaking the Silence!" *Agenda,* no. 8 (1990): 2.

Horn, Pat. "ANC 48th National Conference." *Agenda,* no. 11 (1991): 15 –18.

———. "Post-apartheid South Africa: What about Women's Emancipation?" *Transformation* 15 (1991): 26 –39.

———. "Whither the WNC?" *Agenda,* no. 23 (1994): 64 –66.

Howarth, David, and Aletta Norval, eds. *South Africa in Transition: New Theoretical Perspectives.* Basingstoke, U.K.: Macmillan, 1998.

Hudson, Peter. "The Freedom Charter and the Theory of National Democratic Revolution." *Transformation* 1 (1986): 6 –38.

Hyslop, Jonathan, ed. *African Democracy in the Era of Globalisation.* Johannesburg: Wits University Press, 1999.

IBR (Institute for Black Research). *Resistance in the Townships.* Durban: Institute for Black Research, 1989.

Imam, Ayesha, Amina Mama, and Fatou Sow, eds. *Engendering African Social Sciences.* Dakar: CODESRIA, 1997.

Jacquette, Jane S., ed. *The Women's Movement in Latin America: Feminism and the Transition to Democracy.* Boston: Unwin Hyman, 1989.

Jacquette, Jane S., and Sharon L. Wolchik, eds. *Women and Democracy: Latin America and Central and Eastern Europe.* Baltimore: Johns Hopkins University Press, 1998.

Jaffee, Georgina. "Women in Trade Unions and the Community." In G. Moss and I. Obery, eds., *South African Review.* Vol. 4. Johannesburg: Ravan Press, 1987.

James, Bronwyn. "Energy." In *Agenda Monograph: Translating Commitment into Policy and Practice: Three Case Studies.* Durban: Agenda, 1999.

Jayawardena, Kumari. *Feminism and Nationalism in the Third World.* London: Zed, 1986.

Jenson, Jane. "Changing Discourse, Changing Agendas: Political Rights and Reproductive Policies in France." In Mary Fainsod Katzenstein and Carol McClurg Mueller, eds., *The Women's Movements of the United States and Western Europe:*

Consciousness, Political Opportunity, and Public Policy. Philadelphia: Temple University Press, 1987.

————. "Extending the Boundaries of Citizenship: Women's Movements of Western Europe." In Amrita Basu, ed., *The Challenge of Local Feminisms.* Boulder, Colo.: Westview, 1995.

Jonasdottir, Anna. "On the Concept of Interest, Women's Interests, and the Limitations of Interest Theory." In Anna Jonasdottir and Kathy Jones, eds., *The Political Interests of Gender.* London: Sage, 1988.

Jones, Kathleen. "Citizenship in a Women-Friendly Polity." *Signs: Journal of Women in Culture and Society* 15, no. 4 (1990): 781–813.

Joseph, Helen. *Side by Side: The Autobiography of Helen Joseph.* London: Zed, 1986.

JSCIQLSW (Joint Standing Committee on Improving the Quality of Life and Status of Women). *Annual Report.* Cape Town: Parliament, 1999.

Kabeer, Naila. *Reversed Realities: Gender Hierarchies in Development.* London: Verso, 1993.

Kaganas, Felicity, and Christina Murray. "Law and Women's Rights in South Africa: An Overview." In Christina Murray, ed., *Gender and the New South African Legal Order.* Cape Town: Juta, 1994.

Kandiyoti, Deniz. "Identity and Its Discontents: Women and the Nation." *Millennium* 20, no. 3 (1991): 429–33.

Kaplan, Temma. *Crazy for Democracy: Women in Grassroots Movements.* New York: Routledge, 1997.

————. "Female Consciousness and Collective Action: The Case of Barcelona, 1910–1918." *Signs: Journal of Women in Culture and Society* 7, no. 3 (1982): 545–66.

Karam, A., and J. Lovenduski. "Women in Parliament: Making a Difference." In IDEA, *Women in Parliament: Beyond the Numbers.* Stockholm: International IDEA, 1998.

Kathree, Fayeeza. "Where Have All the Women Gone?" *Agenda,* no. 24 (1995): 21–26.

Katzenstein, Mary. Introduction to Mary Fainsod Katzenstein and Carol McClurg Mueller, eds., *The Women's Movements of the United States and Western Europe: Consciousness, Political Opportunity, and Public Policy.* Philadelphia: Temple University Press, 1987.

Katzenstein, Mary Fainsod, and Carol McClurg Mueller, eds. *The Women's Movements of the United States and Western Europe: Consciousness, Political Opportunity, and Public Policy.* Philadelphia: Temple University Press, 1987.

Kemp, Amanda, Nozizwe Madlala, Asha Moodley, and Elaine Salo. 1995. "The Dawn of a New Day: Redefining South Africa Feminisms." In Amrita Basu, ed., *The Challenge of Local Feminisms: Women's Movements in Comparative Perspective.* Boulder, Colo.: Westview, 1995.

"Key Questions for Election Candidates." *Agenda,* no. 20 (1994): 7–15.

Klugman, B. "Mainstreaming Gender Equality in Health Policy." *Agenda Monograph: Translating Commitment into Policy and Practice: Three Case Studies.* Durban, 1999.

Kruks, Sonya, Rayna Rapp, and M. Young, eds. *Promissory Notes: Women in the Transition to Socialism.* New York: Monthly Review Press, 1989.

Letseme. "Women's Contribution to the Liberation Struggle." *African Communist* 94 (1983): 101–3.

Lewis, Desiree. "Theorising about Gender." Paper presented to African Association of Political Science/Southern African Political Science Series Conference on South Africa: Which Way Forward? Cape Town, 1992.

Liatto-Katundo, Beatrice. "The Women's Lobby and Gender Relations in Zambia." *Review of African Political Economy* 56 (1993): 79 –125.

Liebenberg, Sandy, ed. *The Constitution of South Africa from a Gender Perspective.* Cape Town: David Philip, 1995.

———. "Social Citizenship—A Precondition for Meaningful Democracy." *Agenda,* no. 40 (1999): 59 –65.

———. "Social Security and Human Rights: Current Issues." *Economic and Social Rights in South Africa Review* 1, no. 2 (1998): 2–3.

Liu, Lydia. "The Female Body and Nationalist Discourse: The Field of Life and Death Revisited." In Inderpal Grewal and Caren Kaplan, eds., *Scattered Hegemonies: Postmodernity and Transnational Feminist Practices.* Minneapolis: University of Minnesota Press, 1994.

Lodge, Tom. *Black Politics in South Africa since 1945.* New York: Longman, 1983.

———. "State of Exile: The African National Congress of South Africa, 1976 –86." In Philip Frankel, Noam Pines, and Mark Swilling, eds., *State, Resistance, and Change in South Africa.* Johannesburg: Southern Book Publishers, 1988.

Lodge, Tom, and Bill Nasson. *All, Here, Now: Black Politics in South Africa in the 1980s.* Cape Town: David Philip, 1991.

Lovenduski, Joni. *Women and European Politics: Contemporary Feminism and Public Politics.* Brighton, U.K.: Wheatsheaf, 1986.

Lovenduski, Joni, and Pippa Norris, eds. *Gender and Party Politics.* London: Sage, 1993.

Lovenduski, Joni, and Vicky Randall. *Contemporary Feminist Politics.* Oxford: Oxford University Press, 1993.

Lund Committee. *Report of the Lund Committee on Child and Family Support.* Pretoria: Government Printing Services, 1996.

Lund, Francie, Libby Ardington, and Mary Harber. "Welfare." In Debbie Budlender, ed., *The Second Women's Budget.* Cape Town: Institute for Democracy in South Africa (IDASA), 1996.

Mabandla, Brigitte. "Choices for South African Women." *Agenda,* no. 20 (1994): 22–29.

Madonsela, Thuli. "Beyond Putting Women on the Agenda." *Agenda,* no. 24 (1995): 22–29.

Mahon, Rianne, and Jane Jenson. "Representing Solidarity: Class, Gender and the Crisis of Social Democratic Sweden." *New Left Review* 201 (1993): 76 –100.

"Making Our Voices Heard." *Speak* 15 (1987): 4 –7.

Mama, Amina. "Women's Studies and Studies of Women in Africa during the 1990s." Working Paper Series 5/96, CODESRIA, Dakar, 1996.

Mamdani, Mahmood. "Africa: Democratic Theory and Democratic Struggles." In Mai Palmberg, ed., *National Identity and Democracy in Africa.* Pretoria: HSRC Press, 1999.

Mansbridge, Jane. "An Anti-essentialist Argument for the Descriptive Political Representation of Gender, Race and Sexuality." Paper presented at the Conference on Politics, Rights and Representation, University of Chicago, 1999.

Marais, Hein. "All GEAR-ed up." *African Communist* 145 (1996): 30–42.

———. *South Africa, Limits to Change: The Political Economy of Transition.* London: Zed, 1998.

Marie, Shamim. "Women Face the Challenge." *Agenda*, no. 1 (1987): 70–74.

Matiwane, Mmabatho. "Translating Commitments into Practice." Workshop sponsored by African Gender Institute and the Commission on Gender Equality, Johannesburg, May 6–7, 1999.

Matland, R., and M. Taylor. "Electoral Systems Effect on Women's Representation: Theoretical Arguments and Evidence from Costa Rica." *Comparative Political Studies* 30, no. 2 (1997): 186–210.

Matynia, Elzbieta. "Finding a Voice: Women in Postcommunist Central Europe." In Amrita Basu, ed., *The Challenge of Local Feminisms: Women's Movements in Global Perspective.* Boulder, Colo.: Westview, 1995.

Mayne, Ann. "Discourse on Damage." *Agenda*, no. 16 (1993): 19–32.

Mbete-Kgositsile, Baleka. "National Machinery for Promoting the Status of Women." In Sandra Liebenberg, ed., *The Constitution of South Africa from a Gender Perspective.* Cape Town: David Philip, 1995.

———. "Women at the Crossroads: Women and Governance." Paper presented at the Association of Women Parliamentarians for Africa (AWEPA)/Gender Advocacy Programme (GAP) Conference, Cape Town, 1998.

MBM Change Agents and Ruby Marks Associates. *Needs Assessment of Women MPs and MPLs.* Pretoria: MBM, 1998.

McAdam, Doug, John D. McCarthy, and Mayer N. Zald, eds. *Comparative Perspectives on Social Movements.* Cambridge: Cambridge University Press, 1996.

McClintock, Anne. "Family Feuds: Gender, Nationalism and the Family." *Feminist Review* 44 (1993): 89–112.

Meehan, Elizabeth, and Selma Sevenhuijsen, eds. *Equality Politics and Gender.* London: Sage, 1998.

Meer, Shamim. "Constraints to Land Reform and Gender Equity Goals." *Agenda Monograph: Translating Commitment into Policy and Practice: Three Case Studies.* Durban, 1999.

———. "The Demobilisation of Civil Society: Struggling with New Questions." *Development Update* 3, no. 1 (1999): 13–21.

———. *Women Speak: Reflections on Our Struggles, 1982–1997.* Cape Town: Kwela Books, 1998.

Meintjes, Sheila. "Dilemmas of Difference." *Agenda*, no. 19 (1993): 37–42.

———. "Gender, Nationalism and Transformation: Difference and Commonality in South Africa's Past and Present." In R. Wilford and R. L. Miller, eds., *Women, Ethnicity and Nationalism: The Politics of Transition.* London: Routledge, 1998.

———. "Looking for the Women's League? Leave a Message . . ." *Work in Progress* 70–71 (1990): 15–16.

———. "The State, Civil Society and Gender Violence: A Case Study of the Domestic Violence Act." In Catherine Albertyn, ed., *Engendering the Political Agenda: A South African Case Study.* Johannesburg: Centre for Applied Legal Studies, 1999.

———. "Winnie Madikizela Mandela: Tragic Figure? Populist Tribune? Township Tough?" *Southern Africa Report* (August 1998): 14–20.

———. "The Women's Struggle for Equality during South Africa's Transition to Democracy." *Transformation* 30 (1996): 47–64.

Mohanty, Chandra Talpade. "Under Western Eyes." In Chandra Talpade Mohanty, Ann Russo, and Lourdes Torres, eds., *Third World Women and the Politics of Feminism.* Bloomington: Indiana University Press, 1991.

Molyneux, Maxine. "Analysing Women's Movements." *Development and Change* 29, no. 1 (1998): 219–45.

———. "Mobilization without Emancipation? Women's Interests, the State and Revolution in Nicaragua." *Feminist Studies* 11 (1985): 227–54.

———. "Mobilization without Emancipation? Women's Interests, State and Revolution." In Richard R. Fagen and Carmen Diana Deere, eds., *Transition and Development: Problems of Third World Socialism.* New York: Monthly Review Press, 1986.

Molyneux, Maxine, and Shahra Razavi, eds. *Gender Justice, Development and Rights.* Oxford: Oxford University Press, 2002.

Moon, Jeremy, and Imogen Fountain. "Keeping the Gates? Women as Ministers in Australia, 1970–96." *Australian Journal of Political Science* 32, no. 3 (1997): 455–66.

Morrow, Sean, Brown Maaba, and Loyiso Pulumane. *Education in Exile: SOMAFCO, the ANC School in Tanzania, 1978–1992.* Pretoria: HSRC Press, 2004.

Mosadi wa Sechaba. "Women Arise and Fight for People's Power." *African Communist* 98 (1984): 56–65.

Moss, Glenn, and Ingrid Obery, eds. *South African Review.* Vol. 4. Johannesburg: Ravan Press, 1987.

Mouffe, Chantal. "Feminism, Citizenship and Radical Democratic Politics." In J. Butler and J. W. Scott, eds., *Feminists Theorize the Political.* New York: Routledge, 1992.

Mtintso, T. E. "The Contribution of Women Parliamentarians to Gender Equality." Unpublished master's thesis, University of the Witwatersrand, 1999.

———. "Representivity: False Sisterhood or Universal Women's Interests? The South African Experience." *Feminist Studies* 29, no. 3 (2003): 569–80.

Murray, Catherine, and Kate O'Regan. "Putting Women into the Constitution." In Susan Bazilli, ed., *Putting Women on the Agenda.* Johannesburg: Ravan Press, 1991.

Muthien, Y. "Representivity in the Public Service." Unpublished report, Public Service Commission, Pretoria, 1998.

Myakayaka-Manzini, Mavivi. "Past and Present Debates on the Establishment of National Machinery for the Advancement of Women." Presentation to the Constitutional Assembly workshop on national machinery, Cape Town, June 2–3, 1995.

Naidoo, M., and V. Bozalek. "Maintenance Grant Parity: Women Pay the Price." *Agenda,* no. 33 (1997): 26–32.

Nasta, S., ed. *Motherlands: Black Women's Writing from Africa, the Caribbean and South Asia.* London: Women's Press, 1991.

"Natal Organisation of Women." *Speak* 7 (1984): 17.

Neocosmos, Michael. "From People's Politics to State Politics: Aspects of National Liberation in South Africa, 1994–1999." *Politieia* 15, no. 3 (1999): 73–119.

Neophytou, Vanessa-Lynn. "Developing the Commission for Gender Equality." *Agenda,* no. 26 (1995): 60–65.

Nkomo, Susie. "Organising Women in SANSCO: Reflections on the Experience of Women in Organization." *Agenda*, no. 10 (1991): 10–15.

North, Douglass C. *Institutions, Institutional Change and Economic Performance.* Cambridge: Cambridge University Press, 1990.

"Northcroft Women Organise." *Speak* 3 (1983): 13.

"No to Rape, Say Port Alfred Women." *Speak* 13 (1986): 9.

No Turning Back: Fighting for Gender Equality in the Unions. Johannesburg: LACOM (SACHED), Speak, COSATU Wits Women's Forum, 1992.

Ntone, D., and N. Meth. "New Forms of Racism in the Western Cape: Implications for Black Gender Activists in the Western Cape." *Agenda*, no. 34 (1997): 71–76.

Okin, Susan Moller. *Is Multiculturalism Bad for Women?* Princeton, N.J.: Princeton University Press, 1998.

Orloff, Ann Shola. "Gender and the Social of Citizenship: The Comparative Analysis of Gender Relations and Welfare States." *American Sociological Review* 58 (June 1993): 303–28.

Orr, Liesl, Jeremy Daphne, and Claire Horton. "COSATU Congress: Did Women Reject the Quota?" *Agenda*, no. 35 (1997).

"Our Men Must Stop Beating Us." *Speak* 19 (1988): 4–7.

Paley, Dawn. "Women Pushed Aside as Men Seek Power." www.rabble.ca/news_full_story_shtml?=31275, accessed August24, 2005.

Parker, Andrew, Mary Russo, Doris Sommer, and Patricia Yaeger. *Nationalisms and Sexualities.* London: Routledge, 1992.

Parpart, J. L., and K. A. Staudt, eds. *Women and the State in Africa.* Boulder, Colo.: Lynne Rienner, 1989.

Patel, Leila. "South African Women's Struggles in the 1980s." *Agenda*, no. 2 (1988): 28–35.

Phillips, Anne. *Engendering Democracy.* Philadelphia: University of Pennsylvania Press, 1991.

———. *The Politics of Presence.* London: Polity Press, 1995.

PRC (Presidential Review Commission). *Developing a Culture of Good Governance: Report of the Presidential Review Commission on the Reform and Transformation of the Public Service in South Africa.* Pretoria: Presidential Review Commission, 1998.

Primo, Natasha. "Parliament, the President and Deputy President, South Africa Communication Service, and Premiers' Votes." In Debbie Budlender, ed., *The Third Women's Budget.* Cape Town: Institute for Democracy in South Africa (IDASA), 1998.

Pringle, Rosemary, and Sophie Watson. "Women's Interests and the Post-structuralist State." In Michele Barrett and Anne Phillips, eds., *Destabilizing Theory: Contemporary Feminist Debates.* Cambridge: Polity Press, 1992.

Public Service Commission. "The Progress of Representativeness in the Public Service: Report." Unpublished report, Public Service Commission, Pretoria 1996.

Quincy. "On the Emancipation of Women." *African Communist* 122 (1990): 22–24.

Radcliffe, Sarah A., and Sallie Westwood, eds. *"Viva": Women and Popular Protest in Latin America.* London: Routledge, 1993.

Rai, Shirin, and Geraldine Lievesley, eds. *Women and the State: International Perspectives.* London: Taylor and Francis, 1996.

Ramgobin, E. "The ANC Women's League Returns." *Agenda,* no. 7 (1990): 21–24.

Ranchod-Nilsson, Sita, and Mary Ann Tetreault, eds. *Women, States and Nationalism.* New York: Routledge, 2000.

Randall, Vicky. *Women and Politics: An International Perspective.* London: Macmillan, 1987.

Rantao, Jovial. "Much for Women to Do." *Saturday Star,* May 4, 1991.

"Rape in Marriage." *Speak* 17 (1987): 8.

Razavi, Shahra, and Carol Miller. "Gender Mainstreaming: A Study of the Efforts by the UNDP, the World Bank and the ILO to Institutionalize Gender Issues." UN Research Institute for Social Development Occasional Paper 4, Geneva, 1995.

Reagon, Bernice Johnson. "Coalition Politics: Turning the Century." In Barbara Smith, ed., *Home Girls: A Black Feminist Anthology.* New York: Kitchen Table–Women of Color Press, 1983.

Reddy, E. S., and Fatima Meer, comps. *Passive Resistance, 1946: A Selection of Documents.* Durban: Madiba–Institute for Black Research, 1996.

Redefining Politics: South African Women and Democracy. Johannesburg: Commission on Gender Equality–Parliamentary Women's Group, 1999.

"Restructuring the National Office: Interview with Baleka Kgositsile." *Rock,* March 1992.

Reynolds, A., ed. *Election '99 South Africa: From Mandela to Mbeki.* Cape Town: David Phillip, 1999.

———. "Women in African Legislatures and Executives: The Slow Climb to Power." Research report. Johannesburg: Electoral Institute of Southern Africa, 1999.

Routledge-Madlala, Nozizwe. Address to the Conference on Transformation for Gender Justice and Organisational Change. African Gender Institute, Cape Town, 1998.

———. "What Price Freedom? Testimony and the Natal Organisation of Women." *Agenda,* no. 34 (1997): 62–70.

Rule, Wilma. "Electoral Systems, Contextual Factors, and Women's Opportunity for Election to Parliaments in Twenty-three Democracies." *Western Political Quarterly* 40, no. 3 (1987): 477–98.

———. "Women's Under-representation and Electoral Systems." *PS: Political Science and Politics* 27, no. 4 (1994): 689–92.

Russell, Bev, and Mark Swilling. "The Size and Scope of the Non-profit Sector in South Africa." School of Public and Development Management and the Centre for Civil Society, Johannesburg and Durban, 2002.

Russell, D. 1989. *Lives of Courage.* New York: Basic Books.

Sachs, Albie. "Judges and Gender: The Constitutional Rights of Women in a Postapartheid South Africa." *Agenda,* no. 7 (1990): 1–11.

SADC (Southern African Development Community). "Beyond 30% in 2005." Report on Programme of Action for Women in Politics and Decision-Making in SADC, conference, Botswana, May 1999.

Sainsbury, Diane. *Gender Equality and Welfare States.* Cambridge: Cambridge University Press, 1996.

Saporta Sternbach, Nancy, Marysa Navarro-Aranguren, Patricia Chuchryk, and
    Sonia E. Alvarez. "Feminisms in Latin America: From Bogota to San Bernardo."
    Signs: Journal of Women in Culture and Society 17, no. 2 (1992): 493 –533.
Saul, John. "Liberation without Democracy?" In Jonathan Hyslop, ed., *African De-
    mocracy in the Era of Globalisation.* Johannesburg: Wits University Press, 1999.
———. "South Africa between Barbarism and Structural Reform." *New Left Review*
    188 (1991): 3 –44.
Sawer, Marian. "Femocrats and Ecorats: Women's Policy Machinery in Australia,
    Canada and New Zealand." UN Research Institute for Social Development Occa-
    sional Paper 6. Geneva, 1996.
Schefer, Ronel. "Women Talk Votes and Power." *Democracy in Action* 6, no. 7 (1992):
    6 –9.
Schmitter, Phillipe C. "The Consolidation of Democracy and Representation of
    Social Groups." *American Behavioural Scientist* 35, no. 4 –5 (1992): 422–49.
———. "Contemporary Democratization: The Prospects for Women." In Jane S.
    Jacquette and Sharon L. Wolchik, eds., *Women and Democracy: Latin America
    and Central and Eastern Europe.* Baltimore: Johns Hopkins University Press, 1998.
Schneider, Elizabeth. 1986. "The Dialectic of Rights and Politics: Perspectives from
    the Women's Movement." *New York University Law Review* 589 (1986): 507–25.
Schwartz, Pat. "Liberation—A Feminist Issue?" *Sash,* August 1987.
Sechaba, Mosadi wa. "Women Arise and Fight for People's Power." *African Commu-
    nist* 98 (1984).
Sechaba, Tshepo. "Towards the Emancipation of Women." *Sechaba* 24, no. 8 (1990):
    56 –65.
Sechaba, Tshepo, and Stephen Ellis. *Comrades against Apartheid: The ANC and the
    South African Communist Party in Exile.* London: James Currey, 1992.
Seedat, Fatima, and Lilian Kimani. "Gender Profile of Parties." In *Redefining Poli-
    tics: South African Women and Democracy.* Braamfontein: Commission on Gen-
    der Equality–Parliamentary Women's Group, 1999.
Seekings, Jeremy. "The Broader Importance of Welfare Reform in South Africa."
    Social Dynamics 28, no. 2 (2002): 1–38.
———. *The UDF: A History of the United Democratic Front in South Africa, 1983–
    1991.* Cape Town: David Philip, 2000.
Seidman, Gay. "Institutional Dilemmas: Representation versus Mobilization in the
    South African Gender Commission." *Feminist Studies* 29, no. 3 (2003): 541–63.
———. " 'No Freedom without the Women': Mobilization and Gender in South Af-
    rica, 1970 –1992." *Signs: Journal of Women in Culture and Society* 18, no. 2 (1993):
    210–39.
Seidman-Makgetla, Neva. "Women and the Economy." Paper prepared for the Gen-
    derstats Project, www.womensnet.org.za/genderstats/economy.
Sen, Gita. "Gender Mainstreaming in Finance Ministries." *World Development* 28,
    no. 7 (2000): 1379 –90.
Serote, Pethu. "National Liberation Equals Women's Liberation: A Myth Totally Ex-
    ploded." *Agenda,* no. 11 (1991): 5 –6.
Serote, Pethu, Nosipho January-Bardill, Sandy Liebenberg, and Julia Nolte. "What
    the South African Parliament Has Done to Date to Improve the Quality of Life
    and Status of Women." Parliament, Cape Town, 1995.

"Should the Sisters Do It for Themselves?" *Speak* 67 (1994): 10–12.

Siim, Birte. "Welfare States, Gender Politics and Equality Politics: Women's Citizenship in the Scandinavian Welfare States." In Elizabeth Meehan and Selma Sevenhuijsen, eds., *Equality Politics and Gender*. London: Sage, 1998.

Stadler, Alf. "The Rise and Decline of Party Activism in South Africa." Paper presented to the African Studies Seminar Series, Wits University, October 1997.

Staudt, Kathleen. *Women, Foreign Assistance and Advocacy Administration*. New York: Praeger Special Studies, 1985.

Stetson, Dorothy McBride, and Amy G. Mazur, eds. *Comparative State Feminism*. London: Sage, 1996.

Stevens, Marion. "Health." In Debbie Budlender, ed., *The Second Women's Budget*. Cape Town: Institute for Democracy in South Africa (IDASA), 1996.

Summers, Anne. "Mandarins or Missionaries: Women in the Federal Bureaucracy." In Norma Grieve and Ailsa Burns, eds., *Australian Women: New Feminist Perspectives*. Melbourne: Oxford University Press, 1986.

Taitz, Laurice. "Dragon or Dragon Slayer? The Loathing Zuma Invokes May Say More about Detractors Than Her." *Sunday Times* (Johannesburg), October 25, 1998.

Tamale, Sylvia. *When Hens Begin to Crow*. Kampala, Uganda: Fountain, 1999.

Tambo, O. R. Speech at the concluding session of the Conference of the Women's Section of the ANC, September 14, 1985, Luanda, Angola. ANC Archives, Mayibuye Centre, University of the Western Cape.

Tarrow, Sidney. *Power in Movement: Social Movements, Collective Action and Politics*. Cambridge: Cambridge University Press, 1994.

Taylor, Vivienne. "Economic Gender Injustice: The Macro Picture." *Agenda*, no. 33 (1997): 9–25.

Thornton, Robert, and Mamphele Ramphele. "The Quest for Community." In E. Boonzaier and J. Sharp, eds., *South African Keywords: The Uses and Abuses of Political Concepts*. Cape Town: David Philip, 1988.

Threlfall, Monica, ed. *Mapping Women's Movements*. London: Verso, 1996.

Tilley, Alison. "Is Parliamentary Advocacy All It's Cracked Up to Be?" *Black Sash National Newsletter*, August 1997.

Tripp, Aili Mari. *Women and Politics in Uganda*. Kampala: Fountain, 2000.

———. "Women and the Politics of Diversity in Uganda." UN Research Institute for Social Development, Geneva, 2000.

Tsikata, D. "Gender Equality and the State in Ghana: Some Issues of Policy and Practice." In Ayesha Imam, Amina Mama, and Fatou Sow, eds., *Engendering African Social Sciences*. Dakar: CODESRIA, 1997.

Tsikata, E. "Women's Political Organizations, 1951–1987." In E. Hansen and K. Ninsin, eds., *The State, Development and Politics in Ghana*. Dakar: CODESRIA, 1989.

Turok, Mary. "The Women's Quota Debate: Building Non-sexism." *Work in Progress* 76 (1992): 12–17.

Udit, Pingla. "Engendering the National Liberation Struggle in South Africa, 1945–1995." Ph.D. diss., Department of Sociology, University of Essex, 1997.

Unterhalter, Elaine. "The Work of the Nation: Heroic Masculinity in South African Autobiographical Writing of the Anti-apartheid Struggle." *European Journal of Development Research* 12, no. 2 (2000): 157–78.

Urdang, Stephanie. *And Still They Dance: Women, War and the Struggle for Change in Mozambique.* London: Earthscan, 1991.

Valenzuela, Maria Elena. "Women and the Democratization Process in Chile." In Jane S. Jacquette and Sharon L. Wolchik, eds., *Women and Democracy: Latin America and Central and Eastern Europe.* Baltimore: Johns Hopkins University Press, 1998.

Valodia, Imraan. "Finance, State Expenditure, SA Revenue Service and Central Statistical Service." In Debbie Budlender, ed., *The Third Women's Budget.* Cape Town: Institute for Democracy in South Africa (IDASA), 1998.

Van der Merwe, Esmare. "Winnie's Future Hangs on Vote." *Star,* April 25, 1991.

Van Kessel, Ineke. *"Beyond Our Wildest Dreams": The United Democratic Front and the Transformation of South Africa.* Charlottesville: University of Virginia Press, 2001.

Van Zyl, Mikki. "Invitation to Debate: Towards an Explanation of Violence against Women." *Agenda,* no. 11 (1991): 66–77.

Vargas, Virginia. "Women's Movements in Peru: Rebellion into Action." In Saskia Wieringa, ed., *Subversive Women: Women's Movements in Africa, Asia, Latin America and the Caribbean.* London: Zed, 1995.

Vetten, Lisa. "'The Budget Appears to Be Less Than Required': Four Government Departments' Expenditure on Activities Addressing Violence Against Women." Unpublished draft report, Centre for the Study of Violence and Reconciliation, Johannesburg, 2003.

Volbrecht, Ginny. "Marxism or Feminism." Paper presented to the Association for Sociology in South Africa, Cape Town, 1986.

Vos, Suzanne. "Women in Parliament: A Personal Perspective." In *Redefining Politics: South African Women and Democracy.* Braamfontein: Commission on Gender Equality–Parliamentary Women's Group, 1999.

Walker, Cherryl. "Women and Resistance: In Search of South African Feminism." *Work in Progress* 36 (1985): 25–30.

———, ed. *Women and Gender in Southern Africa to 1945.* Cape Town: David Philip, 1990.

———. *Women and Resistance in South Africa.* London: Onyx, 1982, 1991.

Watson, Sophie, ed. *Playing the State.* Sydney: Allen and Unwin, 1990.

Waylen, Georgina. "Gender and Democratic Politics: A Comparative Analysis of Consolidation in Argentina and Chile." *Journal of Latin American Studies* 32 (2000): 765–94.

———. "Women and Democratization: Conceptualizing Gender Relations in Transition Politics." *World Politics* 46 (1994): 327–54.

"We Are a Force to Reckon With—Hambanati Women's Action Group." *Speak* 8 (1985): 8–10.

Webster, David. "Repression and the State of Emergency." In G. Moss and I. Obery, eds., *South African Review.* Vol. 4. Johannesburg: Ravan Press, 1987.

Webster, Edward, and Glenn Adler. "Towards a Class Compromise in South Africa's 'Double Tradition': Bargained Liberalization and the Consolidation of Democracy." *Politics and Society* 27, no. 3 (1999).

"We Don't Want to Be Tails—Taking the Struggle Home." *Speak* 18 (1988): 4–7.

Wells, Julia C. *"We Now Demand!" The History of Women's Resistance to Pass Laws in South Africa.* Johannesburg: University of Witwatersrand Press, 1993.

"We've Got the Future Looking at Us." *Speak* 36 (1991): 5 –8.

Wieringa, Saskia. *Subversive Women: Women's Movements in Africa, Asia, Latin America and the Caribbean.* London: Zed, 1995.

Wilford, R., and R. L. Miller, eds. *Women, Ethnicity and Nationalism: The Politics of Transition.* London: Routledge, 1998.

Williams, Melissa S. *Voice, Trust, and Memory: Marginalized Groups and the Failings of Liberal Representation.* Princeton, N.J.: Princeton University Press, 1998.

"Women in MK." *Voice of Women,* December 16, 1982.

"Women in Power." *Speak* 62 (1994): 15 –17.

"Women, Politics and Elections: A Gender Dialogue Report." Commission on Gender Equality, Johannesburg, 1998.

Women's Empowerment Unit. "Annual Progress Report for the Period 6 October 1997 –31 March 1998." Swedish International Development Agency, Pretoria, 1998.

"The Women's League —A Fighting Force?" *Speak* 35 (1991): 4 –6.

Women's National Coalition. *Women's Charter for Effective Equality.* Braamfontein, Johannesburg: Women's National Coalition.

Women's National Coalition and Lawyers for Human Rights. "Report on Conference 'Ensuring Gender Equality in the New South Africa.'" Johannesburg, May 7 –9, 1993.

Work in Progress. "Debating Alliance Politics." *Work in Progress* 34 (1984): 12 –15.

Young, Iris Marion. *Inclusion and Democracy.* Oxford: Oxford University Press, 2000.

———. *Justice and the Politics of Difference.* Princeton, N.J.: Princeton University Press, 1990.

Yuval-Davis, Nira. *Gender and Nation.* London: Sage, 1997.

Yuval-Davis, Nira, and Floya Anthias, eds. *Woman-Nation-State.* London: Macmillan, 1989.

Zondo, Ntomb'futhi. "Women and the Vote." *Agenda,* no. 20 (1994): 57 –61.

Zulu, Paulus. "Resistance in the Townships: An Overview." In Fatima Meer, ed., *Resistance in the Townships.* Durban: Madiba Publishers, 1989.

Index

abortion, 92, 149, 201, 261

Abrams, S. Kristine, 145

academics, role in women's organizations, 163

accountability: bureaucracy and, 215; centralized government and, 197; decline in emphasis on, 217; formal accountability, 193; institutionalization of, 222–25; moral accountability, 193–94; political parties and, 193, 196, 197–98; representation and, 192–98, 208–9

Ackermann, Denise, 81

Adler, Glenn, 18

affirmative action, 150, 151, 184; quotas and, 126–28, 175, 177–82, 183, 228, 262, 312n99; representation in bureaucracy and, 226

African Christian Democratic Party, 309

African Communist (journal), 30, 105

African Gender Institute, 223

African National Congress (ANC): autonomy and alliances with, 13, 25–26; Communal Land Rights Bill and, 203; Communist Party, 41; "Constitutional Guidelines for a Democratic South Africa" of, 111–12; Consultative Congress (Durban), 122; customary law and, 157; Democratic Party's differences with, 149–51; Deployment Committee of, 196; feminism as ideology and, 160; feminism opposed within, 138; 48th National Congress of ANC (Durban), 126; GEAR and, 231–32; gender equality and, 134, 162, 186, 190–91, 195–96, 214,

341

83; inclusionary politics and, 155 –56; representation and, 178, 182; women and democratization, 131–32

Democratic Party, 135, 137, 162; Commission on Gender Equality and, 222–23; gender equality legislation and, 100; gender equality within, 195 –96; opposition to quota systems, 178, 179; quota systems and, 188; WNC and, 164; *Women's Charter for Effective Equality* and, 141, 143, 149 –51

demographics: age of women in NOW, 66; ANC and, 95; of ANC Women's League, 125; of Women's Section of ANC, 108

de Swardt, Cobus, 34

Didiza, Thoko, 203

directed collective action, 11, 86, 114 –15, 249

discourse, political, 17 –18

Domestic Violence Act, 201, 230

Driver, Dorothy, 111–12, 114

Duarte, Jessie, 61

Durban Women's Group, 57

Eduards, Maud, 34

education: political education for ANC Women's Section, 101, 104; skills training by ANC Women's Section, 90–91

Edwards, Rita, 238

Elections Bulletin, 191

Electoral Act, 309n36

Electoral Institute of South Africa, 191

emergency regulations. *See* states of emergency

Employment Equity Act, 202

engagement with the state. *See* bureaucracy; Parliament

equality: formal *vs.* substantive, 45; substantive equality, 45, 148 –49, 171, 172, 231; universalist interpretation of, 158; in UWO constitution, 59. *See also* gender equality

Erlank, Natasha, 36

Eurocentrism, 44

exile of ANC: armed struggle emphasized during, 95 –96; communication during, 93 –94; as context for women's activism, 85 –87, 103, 114, 130, 247; demographics of participants, 95; gender equality as commitment during, 86,

130, 142, 212; impacts on women's organizations in aftermath of, 118; intelligence network and, 94; mental illness among women and, 88 –89; mobilization of women as low priority during, 94 –95; organizational structure and culture of, 145; resource allocation and, 88, 101–2; sexism during, 90–91; violence against women and children during, 92; youth and, 90

exile of liberation movements, 24; as context for feminism, 77, 247; NOW during, 72; unbanning and, 134. *See also* exile of ANC

Federation of South African Trade Unions, 25

Federation of South African Women (FEDSAW), 61, 103; alliances and, 45 –46; ANC and, 45 –46; ANCWL and, 26; autonomy of, 13 –14, 249; disbanding of, 303n16; formation of, 21–22, 25; NOW and, 60; organizational structure of, 79; revival of, 133 –34; Women's Section of ANC and, 107

Federation of Transvaal Women (FEDTRAW), 47–49, 104, 134, 254; COSATU and, 291n241; origins and organizational structure of, 61–64; UDF Women's Congress and, 73

FEDSAW. *See* Federation of South African Women

FEDTRAW. *See* Federation of Transvaal Women

Feinstein, Andrew, 311n90

feminism: as challenge to existing gender order, 28; "deradicalization" of, 189; as divisive or separatist, 29, 69, 77 –78; Eurocentrism and, 44; exile as context for, 77; "feminine" *vs.* "feminist" women's movements, 7; feminist discourse, 34 –35, 140; femocrats in bureaucracy, 228, 241; hostility or indifference toward, 68; as ideology, 21–32, 35, 160; indigenous feminism, 76 –81; Marxist feminism, 32–33; motherism as alternative to, 75 –76; nationalism as antagonistic project, 38 –39, 40; objectives and strategies of, 144 –45; opposition to, 138; political party structures and, 188 –89, 208; postcolonial, 5; race and,

nationalist movement: as antagonistic to women's liberation, 38–39, 43; authority of, 34; as conservative, 39–40; as context for women's liberation, 40; feminism and, 29, 38–39; Freedom Charter and, 41; as gendered, 39; gender equality and, 36–37; marginalization of women's issues, 37, 250; as racially defined, 36–37; subordination of women's liberation to, 32–33, 160, 250; trade unions and, 289n78; women relegated to supportive, private sphere roles in, 39; women's liberation as integral to, 108–9; women's movements in, 20–21; women's organizations in context of, 18, 247

National Network Against Violence Against Women, 168

National Party, 137, 162, 179–80; organizational structure and culture of, 145; *Women's Charter for Effective Equality* and, 143

National Union of South African Students, 135

National Women's Executive Committee (NWEC), 90, 95

national women's organization: efforts to create, 73, 103, 119, 134, 251; FEDSAW as, 135

needs-based politics: mobilization, 50–51, 247; *vs.* rights-based approaches to women's interests, 44–45, 233. *See also* practical needs

Neocosmos, Michael, 167, 168

New National Party (NNP), 179; gender equality within, 195–96

New Women's Movement (NWM), 169, 237–38, 244

Ngcuka, Phumzile, 67, 185

NGOs. *See* nongovernmental organizations

Ngubane, S., 206

Nhlanhla, Joe, 104

Nhlapo, Mavis, 89, 95, 98–99, 101, 297n109

Nisaa, 191

Nkobi, Tom, 114

Nkomo, Susie, 78

Non-Aligned Movement, 107

nongovernmental organizations (NGOs), 191, 206, 225, 238, 254

nonracialism, 42–43, 159; ANCWL and loss of, 120; motherism and, 77, 78; poverty reduction and, 236–40, 244; Women's Alliance and, 135; women's movements and, 23, 24, 63, 78–81

NOW. *See* Natal Organization of Women

Ntombela-Nzimande, Phumelele, 58, 118, 120, 125

Ntone, Dorothy, 135

Nujoma, Sam, 106

Nutt, Anne Marie, 307n132

NWM. *See* New Women's Movement

Nyembe, Lucy, 118

Office on the Status of Women (OSW), 218–19, 223, 225, 226, 227, 244, 264

"Operation Big Ears," 142–43, 147

oppression *vs.* subordination, 150

O'Regan, Kate, 152

organizational culture: of ANC, 86; grassroots democracy and, 83; proportional representation systems and, 183; transitional politics and, 114; of UWE, 64; variances in women's organizations, 118, 136, 145

organizational structures: agenda setting and, 83–84; of ANC, 86, 104–5; "branches" and nonracialism, 78; communication obstructed by, 94–95; cross-class organization, 78; federal model of Federation of South African Women, 79; grassroots democracy and, 48; "intellectual dominance" and, 80; leadership as male dominated, 52; local level organization and women's mobilization, 83; of MK, 99; as multiracial, 63; of regional women's organizations, 59–69; of women's organizations, 3

Orloff, Anne, 315n68

OSW. *See* Office on the Status of Women

PAC. *See* Pan Africanist Congress

Pahad, Amina, 25

Pahad, Essop, 264

Paley, Dawn, 258

Pan Africanist Congress (PAC), 24, 91, 140, 162, 178; African Women's Organisation, 180

WOMEN IN AFRICA

AND THE DIASPORA

Engaging Modernity: Muslim Women and the Politics of Agency in Postcolonial Niger
Ousseina D. Alidou

Tired of Weeping: Mother Love, Child Death, and Poverty in Guinea-Bissau
Jónína Einarsdóttir

Women's Organizations and Democracy in South Africa: Contesting Authority
Shireen Hassim

Surviving the Slaughter: The Ordeal of a Rwandan Refugee in Zaire
Marie Béatrice Umutesi
Translated by Julia Emerson